MELANESIA

MELANESIA
Travels in Black Oceania

HAMISH MCDONALD

HURST & COMPANY, LONDON

First published in the United Kingdom in 2025 by
C. Hurst & Co. (Publishers) Ltd.,
New Wing, Somerset House, Strand, London, WC2R 1LA

Copyright © Hamish McDonald, 2025

All rights reserved.

The right of Hamish McDonald to be identified as the author of this publication is asserted by him in accordance with the Copyright, Designs and Patents Act, 1988.

A Cataloguing-in-Publication data record for this book is available from the British Library.

ISBN: 9781805263951

www.hurstpublishers.com

Book design and typesetting by Beau Lowenstern
Cover image by Adobe Stock / Hakinmhan
Index by Garry Cousins
Map on page 272 by Alan Laver
Map on page 286 by Timothy Skewes
All other maps reproduced with the permission of CartoGIS Services, Scholarly Information Services, the Australian National University.

CONTENTS

PREFACE   1

1. Melanesia   5
2. Fiji   27
3. Vanuatu   51
4. Espíritu Santo   75
5. New Caledonia   95
6. Solomon Islands   121
7. Malaita   139
8. Bougainville   153
9. Papua New Guinea   177
10. Port Moresby   201
11. Western Province   223
12. The Highlands   243
13. The Sepik   261
14. West Papua   273

EPILOGUE 287

Acknowledgements 299
Endnotes 303
Index 311

PREFACE

AS A REPORTER I WAS NEVER a Pacific specialist. Back in Australia between postings in Asia, I had short immersions in the island nations, mostly in reaction to political shocks such as the military coups in Fiji, the Kanak unrest in New Caledonia and the crises of governance in Papua New Guinea and Solomon Islands.

I travelled by air, stayed mostly in tourist-class hotels, and interviewed articulate English or French-educated locals. But exploring the towns on foot, I'd come across docks busy with small, rusty ships loading people and freight for remote settlements, river landings where people and their belongings boarded dinghies and canoes, dusty transport terminals where villagers headed home from town and school on battered buses and trucks.

The Polynesian nations, with their chiefly hierarchies, orderly administrations and stern Methodism, interested me less. It was the tangled, impossibly diverse mix of the Melanesian world that fascinated. Every discovery led to more intricacy; every book and academic article led to a dozen others. The crowds in the markets, the election rallies, the peace ceremonies enveloped me in a mix of wood smoke, sweat and coconut oil.

Meanwhile, profound demographic change, notably the multiplying population of Papua New Guinea, presaged a new balance of power and influence in the region. Huge new resource projects were bringing in flows of revenue and the risk of more local conflict. Wide access to wireless telephony and data was revolutionising patterns of authority, empowering individuals. Then, as has happened before, the arrival of a distant and alien great power – in this case China – jerked the Pacific's traditional metropolitan patrons in the West (the United States, Australia, New Zealand) out of complacency.

For me, there came a growing awareness that many new things were happening. People like me needed some education about them. And having met many impressive men and women in my previous travels, it was time to try putting to rest the disparaging stereotypes and civilisational rankings that nineteenth-century evolutionary thinkers attached to Melanesia, as described in the first chapter. It was time for a new exploration. Hence this book, intended as a first step into this Melanesian world for the non-specialist.

I still wanted to get on those ships, dinghies and inland buses. And after finishing regular work, I now had the time. The original concept was a single journey through Melanesia, from its southeastern edge in Fiji to its other margin in Papua and Maluku, travelling as much as possible at ground and sea level, listening to local voices about their transition from customary life into modernity.

As it turned out, a continuous single journey proved impossible within the constraints of time, visas and funds. While there were several arduous trips by road and sea, there had to be connections by air to seize opportunities. In addition, several countries in the region closed their borders for two years during the Covid-19 pandemic. So there were wide gaps between bursts of travel, and the actual sequence of my journey was not as bolted together as it may appear here. An application to the Indonesian government for a visa to revisit the Papua provinces has gone unanswered, so Chapter 14 draws on my previous visits as a journalist in 1976 and 2013.

The enforced spells between travel had the benefit of allowing me to catch up on what has been written before about this region – or at least some of the immense body of academic research and personal accounts lying in

PREFACE

library stacks. This book is the result of this eclectic immersion in present-day Melanesia and what we know of its history.

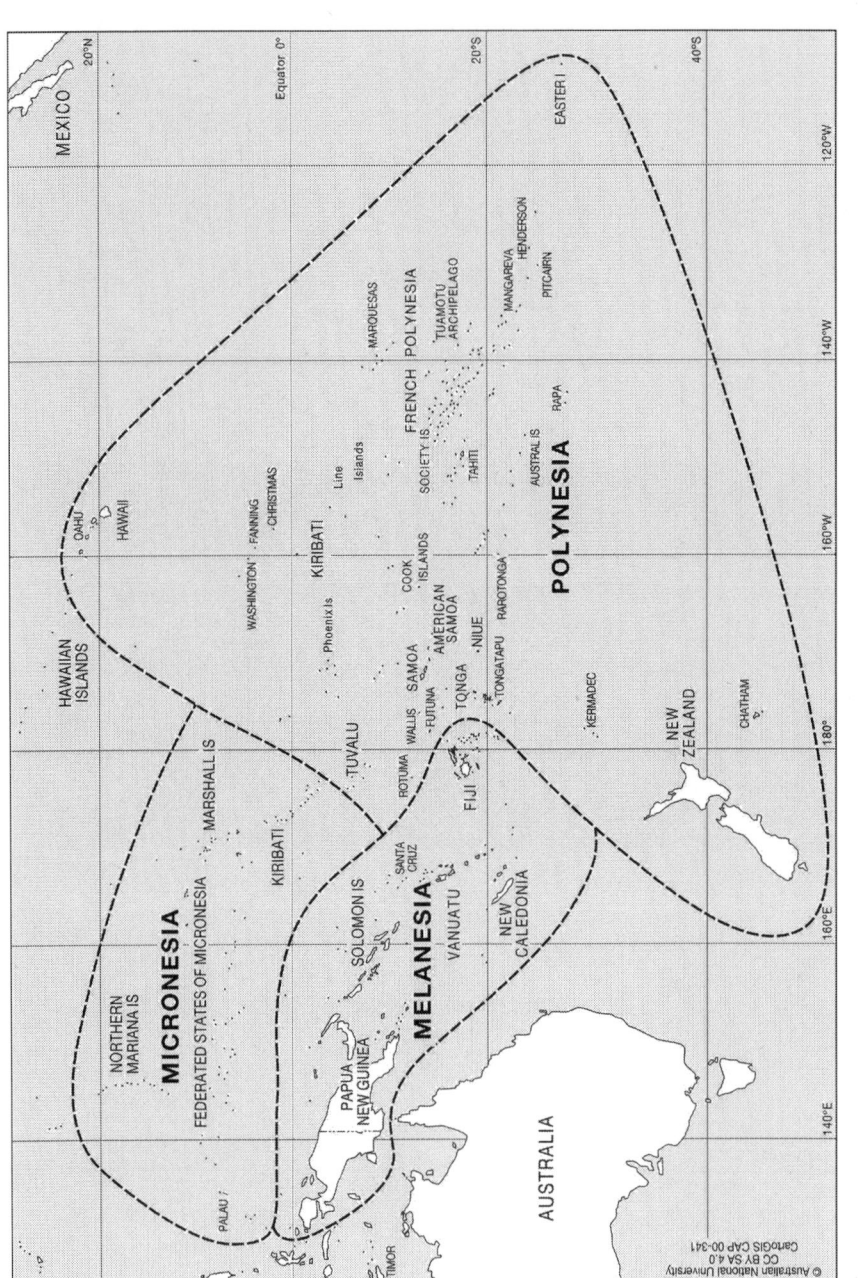

Melanesia, Micronesia and Polynesia: this nineteenth-century classification of Oceania is still widely used, despite the many discovered overlaps between the three regions.

1

MELANESIA

Noble and Other Savages

FIRST, BEFORE OUR TRAVELS, who are the Melanesians?

The people of the arc of islands in the southwest Pacific now known as Melanesia – stretching from Fiji through the great bird-shape of New Guinea to the Moluccan islands – are still among the least known and least understood of their hemisphere.

They suffered invidious comparison from the start.

The early European explorers, notably Louis Antoine de Bougainville and James Cook, navigated through the passages of Patagonia into the vastness of the Pacific and landed like gods at Tahiti. The chiefs welcomed them on shore, along with a populace of great physical beauty to the European eye – tall, light-skinned and wavy-haired. The Europeans found a society that needed little labour for the food of forest and reef, lived in open-sided houses, went about largely naked without shame, and offered and performed the sexual act openly.

It seemed that here was the "noble savage" conceived by their contemporary, philosopher Jean-Jacques Rousseau, who postulated an intrinsic virtue in people living in a "state of nature", uncorrupted by notions of individual property and civilisation.

"One would think himself in the Elysian fields," wrote Bougainville; Tahiti seemed a "garden of Eden", its inhabitants living in a "state of innocence". His accompanying naturalist, Philibert Commerson, found the Tahitians "without vice, without prejudice, without wants, without discord"; they knew "no other god but love".[1]

Some two years later, Cook's crew aboard the *Endeavour* found the same embrace. His botanist, Joseph Banks, wrote of an "Arcadian" landscape of beauty and plenty, in which he and other members of the ship's complement immersed themselves in lovemaking, tattooing and feasting between their duties of victualling, repairs and scientific observation.[2]

The British and French explorers found similar societies as they proceeded westwards, although none as Elysian as Tahiti, in the Marquesa Islands, the Friendly Islands (Tonga) and even in the cool climate of New Zealand, where the Māori also qualified as Noble Savages, despite some reservations on account of cannibalism.

When these explorers turned their ships northwest, to round the southern or northern coast of New Guinea and reach the Dutch settlements of the East Indies on the way home, they encountered a different world.

During his second voyage, in 1774, Cook put his ship HMS *Resolution* into a bay he called Port Sandwich, in what we now know as the island of Malekula, part of the archipelago he named the New Hebrides, now the Republic of Vanuatu. It was his first encounter with Melanesians and he was not impressed.

"The People of this country are in general the most Ugly and ill-proportioned of any I ever saw," Cook wrote in his journal, adding that "we saw but few women and they were full as Disagreeable as the men." Six years earlier, in nearby islands, Bougainville had formed a similar view. The natives were black, with thick lips, woolly hair and noses pierced with sticks and other ornaments; he described them as generally short and ill-proportioned.

Cook thought the Malekula islanders unreliable. Sometimes they accepted small gifts and allowed working parties ashore to replenish water casks and gather firewood. Other times they tried to swarm aboard the ship and pilfer things, or let fly with arrows that the British sailors suspected were poison-tipped (tested on a ship's dog, this proved not to be the case).

Not tempted to stay by what seemed a meagre supply of water and fruit, Cook sailed the *Resolution* southwards, to the island of Erromango. There the islanders appeared receptive, offering yams and coconuts. But then they rushed the ship's boats, trying to drag them ashore. Arrows, stones and spears hit the boat crews, and Cook ordered his marines to open fire with their flint-lock muskets. With several wounded on both sides, Cook abandoned any attempt to open cordial relations and sailed the ship to the large island visible to the south.

At the southeastern end of this island, Cook found a deep bay and cautiously took the *Resolution* in to anchor. He found the islanders more co-operative, with two coming forward as intermediaries. The crew were able to collect water and fell some trees for timber to repair the ship.

The inhabitants called their island Tanna, a name that still applies, though they still use the name Cook gave the bay, Port Resolution. Cook seems to have found the Tanna people somewhat more attractive than the Malekula natives. They were also middle-sized and dark, dressed much the same way: the men in a plaited belt holding up a penis sheath, the women in leaf skirts. While the women, as elsewhere in these islands, had their hair cropped short, the men struck Cook as popinjays. In Tanna, their crisp and curly hair was stretched and plaited around a plant stem so that it "looks like a parcel of small strings, hanging down from the crown of their heads". Cook continued:

> the most of them have good features and agreeable countenances, are like all the Tropical Race, active and nimble, but these seem to excel in the use of Arms, but do not seem fond of labour, they never would put a hand to assist in any work we were carrying forward, which people of the other islands would take a delight in, but what I judge most from, is their making the Women do the most laborious work, of them they make pack-horses ... I cannot say the women are beauties but I think them handsome enough for the men and too handsome for the use that is made of them.

Cook and his travelling scientists "at first thought the Tanna people a race between those of the Friendly Islands [Tonga] and those of Mallicollo [Malekula] but came to think no affinity to either, except in hair with

Mallicollo". Much later, this suspicion has been shown not entirely wrong, as the southern islands of the New Hebrides had been visited by Tongan canoes. Cook's second-hand report, from people on Tanna, that the island of "Erronan" further south, now known as Futuna, had a language close to Tongan, turned out to be correct.

Although Cook and his officers were ready with warning shots when threats of attack and pilferage occurred, the spirit of the Enlightenment continued to inspire the commander. Cook was furious with a marine who shot and killed a man who fitted an arrow to his bow. If the Tanna people were reluctant to welcome the explorers ashore, or assist their work, who could blame them? "In what other light can they ... at first look upon us but as invaders of their Country; time and some acquaintance with us can only convince them of their mistake."[3]

To Cook's mind, the Melanesians only improved further on his next stops, along the coast of the island he named New Caledonia, where the islanders were "strong robust active well-made people, courteous and friendly and not in the least addicted to pilfering". They were dark, like the people of Tanna, and had similar hair and beards, but "these have better features, more agreeable countenances and are a much stouter race, some who measured Six feet four inches".[4]

Still the dichotomy of the Pacific Ocean was set in European minds. The islands stretching from Hawai'i and Tahiti to New Zealand were the realm of the Noble Savage. Cook himself wondered in his journals whether their peoples should be left alone. Denis Diderot, the friend of Rousseau, raged in a commentary on Bougainville's journal that the pagan idyll of Tahiti should be left undisturbed by the guilt and hypocrisy that Christianity was bound to introduce, "with crucifix in one hand and the dagger in the other".[5]

The islands of the western Pacific were seen to need no such preservation. The later French explorer Jules-Sébastien-César Dumont d'Urville in 1832 put them into a separate racial category, "Melanesia", based on the Greek words for "black islands", distinguishing them from the noble Polynesians to the east and the Micronesians to the north. The peoples of Melanesia were dismissed as savages, beyond friendly tutelage and to be avoided because of cannibalism, head-hunting and blackwater fever (malaria).

Diderot's plea was soon ignored. The fall of the Pacific Eden happened without clergy. By the time William Bligh visited Tahiti in 1792, the Tahitians had been corrupted, largely by the whaling ships from Nantucket and their multinational crews of press-ganged desperadoes (as portrayed accurately enough later on by Herman Melville). Many of the Tahitians were now addicted to alcohol, no longer bathed as frequently as before and wore dirty, cast-off clothes. Venereal diseases, probably first brought by the Cook and Bougainville expeditions, had ripped through the population.

Then came the bibles. The emerging wave of Christian evangelism that would come to full flower in the nineteenth century had noticed the more repugnant features of Polynesian society recorded by Banks and others: infanticide among the priestly caste, human sacrifice, cannibalism and of course sexual licence. In helping to found the London Missionary Society in 1795, the Rev. Thomas Haweis declared in a sermon that the lands of the South Seas:

> seem to realise the fabled Gardens of the Hesperides, – where the fragrant groves, which cover them from the sultry beams of day, afford them food, and clothing; whilst the sea offers continual plenty of its inexhaustible stores; and the day passes in ease and affluence, and the night in music and dancing. But amidst these enchanting scenes, savage nature still feasts on the flesh of its prisoners – appeases its Gods with human sacrifices – whole societies of men and women live promiscuously, and murder every infant born amongst them.[6]

The missionary ship *Duff* arrived in Tahiti in 1797 and landed four clergymen, supported by various tradesmen and their families. By the time the Russian explorer Thaddeus von Bellingshausen visited in 1820, the island was transformed. Not only had cannibalism and human sacrifice gone. The people now covered up in European clothes, their hair was cut short, tattooing was discouraged, liquor was banned, dancing and music were discouraged, and houses had walls. Converts acted as morality police who interrupted lovers, the sabbath was observed, and Tahitians were made to work.[7]

MELANESIA

The missionaries moved through the Pacific, finding their most willing flocks of converts on the Polynesian islands that had welcomed the first European explorers. The adoption of Christianity by various high chiefs in Tonga and Fiji in the first decades of the nineteenth century came in parallel with their efforts to construct higher, unified forms of government to deal with the growing incursions of the Europeans and Americans. The pyramid of chiefly authority helped Tonga's high chiefs to formalise a monarchy by 1875, which then agreed to British protection without ceding sovereignty. Elsewhere these efforts were less successful. The Fijian high chief Seru Epenisa Cakobau, who had adopted Christianity in 1854, declared himself king of Fiji in 1871 and attempted to build a modern state with guidance from European traders. It went bankrupt in 1874, forcing Cakobau to put Fiji under the British crown. The belated Māori attempt to unify, in the Kīngitanga movement in 1858, came too late to counter British settlement. The Tahitian kingdom, founded soon after Cook's visits, ended with cession of sovereignty to France in 1880. The Hawai'i kingdom, formed in 1795, had quickly got the idea of modern trade; its people were as active across the Pacific as the Americans and the Australian-based British early in the nineteenth century. But the kingdom was rendered unstable by the manoeuvring of white settlers and their armed militia. It was annexed by the United States in 1898.

Notwithstanding these reverses, the Polynesians came to be considered in the West, particularly in Britain, as loyal servants of God and soldiers of the King. The Māori and the Fijians had transferred their ancient battle skills to modern arms. The Tongan kingdom was considered a quaint imitation of the British monarchy and aristocracy. Tongans and Samoans became lay preachers for the missionaries, sent into Melanesian islands as advance parties for the white ordained ministers, often at the cost of their lives.

But having constructed the Melanesian category, the Europeans found it raised more questions and challenges. As a patrolling Royal Navy officer remarked on a voyage back from Tonga to Sydney in 1867, "the natives became more barbarous as we went westward". A decade later, the commander of the Royal Navy's Australian Squadron, covering the Pacific from

Sydney, pronounced that "Melanesians were too much of a wild beast to appreciate anything but the logic of force."[8]

The Melanesians, some of whom remained uncontacted by the outside world until the middle of the twentieth century, continued to be viewed as inferior, as the emerging science of evolution turned its attention to humanity. In Dumont d'Urville's racial hierarchy, later reinforced by Charles Darwin's writings (Darwin had closely studied the Pacific during the voyage of HMS *Beagle*), the Melanesian islanders were below the Polynesians, although above the Aboriginals of Australia and Tasmania, whom d'Urville also included in his Melanesia. European ideals of beauty contributed to this hierarchy.

Appearances aside, Melanesian political systems tended to be highly localised and based in many cases on haphazard ascendency of "big men". Their cultures were derided for superstition. "So we have the essentially universal European beliefs that, whereas all the native peoples in question are primitive, the Polynesian and Micronesian ways of life are relatively 'high' and the Melanesian cultures comparatively 'low'," wrote Valentine, noting the "absurdity" of the assumption that the lighter-skinned Polynesians and Micronesians, being more like Europeans, represented a higher form of humanity than the dark Melanesians.[9]

The three categories are actually nonsensical, says Paul Geraghty, the eminent linguist of the Fijian islands and beyond. "Even within geographical Melanesia there are two totally different language groups," he told me, sitting between piles of books in his room at the University of the South Pacific in Suva. "So, some parts of the Solomons and Papua New Guinea speak what are called Papuan languages and other parts speak what are called Oceanic languages. Still they don't have very much in common. The only things they have in common are what they also have in common with Polynesia and Micronesia. There's no such thing as a Melanesian culture or a Melanesian language. There's just what's left after you've taken away Polynesia and Micronesia."

Geraghty pointed to the example of the people of Rotuma, an island now included in Fiji but with a distinctive culture. "Rotuma is not Polynesian, as a lot of people think, and it's not Micronesia, and so by default you have to put it in Melanesia if you insist on having those three divisions," he said. "But to me it's more accurate to say … they are just Pacific people. They occasionally relate to Fijians, they occasionally relate to Polynesians, they are different, and it's the same with all these other parts of Melanesia, from New Caledonia to the Solomons and Papua New Guinea. They have certain things in common, but the fact they are called by this term *Mélanésie*, coined by Dumont d'Urville in 1840, is of no interest or relevance in terms of what's happening on the ground in language and culture."

Geraghty does agree that the people in Melanesia have had a bad rap among Europeans from the start, and that this persists today. "That was the perception," he said. "That is the perception … The Polynesians put their foot in the European door before the Melanesians did."

Part of the problem was that the European explorers approached Melanesia from the east. The biggest island in Melanesia – and the world's third largest island, after Australia and Greenland – remained just an outline on the map until the last quarter of the nineteenth century. The Portuguese who touched on its western and northern coastline called its people Papuans, possibly derived from words meaning "frizzy-haired", and wrote of them as *cafres* (kafirs, or heathens). Cook made only short forays ashore from the *Endeavour* on his passage home through the Torres Strait. He met hostile natives on a beach and described them as having much the same appearance as the "New Hollanders" of Australia, although their skin was not so dark.

However, the great naturalist Alfred Russel Wallace, who reached New Guinea via the East Indies and based himself in Manokwari, Western New Guinea, in 1858, was taken with the Papuans. His first glimpse of them had been in the Kai Islands in 1836, when about forty young men came out in canoes to meet him. He contrasted them with the "unanimated" Malays: "These forty black, naked, mop-headed savages seemed intoxicated with joy and excitement." Later he wrote that it was difficult to judge the "intellect" of the Papuans, but he was "inclined to rate it somewhat higher than that of the Malays, notwithstanding the fact that the Papuans have never yet made any advance towards civilisation".[10] In the Malays' defence, it might be said that after four centuries of subjection to Portuguese, Dutch and British inroads, they had much to be unenthusiastic about.

The Malays and other Asians had made forays of their own into the western fringes of New Guinea for many centuries. Some of the Moluccas had come under the kings of the eastern "spice islands", and some of their peoples had been the first in Melanesia to take up a monotheistic religion, Islam. Traders aboard prahus and junks swapped bronze drums and axes from present-day Vietnam for exotic forest and sea items such as bêche-de-mer and the aromatic massoy bark. Bird of paradise plumes found their way into the headdresses of the kings of Nepal and the Janissaries guarding the Ottoman sultans, and into the tribute sent to the Chinese emperor by the eighth-century kingdom of Sriwijaya in Sumatra.[11]

The missionaries and evolutionists were meanwhile wrangling over the question of whether all humanity belonged to the same species or was made up of several species at different stages of advancement. In modern terms, the question was essentially whether the assumed ascendency of Europeans was innate or created by environment. If it was the former, what was the point of trying to convert the heathen to the highest form of religion, Christianity? Although Charles Darwin argued that some peoples showed no sign of religious belief at all, the missionaries came to think that all savages were open to conversion. Any form of religion was an encouraging sign of their yearning for the spiritual, for answers to the big questions about the meaning of life, that distinguished humans from animals. It prepared the pagans for receiving the gospel, as scholars Helen Gardner and Christine Weir have written. "The Protestant call to translate the Bible into all tongues was based on the belief that every language had been created by God and therefore contained the means to describe the revelation of Jesus."[12]

Nearly all things about the New Guineans remained open to conjecture. In 1875, one "Captain J.A. Lawson" published *Wanderings in the Interior of New Guinea*, in which he claimed to have crossed the island from south to north and back again, to have seen a waterfall bigger than Niagara, a mountain taller than Everest, spiders as big as dinner plates, deer with long silky manes, huge apes and a 3-ton striped feline bigger than the tiger.

Within a few years, expeditions up the rivers and across swamps and razorback ranges, mounted at great cost in lives, dispelled such fantasies.

But the aura of darkness and danger was slow to vanish. Explorer after explorer reported hostile encounters, showers of barbed arrows met with volleys from Lee-Enfield and Snider-Enfield rifles. The New Guineans, like the peoples of the islands just to the east, remained associated with cannibalism, treachery, savagery, polygamy and poor treatment of women.

By the end of the century, however, Europeans were starting to question whether their own intrusion and shows of force might be creating that hostility. In 1871, the Russian nobleman Nikolai Miklouho-Maclay landed at an apparently deserted beach at Astrolabe Bay on the north coast with a display of European force: a Russian cruiser. Its crew helped him for a week to build a house before leaving him there "alone" with his servants. According to one possibly over-romanticised account, when a mass of armed local warriors approached, Maclay unrolled a mat and lay down as if to sleep, and they accepted his good intentions. He stayed there unharmed (except for malaria) for fifteen months, making forays into the mountains behind the coast. He spent another year there in 1876 and made a third visit in 1878. Another example of peaceful coexistence came in 1937, when Australian patrol officers Claude Champion and George Anderson led an expedition into the southern highlands and were confronted by thousands of warriors. They had the inspired thought to have their cook, Naisi, sit down in front of the warriors and play his mouth organ. All thought of conflict soon evaporated.[13]

Like Wallace, some Europeans were beginning to see Papuans in a different light. In 1876, the Italian Luigi Maria D'Albertis began exploring the great Fly River system. "Unlike the Anglo-Saxon explorers of New Guinea, D'Albertis acknowledged beauty when he saw it," wrote Gavin Souter. D'Albertis wrote of kissing his hand to one Papuan maiden. "My eyes, too, had told her that hers were the most beautiful eyes in Bioto, and that her form was more perfect than that of any of her companions." Later he wrote of an ambush in which six local sirens lured his boat to the bank; two of them were "handsome in their own style".[14]

Around the same time as Maclay's landing, missionaries were taking up the great challenge of New Guinea. In 1872, the prominent evangelist John Dunmore Lang lectured in Australia on "New Guinea: A Highly Promising

Field for Settlement and Colonisation", even though his own efforts among the Aboriginal peoples of Queensland had not been encouraging. The London Missionary Society sent in lay teachers from the Loyalty Islands (now attached to New Caledonia) and Samoa to villages around the Gulf of Papua, with European preachers following. It started a precarious foothold for Christianity, set back by periodic acts of cannibalism.

Others were interested not in saving souls but in making fortunes. In 1878, a small gold rush started inland from the harbour found by Captain John Moresby five years earlier on the south coast of Papua. On the Laloki River, about sixty fossickers panned for gold. A storekeeper acted as agent of the Queensland government until he was killed by sea-pirates. The gold discoveries petered out and by 1883 only five white people lived in what had come to be called Port Moresby – two missionaries, the wife of one, and two storekeepers. They were the only Europeans in the whole of New Guinea except for a few in Dutch mission stations at the Vogelkop (Bird's Head) at the island's far western end.

In London and other European capitals, entrepreneurs floated schemes for settlement and exploitation of New Guinea and nearby islands, using the East India Company and the Hudson Bay Company as models. The colonial office warned them off, saying the Royal Navy would stop them landing settlers. The Australian colonies, Queensland in particular, were causing enough unease about the unabashed "dispersal" of the Aboriginals to allow European settlement.

Britain was being drawn reluctantly into the Pacific Islands. It had stepped in to take over Cakobau's bankrupt kingdom in Fiji and appointed a high commissioner for the western Pacific to try to regulate the notorious "blackbirding" trade in Melanesian labourers for the new sugar plantations of Fiji, Queensland and Samoa. The colonial secretary, Lord Derby, hoped that was it. The empire already had "enough black subjects".

Yet pressure was building up in the Australian colonies. The interest shown by the Italian and Russian expeditions, stronger assertions of Dutch sovereignty over western New Guinea, and German preparations for commercial investment in northeastern New Guinea caused anxiety in Brisbane,

Sydney and Melbourne. Few Australians had plans to move or invest there. But by jingo, no non-British power should be allowed to seat itself just above the Australian mainland. A pattern was being set. Australians showed interest in the Pacific mainly when others showed up.

In April 1883, Queensland ordered its magistrate on Thursday Island, in the Torres Strait, to proceed to Port Moresby and annex the eastern half of New Guinea island for Queen Victoria. This he did, to great applause in Australia, although one of the missionaries on shore, William Lawes, said it would be better annexed as a crown colony than as an "appendage" to Queensland. "Nowhere in the world have aborigines been so basely and cruelly treated as in Queensland," Lawes wrote.[15] The British government learned about it from a Reuters report. Its prime minister, William Gladstone, was swayed by the arguments that Queensland, with its grim blackbirding trade and massacres of Aboriginal people, was unfit to govern a native population. The annexation was annulled.

This set off another recurrent feature of Australian engagement in New Guinea and Pacific: the journalistic race. The adventurous young George Ernest Morrison persuaded David Syme, publisher of the liberal Melbourne newspaper *The Age*, to finance an expedition to explore New Guinea. The conservative rival newspaper, *The Argus*, then appointed a former Queensland native police officer, Captain William Armit, to mount its own expedition. Both forays, with huge retinues of native carriers, wasted much money in penetrating short distances into the mountains behind Port Moresby before retreating. Morrison suffered near fatal arrow wounds after ignoring clear signs – a shield and crossed spears placed in his path – that he should go no further.[16]

In 1884 Germany made its move, annexing the northeastern portion of New Guinea island and the arc of large eastern islands down to the northern Solomons, all to be run by a commercial enterprise, the Deutsche Neuguinea Kompagnie (German New Guinea Company). Britain followed by declaring the southeast of the mainland a protectorate in November that year.

While their empire lasted, the Germans got the best of it. The big eastern islands provided flat, fertile land suitable for producing copra (dried coconut flesh) for the soap factories of Europe. The British domain, handed to Australia in 1906, was more difficult terrain and its administration, under the former judge Hubert Murray from 1908 to 1940, emphasised protection of the native peoples over commercial exploitation.

In the islands between New Guinea and Fiji, the British had meanwhile tried to avoid being drawn into responsibility for their native populations. The commissioner in Fiji and the commodore of the Royal Navy's Australian Station attempted to protect missionaries and traders in the Solomons and New Hebrides and to regulate the labour trade.

They largely failed at the latter task. The blackbirding schooners were too numerous and were quick to hoist non-British flags when approached. If their captains were arraigned in Australian courts for their more egregious atrocities, sympathetic juries let them off.

As for protecting the missionaries and traders, the British response to the killing and consumption of Europeans was usually a punitive expedition, weeks or months later, with carronades fired into jungles and shore parties burning down deserted villages. Ship captains walked a fine legal line: such futile blasts were "acts of war" and thus legal. The alternative of arresting a native and taking him for trial in Suva or Sydney posed problems of jurisdiction and reliable testimony.

The French had annexed New Caledonia in 1853 and developed plantations and mines using labour imported from the Loyalty Islands and the New Hebrides. France showed an interest in extending its rule over the New Hebrides in 1886, to the alarm of the Australian colonials. Britain was induced to intervene, forming a Joint Naval Commission with France in 1887 that ran combined punitive operations when required. In 1906, the two powers agreed to run the New Hebrides as a "condominium" with parallel administrations, and a top judiciary with the chief justice appointed by the King of Spain. The first judge he sent spoke neither English nor French and was deaf into the bargain. In 1893, the British declared a protectorate over the southern Solomon Islands and later traded Western Samoa to the Germans for Choiseul and other islands just south of Bougainville.

All this greatly exercised the politicians of the Australian colonies and impelled their negotiations to form a federation. Together in a combined new nation, the Australians on one side of the Pacific, with the Americans on the other, could wield the power to keep the Pacific Islands under safe Anglo-Saxon supervision. The new constitution, which came into effect in 1901, conferred the federal government with general powers over foreign relations and defence, as well as the power to make laws concerning "the relations of the Commonwealth with the islands of the Pacific". Edmund Barton, who would become Australia's first prime minister, declared: "here are a very large number of people who look forward with interest to the Commonwealth undertaking, as far as it can as part of the British Empire, the regulation of the Pacific Islands."

An early investment in this responsibility was the formation of the Royal Australian Navy and the purchase of a new fleet, including heavy and light cruisers, destroyers and submarines, which sailed into Sydney Harbour in 1911. In perhaps the earliest strategic study by the new federation, in 1913 a naval officer identified a "flexible tripwire" running from Singapore through Java and Timor to Papua, the Solomon Islands and Fiji: in case of war, "on this line we should attack the enemy", the officer observed.[17] It was not clear who might be the enemy, but outlying Australia was feared to be a tempting target for a whole range of alien powers.

The new fleet enabled Australia to assist in the seizure of Germany's Pacific colonies at the outbreak of the First World War and to take over Pacific duties such as punitive expeditions from the Royal Navy's Australian Station.

While the founding fathers of Australia asserted their rights of tutelage and control over the Pacific Islanders, they wanted Islanders to stay at home. The earliest legislation of the new federal parliament established the White Australia policy, barring cheap labour from impoverished Asia and the Pacific that would depress wages for the European working man and keeping the new nation's population comprised of "superior" British stock. The importation of Pacific Islands labour was banned from 1901, and most of the remaining "Kanakas" (a colloquial name derived from the Hawai'ians' word for themselves), as many as 7500 people, were sent back to their home islands or to plantations elsewhere. About 1600 were allowed to stay in

Australia because of local marriages or long settlement, seeding a small community of descendants identifying as "Australian South Sea Islanders".

The Allied victory in the First World War gave Canberra the opportunity to hold on to its conquests. The Australian prime minister, William Hughes, was talking about a "Monroe Doctrine for the Pacific", modelled on the American warning to European powers to stay out of Latin America. Australia needed to ensure that "the great rampart of islands stretching around the northeast of Australia" would "be held by us or by some Power in whom we have absolute confidence".

At the Paris Peace Conference in 1919, Hughes fought opposition from the US president, Woodrow Wilson, for Australia's right to hold on to the former German territories of New Guinea and nearby islands. Hughes did not get his wish for outright annexation. Instead, the former German territories were subject to a League of Nations mandate that required a level of supervision from Geneva. However, Hughes secured acceptance of Australia's right to control immigration to the New Guinea territories, ending Germany's looser regime, which had allowed a thriving Asian trading community of about 1500 people, mostly Chinese, to settle in Rabaul and other towns. Under the new Australian rule, in a bizarre application of the White Australia policy, Asian men found it difficult to get permits for their brides to join them, or indeed for any female relatives of childbearing age. Many lasting marriages between Chinese men and Melanesian women were the result.

In contrast to Papua, where Hubert Murray gave more weight to the protection of native life and customs than to economic exploitation, the separately administered territory of New Guinea saw a full-blooded continuation of the German emphasis on commerce. The Australian trading companies Burns Philp and W.R. Carpenter assisted in the carve-up of confiscated German assets. W.R. Carpenter ran a dummy ownership scheme, installing Australian war veterans as nominal owners of small land allocations from the extensive German plantations. When those veterans actually running their own little and quite uneconomic plantations got into trouble, as many did, the trading firms were there to foreclose on their debts. Indentured labour was the norm on these plantations.

Flogging was officially banned but widely practised.

In 1926, the discovery of gold on the eastern coast of the main island set off a rush. Adventurers from around the Pacific flocked to Papua, including the Tasmanian-born future film star Errol Flynn. To get their tools and camping gear into these remote places, prospectors recruited young men from coastal villages as porters by bribing their chiefs; they fared wretchedly in the damp and cold high mountains they had to cross under heavy loads. The advent of aircraft helped to develop the mines. By 1933, the grass airstrip at Wau was the busiest airfield in the world, measured in take-offs and landings. Stripped of fittings and carrying minimum fuel, the new all-metal aircraft, such as the Junkers and Ford tri-motors, could ferry in the components of massive dredges to be assembled on the goldfield.[18]

Aircraft also scouted further into the highlands, ahead of expeditions on foot by goldminers such as the Leahy brothers. There they discovered relatively large populations living in wide, fertile valleys marked by intensive agriculture. More recently, some of these communities have been found to date back thousands of years.

The nineteenth-century belief in a hierarchy of racial types was only slowly fading. In a fundraising pamphlet, "The Call of the Pacific", published in 1912, the missionary John Burton ranked Fijians below the Tongans, Samoans, Tahitians and Māori, but above "the Western peoples of the New Hebrides, New Britain and New Guinea". "They have not the same intellectual development, and their civilisation is of a coarser order," he wrote. "There seems a sort of arrested development."[19] Even in the 1920s, some anthropologists pushed the same line. Popular books warned that the supremacy of the European race was being challenged by intermarriage, which threatened to dilute its superior capacities. The pseudoscience of eugenics flourished, giving rise to political movements stressing racial purity.

In the Pacific colonies, Europeans stayed a remote distance from their local subjects. Papuan men were forbidden to wear shirts, in case they did not keep them clean. They were barred from consuming alcohol and not allowed into the same cinemas as Europeans. A "White Women's Protection Ordinance" made Papuan men fearful of even greeting European women.

Only on the cricket pitch was there significant social mingling. Many of the European men nevertheless had local women as mistresses, and a small population of mixed-race children resulted. Some of these children were ignored; others were acknowledged and educated in Australia. Less clearly recorded, there were also relationships between European women and Melanesian men. Between 1924 and 1940, however, no mixed-race marriages were recorded in the territories of Papua and New Guinea.

The "great rampart of islands" fell rapidly after Japan attacked the Western powers in December 1941. In January 1942 a huge invasion force stormed into Rabaul, which became the base for air and naval operations further afield. Other Japanese forces landed along the northern coast of New Guinea. Soon after the British surrendered in Singapore, the Dutch were overwhelmed and surrendered the Indies in February, with elements of their administration and local forces escaping to Australia and some holding a last toehold in the swampy southeast corner of their New Guinea territory. Then began years of counter-operations. American forces pushed up from the New Hebrides to wrest the Solomons from the Japanese, while Australian and American troops pushed the Japanese back along the Kokoda Track to the north coast. All the while, great naval and air battles raged around the islands.

As elsewhere, the war disrupted the relationship between colonial rulers and the ruled. In the Americans, Pacific Islanders saw a much wealthier power than the Australians, British and French. They gained in some instances much better wages for their labour than before. They saw African Americans in command of modern technology, and they found American soldiers more inclined to be friendly than the old colonial settlers and officials. The Americans were often deeply appreciative of the care given by local staff to their wounded.

Much sentimentality has washed over this wartime encounter. The "fuzzy-wuzzy angels" who carried ammunition up the Kokoda Track and the wounded back to Port Moresby were conscripted without much choice, and they were paid meagrely for their arduous and risky work. In some regions, local people welcomed the Japanese and their promise of a new, equal order. Australian patrols handed out harsh justice to these collaborators. After the war, Australian administrators and businesses returned. Australian expat communities gathered in bowling clubs and supermarkets. The two territories of Papua and New Guinea were now administered as one, and a new governor in Port Moresby started inviting Papua New Guineans to tea and dinner.

By the 1960s, it was accepted for kiaps (Australian patrol officers) to marry their local girlfriends. Australian governments generally thought that independence for Papua New Guinea was a distant prospect, requiring decades of education and development, but this belief was challenged by examples of decolonisation elsewhere. Fiji gained independence in 1970, and Papua New Guinea followed in 1975. The Solomons secured independence in 1978 and the New Hebrides became the independent Vanuatu in 1980, the only one of the Melanesian states to reach independence via a degree of armed struggle. (New Caledonia's sometimes violent independence movement is still unresolved.)

In the decades since, scholars have continued to work on the riddle of the Melanesians and their origins. How did these mostly dark people, with their 1100 or so languages, come to be interposed between the Malays to the west and the Polynesians of the central and eastern Pacific, whose fewer languages share many common words?

Linguists have long found that many of the languages of island Melanesia, east of New Guinea, shared common antecedents with those of the Southeast Asian and Polynesian archipelagos. Archaeologists have carbon-dated shards of a distinctive decorated "Lapita" pottery across the island chain and out to Tonga and Samoa, indicating a southeastward maritime traffic around 3500 years ago. But geneticists have found that some speakers of those languages had DNA closer to the Papuans isolated deep in New Guinea: about 90 per cent of the genetic make-up of many present-day Vanuatu people is shared with populations in New Guinea, and the percentage is also high among the Fijians. Even the remote Polynesians had significant Papuan ancestry.

The Papuan presence in the northwest of the island chain – the Bismarck Archipelago in present-day Papua New Guinea and the northern Solomons (including Bougainville) – was known to be ancient. They had been part of the "Out of Africa" movement of humanity many tens of millennia ago. The last great ice age, with sea levels as much as 125 metres below present levels, produced two great shelves of land: Sunda in the west of present day Indonesia, and Sahul, linking New Guinea, mainland Australia and Tasmania as a continuous land mass. Across the intervening zone of deep sea and islands, known as Wallacea, the Papuans migrated in bamboo rafts and small canoes between 60,000 and 50,000 years ago. As winds and currents reversed with the monsoon seasons, it was not an irrevocable step, although there were times during the voyage that the island behind dropped out of sight before the next one ahead appeared, in sea gaps of up to 90 kilometres.

One branch of this migration went across the north of Wallacea to the New Guinea mainland, and then beyond, reaching New Britain and New Ireland in the Bismarcks 39,000 years ago, and Bougainville and its nearby islands 32,000 years ago. A second branch of migration followed the present Nusa Tenggara and Timor chain before crossing to the Sahul Shelf south of present-day New Guinea. Some people stayed in New Guinea. Others walked south and dispersed across Australia as far as Tasmania. Long before the global warming cycle raised the sea level and separated Papua from Australia (and Australia from Tasmania) some 8500 years ago, their cultures evolved distinctly, despite some contact in northern Australia.

Then came the Austronesians, an Asiatic maritime people originating in Taiwan and nearby coasts of mainland China. They crossed into the Southeast Asian archipelago about 5000 years ago. Then from about 3350 years ago they ventured around the north of New Guinea Island to the Bismarcks and the northern Solomons, evidenced by the remains of the Lapita pottery they produced.

They developed the technology for fast, long-distance voyages. They built up the sides of their dugout canoes with planks, lashed an outrigger for stability, and used an inverted-triangle sail of woven matting that, as with a present-day sailboard, pivoted fore and aft on its lower point and allowed passage close to the wind. The new sail design allowed them to cross the 350-kilometre ocean gap from the main Solomon Islands to the Santa Cruz group, near present-day Vanuatu, and then beyond to Fiji, Tonga and Samoa.

Later the Austronesians developed the double-hulled canoe, its wide platform allowing passengers, domestic animals, food supplies and stocks of seed and tuber roots to migrate across hundreds of kilometres of open sea, guided by the stars and knowledge of seasonal winds and currents. They reached the Marquesa Islands by about 200 BC, Hawai'i and Rapanui (Easter Island) by about 500 AD and New Zealand by about 1200 AD. To the far west, Austronesian voyagers reached Madagascar and East Africa by about 700 AD.

Yet the sequence of migration across the near and middle Pacific remained a matter of contesting theories until 2015, when geneticists managed to build entire genome sequences from the bone of ancient individuals buried close to the Vanuatu capital Port Vila. It was revolutionary. These people seem to have been the first humans to live there, and they show little or no Papuan ancestry.

So it appears the Austronesians of distant East Asian ancestry moved through the Bismarck Archipelago without much admixture with the Papuans, possibly for cultural reasons, bypassing the main Solomon Islands, and settling remote Oceania as far as Tonga and Samoa. Only later did a secondary steady migration of people with a high-degree of Papuan ancestry happen, spreading Papuan genes across the Pacific, and in Vanuatu's case producing the unusual result of a near-total genetic switch without replacing the languages of the first settlers. In later centuries, back migration spread Austronesian languages further into the Solomons. Then from about 1000 years ago, Tongans voyaged northwest, establishing settlements in the Loyalty Islands of New Caledonia and the "Polynesian" outliers of the Solomons, notably Ontong Java east of Malaita, and the Rennell-Bellona group, where they exterminated an early race of smaller, darker inhabitants.[20]

But it was not a one-way movement. Edible bananas, sugar cane and other staples came back to Southeast Asia. Wallace had found it impossible to fix an ethnological boundary between Asia and Melanesia like his famous line separating their flora and fauna. Pockets of Papuan languages and cultural traits can be found deep into Indonesia's eastern islands and Timor-Leste. The westernmost was on the island of Sumbawa, until it was wiped out by the eruption of Mount Tambora in 1815.

Today, Melanesian islanders are pondering their place in the world. The old colonial image of Melanesians as barbarous and unpredictable still lurks in the Western perception and even among Melanesians themselves. These negative representations, says Solomon Islands scholar Tarcisius Kabutaulaka, "have over time been internalised by Pacific Islanders, including Melanesians, and used to perpetuate relationships with Melanesia that have racist, essentialist, and social evolutionary elements."

But more recently, Melanesians have been breaking free of this perception, Kabutaulaka notes:

> since the 1970s, Melanesians have appropriated the term Melanesia and used it for self-identification, turning it from a derogatory term to a positive one: a source of pride and self-identification. They have appropriated a colonial concept and deployed it as an instrument of empowerment. Since the late 1980s, they have used it to mobilise through subregional organisations such as the Melanesian Spearhead Group and events such as the Melanesian Festival of Arts and Culture. This has enabled Melanesian countries to assert political and economic power in Oceania and to redefine and re-present themselves.

The result is a movement called Melanesianism, full of ambiguities and largely undefined, like the earlier expression of a "Melanesian way" in political activity by the Papua New Guinean writer Bernard Narokobi. "Melanesianism is rooted in and draws strength from the past but is not confined by it," Kabutaulaka says. "It exists and is real because it is talked about, lived and experienced, not because it is defined."

This discourse or *tok stori* celebrates the idea of Melanesia for its peoples. "They have subsequently created 'alter-natives' who are clawing their way out of the ignoble savage cocoon where they have been encased for centuries," Kabutaulaka concludes. "Melanesians, armed with diverse and rich cultures, have captured the ignoble savage, turned it on its head and used the term Melanesia to establish their place in Oceania and beyond, creating new and empowering images. Melanesians are asserting their 'place in the sun in Oceania.'"[21]

This book is about journeys to discover these "alter-native" Melanesians.

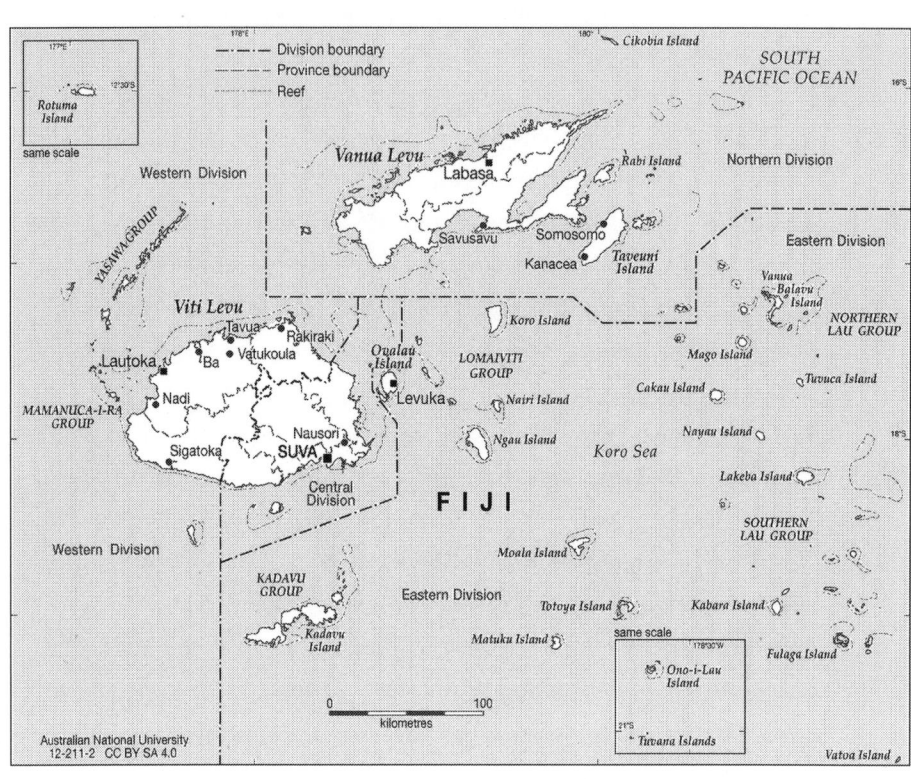

2

FIJI

The God in the Mountain

MY SEARCH FOR MELANESIA began in Fiji, where the indigenous peoples had encountered two very different waves of outsiders. One was the military and cultural invasion through the eastern islands by Polynesian chiefs and their warriors. This put the Fiji islands across that blurry boundary of Melanesia and Polynesia. Then came the nineteenth-century sugar industry that imported plantation and factory workers from India, leaving a diaspora that threatened the i-Taukei (indigenous Fijian) hold on their own country.

One morning in the rainy season found me climbing the Nakauvadra Range in the north of Viti Levu, the main island. This wall of mountains, shading from the green of the valley below up to an ominous black along the continuous ridge at the top, contains the essence of Fiji in more ways than one.

In a gleaming well-guarded factory off the King's Highway on the coast below, the Fiji Water company bores into aquifers beneath these mountains, bottles the artesian flow, and markets it as "Earth's finest water". An astute contribution got it product placement in Barack Obama's first election campaign.

Nakauvadra is also the home of Degei, paramount god and founding father for the Fijians before the missionaries came, and still a deity ranking somewhere just below Jehovah and Jesus. Degei lived in a vast cave at the highest point of this range, sometimes taking the form of a giant snake. It is unclear, from what Fijians have told researchers, how benign a god he is.

Three hours into the ascent, I was beginning to wonder myself.

The journey to this village and this mountain had begun out of a sense of something missing from the Fiji Museum.

The museum is a very interesting one. It has some examples of Lapita pottery dug up around the Fijian islands, the earliest evidence of human habitation dating back about 3000 years. The display calls the Lapita people "proto-Polynesians". It has a magnificent full-size sailing canoe, nearly 14 metres in length, one of the fast and sturdy outriggers that in more recent centuries linked the islands of Oceania. There was a room full of *tabua*, sperm whale's teeth exchanged as ceremonial gifts to show good intentions, make amends or get a wife.

There is mention of the earliest days of Fiji's encounter with Europeans. There is a cabinet full of images of Cakobau's brief attempt to create a Fijian kingdom, including photographs of a pygmy priest, two warriors taken as prisoners of tribal war and the pickled arm of a slain chief, all sold by Cakobau's government to P.T. Barnum's circus in the United States.

As well as Cakobau, the display features Ma'afu, the Tongan prince who invaded the Lau Islands in the east of Fiji in 1848 and contested power with Cakobau. There is a whole display case for the Rev. Thomas Baker, a Methodist missionary killed and eaten in central Viti Levu in 1867, along with seven Fijian assistants. It includes a shoe the killers put into the earth oven, believing it part of Baker's body.

There are photographs of early colonial governors and offices after the cession in 1874, when the British set up the *Bose Levu Vakaturaga*, the Great Council of Chiefs, as a deft strategy to keep traditional authority on their side.

There are respectful pictures and relics of Ratu Sir Lala Sukuna (1888–1958), a talented scion of the chiefly line of the eastern Bau Islands who became the first Fijian to earn a university degree (from Oxford) and to be admitted to the English bar. From the interwar years he rose to be a senior statesman, shaping the British perception of Fijians as trusted members of the empire, partly by raising a Fijian battalion to fight the Japanese in 1943. He also helped develop the linked institutions of state and traditional chieftainship that led to independence in 1970, with the high chief of Lau, Ratu Sir Kamisese Mara, a relative, as founding prime minister.

But about what went before, there is only a wall chart against the back wall, titled "Old Religion" with inverted commas, as if to apologise for calling it religion. Three paragraphs mention faith in *kalou vu*, or founding ancestor gods, and the practice of communicating with them through possessed priests, often with the help of *yaqona* (kava). There is a small display case of rattles and other paraphernalia used for casting spells.

It's as though the official culture accepts that before the Methodists brought the Bible and their Victorian morality, and before Cakobau and Ma'afu established the Tongan paramount chieftainship model and teamed up with imperial Britain, Fiji was a place of utter savagery and chaos.

Yet when I asked Elia Nakoro, a senior curator, whether the old religion had completely gone, he said that in many or most villages, *vakatevoro*, or "witchcraft", was practised alongside Christianity. A particular person, often from Ra (the province around Drauniivi and Rakiraki on the north side of Viti Levu) or the other big island, Vanua Levu, would, for the gift of a bag or two of kava and a pack of cigarettes, go into a trance and divine who was making someone sick, or who had stolen something. Sometimes, Fiji's police employed such a person to find offenders.

The linguist Paul Geraghty came to Fiji as a young man to compile a dictionary of Fijian and has stayed for decades. Everyone I met in Fiji knew him. They called him Paul nGereti, giving his Irish name a Fijian twist. When I went to see him at the University of the South Pacific, a leafy campus on the site of an old New Zealand flying-boat base on the edge of Suva, I tentatively and almost apologetically broached the subject of witchcraft.

"What you say is true, and you are understating it," Geraghty said. "The belief in traditional powers and traditional spirits is absolutely everywhere. If someone is ill, the first question will be: Who's making him ill? And then they will go to someone else to counter that.

"In Nadi recently, visiting an adopted family of mine, they have a little boy who's named after me. They said, 'Did you know your namesake can cure burns? I said, 'I didn't know that, how?' Well his grandmother is from Beqa. And the Beqa people are famous for fire walking and they're also famous for just being able to touch the burn and it heals. And they said, without blinking an eye, 'The grandparent passed this on to your namesake, who's a boy of about twelve, and he can do it.' And they all believe it…

"In a way it's what holds Fijian society together," Geraghty went on. "If you didn't have that then you wouldn't have a Fijian society. Every Fijian child knows there are certain places where you don't go because they're haunted."

Did this belief include the old gods such as Degei? "Yes, it can do. Most people know who their ancestor god is. And they also know that their ancestor god has what they call *waqa* or *waqawaqa*, which is a form in which they are visible. And that can be an animal or bird, like a white dog, or sometimes even a person like a dwarf. So when I see a white dog I know it's my ancestor calling, I know something is going to happen."

And what do the Fijian churches say about all of this? "They might have preached against it in the nineteenth century," Geraghty said. "[But] I know priests who go and get traditional medicine. They say it's all god-given."

Fiji is unique among the Melanesian nations in having a common language among its native people, even if, as Geraghty has documented, there are some 300 dialects. "Fiji people do understand each other," he told me, but then adds: "It's like British dialects going back 200 years. Today they generally understand each other, but 200 years ago a Geordie would not understand a Cornishman. Not a word. That's the same in Fiji."

Geraghty recalled talking to Fijians from the eastern islands who had travelled to Nadroga, in the southwest of Viti Levu. "They said the people there might as well be speaking Hindi," he said. "Many would say there are two distinct languages, Eastern Fijian and Western Fijian, but it's being gradually standardised, in the eastern direction. There are some exceptions, but people are drifting towards what they call Bauan language."

But are they Melanesians? "Fijians do sometimes say 'We are Melanesians and proud of it', when it's to their advantage," Geraghty said. He pointed to the example of a regional grouping called the Melanesian Spearhead Group. "They happily belong to that." Frank Bainimarama, the coup leader turned elected prime minister, had become an enthusiastic member when his initial military government was excluded from the wider Pacific Islands Forum and the Commonwealth.

"What I don't hear is Fijians being jealous of Polynesians," Geraghty said. "They are a very proud people. There was a famous German botanist who wrote that just as every Roman citizen was proud to say they were Roman, every Fijian was very proud to say they were Fijians ... If you look at the history of the nineteenth century, when the Tongan chief Ma'afu conquered what you could say was a great deal of Fiji, nevertheless Fijians will say he was actually one of them, as his mother was from Fiji and he had certain rights because of it. Though I would say it was due to the fact he had firearms, which the Fijians didn't."

If there is a cultural spectrum from Polynesian to Melanesian in Fiji, it is widely seen as running from east to west. So, to look for the underlying, original Fiji, I went west, to the place where Fiji was founded, according to legend, in a journey that culminated in my climb up the Nakauvadra Range.

The village of Viseisei sprawls over low-lying flat land alongside the wide lagoon that is the outer anchorage for Fiji's second largest city and port, Lautoka. Viseisei is an ethnic Fijian node in a region built up on sugar cane, and hence with a large Indo-Fijian population.

A travel agent living in Viseisei, Finau Moce Bavadra, invited me to stay with her and her husband, Api. When I got to their two-bedroom cement-block house, it was already dark. A group of men sat on the porch next door around a *yaqona* bowl. Finau was a convivial woman around sixty years old with curly hair, wrapped in a sarong patterned in the black, brown and white of traditional bark-cloth. She gave me dinner: a slice of fish cooked in coconut milk, cassava slices, and spinach. Api was a big man, temporarily out of work; his usual job was as a singer in a nearby resort. They had no children of their own, but a procession of adoptees came in and out of the house. After dinner we all went to sleep, me in one of the bedrooms, the family stretched out on woven mats in the main room.

When I woke the following morning, Finau had already taken the early bus to Nadi Airport to meet some tourists, whom she would put on a boat out to the Yasawa Islands. The Bavadras' adopted daughter, Kailesi, was ironing her school tunic on a towel laid on the floor. Api made us tea. I walked out to look around. Coconut palms and breadfruit trees were lit by the sun coming over the mountains to the east. In the centre of the village was a green with a white-painted monument to the arrival of Methodist missionaries in 1835 and a simple white masonry church. The sound of a choir came from inside. On the other side of the green were some formal-looking buildings in semi-traditional style, with the Fijian flag, a pale-blue ensign, flying from a post. The lagoon beyond was calm, pale blue like the flag.

Back at the house, Api told me that the village was on a five-day limited fast, imposed by the pastors at the church. No kava, no alcohol, no cigarettes. "It might help our population growth," Api said. "Men get on the kava, then all they want to do is go to sleep." The women and children were keeping up a relay of hymn singing for the entire five days; husbands would have to take their chances between choral shifts.

Mid-morning, a pastor, introduced as Kata, came to visit. He was a tall, lean man with a lantern-jaw face. He was dressed in a long-sleeved pink shirt, iridescent mauve tie and dark grey *sulu*, the kilt that is Fijian male formal dress. He was filling in a ledger with details of each household's residents.

I asked him about the belief in spirits among his flock. "Yes, it is there," he said. "The *kalou vu*, the spirits of the ancestors. They are like good angels for the people." But what about the bad spirits, the people who use spells? "I advise people to believe in Jesus, to maintain good relations with your neighbours, and follow your leaders, from the household to the *mataqali* [clan] to the *yavusa* [village] to the *vanua* [chiefdom]." The Methodist Church and the chiefly system again, reinforcing each other.

Before leaving, Pastor Kata said a prayer, partly in Fijian, partly in English. He asks for a blessing for "this visitor from Australia, to help him learn about our path from un-Christianity to Christianity."

Just around the coast from Viseisei is Vuda, a point projecting into the lagoon where the first canoe is said to have landed after the original Fijians' long sea voyage from the west. The canoe hit the reef and was holed. The canoe is named Kaunitoni, which roughly translates as "a log under water". Viseisei means "dispersal", and legend says that the Fijians scattered and settled all over the islands after this first landing.

When asked, Fijians will often say that they came ultimately from "Tanganyika", the region of East Africa south of Kilimanjaro. This history is even found in school textbooks. Tanganyika, a name from old atlases, is always used instead of Tanzania, the modern state that includes it. Somehow the proto-Fijians circled the Indian Ocean and came down through the islands to here. Some talk of a diversion via Egypt.

The legend seems designed to reinforce Fijian exceptionalism. One of Api and Finau's adoptive sons told me Fiji was a special place because of its location on the international dateline: yesterday on one side, today on the other. Graham Davis, a Sydney television journalist who grew up in Fiji as the son of the head of the Methodist Church, told me of the affinity *iTaukei* (ethnic Fijians) feel for the Israelis. Both are "chosen people", and a Fijian head of state once said as much on a visit to Israel.

There are scholars who think the Kaunitoni legend is recent propaganda. They point out that it was not noted by any of the missionaries, amateur ethnologists or colonial officials who took down much else from Fijians in the nineteenth century. Its first reported mention came in 1895, and it next appeared in 1913. Unusually for an oral legend, it is told from one end of the Fijian islands to the other and is included in official histories. Sceptical scholars suggest it was a modern construct used in nation-building.[1]

But other scholars believe there can be historical truth in legends, and maybe this can help uncover Fiji's more Melanesian past. Aubrey Parke (1925–2007) was an experienced archaeologist when he came to Fiji as a colonial civil servant in 1951. Also a skilled linguist, he soon mastered Fijian and became an assiduous collector of traditional legends. From these he outlined a tentative history. He pictured a landing at Vuda by an ancestor-god or chief named Lutunasobasoba who stayed and settled around Viseisei, while Degei split off and sailed around to the Ra coast before moving up into the Nakauvadra mountains.[2]

Inland from Viseisei was an ancient settlement, close to a long tidal creek, perhaps more easily defended. It is now a nondescript village called Lomolomo, off the Queen's Road towards Nadi. The hill behind, known as Edronu, was where Fijians traditionally went to seek *mana* – spiritual power – from two caves where ancestor-spirits dwelt. In 1943, Fijian soldiers reportedly went there to seek *mana* before heading off to fight in the Solomons.

Api and I rented a car and bought a couple of *sevu-sevu* (gift) bundles of kava.

At Lomolomo we walked up to the village council house and sat on the edge of a wide woven mat. After a wait, the village headman came from a side door and sat on the opposite side of the mat. A former policeman with a military-style moustache, he looked irked at being disturbed. Api slid one of the *sevu-sevu* packages across to him. I tried to maintain a dignified cross-legged position as long as I could, while I asked permission to climb to Edronu.

The headman pondered this. "You are a writer, and you want to go and see all this, and then write it up and make money from a book?" he asked. I explained that the prospects of profit were not great from a project like this. I eased my clamped legs. "Sit properly!" he barked, and he shook his head dismissively. It was outrageous, he was effectively saying, that someone would come in like this and try to make money from their legends.

The interview was over. He kept the kava.

We got a better reception next morning from Ratu Tevita Momoedonu, one of the upper-middle chiefs of Viseisei and a nephew of the paramount chief of the Vunda region, the late Josefa Iloilo. He had been close to Timoci Bavadra, founder of the Fiji Labour Party and leader of the ill-fated government overthrown by Colonel Sitiveni Rabuka in 1987. Bavadra, a medical doctor, came from Viseisei. He died of cancer two years after being deposed, something that inevitably got Fijians gossiping about spells and divine retribution.

In 1999 Ratu Tevita stood for Labour and won the local seat in parliament. Labour formed government under Mahendra Chaudhry, the country's first Indo-Fijian prime minister, with Bavadra's widow as his deputy. A year later, Ratu Tevita was thrust into prominence when a mixed-race businessman, George Speight, led disaffected special forces soldiers in a coup against Chaudhry, whom he held hostage in parliament along with all but one MP: Tevita, who was away from parliament at the time. The president, Ratu Sir Kamisese Mara, swore Tevita in as prime minister so that he could give the necessary advice that a state of emergency should be declared. That constitutional task done, Tevita resigned fifteen minutes later. He would later go to Japan as ambassador. By the time Api and I met with him, he was retired from politics, running a trading business and living in a large house by the lagoon.

Tevita sat me down in a chair next to him. Api felt more comfortable sitting lower, on the floor. Tevita laughed at the story of our encounter at Lomolomo the previous day and gave us his take on the Kaunitoni story. The first-landing ancestor was followed by his eldest son, who remained in Viseisei – something the history books suppressed, he said. Worship of these ancestor-gods had been very much part of local life but had weakened with the arrival of the churches. "They converted the chief, so the missionaries were not clubbed to death," he said.

However, belief in the old gods persisted. "Despite the fact that Christianity is very prevalent here, there are still some remnants of people who cling to the worship of these devils. I call them devils. They are devil-worshippers!"

Not guardian angels, like the pastor had said? "Guardian angels come from God, not devils."

Ratu Tevita had no regrets for the passing of the old ways. The devils told you to club your brothers. They demanded that when a chief died, his wives be buried alive alongside him. The custom was also to bury women in the foundations of chiefly *bure* (meeting halls) for auspicious effect. Before he converted to Christianity, the nineteenth-century great chief Cakobau had an island for fattening people up for cannibal feasts.

Vuda had been spared this. "Some guardian angel intervened: Don't eat your brothers."

The chiefly system was a disguise for naked force in the old days: the rule of the club. Now this history was repeated as farce. "The chiefs now take it for granted that they are born leaders," he said. "But they lack the brains, they are uneducated." In some meetings of the chiefs, "they just sit down and say, 'Give us the grog [kava].'" The Great Council of Chiefs had become an irrelevance before it was abolished by Bainimarama for not approving his seizure of power in 2006. "If you should have attended one of its meetings, you'd see that members slept, literally were asleep," Ratu Tevita said. "All the issues that were raised came from politicians controlling the meetings. But the chiefs themselves, in their capacity as traditional leaders, were a bunch of hooligans: no vision, no drive, no nothing but carrying the attitude that 'I am a chief.'"

This was why he had joined the Labour Party: to fight the corruption that had grown up under the mutually supportive rule of Mara's Alliance Party and the chiefs. "Mara would come there like a god!" he said. "Where would you sit when Ratu Mara was there?" But Bavadra only lasted a month as prime minister, thanks to the fear among native Fijians that Indo-Fijians would take over. "I tell you, without the presence of the Indians in this country, Fijians would have been worse off than any undeveloped country in the Pacific," Tevita told me. "The Indians turned the economy of this country. We still have a lot to learn from them. They till the land, get paid, when the iTaukei people only drink grog and sleep."

In 1987, Tevita had been among several busloads of people from the west of Viti Levu who'd gone to Suva to try to save Bavadra's government. They drove onto the landing for the boat to Bau Island, with the intention of meeting the retired governor-general Sir George Cakobau, the revered great-grandson of the nineteenth-century high chief and a war hero himself. They were intercepted by a group of Colonel Rabuka's supporters, well-educated iTaukei people. "They said, 'You people from the West, you go back, otherwise it will be big trouble,'" Tevita recalled. "So I told the team, 'Don't give them the excuse, we don't want to get hurt unnecessarily.

Board your bus. Let's go back.'"

Ethno-nationalism was still a powerful force in Fiji, Tevita told me. "What I am scared of is: we have not eradicated that racial feeling among iTaukei people, despite the fact that we have received Christianity, we worship God ... A slight thing like that could trigger the whole thing, and that could be another repetition of what happened in 2000." Speight's 2000 coup against Chaudhry, the first Indo-Fijian prime minister, was accompanied by violence against Indians. Should Bainimarama become president and leave his Indo-Fijian attorney-general and finance minister Aiyaz Sayed-Khaiyum as prime minister, there could be an even worse backlash, Tevita said. "If it came to Fijians hurting Fijians, then *kalou vu* can come up." (In elections two years after this conversation, in 2022, Rabuka defeated Bainimarama. He has since restored the Great Council of Chiefs.)

"Then we have the biggest devil of all, the Methodist Church, a wolf in sheep's clothing," Tevita added. In his view, the church was spreading a dangerous message that "this land was created for iTaukei, full stop", and that "If the Indians want to rule a country [they should] go back to India". "That message is coming out from the pulpit," he said. "In the 1987 coup, Rabuka was endorsed by two institutions: the Methodist Church and the Great Council of Chiefs."

Our meeting was over. Tevita pushed back the *sevu-sevu* of kava. "I don't drink this, it makes you stupid and lazy," he said. "If I have an evening meeting, I tell my men: 'You do your homework between eight and ten, then come to the meeting.'"

My conversation with Tevita had highlighted a clear division in Fiji, not between Melanesian and Polynesian cultures, but between western Viti Levu, where people had tended to support Bavadra's government, and the eastern Tailevu region (around the Bau landing), where there had been support for the 1987 and 2000 coups. The west's resistance to the power nexus of the eastern chiefs, to the colonial government and its heirs and to the Methodists went back a long way, to the early decades after Fiji's cession to the British crown. It had been strongest near the northern coast of the island, in Ra Province, in particular around the village of Drauniivi.

In reading about Fiji's history, I had jotted down some notes on a sheet of paper: place names, some local personages and historical characters in two key movements of resistance. One of these movements, Tuka, was religious. The other was an economic cooperative called the Viti Kabani, or Fiji Company. Among the contemporary sources was Leone Naisua, a man from Drauniivi whom a historian from the University of the South Pacific, Robert Nicole, had acknowledged as being a great help for a book largely about these two movements.[3]

Api had looked at these notes and recognised Naisua's name. "I remember him: we worked together maybe thirty years ago at the Treasure Island Resort," he said. My plan to take a bus to Drauniivi and arrive unannounced was put aside. Api would drive me there and introduce me in person.

So we set off around the western and northern coast: an open county of treeless hills, fields of sugar cane, narrow-gauge rail tracks running alongside the road, mangrove forests, little houses with boats in their yards. Past the towns of Ba and Tavua, full of Indian shops, canteens and taxis, then into less settled Ra. A sign indicating the road to the Fiji Water plant on the right, a ranch-style gateway to a government cattle project, and then Drauniivi, a low-lying village between the highway and the mangroves.

We turned off the main road and found some people gathered under a shady tree. Api got out and asked for Leone Naisua. There was a shout, and suddenly an old man was embracing Api. Leone had died some time back, but this was his younger brother, Tava, who had also worked at Treasure Island with Api and Finau all those years ago. We retrieved the *sevu-sevu* from the car and passed it over, and it was arranged I should come back two days later and stay.

To fill in the time back at Viseisei, I quizzed the Bavadras' adoptive daughter, Kailesi, about what she was being taught about the old legends at the local high school. Her teacher had described Degei as a "shapeshifter" – sometimes in the form of a human, sometimes a snake. I couldn't think of a better way to explain it to a class of thirteen-year-olds.

Api, his son and another man were going up to their patch of traditional land in the nearby hills to collect firewood for earth ovens at a marriage feast in the village, and I went along in their borrowed car. From the nearest road, we walked down a track through bushland and swam across the muddy Vuda River to get to this little farm of cassava and papaya. We piled the firewood by a track that a truck could reach later and picked a bag of wild spinach for dinner. We then drove home on to Viseisei via a different route. Api pointed to a steep rock tower above the river: an ancient fortified village had once been on top, its approach a narrow, easily defended gorge. I got the impression it was tabu, not a place he wanted to take me.

On the appointed day, Api and Finau drove me and my bag back to Drauniivi and we said our farewells. I was billeted in the house of a relative of Naisua, Temesi Namulo, whose large house had a large room with a floor covered in mats of woven pandanus leaf and purple cloths hanging from the roof beams. There were beds around the walls, screened somewhat by mosquito nets. Family life played out on the mats in the middle of the room: snacks and meals, the kids' homework before and after school, watching television. In an old, more ramshackle part of the building, the women cooked on a fire, and the bathroom held an oil drum full of water for dousing yourself with a dipper.

Tomasi, son of the late Leone Naisua, came in and took me in his charge. A strong young man of medium height, he'd worked as a bar manager in resorts but was now looking for another job. He questioned me intensely about why I had come to Drauniivi. I said it was because of a book by an American anthropologist, Martha Kaplan, who'd stayed in the village in the 1980s to research her thesis on the Tuka movement. Some years before, Tuka had been classed as a cargo cult in a famous academic book called *The Trumpet Shall Sound* about the millenarian movements that spread through the Pacific following colonisation.[4] Yet Kaplan's book was titled *Neither Cargo Nor Cult*.[5]

Kaplan took a much more sympathetic view of Tuka, putting it in the context of late-nineteenth-century resistance in inland and western Fiji to the pressure for change coming from the Cakobau hierarchy, the Methodists and the British administration. More recently, historian Robert Nicole pushed this thesis further in his book *Disturbing History*. These two books countered the popular and official image of Fiji's emergence into the modern world. As Nicole puts it, the official narrative cast Fiji as "a country that excelled under British tutelage and the wise rule of its chiefs", backed by Indians who toiled endlessly. Instead, Nicole paints a picture of class dominance by the chiefs and their European allies. But class divisions were disguised by ethnicity and enforced by war. Evangelism became a pretext for subjection.

In the late 1860s and early 1870s, as Cakobau pursued his claim to be Tui Viti, supreme chief of all Fiji, and later king of the islands, he was egged on by a claque of European traders and planters calling themselves the "Nadi Swells". He imposed a head tax, sent recruiters out for plantation workers and signed over large tracts of traditional lands to Europeans. The entire Yasawa island group was sold off for guns and ammunition. The inland people were derided as *kaisi* (low-class, barbarous) and *tevoro* (devils, infidels).

In 1862, a party of Wesleyan teachers went to the Nakauvadra Range and stripped a temple to Degei of its relics. In 1873, a Fijian recruiter from Bau landed at Ra and went up into the hills behind Drauniivi. He was killed with an axe and eaten. Next month, a schooner landed Fijian troops under a British officer at a neighbouring village, where one of the Wesleyan teachers had settled. Reinforced by European volunteers, the troops marched several kilometres inland to Nakorowaiwai, the village where the killers lived. Massed warriors, painted for war, waited behind a priest who had performed rites believed to confer invulnerability. The priest was shot immediately and the warriors hit by fusillades. The soldiers went house to house, killing and burning. The European volunteers saved some of the women and children, but the attackers killed up to 300 of the villagers.

As I've noted, Cakobau's kingdom collapsed financially in 1874, and Queen Victoria's rule started after an act of cession was signed by coastal and eastern chiefs, none from the Ra region. Murders of missionaries and planters led to wars of subjugation in the interior of Viti Levu. A measles epidemic in 1875 killed one in five Fijians. Some saw it as the wrath of the traditional gods.

The region of Ra was seething. What later British official historians called "Fiji's Holy Land" or the "Mount Olympus of Fiji" – indeed, the fount of divinity for the entire world in the eyes of old Fiji – had been invaded and defiled.

Soon after the massacre at Nakorowaiwai, a young man from Drauniivi, Mosese Dukumoi, son of a traditional *bete* (priest), returned from working on a plantation. At a place called Vale Lebo at the foot of the Nakauvadra Range, he began rites to communicate with the old gods. Vale Lebo became a place of pilgrimage, where people came and presented whale's teeth, kava and other gifts in return for a sip of the *wai ni tuka* (water of immortality), from which the Tuka movement would take its name. Dukumoi soon became renowned as a seer and miracle worker, referred to as Navosavakadua, meaning "He who needs only speak once." He preached about the return of the twin sons of Degei (they had been exiled for killing Degei's favourite bird because it was too noisy), about the coming departure of the Europeans and about an imminent judgement day.

This alarmed the colonial administration. In 1878, police destroyed the Vale Lebo settlement and took Navosavakadua to the eastern Lau islands for five years of exile. On his return, he restarted Tuka, this time mixed with Biblical elements, making Degei and his twins the avatars of Jehovah and Jesus. The world would be turned upside down, he prophesied, with the whites serving the natives, the chiefs becoming commoners, the churches sent away. Resistance to the colonial administration grew, but not violently. "Rather, people simply refused to follow the orders of government officials and Wesleyan teachers," writes Nicole. But alarmingly for officials, Tuka followers began practising marching.

When Navosavakadua came to attend the trial of followers for unauthorised drilling and "disturbing the peace" in December 1885, he was arrested. In March 1886 he was sentenced to a year's hard labour for the newly invented offence of "conduct calculated to raise evil in the land". A colonial official, A.B. Joske, who witnessed proceedings ("a thrilling moment") described Navosavakadua:

He was certainly not much to look at, being very black and of a decidedly Melanesian type. He looked bilious and overfed, and had a dazed, far-away look as if he was continually under the influence of narcotics. Undoubtedly he was always more or less stupid with the unlimited drinking of yangona [sic] and smoking of coarse rank native tobacco.⁶

Ah yes, a *Melanesian type*. Navosakadua was imprisoned, but the legend surrounding him was not so easily contained. A rumour spread that when jailors came to prepare him for the cells, their scissors bent when they tried to cut his hair. This has morphed further into stories, still told and believed, that attempts to kill him in jail were unsuccessful because of his powers.

Colonial officialdom meanwhile tried to dispel his aura with a disinformation campaign. They spread stories that the Tuka women were getting fed up with constantly chewing kava for the men and providing sexual services. The latter accusation would often be levied against the leaders of dissident movements around the islands, as we will see. The Great Council of Chiefs declared Navosavakadua a "monomaniac". On his release, the administration used a new ordinance to exile him to the far-off northern island of Rotuma for ten years.

The loyalty of his followers was not extinguished. They built a new *bure* or spirit house in the Nakauvadra foothills. In 1891, officials arrived and had hundreds of local men flogged. The houses of Drauniivi were destroyed and its inhabitants deported en masse to the southwestern island of Kadavu. A.B. Joske, the colonial official who reported on Navosavakadua's trial, explained the thinking behind this deportation:

> The Kadavu Islanders, possessing a large intermixture of Tongan blood, are perhaps the most advanced and intelligent ... of our Fijian population. There is therefore no fear of the "Tuka" doctrines being received by them otherwise than with ridicule and it may reasonably be hoped that finding themselves among a strong but law-abiding and civilised community the Drau-ni-ivi people will profit by their association with

them by qualifying themselves for what they will certainly long for – a permission to return to their own mountain district.⁷

It was not until 1907 that the villagers were allowed to return and rebuild on the present site of Drauniivi, close to the highway and thus the attention of passing authorities. Navosavakadua never returned. He died in 1897 on Rotuma, where he had married a local woman and had children. His fame continues, and his descendants from Rotuma meet periodically. He may not be mentioned in the Fiji Museum, but Drauniivi has a small museum of his relics.

In the second decade of the twentieth century, another form of resistance began. Apolosi Nawai, born in 1885 and the son of a Methodist teacher, had been a troublemaker at school before travelling widely around the country on church business and as a carpenter. He knew the ethnic Fijians' fears. They were being talked about as a "dying race", and a new governor was trying to lease out native lands on a large scale, with Bauan chiefs getting a cut for their support.

Nawai opened a produce business, initially buying and selling bananas, Fiji's second most valuable export after sugar. It became the Viti Kabani (Fiji Company), headquartered on the Rewa River just east of Suva, eventually trading a range of products and building up its own shipping fleet. Stories spread that Degei's twins were the spiritual force behind the company's success. Nawai was a compelling orator. "Once [he] opened his mouth, your mind was no longer your own," said one person who had seen him speak.⁸

Nawai continued to build the company as the First World War raged on the other side of the world. He issued shares to raise capital and hired skilled expatriates. The colonial administration was perplexed. On one hand, it had long wanted to encourage individual enterprise among the Fijians. On the other, some chiefs and European traders worried that the company was becoming like a second administration, as well as cultivating a return to "dark and pagan customs". This view intensified when Nawai started a new secondary school and established the company's own police force.

Racial jealousy intruded. Nawai got about not in a traditional *sulu* but in Western-style suits, tailored by the fashionable Peapes of Sydney. The colonial establishment hated the fact that European men and women worked with him. When one of them, Stella Spencer, slapped the face of a Fijian man who called her a "loose woman", she was charged with assault. "A woman who goes about with natives, making love to them – a woman like that is an absolute danger to the community ... a disgrace to her colour," said the English prosecutor.

In 1915, police arrested Nawai and intercepted his fleet of trading cutters. Charged with resisting arrest and embezzling company funds, he was sentenced to eighteen months' hard labour. Seven others in the business received lighter sentences. The company continued to operate, and Nawai rejoined it on his release in 1916. Searching for a way to wind up the Viti Kabani, officials found it in the criminal code of colonial Nigeria, which included restrictions on "unlawful societies". The Fijian administration enacted the Native Companies Law, giving the government wide powers to deregister and intervene in such companies "to protect natives". A few months later, two policemen said they had been in a crowd at Tavua and heard Nawai say, "I am the enemy of the government. I am the strong man." It was a dubious charge of sedition and was never tested in court: Nawai was exiled to Rotuma without trial. That was effectively the end of the Viti Kabani, a prime example of indigenous capitalism that might, if it had been encouraged and wisely shaped rather than suppressed, have led to a greater sense of control among the Fijians and helped to avoid the racial conflict that unfolded decades later. Nawai lingered in obscurity until he died in 1946. There are no memorials, no streets named after him. There are plenty for Ratu Sukuna, whom Nicole calls "the great collaborator chief".

In Drauniivi, I continued talking with Tomasi on the mats at his uncle's house. When visitors came, Martha Kaplan's book was passed around and her genealogical chart of Degei, his wives and descendants closely studied and criticised.

The villagers of Drauniivi were not doing well. Money was short. The government-owned cattle ranch restricted their access to traditional lands.

The Fiji Water company was no longer giving locals preference for jobs. While Fiji Water was making large profits, Drauniivi's supply of water for cooking and bathing came from a separate bore, which individual households paid for. It seemed many families struggled to make their weekly payments for water. By the second day of my stay, the oil drum in the bathroom was nearly empty and the toilet had no water in the cistern to flush. Some of the younger men were already in touch with the Australian and New Zealand high commissions in Suva about seasonal work.

Tomasi's cousin Makareta had returned. Early that morning, she and another woman had taken an outboard dinghy through one of the channels in the mangroves and gone to the outer reef, about 8 kilometres offshore. There they had caught about three dozen fish with handlines. Twelve hours later, on the next tide, they'd returned. But traditional duties for this unusual all-female crew continued. Makareta and her mother had cooked some of the fish. A meal was laid out on a tablecloth spread on the mats. As her guests ate, Makareta supervised her children's homework.

Later that night, Tomasi called in before I went to sleep. "Be ready to leave at five o'clock in the morning," he said. Sure enough, at 5.15 am, there was a soft tap on the window nearest my bed. I dressed quickly, grabbed my backpack and found the gap in my mosquito net. After stepping around the children sleeping on the mats, I pulled on my shoes at the door. Tomasi was waiting with two other young village men next to a four-wheel-drive pickup we'd engaged. Our driver, Ovea, was a local man. We got into the vehicle, bumped along the muddy track out of the village, and turned east on the King's Road. The hills inland turned from black to velvet green as daylight came. To our left, gaps in the mangroves showed a pale, calm sea. The highway twisted around coves and past little one-room houses of board and corrugated iron, occasionally revealing a sudden peak of black volcanic rock.

We turned into the small township of Vaileka. Most of the shops still had their shutters down, and the single street was empty of traffic. But at the far end, one Indian store was open. The warm smell of fresh bread wafted out from behind the counter. The shopkeeper passed us twelve loaves of white bread. Tomasi added six tins of tuna and a tub of butter. As the corpulent shopkeeper squeezed behind the till and totted up the bill, the baker appeared, waving a coconut shell filled with kava. The soporific drink seemed a strange heart-starter at 6 am, and not the best way to start a hike. We declined. However, at a nearby house we bought bundles of kava roots to bring as gifts.

Ovea drove us up a winding road through low hills, mostly treeless grazing land. After twenty minutes, the road ended in Vatukacevaceva village: small houses made of corrugated iron and timber, scattered over clipped grass. Under shady trees, children in pressed cotton shorts and tunics waited with their mothers, who wore loose, bold-patterned dresses. Buses, open to the breezes with glassless windows, pulled up to take them to school down in the town.

We met Peni Vunica, the village headman, and handed over the kava *sevu-sevu*. He guided us to a one-room house, where we took off our shoes and sat on the mat. A woman brought a pot of tea and a plate of our bread and tuna made into sandwiches. A young man, Seremaia Votai, was recruited to guide us up the mountain. It was 8 am by the time we set off.

What started as an easy stroll out of the village, across pastures and a small stream, turned into a steady upward slog over broken rocky ground. We passed the vestiges of an old pine plantation. The sun was hot now. After two hours, we paused beneath a line of shady trees. Tomasi showed me leaves that were used by Fijians as flavouring before the arrival of Indian spices. Then we went back out into the sun. On one side of the path, the ground fell sharply away. Cau-Cau, one of the young men from Drauniivi, stayed behind me in case I faltered.

Our trek was soon more a climb than a hike: we pulled ourselves over rocks, fallen logs and muddy slopes by holding onto saplings, bushes and tree branches. Finally we reached the ridge, three hours after setting off from Vatukacevaceva. But the ordeal was not over. The track to the highest point of the ridge leads off to the west. Soon Seremaia and Tomasi were far ahead, out of sight in the bush. Cau-Cau came up behind and urged me to speed up. "We are running out of time," he said.

The ridge was not level, but an up and down sawtooth, the path strewn with obstacles. One last haul over a jumble of huge boulders, and we emerged into the open at the top. The view was splendid. The Nakauvadra ridge curved around to the northeast. Vatukacevaceva was tiny, down in the valley. To the north, we looked over the coastline out to the reef several kilometres beyond. The resort islands of Rakiraki were clear but it was too hazy to see the other big island, Vanua Levu. At our backs was another deep and wide valley, the source of the Rewa River flowing down to the southern coast.

There was no cave. Instead, there were the rusty remnants of a large iron cross, about 3 metres high. A group of Young Methodists had carried it up many years earlier and cemented it in, no doubt intending to show the triumph of Jehovah over Degei.

Sitting among the rocks under a wild lime tree, we ate the rest of our tuna sandwiches and gulped Fiji Water laced with a pink energy-boosting drink. A curtain of rain was coming up the valley. It was time to go.

Going down was worse than going up. I resorted to a crab-like crawl, using my hands and feet. By the time we were back on the sloping tussock, I could no longer stand up. Tomasi came back and walked in front of me so that I could lean on his shoulders. At the trees where we'd rested on the way up, a villager, Kalaveti Ravulo, was waiting with a sturdy mare, its foal running loose alongside, occasionally suckling its mother and nervously kicking when humans got near. I climbed up and rode bareback behind Kalaveti. The mare's backbone, as she picked through the tussock and rocks, produced a new kind of pain.

At 5 pm, we got back to Vatukacevaceva and sprawled in the village meeting house. Outside, men pounded up the kava we had brought in an iron pestle. A rainstorm came and went. As dusk fell, the ground-up kava was put into a sock-like filter, soaked, and squeezed into a bowl. Peni Vunica, the village head, arrived, along with other older men. The first shell of *yaqona* was passed out, accompanied by claps of appreciation. The custom was to down each shell in a single gulp.

More rounds followed. Tomasi made a formal speech of thanks to the village for allowing us to come to this sacred spot and guiding us to the top.

I followed with an explanation of my purpose, how I wanted to get a glimpse of the ancient, deep Fiji, how thankful I was for Seremaia's guidance and for Kalaveti and his horse.

As the evening went on, there was more talk and questions. What were the prospects of work in Australia? What did I think of the footballer Israel Folau describing the recent Australian bushfires as God's punishment for the legalisation of same-sex marriage? Ovea, our taxidriver, had not turned up. He had taken another job some distance away in Tavua and would not be with us until 9 pm. There was nothing for it but to donate some more kava, this time in the form of a ready-made powder from the village store.

A village storyteller, Sainivati Rairi, told us what he knew about Degei's cave. The cave was there, he said, but the old god picks and chooses when it is open. One time long ago, some local men were chasing a wild boar up the mountain with their dogs. The cave opened and swallowed up the pig.

Rairi went outside and came back with a small but heavy-looking bag. It held a perfect sphere about 25 centimetres in diameter and dark brown in colour, which was passed around. It had the weight of iron, and I thought it might be an old cannon ball, but my little voice-recorder, which draws coins and metal things to its speaker, showed no sign of magnetic attraction. Rairi launched into a long story about how this mysterious ball had been found beneath a certain fish in a pond, and how it had magical healing properties if rolled along an injured limb.

Before Ovea turned up, I posed one last question. Were they Melanesian or not? The circle of drinkers looked at one another and shook their heads. It seemed a preposterous thought. The Fijians did not bow to the Polynesians to the east, but clearly they were a cut above the peoples to the west.

We got back to Drauniivi. Awash with *yaqona*, sleep came easily. Next morning I wrote down the email addresses of the family who had welcomed me in. Tomasi came and stood with me by the highway while I waited for the bus to Suva. Next stop, Vanuatu. If Fiji was the eastern cultural border zone where Melanesia shaded into Polynesia, I was now going to a place unambiguously in the Melanesian world. I wanted to see first-hand what I'd been reading about: how its old ways and beliefs were actually helping hold this young nation together.

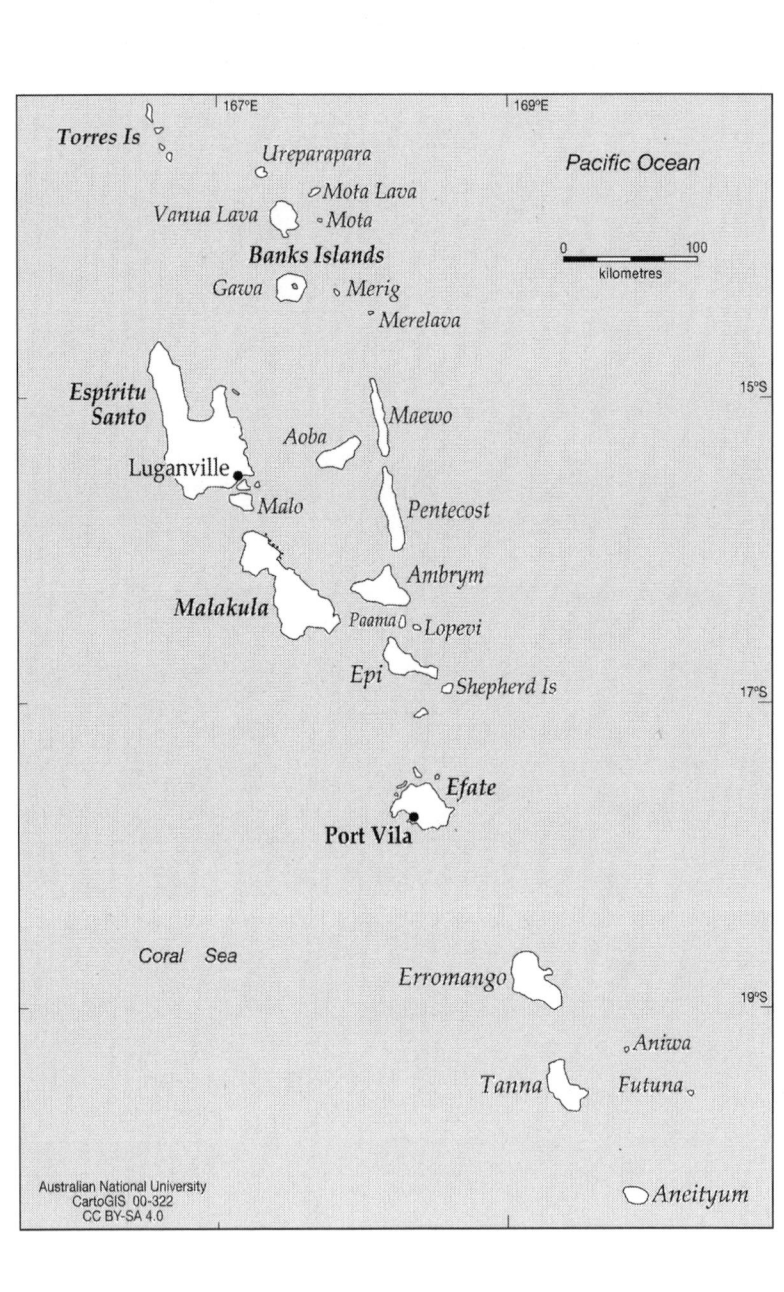

3

VANUATU

Condominium of Bibles and Plunder

EACH OF THE ISLAND COUNTRIES has its own internal ferry services, but passenger shipping between countries is all but extinct. There were some regular cargo services, including a ship called the *Southern Moana* that did a regular circuit from New Zealand around Fiji, Vanuatu and New Caledonia.

One afternoon in Suva, I presented myself at the Queen's Wharf and walked up the gangway to the *Southern Moana*'s deck. The captain, an Indian from Bangalore named Hoolikantimath Prasad, and the chief officer, a Chinese from Shandong, Liu Xueqiang, welcomed me aboard and got a crewman to take me to the cabin normally reserved for the shore pilot.

For the next three days, by special permission from the shipping line's chairman, I was a "supernumerary" in the ship's crew list as the *Southern Moana* rolled and pitched gently towards Vanuatu. I imagined how a great sailing canoe like the one in the Fiji Museum would have raced through this water, wind on its quarter, faster than the 12 knots of the container ship. A day and a half out of Lautoka, in the early dawn, the radar picked up a corner of Vanuatu's Efate Island, and the ship nosed between turquoise shallows up the deep blue channel into Port Vila's harbour.

A few days later, I was back at the harbour waiting to catch a ferry north. Passengers milled around piles of luggage. Women nursed their babies. A group of young Americans turned out to be on a mission from God, coming to share the Bible with the ni-Vanuatu for a month, as if they needed it. Trucks kept arriving with cargo. About four hours behind schedule, we all walked up the ramp and climbed a stairway to the upper deck and the ship sailed. It was crowded and, with the air-conditioning not working, we were soon sweltering inside the cabin. Groups covered all the floor pace on the outside decks. I tried to sleep on a sarong spread in an aisle, my rucksack for a pillow. A group of French-speaking ni-Vanuatu nuns in blue cotton vestments were my nearest sleeping companions.

Morning found us between Ambrym on the right, its volcano smoking, and Malekula on the left. There was no sign of human dwellings, just a shoreline of mangroves, a line of coconut palms behind and jungle-covered hills rising beyond, pretty much as James Cook would have seen it from the *Resolution* in 1774. Only when the ferry nosed into Malekula at Litzlitz, a spit of landfill out from the mangroves, could houses of thatch and corrugated iron be seen. Passengers disembarked. Cargo was stacked on the jetty. Trucks and utilities arrived to collect people and goods. Mid-morning, the ferry set off north, less crowded now. I found a space on the outside deck. A family group offered me a portion of the baked fish and cassava they'd bought at Litzlitz. I gave them some of the oranges I'd bought in Vila. One of the young American evangelists sat down near me and opened her black-covered Bible to study.

It was night when the ferry steered through low-lying small islands and reached the wharf in Espíritu Santo. The town of Luganville is an unlikely portal to the island of the Holy Spirit, a long treeless stretch lined with shabby trade stores, petrol stations and offices. In the morning I walked around. Behind the main strip were quiet streets with bungalows shaded by tall trees and hibiscus bushes. Here and there were the curved, corrugated steel humps of wartime Quonset huts. One had been converted into the Lau Chung Yau garage. Another had been turned into a dwelling, with windows cut into its sides.

On the seaward side of town was a wide, deep channel running east to west, called the Segond Canal, with the low island of Aore on the far side. Between 1942 and 1945 it had up to a hundred warships at anchor, including heavy cruisers and battleships. Under the water is the hulk of the SS *President Coolidge*, a giant troopship that sank after hitting a defensive mine. Now it's a popular diving attraction.

Up to 100,000 Americans were in and around Luganville at any given time between 1942 and 1945. About half a million passed through. As well as five airfields and floating docks, the base included fifty-four cinemas, cafés, tennis courts and sports grounds, and stores of all kinds. Across the canal on Aore there was a big rest and recreation camp, depicted as the island paradise of "Bali Hai" in James A. Michener's book *Tales of the South Pacific* and the musical film adaptation. Unlike in the film, however, there were few local beauties to be seen: villagers around Luganville sent their young women away to other islands for the duration of the American occupation.

Some 10,000 islanders came to work for the Americans as labourers and servants. At war's end, Luganville became a giant second-hand market for surplus trucks, Jeeps, small ships and electrical goods, attracting buyers from around the Pacific. The leftovers were dumped into the sea at the eastern end of town, in what became known as Million Dollar Point.

The town then regained its French atmosphere. The French government had eyed the unclaimed New Hebrides in the late nineteenth century as an extension of its New Caledonia possession and encouraged French citizens to settle there. By the time the Anglo-French condominium was formed in 1906, 401 Frenchmen were cultivating 20,000 acres across the islands, compared with 228 British holding 7000 acres. The French were mostly clustered in the northern islands, on the flat lands of southern Espíritu Santo and Port Sandwich in the south of Malekula. Their numbers grew from 1906, while British settlement was little changed. By 1939, French settlers outnumbered British ten to one. In 1923, French planters were allowed to import labour from Tonkin, the northern region of Vietnam, on five-year contracts. About 5000 Vietnamese labourers had arrived by 1926.

Luganville was a French town. The French district agent had a corrugated-iron bungalow with an attached police station and jailhouse, and the Compagnie Française had warehouses around the small river that runs into the canal, where an open-air market and a row of food stalls are now located. The British agent on Santo was on the east coast, at Hog Harbour. The Australian island traders Burns Philp and W.R. Carpenter battled the French for business. Before the Second World War, the social highlight was the arrival of a steamer, when the planters would pile on board for drinking sessions.

Against the brutality of plantation labour was a largely French scattering of Catholic priests. From 1887, Port Sandwich, Cook's old anchorage in the south of Malekula, became the base for the Catholic Church to take Christianity to the northern islands. Many priests were noted for their understanding of *kastom* and patient approach to conversion. Tom Harrisson, a British ornithologist turned colonial official in the 1930s, wrote of one priest, Père Bancarel: "he has given thirty-five years of his small body to his work, never taking a holiday for one day; receiving only a nominal wage and some wine; celibate; in this land of a thousand false accusals and lies, accused by no-one; in a tiny hut by a great church."[1]

The Second World War stimulated the local economy. French settlers and Tonkinese (as people from northern Vietnam were called) opened restaurants, laundries and curio shops. They sold local food to commissaries, took soldiers on excursions, sold liquor on the sly and pilfered vehicles and other property. But at the end of the war the French and Australian trading companies encountered new competition from Asian immigrants.

About 2000 of the Tonkinese were repatriated in 1946, and most of the rest went back in 1963 in ships sent by Ho Chi Minh's government. A few hid out and re-emerged after the repatriation ships had left. Some became successful businessmen, such as Dinh Van Tho, who in the 1970s started the Hotel Santo, still the main place to stay in Luganville for visiting business travellers, sports teams and diving groups. Racial lines blurred. Dinh married a young British-African traveller from Zambia, Mary-Jane, who has run the hotel since his death, together with their son Kim.

Then canny individuals from southern China arrived. At the LCM Store on Luganville's main street, I met Puchy Lo in his office out the back. His desk was cluttered with invoices and samples of the foodstuffs, hardware and apparel stocked in the shop. Against one wall was a shrine, with a scroll of Chinese writing, a statuette of an ancient sage in robes, a lily, an incense burner and some fruit.

Puchy's father, Lo Sin Chao, arrived from Tongguan in Guangdong Province around 1950, following a cousin who worked for a French settler. Once in Hong Kong it was easy for Cantonese to travel to other British territories, and he shipped out on a cargo boat without a passport. Soon he branched out with his own shop and sent for his wife to join him. Puchy was born in 1956, one of three brothers.

Awa Leong, who runs the Unity store and petrol station further down Boulevard Higginson (named for the Irish-born founder of the first French settlement company), told me about his father, Ah Po. Ah Po left China at seventeen and made his way to Port Vila. He grew vegetables and worked in a bakery, then started trading and moved his business and family to Santo in 1962.

Richard Lo runs the most upmarket supermarket on Luganville's main street, with a row of glass-fronted freezers holding the imported foods sought by foreign tourists and expat residents, and racks of high-end sports equipment. His father, Lo Chan Moon, crossed into Hong Kong from Guangdong as the Chinese civil war ended and joined a cousin who was trading with the Pacific Islands. He went initially to the Solomon Islands, and there heard about the Tonkinese in the New Hebrides. The senior Lo had done some business in Vietnam and knew some of the language, so he came down to Santo and looked for opportunities. Out of this came the idea to import food. He wrote to his cousin and asked him to send an initial cargo of rice on trust. When it arrived five months later, his father sold it in three days at a good profit. "People were on ration tickets, so it was a gold mine," Richard relates. His father repaid his cousin and ordered a second rice shipment, double the size.

Richard and his brothers all completed their primary education in local Anglican schools. The manager of Burns Philp, the Australian shipping line and agency, was an old boy of Cranbrook, a prestigious school affiliated to the Anglicans in Sydney. The fees were no problem for the Chinese traders, and in 1969, classmates Puchy Lo, Richard Lo and Awa Leong all went off to school there, flying to Nouméa in a DC-3 and then on to Sydney in a Caravelle jet.

They settled in reasonably well. "If you were good at sport, no one picked on you," Puchy told me. Richard was also a good mixer and happy at games. Awa hated sport and would hide in the library when the others were out on the playing field. They all went home for the long summer holidays, but the shorter breaks between terms left them at loose ends, as boarders had to leave the school. If they weren't invited to stay with fellow boarders or friends of their parents, they went to the People's Palace, a spartan doss-house run by the Salvation Army at the rough end of central Sydney. After finishing school Awa came back to work with his father. Puchy and Richard went on to complete commerce degrees at the University of New South Wales and then came back too.

As well as creating economic opportunities, the Second World War changed the people of Santo. Even before the Pacific War, the island had seen resistance to the European inroads, drawing on *kastom* and belief in magical powers. In 1923, an islander named Runovoro became a renowned prophet, claiming the ability to restore life to the dead. If white men were killed, he said, the ancestors would return from a far-off land with a great white ship loaded with valuables. Then Runovoro's wife died, and he declared that a British planter named Clapcott had slept with her and then given her poison. Clapcott must be killed to bring her back to life. Runovoro and two others thereupon shot Clapcott, cut up his body and distributed parts around villages. Then, believing in their own immortality, they surrendered and went calmly to the gallows (the French authorities used the guillotine for capital offences, but because of Clapcott's nationality, the British ran the case and applied their own method of execution). An Australian warship came and bombarded Runavoro's village, whose residents had fled into the bush.

In 1946, Santo was swept by the teachings of a man named Tsek. He preached that depopulation was the result of disputes over possessions. If everyone cast off their clothes, destroyed their goods and livestock, dropped all kinds of tabu and had sex in the open with whoever agreed, then

America would bring prosperity. This "Naked Cult" spread all over Santo. At Tasmalum, site of the Clapcott killing, the cult's followers built a long road down to the sea and a jetty for the expected ship. The administration destroyed the jetty and launched a campaign against the waste of household livelihoods. Together with a backlash from traditional-minded villages, this saw the Naked Cult peter out.

Not all resistance was based on magic. On the "dog's head" of Malekula Island, just south of Santo, the Big Nambas put up a strong fight against the intrusion of European settlers and missionaries early in the twentieth century. Their name referred to the large penis-sheaths they wore attached to their belts, in contrast to the smaller sheaths worn in Malekula's east and south by people known as the Smol Nambas. Following the murders of isolated settlers, punitive expeditions involving French native police from the Loyalty Islands were launched, along with naval bombardments.

By 1916, the Big Nambas were coming to accept that they could not win, and welcomed the first Seventh-day Adventist mission. In 1939, three islanders (Paul Tamlumlum, Kaku and Ragh Ragh) set out to beat the Europeans at their own game by forming a cooperative to produce and market copra, with profits going into a community bank, with some help from British officials. Its activity waned during the war, when many men went to Santo to work for the Americans, but picked up again from 1945.

Ragh Ragh, also known as Charley, then tried to take it down the cargo cult path, urging the building of airstrips and roads for the landing of American largesse. His followers started military-style drilling, and he issued medals and badges of rank. Dissociating themselves from this millenarianism, Paul Tamlumlum and a powerful chief named Etienne expelled Ragh Ragh from the cooperative and formalised it as the Malekula Native Company to carry out purely economic and development activities. It went ahead, subject to the periodic wrangles over finances and share ownership typical of Melanesian enterprises cutting across traditional lines.

Hoping to see more of present-day life in these islands, I'd asked Puchy Lo who ran the trading boats around the nearby islands. He got me the phone number of "Peter Karaapha", who turned out to be Peter Terry, a

Big Namba from northwest Malekula who was now operating a small ship called the *Karaa Pha*. It was heading to Malekula the following evening at 6 pm and he agreed to have me aboard as a passenger.

The *Karaa Pha* was a steel boat painted grey and blue, with a high bow and long after-deck with a hard roof. It was already stacked with assorted cargo: a clutch of whipper snippers (grass cutters), a bundle of rakes, two fibreglass water tanks, a bicycle, a petrol genset, corrugated steel roofing, steel reinforcing rods, cut timber, and bags of rice, cement and flour. About two dozen passengers waited on the wharf with boxes and bundles. Lolo, another Big Namba, was stringing and tuning a ukulele for his son Ben, fourteen. Lolo told me he had been to New Zealand twice for seasonal work, bringing back up to NZ$15,000, which went towards building a house and school fees. He wanted to try Australia next, where wages were higher.

The islanders boarded and placed themselves on mats around the cargo. I was ushered up to the wheelhouse and met the captain, Api Ruben. The ship cast off on time, but immediately a problem was apparent: the steering was locked hard to port. Api cut the engines, and a crewman jumped into an outboard-powered dinghy and used it as a tug to nudge the ship back to the wharf. Passengers were ordered off; crewmen unloaded bags of cargo to allow access to the hatch over the steering mechanism. The engineer went down the hatch, discovered a broken hydraulic line, and went into town with Peter Terry to get a new one.

We waited.

Peter and the engineer returned and fitted the new hydraulic line. At 8.30 pm everyone reboarded, and the *Karaa Pha* set to sea again, the helmsman guiding us down the channel using a GPS on a small screen. Clear of the smaller islands, the ship headed south. At 10 pm, the cook brought me rice and tinned tuna on an enamel plate. I tried to sleep on a shelf in the wheelhouse. The southeast trade wind got stiffer, building up a short swell that hammered the ship's bow, sending up a shower of spray. At 12.30 am, I made it out of the wheelhouse to the side-rail and puked my dinner over the side, watched with amusement by the passengers huddled on deck. I stayed there, sitting on a couple of stacked tyres and resting my head on the rail. An hour later the ship turned west, across the sea, so the pitching turned into heavy rolls. Then we were in the lee of Uripiv and Uri Islands and slid alongside Litzlitz jetty at 2.30 am. It was deserted. The Milky Way blazed overhead. Api gave me the captain's cubbyhole on the side of the wheelhouse while he stretched out on the chart table. I slept for three hours and woke at dawn. Crewmen were piling cargo on the wharf. Utes and trucks came down the causeway out of the mangroves. The ship was staying there two days, so Api walked me to a nearby guesthouse, where I took a thatched cabana and a shower in the shared bathroom block.

Jack Waiwo, a local tourism official with a degree from the University of the South Pacific, lived at the back of the resort. The next morning he drove me through Lakatoro, then west up a partially paved road through plantations and bush to the other coast. From the central spine of hills, the road twisted down to a pretty bay called Losinwei.

A small resort stretched through a garden down to the water. In the open-sided dining room, the owner, Sethla Amil, a wiry, bearded man who gave his age as eighty-seven, sat down to talk. When he grew up here, the Big Nambas and Smol Nambas were still fighting. Wandering strangers were killed. Women and girls were abducted. Missionaries got attacked with bows and arrows. As a small boy, he saw a man killed with a club, and the elders take the body away to be dismembered and eaten. Back then, the village had been surrounded by concentric fences. When there was word of fighting, the men would blow into conch shells and beat drums of hollowed logs.

His father and grandfather told of a sailing ship from New Zealand that arrived in the bay and sent men ashore to trade tobacco for food. One crewman disputed a transaction and was promptly clubbed and taken off to be killed. The others escaped and sailed off. Three months later a warship arrived and shelled the village. The people hid in a cave. No one was hurt.

Sethla went outside and came back with a plastic shopping bag, from which he produced a skull. It was the skull of the man he saw killed, he said. It seemed to have a crack on one temple. The god of the local people was named Dramdram. "For my tribe, the belief in him still exists," Sethla said. "The tabu place to pray to the god is there. People who are already dead are there. If someone wants something, has some issues with family, or is going to court, or wants some land protected, he takes pig's tusks and food, and goes there to pray. If he wants to kill someone in Vila or Santo, he calls that person's name, and offers something, like animal's blood. Then that person will die."

The fighting died down in the 1950s. Men from different tribes and places had gone to work for the Americans in Luganville and become friends. Sethla saw his first white man when he was eight, working a tractor in a plantation. People came from all around to watch. "The bad days of black-birding were at the beginning," he said. "Then it got better." Now people were anxious to get work abroad. His own son, Bruce, had left three weeks earlier for seven months' seasonal work in New Zealand. The money Bruce saved helped to expand the resort, which had hosted guests from Australia, America, Israel, Germany and China. Sethla showed me the guest cabins and the beach where turtles came to bury their eggs.

Chinese government money was now funding a better road across the island. Graders were preparing a construction base up on the hill. Further round the coast, inland from Unmet village, New Zealand aid was reviving a hydro-electric dam project that had been started by the Chinese in 1996. Midway, the Chinese had packed up and left, leaving equipment to rust. I heard two explanations: some said that a downstream community had objected to the interruption of their water flows; others that landowners not included in the project's compensation scheme had put a tabu on the project.

Such jealousy was not uncommon. In 2000, landowners who felt they were missing out burnt down the terminal at Malekula's main airstrip at Norsup. In Pentecost, visits by cruise ships had been halted by disputes over who got the landing fees.

On my third morning at Litzlitz, I woke at 5.30 am, packed up and walked down to the jetty where the *Karaa Pha* was tied up. We cast off and headed north along the coast, calling in at small villages where people waited on the beaches. The crew ferried people and cargo between ship and shore in the battered aluminium dinghy. Superbly fit young men, they tossed 25-kilogram bags of cement and rice to one another like beach volleyballs.

There was a joy in their work. I thought of Alfred Russel Wallace's reaction to the first Papuans he saw, who seemed to him "intoxicated with joy and excitement".

All day the *Karaa Pha* pottered around the northern coast of Malekula. At the last stop, a village called Tenmaru, I went ashore in the dinghy. Up from the rocky beach, we walked under tall trees into the village. There was a large church built with rendered cement blocks. Inside was a faded and creased photograph of Norman and Alma Wiles, two Americans who landed here in 1916 to start the Seventh-day Adventist mission among the Big Nambas. Norman Wiles lasted four years before dying of blackwater fever. Alma went back to the United States. The mission somehow survived.

We got back to the *Karaa Pha* and the last cargo was loaded. Some of the crew jumped into the sea, clothes and all, and came out shaking water out of their dreadlocks. The ship pointed north for the transit to Luganville, in calm water thanks to the lee of Malekula. We got back to the Melkofi jetty close to midnight.

Peter Terry had another ship, a longer and lower vessel, the *Lara Star*. A few nights later it would set off to Pentecost, and I made arrangements to join it. Awakening at dawn after a night's passage, I came out to see the ship nosing through teal-blue water towards a jungle-covered hillside. Smoke rose from cooking fires up the hill, but the narrow beach was deserted. The crew loaded timber from the ship onto the dinghy and dumped it ashore while cargo supervisor Elten Mathias phoned the customers to come and collect it. Vehicles drove down a narrow road. Consignment documents signed, our captain, Adrien Jean-Marie Pakoro, ordered the anchor up and a course south along the Pentecost coast.

Throughout the day we made a half-dozen similar stops. At Abwatuntora, the crew pushed a large watertank off the ship's top deck and floated it to shore. At Loltong, where snorkellers staying at the local resort spouted like small whales, we delivered cartons of Hardy's Merlot, slabs of VB and Tusker beer, boxes of biscuits, mats, steel dishes, nappies, noodles and tins of pork luncheon meat and curried chicken. At Bwatnapne, the *Lara Star* docked alongside a larger vessel, the *Tevanu Star*, and unloaded five barrels of fuel. Huge bundles of kava were being loaded onto the *Tevanu Star*, each requiring four men to carry them. Kava was the most lucrative crop here.

Jean-Marie took the *Lara Star* out into the bay and dropped anchor for the night. The crewmen put handlines baited with balls of rice down to the seabed. Soon they were hauling up large fish, fat vertical discs of a glassy grey with tiny yellow fins and tail, which they called *papillons* (butterflies). They caught eight of them and put them in the freezer.

At 6.30 am, the anchor was hauled up. The electric capstan was powered by the starboard diesel, which had been out of action the night before. The engineer, Ated Suma, had managed to clear a fuel-line blockage by ingeniously borrowing the little squeeze-pump from the fuel hose of the dinghy's outboard. It was a Sunday, and one group of passengers with a boom box was playing American country songs about Jesus. We stopped at a large village, Melsisi, and then a place unmarked on the map. "The prime minister comes from here," a passenger told me. Pentecost was better known for *nangol* or "land diving", the ritual of young men jumping from bamboo towers with vines attached to their ankles.

At Ranmawat, a tall young woman accompanied by a girl of about ten got on. As the ship chugged down the coast, she introduced herself as Sophia Buleban. She spoke fluent English and French and used to work in a computer business in Vila. Her passion was singing, both solo and in a choir. She had spent time in Australia with Hillsong and other church groups. Now, aged thirty-three, she just wanted to go back and live a *kastom* life. She had built a house on family land and planted kava. "I want to live this life," she explained. "Each moment I enjoy it." She has no qualms about her safety living alone. "Respect is very durable here. It's part of the *kastom*, very strong." She and her niece got off the ship at Hotwata, a beach named for the nearby thermal springs. It was raining, and I watched them walk along the beach under an umbrella.

By midday, deliveries were finished and the *Lara Star* began the long trip back to Luganville, past Ambae. At sunset, the crew cleaned and cut up their catch of *papillons*. They cracked open fresh coconuts, grated the flesh with a knife, soaked it and squeezed it onto the fish. The stew was served on rice. Our arrival time was estimated at 9 pm. I had booked a hotel room. But the tide pushed us back, and it was midnight when we tied up at Melkofi wharf. Not a vehicle was stirring. I settled down for a third night on the bunk and made my way into town soon after dawn.

To visit the most famous island in Vanuatu's south, I had to break my rule and travel by air. When I walked out of the little terminal at Whitegrass Airport on Tanna, Werry Narua was waiting in his four-by-four and waved me over. His wife, Monique, was in the back seat, holding a squirming naked two-year-old, Elizabeth. We drove south to Lenakel, the main township on the island, and stopped to fuel up the vehicle with diesel, buy a jerry-can of petrol for a generator and stock up with bread and other food. Then we headed east across the island, into lush green hills that became steeper and steeper. At the summit, cloud pervaded the trees. Women and children sat under an awning, clutching cloths around themselves to keep warm. We bought some vegetables from them.

Werry now drove us down the other side of the range, a deeply cut road through a forest of tree ferns, strange succulents and lichen-covered tree trunks. Heavy rain had left deep channels in the dirt road. We lurched around them precariously. Then suddenly the forest was gone; we were driving across a bare, dark-grey slope. This was the ash plain, deposited over centuries during eruptions at Mount Yasur, which loomed up into the mist to the left, a steepening slope of grey.

Tyre tracks led us down to the steep bank of a river, incised deeply into the soft ash. Werry shifted gears and we plunged into the stream, then climbed up the other side with a roar of the engine, back onto the ash plain. We passed a white box on a pole, part of an automatic system monitoring Yasur's volcanic activity. "Up to level two, which it is now, it's fine," he said. "The rocks being shot up drop back inside the crater. When it gets to level three, it's more dangerous nearby. Level four, we all get evacuated."

Back in vegetation, we passed an elaborate fence and gateway, the entrance to a tourist track up to the volcano's rim, only 361 metres above sea level. Trekkers who make the climb can look down into the volcano and see gobs of red-hot magma shooting out of vents. Soon the road levelled out.

We passed isolated houses and an occasional pedestrian, and then reached the village of Ireupuow, with its small homes of corrugated iron and palm thatch and an uneven soccer pitch with a small spectator stadium and a row of flagpoles.

On through the village, then up a forested track and around a spectacular banyan tree. At last we reached Werry and Monique's domain: the Port Resolution Yacht Club. In its main room, flags and club pennants from many nations hung above the dining tables and tattered sofas. There was no electricity, except for three hours in the evening, when Werry ran the petrol generator. But there was mobile phone coverage and internet access.

My room was further up the slope, on the edge of a cliff overlooking the bay. The tree-clad shore opposite at first looked unoccupied, but at dawn and dusk plumes of smoke appeared from cooking fires. Rock pinnacles marked the entrance to the bay. Beyond, way out to sea, was a reef. On a clear day, the small island of Aniwa could be seen from further up the mountain. Like Futuna to the east, Aniwa has a language close to Tongan.

In 1774, on his second Pacific voyage, James Cook anchored here to replenish his ship's water and replace spars. He named the bay after his ship, the *Resolution*. The view would not have changed much since then, although the water is now shallower thanks to volcanic upheavals.

The Tanna men had not leapt at the opportunity to work for these strange interlopers. "One fellow showed us his backside in a manner which plainly conveyed his meaning," Cook recorded. Cook expressed the hope that with "time and some acquaintance" the Tanna people at Port Resolution would get over their view of these Europeans as invaders.

Time and further acquaintance with Europeans proved them entirely justified.

In 1825, an Irish seaman and trader, Peter Dillon, sailed from Sydney and discovered sandalwood growing in Tanna and Erromango, a smaller island to the north. When the natives were not interested in trading it for the implements Dillon offered, he moved on, but others soon took up the business opportunity. The aromatic light timber was highly valued in China for its fragrance; it could be crafted into shrines or burnt as incense. Traders flocked to the islands of Erromango, Tanna and Aneityum. "The riff-raff of Australia came into the sandalwood trade," wrote Harrison. It was a violent, ugly encounter. When attempts to trade with items such as axes and tobacco went awry, the natives attacked, and the white men and their Polynesian crews responded with gunfire. The islanders quickly learned that muskets took some time to reload, so rushed the boats after the first volley. There were massacres on both sides.

The trade became an embarrassment to the distant British government. When citizens of British colonies were indicted, they were hauled before courts in Sydney and Brisbane, where juries were reluctant to convict anyone for the perfectly excusable act of killing a savage. It was to be much the same story when the sandalwood ran out and Australian privateers turned to the human trade. Benjamin Boyd, the pioneer of "blackbirding", brought sixty-five islanders from the New Hebrides and the Loyalty Islands to work on farms in the Riverina District of New South Wales in 1847. Many died of cold and illness. Some walked back to Sydney dressed in their penis-sheaths. Boyd's skull would eventually be taken in a clash on Guadalcanal, in the Solomons, in 1851.

Another merchant from Australia, Robert Towns, made his first financial killing by taking 100 tons of sandalwood from Erromango to China in 1847. By the early 1860s he had shifted to growing cotton inland from what would become the Queensland city bearing his name, Townsville. When the boom in cotton prices caused by the American Civil War ended, he moved on to sugar cane. Both crops required intensive labour, which was supplied by kidnapping men from the Melanesian islands.

The London Missionary Society tried to civilise and convert the islanders. The Rev. John Williams landed at Port Resolution in 1839 and left three Samoan teachers behind when he went on to Erromango. On landing at Erromango, Williams and his English assistant were killed with arrows and clubs, in revenge for the killing of a chief's son by an earlier ship. The rock where Williams was laid out for butchery, the outline of his portly body still engraved in the stone, is now a gruesome tourist attraction.

The missionaries persisted. More Samoans and Cook Islanders were sent, although their language was unintelligible to the islanders and they had little resistance to malaria. They had the scantiest idea of Christian religious doctrine but were there to prepare the way for the real men of Christ. "So Christianity continued to hurl Polynesians at the razor's edge of heathenism," wrote Harrisson.[2] Jehovah and Jesus became just two among many deities for the islanders. The missionaries were blamed for outbreaks of disease. The mission at Port Resolution was withdrawn.

Yet a stern Presbyterian from Nova Scotia established a lasting foothold on Aneityum in 1848. John Geddie was a strict Sabbatarian. As well as opposing violent customs such as cannibalism and widow-strangling, he attacked the more enjoyable aspects of *kastom*, such as kava, dancing and ceremonial exchanges of food. "Geddie was a man with no imagination – an enormous asset in such work," wrote Harrisson. Geddie's evangelism extended to the islanders' dress: "A native could not be a Christian in his own clothes; no Christian woman could show her breasts … Trousers and shirt were the entrance marks to church service."

The arrival of Europeans was devastating for the islanders. A measles epidemic that hit Fiji in 1861 soon reached the New Hebrides. It reduced the estimated population of Erromango from 6000 to 2000. By 1930, the island's people numbered 500. More waves of disease followed: measles again in 1876, Spanish influenza in 1919, whooping cough in 1932. By 1935 the population of the New Hebrides had dropped from an estimated 650,000 in 1870 to about 45,000, according to Harrisson. Commentators at the time blamed this on "degeneracy" and a "loss of interest in life", suggesting that the native "makes up his mind to die". A more convincing explanation, proposed by some ethnographers, is that the suppression of *kastom*, the disruption of trade and the arrival of disease and labour recruiters were shattering communities.

Here in Port Resolution, the missionaries tried again. The Rev. John Paton, a reform church Scot, came in 1858. His wife and child, and a European assistant, died of illness within three years of arriving. Then, in 1861, he was blamed for the measles epidemic. Islanders burnt down his house and drove him away. He returned aboard HMS *Curacoa*, which blasted the shore with its cannons, killing four people, while a shore party burnt all the houses and canoes it could find. Paton was assigned to another island.

Successors gradually gained a permanent footing, backed by displays of force and the replacement of the musket with the repeater rifle. They built a small hospital on Tanna, and some won much affection. Next to Werry's flag-draped resort is the grave of Agnes Watt, a missionary's wife known to the islanders as Misi Bran, who died aged forty-seven in 1894 after twenty-five years on the island. Her tombstone includes a line in the local language: *In rabi nakur ipare*, translated for me as "She died serving us" or "She loved the island people".

The Presbyterians remained dominant in Tanna and other southern islands. When Rev. Geddie spotted some Marist fathers in long robes in 1848, he "recognised at once the mark of the beast ... The battle is no longer to be fought with Paganism alone, but with Paganism and Popery combined".

Generally, it was not a happy regime for the islanders. The missionaries set up their own courts, appointed their own police and installed paramount chiefs of their choosing. People caught breaching the sabbath or drinking kava were made to carry heavy stones up and down beaches or to do unpaid road work. Sacred rocks were thrown into the sea. A government agent, W. Wilkes, called it a "mailed fist kind of evangelism such as I have never seen nowhere else in the Pacific". The British district officers essentially left it to the Presbyterians to run things, and backed them up with police power when required.

Still, Robert Louis Stevenson, who spent the last years of his life in Samoa, wrote that "with all their gross blots, with all their deficiency of candour, humour and common sense, the missionaries are the best and most useful whites in the Pacific". To which Harrisson added that "even if they had come and done nothing they would still be the best people in the Pacific. For everyone else was worse than nothing." Harrisson had a dim view of the resident Europeans, seeing them as out to take what they could, with few scruples.

Traditional society was fraying. Young men went away to plantations and came back with money, new things and new ideas. Converts to Christianity objected to old customary rules, such as having their marriage partners chosen for them. The church imposed new lines of authority. Meanwhile, word was reaching Tanna of other faiths and ideologies. The island was ripe for a new movement of resistance and renewal. For some, this took the form of switching faiths, and inviting in the Catholics and Seventh-day Adventists.

Then, just before the Pacific War, came John Frum. This mysterious visitor prophesied great upheavals: Tanna would join up with Erromango and Aneityum to form one big island; Frum would return to distribute wealth and abolish sickness; the white men would leave.

The British district agent made inquiries in November 1940 and found witnesses to John Frum's appearance. Goats were being slaughtered to feed the gatherings waiting for his return. By May 1941, it had become a mass movement. People spent their savings, buying up in the stores, believing wealth would come. They slaughtered their animals. They stopped working for white men. They disappeared from church. Kava drinking and orgiastic dancing were said to take place nightly.

Police came in from Vila, arrested the movement's leaders and took them back to the capital. The eruptions continued. Some Tanna men claimed to have met John Frum personally and supplied him with choice food. Others said they *were* John Frum. One or two dressed up, with white powder on their faces and yellow colouring in their hair. Others spoke from behind a screen, claiming to be John.

Like other millenarian or cargo cult movements in Melanesia, John Frum is often supposed to have been sparked by the arrival of the US military and the lavish comforts of its bases, and by the sight of African American troops operating complex machinery. However, the John Frum legend predates the US landing at Port Vila in April 1942 and the establishment of huge bases there and at Luganville. Only later, when Tanna men joined the 10,000 New Hebridean workers on the US bases, did John Frum come to be linked to the "King" of America, Rusefel (Roosevelt), and described as half-American in appearance. In these later versions of the story, the wealth he promised would arrive in Jeeps, emerging from mountains, or on aircraft (at least one village in Tanna cleared an airstrip in anticipation).

Before this, John Frum was described as a brother of Karaperamun, the most powerful god of Tanna, who lived in its highest peak, Mount Tukosmeru. Frum's three disciples – Isaac, Jacob and Lastwan – were described as ordinary locals. One theory holds that his name was a corruption of John Brown, the American anti-slavery fighter; islanders may have heard "John Brown's Body", an anti-slavery marching song, sung in church (the lyrics speak of Brown's corpse "a'mouldering in his grave").

John Frum's following thrived despite the arrest of the movement's leaders. When they were exiled to other islands, they took the movement with them. When Irving Johnson, correspondent for *National Geographic* magazine, came to Tanna in 1952, his yacht *Yankee* was swarmed by people in canoes, handing over lists of the things they wanted. In 1957, the arrested leaders finished their terms of exile and returned to Tanna, where they promptly formed a John Frum "army" of men dressed in surplus US Army fatigues and carrying wooden rifles, drilling and raising the US flag. British authorities sent 200 police; the John Frum forces dispersed in the bush; and the British wisely gave up further attempts to suppress the movement. At Port Resolution, I walked from the yacht club down to Ireupuow village. Out in a field, women were cutting grass and weeds with bush knives. One man was operating a petrol lawnmower; another wielded a whipper snipper. One of the women told me, in good English, that the field was being readied for the annual flag-raising ceremony for John Frum.

An old man gestured for me to sit by him on a log under a tree, where he was watching the women at work out in the sun. His name was Samson, and he was sixty years old. A local, he had settled back on the island after working on ships sailing to New Caledonia and Fiji. He pointed to a cement-block and corrugated iron building, the shape of a large shed, under construction behind him. This was the new Presbyterian church, and he was the elder in charge.

The people here were faring better than those on Erromango. "When they killed the Rev. John Williams and cut off his head, it spoke to them," Samson said. "It said the island would lose its people and be left to animals.

Now you can see it. There are few people, and many wild animals roaming around, pigs and snakes."

Samson did not see a conflict between John Frum and the Christianity he hoped to foster in the new church. "The message of John Frum is like the book of St John, chapter one," he said. "It's about preparing yourself, getting an education, going to church, cooperating with each other." The story of John the Baptist has been suggested as another explanation for the origin of the John Frum legend, and John Frum's name; missionaries showed early Biblical movies, such as *The King of Kings*, made in 1927.

Samson and other village leaders offered *kastom* marriage ceremonies for tourists. "You just need to buy a pig and some kava," Samson said. "Our ladies will organise the taro and yams. They will take the bride down to bathe in salt water, and then rub her with coconut oil. The men will take the groom to the sea and paint his face and arms. They put feathers in each other's hair at the *nakamal* [ceremonial house] instead of exchanging rings. It's all legal. The papers are sent to Vila."

The next day, Werry and Monique got me organised early. It was 15 February, the day of Ireupouw's annual John Frum parade. On the village field, the flags of the United States, France and Australia were already hoisted. A short drive away across the volcano's ash field, we reached Sulphur Bay, where bamboo and palm-leaf shelters around the parade ground were heaving with people. Children were running about. Every few minutes, the volcano rumbled like the base pipes of a giant cathedral organ.

On top of an embankment was a single-storey concrete building with three flagpoles, two huge speakers and a microphone arranged in front. A marquee to one side sheltered two rows of special guests sitting on folding chairs. Another open-sided shelter housed foreign spectators: half-a-dozen people in backpacker-style clothes, a Chinese couple with two children, a television crew from Montreal and two Americans in white short-sleeved shirts, dark ties, dark cotton trousers and black plastic sandals. Their name badges announced them as "Elda" Redford and "Elda" Wadsworth. Both looked to be in their early twenties. They were Mormon missionaries, they told me, stationed for two years at a village high up in the hills of south Tanna.

Mid-morning came a flurry of music and announcements. Flags went up on the embankment: those of the United States, the US Marine Corps and Tafea, the local province. On the parade ground, two older men in green fatigues marched up to another tall flag pole and slowly hauled up a giant Stars and Stripes. From a side road, out marched two lines of younger men, also in faded green fatigues. They wore peaked cotton caps and canvas shoes or bare feet. Each shouldered a length of bamboo, sharpened to look like a bayonet and painted red. When they reached the viewing stand, the two lines split before merging again up and down the field, then proudly marched off.

Then came a succession of village dance groups in grass or raffia skirts, anklets of dried pods rattling as they stamped their feet in rhythm. Baskets of food were brought into the middle of the ground and distributed. There were slabs of *laplap*, a glutinous cake of pounded cassava soaked in coconut milk with wild spinach and baked on hot stones underground, and stringy portions of pig meat cooked the same way. I went up to the VIP tent and spoke to the headman of John Frum. Chief Isaac Wan wore an old Marine Corps peaked cap and a royal-blue tunic with epaulettes and several plastic medals attached. His eyes were cloudy. His attention wandered. His father, Meles, had spent ten years in Port Vila's jail and seven years of exile on Malekula Island before returning to become John Frum's chief in 1957. When he died in 1975, Isaac took over. "Johnny talked to my father," Isaac said. "He said there are many nations in the world, but your friend America will help you."

In the adjacent concrete building, I found a crude mural of a volcano with a portal in its side, and the words "Holy Holy Stone" and "The Glory of John Custom". A wall panel explained how the god Ugden had created the land and custom, but missionaries and colonial officialdom tried to destroy these sacred ways. In prison, Meles and other leaders were visited by John, who told them that America would save them. Some US marines gave them American flags, which they raised when they returned to Tanna on 15 February 1957. "From these time on, the British and French knew it was America who gave them Freedom to live their Kastom Life," the wall panel said. "[The] Spirit of John Frum continues to inform the people to always respect their Kastom Life and Friday as a day of rest where everyone gathers to listen to his words. On Fridays the words of John Frum continue to guide this Movement until the day he promised to appear to his faithful believers, here on Tanna."

Back outside, I found Werry and Monique again, and we walked down a track to Sulphur Bay village, next to a broad beach littered with tree branches. A politician was giving a speech at a microphone. Alongside the American, French and Tafea province flags, here a Vanuatuan flag fluttered too.

The chief of this village was Kasiken Poida, aged thirty-nine, who had taken over the role from his father. He explained that this village followed the "Unity" strand of John Frum, as distinct from the "Traditional" John Frum up at the parade ground. "John Frum arrived in a time when a lot of things were working against the *kastom*," Kasiken said. "Unity means that belief and the church can be combined."

Kastom could not be maintained or restored completely. "We want to, but we can't keep it," he said. "It's the trend of life. Our kids are going to school, we need medicine." However, modern ways were also a struggle. The constitution of Vanuatu was in conflict with many aspects of *kastom*, he said, such as when it came to the rights of women and children.

The annual John Frum parade was a forlorn exercise now, Kasiken told me. "It is just a show for tourism. They are not living it." Indeed, the twenty-four marchers we had seen up the hill were a fraction of the 120 or so pictured in a photograph taken in 1979. What was needed was a compromise between loyalty to tradition and adaptation to the past, Kasiken said. "We can keep the spirit of what our forefathers have been doing. We are wearing the clothes, but privately within I am keeping the spirit of that, because that's where my identity comes from."

The people of Tanna were once regarded by Europeans as among the most "difficult" peoples of the Pacific to connect with. Today, many of the men and women of Tanna have a widening circle of links to the outside world. Scores of young Tanna people now head to New Zealand and Australia for seasonal work on farms and vineyards. On the island itself, there are tourism entrepreneurs such as Werry and Monique. Kasiken had worked on other islands for many years and had married a chief's daughter from Ambrym Island, rather than a local woman as *kastom* would strictly dictate. While in Tanna, I had tried to locate three men whom I'd interviewed in the Otago region of New Zealand in 2008, where they had been picking grapes. Werry knew one of them, Josaiah Iaken, from a village called Tanyeba on the west side of the island, and passed on a message, but we hadn't heard anything more. After the parade, he and Monique dropped me off at Lenakel for the ferry to Port Vila. I was sitting under a tree at the landing with other passengers, waiting to board when a vaguely familiar islander came up.

"I hear you are looking for me," he said. It took me a moment to realise it was Josaiah. He remembered our interview in New Zealand, and someone had shown him the story I wrote for *The Sydney Morning Herald* about the seasonal work scheme. He had done several stints of seasonal work and invested the proceeds in a vehicle to run a transport business on the island. He took me to meet his wife, who was travelling to Vila on the same ferry as I was waiting for, en route to Brisbane for seasonal work picking strawberries. "It's my turn to mind the four kids," Josaiah said.

*

Sulphur Bay now has two resident Presbyterians ministers, an Australian (who perhaps judiciously was away on parade day) and a ni-Vanuatu, Maliwan Tarowai, who showed me a copy of his life story, *Cargo Cult to Christ*, written by Robert Charles McKean and published by a small Christian publisher.

The old gods are still invoked as well. "We drink kava and we talk to our gods," Kasiken had told me. "Kava is the dimension to the spirits. We pray to the stones." Karaperamun was the special god of Tanna. "He's the black god," Kasiken said, explaining that he was black in the sense of being a god for black people.

Earlier that day, near the parade ground, I'd asked a local when John Frum might return.

"I don't know," he said. "We have only been waiting about eighty years. You've been waiting 2000 years for Jesus."

4

ESPIRITU SANTO

Long God Yumi Stanap

IT STARTED AS A STIRRING among people of the "dark bush" of inland Espíritu Santo.

With their coconut plantations on the flat coastal plains becoming unprofitable because of the wartime rise in wages, white settlers turned to raising cattle. They got titles to wide tracts of land on the more temperate and well-watered inland plateau and began clearing bush and fencing paddocks for grazing.

Displaced bush people moved down to Luganville, led by a chief named Buluk. There they encountered Jimmy Stevens, a bearded, pale-skinned, charismatic man. His grandfather had been an English sailor, Thomas Carfield Stephens, who cruised around the New Hebrides in the 1890s, then to Fiji and Tonga, where he wooed and wed a daughter of the royal family, Sela Tupou. They had three children, but Stephens got into financial difficulties. One night in 1904 he loaded his family into a whale boat, along with a supply of watermelons for sustenance and did a moonlight flit from his debtors. They sailed through the Fijian islands and eventually to Santo, where they settled. They had more children, about ten, and one of their brood married a girl from the Banks Islands, north of Santo. Among their children was Jimmy, his surname's spelling changed.

Jimmy Stevens worked for the Americans during the Second World

War. When it ended, he dug up and restored caches of generators, refrigerators and batteries and sold them for handsome profits. He operated a bulldozer for a while, then captained a small trading ship for Burns Philp. In the 1960s, Stevens connected with Buluk and his bush people, and guided them to squat on French cattle runs at Vanafo, about 27 kilometres north of Luganville in the uplands. They grew their own food, occasionally feasting on "wild" cattle. In 1966, Stevens and Buluk convened some 800 bush people and issued an "Act of Dark Bush Land", claiming all land beyond existing European coconut plantations. Stevens spent a short spell in jail for trespass and on release moved up to Vanafo, where he planted the flag of his new movement, which he called Nagriamel, combining the names of two plants used in traditional ceremonies. He organised his followers on *kastom* lines and, elected as chief, accepted the perquisites of office, which came to include some twenty-three wives and uncounted children.

The island that Pedro Fernandes de Quirós had mistaken for the great southern continent was meanwhile attracting distant schemers. A Hawaii-based businessman, Eugene Peacock, bought rundown plantations in 1967 and subdivided them into small lots for sale to foreign buyers, mostly residents of Hawaii and US servicemen. Similar schemes were started by American investors in other islands, including Efate, where Port Vila is located.

For all his concerns about land-grabbing, Stevens was friendly towards Peacock's projects. As in Tanna, probably, the American flag meant liberation from British and French masters. Stevens also found American friends in the Phoenix Foundation, formed by Lithuanian migrant Michael Oliver and inspired by a Californian professor of philosophy, John Hospers, who in 1972 stood as the Libertarian Party candidate in the US presidential election.

Stevens was inclining towards separation of Espíritu Santo from the New Hebrides, along with any other nearby islands that might volunteer, under his own rule in a state to be called Vemerana. Oliver saw in this the chance to re-establish a libertarian state, having just had his flag, which he had planted on the Minerva Reef between Tonga and Fiji, ripped down by the crew of the Tongan king's yacht. Oliver gave Stevens money to buy a shortwave radio transmitter, print passports and hire lawyers to draw up the Vemerana constitution. Soon Stevens was on the airwaves at 6 am every morning to talk about Nagriamel and Vemerana. The flag of the proposed new state, a green star on a mid-blue field, flew over Vanafo.

Santo became the focus of a struggle over the pace of independence for the New Hebrides. A nationalist party, eventually named the Vanua'aku Pati, was forming among teachers, civil servants and Protestant clergy, initially in Santo among these Anglophone elements. It was led by Walter Lini, a young Anglican priest trained in New Zealand. Lini went to the United Nations, urging pressure on Britain and France to speed up independence.

In reaction, French settlers and other Francophone groups in Santo formed the Mouvement Autonomiste des Nouvelles-Hébrides, urging "steady evolution towards an autonomous status". It allied itself with Nagriamel and another Francophone group in Santo, Tabwémasana. Further afield, it corresponded with a Francophone grouping in Efate, and in Tanna with John Frum and an even more strict *kastom* grouping in that island's Middle Bush named Kapiel. This broad movement came to be known as the Moderates.

For its part, Britain wanted to shake off its Pacific colonies. Fiji had become independent in 1970 and the Solomon Islands in 1978. But France was worried an independent New Hebrides would stir up Kanak nationalists in New Caledonia and join agitation against nuclear testing in the Tahitian islands. "We have so much more at stake," said the French commissioner in Port Vila, Jean-Jacques Robert. "The British will be leaving only a handful of Anglo-Saxons behind. But we shall be leaving at least 4000 French nationals – planters, traders and so on – and we are working now to safeguard their interests, their language and culture."

Indeed, his side of the condominium was doing just that. Tabwémasana followers attacked Vanua'aku demonstrators in Santo. Stevens kept up declarations of imminent independence for Vemerana on his radio. However, Lini's Vanua'aku Party swept elections held in November 1979, even in Santo, and independence was scheduled for 30 July the following year. Two months ahead of that deadline, hundreds of Nagriamel bushmen descended into Luganville one morning before dawn, armed with bows and arrows, and took the small British police force prisoner. The French police were trusted to stay in their quarters. At 7.15 am, Stevens announced on radio that Santo had seceded and formed the Vemerana Federation.

A revolt broke out on Tanna Island in sympathy. The *kastom* group Kapiel captured the British district officer and his assistant. Port Vila flew in a police mobile force squad, which crossed the island to Kapiel's base in the Middle Bush and freed the captives. Police returned a week later to make arrests around Sulphur Bay. Kapiel and other Moderates then marched across to the district offices at Isamel, on the west coast, and freed the prisoners. Police dispersed the rebels with gunfire, one of them dying from gunshots fired by one side or the other or both. It explains why I didn't see the national flag flying at the John Frum parade.

In Port Vila, Lini as chief minister ordered a blockade of Espíritu Santo, and asked Britain and France to use force to quell the revolt. London sent a company of Royal Marines. Paris sent a company of paramilitaries from Nouméa but withdrew them a day later and vetoed any action by the British forces.

The French commissioner's media adviser helped the growing crowd of international media to evade the blockade and get into Santo to cover a civil war that was low on casualties but high on local colour. "Jimmy Stevens, Casanova of the Jungle at the rate of four virgins a night ..." was how one London tabloid reporter started his story.

Groups of the Moderates in Malekula, Aoba and Ambrym formed provisional governments, announced secession and sent delegates to Luganville to declare a government for the northern islands.

With negotiations getting nowhere, the metropolitan powers sent the British marines and some newly arrived French paratroopers into Luganville, where the bushmen melted away. The European troops watched as the town was looted, but on 30 July kept back jeering crowds as the new flag of Vanuatu was hoisted. In mid-August they departed and were immediately replaced by a battalion of Papua New Guinea's defence force, flown in by the Australian air force. Vanua'aku Party members who had fled the coup now returned. Police and PNG troops began arresting Moderates. French military aircraft evacuated nervous French nationals to Nouméa. Then some 150 PNG soldiers went up to Vanafo and arrested Stevens, who was waiting quietly. He was tried and sentenced to fourteen years' jail. Released in August 1991, he died in Vanafo in 1994.[1]

And so the Republic of Vanuatu came into being. It was the only Melanesian colonial possession to gain independence with a measure of armed struggle and resistance from a metropolitan power (excluding New Caledonia and West Papua, whose independence movements are still in progress).

In Santo, the French settler community was depleted. Some of its members left of their own accord, mostly to New Caledonia. Others were expelled by the new government for having assisted the Nagriamel secession attempt.

Independence brought luck for some. Puchy Lo, back from his studies in Sydney to take over the family business, took over an abandoned French plantation at Norsup. He and Awa Leong bought a small cargo ship, the *Henri Bonneaud*, from its French owners. They ran it for a decade, picking up copra from around the northern islands, until the cost of spares from Germany for its Krupp engine got too much. "We could break even with a hundred tonnes of copra a week, but then we'd have a break-down," Puchy recalled. "It was terrible." They sold the ship for a token amount to be sunk as a diving wreck. Such losses aside, the stores of these established Chinese trading families and the remaining Tonkinese came to dominate the region's business economy. Burns Philp declined and eventually went out of business in 2006.

The new state was a strange hybrid from the start. How could it be otherwise? It had sprung from the unique condominium, in which the French and British ran separate district officers, courts, police and postal services. Schooling had been left to the missionaries, who concentrated on biblical studies. The first secondary school graduates were only emerging in the late 1960s, and the first university graduates in the early 1970s.

The Vanua'aku Party had developed in the 1970s, when liberation theory was in vogue. Another influence was the Black Pride movement in the

United States, the Caribbean and Africa. The new Vanuatuan flag, with its red, black, green and yellow, mirrored the colours of Rastafarianism. Reggae became popular and remains the driving beat of the country's popular music.

Yet the national language was not a native tongue, but Bislama, the lingua franca that had developed when people from different islands dealt with traders or were thrown together on the sugar-cane fields. (The name is thought to come from bêche-de-mer, the sea cucumber traded to China.) English and French were also kept as official languages.

At independence, four-fifths of the population lived in villages ruled by *kastom*, but the towns of Luganville and Port Vila were already cosmopolitan and would become more so. The lack of direct taxes, both personal and corporate, gave Vanuatu an advantage. Suddenly Port Vila had numerous banks along its main street, with foreign lawyers and accountants serving clients around the world. Cruise ships brought tens of thousands of visitors each year to Port Vila's new wharf, finished in 1972, while the city's wartime airfield was extended for passenger jets. Hotels and resorts multiplied, along with duty-free shops and real estate agencies.

This new world co-existed with a distinctively Melanesian style of politics in the government buildings on the hill above the resorts. The bankers and accountants connected Port Vila with the flashier side of global capitalism at the same time as Vanuatu's new politicos extolled the virtues of *kastom* and economic independence.

From early on, in the 1980s, Vanuatu opened diplomatic contact with China rather than Taiwan, and with states shunned by the United States such as Cuba and Libya. Alone in the region, it supported independence for West Papua and East Timor. French apprehensions were correct: it backed the strengthening Kanak nationalists in New Caledonia and strongly opposed French nuclear testing.

For a bit more than a decade, Walter Lini held it together. The Anglican priest from Pentecost, trained and ordained in New Zealand, was respected for his decency and honesty. He was joined in parliament by another respected churchman, Sethy Regenvanu, a Presbyterian pastor from the small island of Uripiv near Malekula, who became lands minister and later deputy prime minister.

However, Vanua'aku split in 1988, with its ambitious secretary-general Barak Sopé in conflict with Lini over the handling of urban land and exiting to form the Melanesian Progressive Party. Vanua'aku lost its majority in 1991. From then, for some fifteen years, Vanuatu politics were characterised by shifting and short-lived coalition governments and frequent corruption scandals.

After Lini died in 1999 at the age of fifty-seven, the date of his death, 21 February, became a national holiday. In Port Vila on that day, I went to the Anglican church at Tagabe for the annual memorial service. It was attended by family members including his widow, Mary, and surviving comrades from older Vanua'aku ranks. It was a familiar communion service, but with the liturgy adapted to local idioms and the hymns sung with the harmonies of the Pacific Islands.

Afterwards, the congregation moved through the church grounds to watch wreaths being placed around a memorial pillar to Lini. Among the wreath-layers was Benny Wenda, the head in exile of the West Papuan liberation movement, who was in Port Vila to lobby for his cause.

Ralph Regenvanu, one of Sethy's five sons, was there, too, with his father and his Australian-born mother, Dorothy, who came to these islands as a Presbyterian pastor. Ralph was then foreign minister. He explained Vanuatu's support for the West Papuans. "Like them, we are the only Melanesian country that had to fight for independence: everyone else was given it on a plate," he said. "There was actually bloodshed, we had to organise, there was violence, to get our independence."

In the years before independence, leaders such as Lini and his father had sat in the corridors of the United Nations with their counterparts from West Papua, Zimbabwe, East Timor and other places. After Vanuatu got independence, Lini declared: "We're not actually independent until all of Melanesia is independent."

"We were part of that group," Ralph Regenvanu said. "We managed to get out, but we said we simply won't forget you. We will get you out."

Foreign policy was a relatively straightforward matter for the new nation. It was the new Vanuatu's constitution that was – and continues to be – problematic.

The motto of the new state was *Long God Yumi Stanap*: With God We Arise. As we have seen, many ni-Vanuatu are not entirely sure whether they follow the Jehovah of the missionaries or the gods residing in their volcanoes. Many give a nod to both. As in other countries of the region, belief in spirits and "witchcraft" is prevalent. Accusations of employing a fatal spell can bring murder in retaliation.

The Christian faith comes in many forms: Vanuatu has some thirty different denominations. The young Americans on the ferry to Santo and the Mormon "eldas" at Sulphur Bay are just two examples of continuing evangelism. Clerical dress is said to occasionally be used as a disguise by overseas entrepreneurs hoping to avoid the 10 million vatu (A$127,000) fee for foreign investments. However, the constitution's enshrinement of "Christian principles" generally satisfies most people, it seems, since it does not bind them to any one church, or to any church at all.

It was the commitment to "traditional Melanesian values" in the constitution's preamble that caused more of a contradiction. The constitution adopted a Westminster structure of government, with a non-executive president chosen by the parliament and six regional presidents. Then it got into muddier waters. The constitution set up a hierarchy of courts and included a bill of rights based on universal freedoms. But it also provided for a Malvatumauri, or National Council of Chiefs, to advise on those traditional Melanesian values, in particular on national land laws. It further stipulated that "All land in the Republic of Vanuatu belongs to the indigenous custom owners and their descendants"; that "The rules of custom shall form the basis of ownership and use of land"; and that "Only indigenous citizens of the Republic of Vanuatu who have acquired their land in accordance with a recognised system of land tenure shall have perpetual ownership of their land."

The duality of the state and *kastom* was hard to reconcile. Someone who got elected to parliament, or a young person who got a university degree and a civil service position, was expected to show gratitude in tangible ways to the community that had supported them along the way. Some find the demands so onerous that they are referred to as "drinking blood".

"The big way in which *kastom* is recognised in the modern state is the clientelist politics," explained Ralph Regenvanu. "That's the main manifestation." As well as introducing codes of conduct and an investigative ombudsman, governments have tried to take the pressure off MPs by giving them an annual personal fund of 3 million vatu, about A$38,000, to spend at their own discretion. By the standards of the slush funds allocated to MPs in Papua New Guinea and the Solomons it is modest, but it is still much criticised. Regenvanu gets much praise for spending most of his on scholarships. He admits it is relatively easy for him to do this, as he represents an urban electorate with voters more distanced from tradition. For some politicians, however, the fund is clearly not enough, judging by the huge sums revealed in kickbacks and embezzlements, including bribes to other MPs for their support in forming government.

"I suppose we're dealing with it totally in Western terms, [in treating it as] corruption," Regenvanu said. "Only when it comes to the election laws do you see some flexibility, like on polling day you're allowed to feed people and provide transport."

Gregoire Nimbtik has wrestled with this. He was born to a chiefly Big Namba family in Amok village in northwest Malekula. His grandfather had fifty wives, his father had ten (most inherited under *kastom* from deceased brothers and other close relatives). Gregoire was one of eleven boys and eleven girls. Part of his village had converted to Seventh-day Adventism and moved to the coast, where the men took wage jobs in plantations; the rest of the village, including Gregoire's family, stayed in the bush. They all came together for pig-killing ceremonies called *nimangki*, in which men acquired higher social grades, a practice found across the northern islands. Gregoire's formal schooling ended at age twelve when his father died and money became too short for school fees. He later studied by distance education with the University of the South Pacific, earning bachelor's and master's degrees. Later he got a scholarship allowing him to complete a doctorate at RMIT University in Melbourne.

His civil service career had started by then, in the education department, where he was supposed to select the brightest students for the tertiary scholarships given by Australia and New Zealand. He found his recommendations overruled by higher-ups, in favour of the children of politicians and other well-connected people.

Coming back from Melbourne, he became director-general of the Prime Minister's Office, the central node of government. He lives in Port Vila with his wife and two children. I met him one morning at a café near his office, and he told me about his doctoral thesis, titled: "Worlds in Collision: An Inquiry into the Sources of Corruption within Vanuatu Government and Society".[2] It explored the clash between what he called the "legal/rational" system of government and *kastom*. "What is moral on one side is immoral on the other side," was how he summed it up in the café, before gulping down a hot chocolate and heading to work.

Later I found his thesis online. *Kastom* was built on reciprocal giving, it explains. "In Vanuatu the *kastom* practice of distributing goods and services to close families and political supporters is in fact considered moral, because a leader is fulfilling their social duty," Nimbtik wrote. "However, in a legal-rational governance system, this practice is labelled as corrupt because a leader is favouring his close relatives and in-groups and therefore distorting the processes of justice, fairness, and equity." From here it is a short step to justifying embezzlement as a necessary part of fulfilling reciprocal *kastom* obligations.

In 2013, when Ralph Regenvanu became minister for lands, having entered parliament in 2008, he found that his predecessor had granted leases over 190 parcels of prime urban land worth millions of dollars to officials under his portfolio, his staff and political associates, and his close family members. Regenvanu convened these recipients and appealed to them to relinquish the leases before legal action started. The recipients were unfazed, telling Rengenvanu he would soon be replaced and his successor would kill any action he started. Indeed, two years later a new minister, noted for previously granting state land to himself and to his kin, announced that all legal action would be dropped.[3]

With four-fifths of the population living in customary communities, the state is foreign to many Vanuatuans: its legitimacy is suspect given its agencies derive from those that tried to break down custom, alienate land and enlist native people for expatriate enterprises. Hence, within a month of independence, Walter Lini went to Pentecost to upgrade his chiefly status at a *nimangki* ceremony. This became the norm, as elected leaders feel they need added legitimacy. As Nimbtik wrote: "The implication is that when there is a clash of traditional values of social obligation with that of the legal-rational state, it is more likely that elected members of parliament will conform to social norms rather than the rule of law."

Before the Europeans arrived, the islands had different political systems. In Efate and other central islands, leadership was based on hierarchies of inherited chieftainship. Around the end of the sixteenth century, a great chief, Roi Mata, established his rule over much of these islands. When he died, he was buried on Eretoka Island, accompanied by the live burial of close relatives and a man and woman from each of his subordinate clans; the men were anaesthetised with kava. But such paramountcy did not flourish. After independence, the National Council of Chiefs lost respect for failing to call out government ministers who trampled on *kastom*, such as by pushing through leases of traditional land without the owners' consent. It was accused of being a "rubber stamp" for government – in private, at least, because chiefs were traditionally held to be protected by magic and sorcery.

Ralph Regenvanu acknowledges that there are still "arguments about chiefs": "are they real or not, are they authentic, are they really *kastom*?" And because the National Council of Chiefs is enshrined by the constitution, "we have to figure it out. We can't say maybe they're not really chiefs, let's get rid of that".

When he became lands minister, he had to address the shambles in land leasing. As well as the urban land scandals, nearly all the customary land around the coast of Efate had been handed to foreign tenants on seventy-five-year leases. When the leases expired, it would return to the traditional owners – that is, if they could afford to buy the villas and resorts constructed on it. Meanwhile, access to beaches and inshore fishing grounds was blocked, with some estate agents advising tenants to acquire guns and fierce dogs to keep locals off the beach.

Regenvanu's solution was land reform, which he pushed through in 2013. "We amended the constitution to exclude resolution of customary ownership of customary land from the jurisdiction of Western courts," he said. Previously, "the constitution had given anyone who felt aggrieved the right of recourse to the Supreme Court. So we had to stop that right when it came to customary land, and uphold the other part of the constitution, which said the rules of custom shall apply to customary land ... we had to say you can't go to court any more, but to the *nakamal*."

In his thesis, Nimbtik noted that the chiefs were solving problems that the government couldn't. When armed members of the paramilitary Vanuatu Mobile Force kidnapped the president and seized key installations in Port Vila over a pay dispute in 1996, a group of chiefs talked them down in a kava ceremony. In 1998, policy holders in the National Provident Fund rioted over reports that politicians were not repaying loans from the fund. They beat off riot police but quietly went home when chiefs were called in. When rioting broke out between Tanna and Ambrym communities in Port Vila in 2007 over an alleged witchcraft killing, the prime minister held pig- and mat-giving ceremonies with chiefs from both islands to restore peace. In 2006, authorities could not get the public to hand over twenty escaped convicts. Chiefs went on the radio and persuaded the escapees to come to a *nakamal* for the night before handing themselves in.

In these cases, it was not the National Council of Chiefs but local leaders, appropriate to each problem, who were called in. In his thesis, Nimbtik argued for more consultation with local communities through their chiefs and *nakamals*, more reliance on traditional conflict resolution and more use of restorative justice rather than the imported punitive system.

Another source of tension is the subordinate position of women in many parts of Vanuatu. Women sit on the outer at *nakamals* and were traditionally not allowed to speak. There are exceptions, such as Pentecost, where Lini's sister Hilda had risen to high chiefly status and was elected to parliament. There was a perception, Nimbtik admitted, that tradition meant male domination and modernisation meant the liberation of women.

Just how heavily tradition can bear down came in the story of one woman, Merilyn Tahi, from Ambae Island in the north. At age twenty she was taken out of school and forced by her family into marriage.

I had one son and was forced to care for three children adopted by my husband, and one son from another woman," she later told a meeting of Pacific women. "I was married to him for twenty-six years ... he died in 1997 ... [When he died] all my things were thrown out of my matrimonial house ... I have since found another partner ... [but] according to custom, because of the bride price, I should have remarried my husband's brother, uncle or nephews. So the uncle has vowed revenge if I remarry someone else ... I still go to the island regularly with my son, but I do not go to my matrimonial home or my husband's family. My husband's sisters no longer speak to me. I have lost everything there.[4]

She did go out to work, first in the civil service and then in non-government bodies, where she became renowned for her work on gender equality and the prevention of violence against women and girls.

This tension between individual and communal rights is "probably the most contentious issue" facing Vanuatu, Ralph Regenvanu told me. "You have the bill of rights in the constitution, which doesn't exist in *kastom* in many ways. What are individual rights, as compared to communal rights under *kastom*? The rights that are much more privileged under *kastom* are community rights. So there's always a tension there. But it's a good thing. It's for us to work it out."

From this, a picture emerges of communities running their lives only lightly touched by the state, with a high degree of self-sufficiency. Their cash needs are met largely by selling kava and other commodities, or by spells of work in the large towns or abroad. People move between islands and language groups, with Bislama, an English-based Creole, their common language. Intermarriage between language groups is not unusual. In all but the most remote traditional villages, mobile phone ownership is the norm and social media is an important source of news, information and entertainment.

For the past decade, Vanuatu has been one of several nations trying to measure progress using more than gross domestic product, including statistics on wellbeing. Bhutan was a pioneer of this with its Gross National Happiness reports. An American statistician involved in Bhutan's effort, Jamie Tanguay, then moved to Vanuatu to apply similar survey techniques at its National Statistics Office. The 2010–11 survey found that the vast majority – 92 per cent – of ni-Vanuatu households in rural areas (where 75 per cent of the population reside) had access to customary lands, and that all but 5 per cent of these households were both housed and fed by their land. People with access to customary lands were, on average, happier than those without access. And 88 per cent reported that access to land was enough or more than enough to meet their family's needs, in combination with access to forest and marine resources.

Indigenous languages remain widely spoken in Vanuatu: 92 per cent of people speak an indigenous language as their first language. Traditional knowledge, including understanding of the traditional planting calendar, family history and place, and local flora and fauna, is quite strong, with 97 per cent of survey respondents reporting a strong or moderate understanding. Traditional wisdom, however, which includes understanding of traditional stories, dances, songs and games passed down for generations, is relatively weak, with 47 per cent deficient in all categories.

Traditional production skills are quite prevalent, including planting and harvesting crops, roasting food, producing medicines and producing materials used for housing. Traditional commodities such as pigs, yams, mats and kava were highly accessible without needing cash. Participation in traditional ceremonial activities, including but not limited to marriage, death, circumcision, status, reconciliation, birth and harvest ceremonies, was very important for nearly all respondents, and it makes them feel happier. Two-thirds were positive about their chiefs' ability to communicate, settle disputes, manage community assets and adhere to customs. In a ranking of select Melanesian values, the top three, considered by 90 per cent or more ni-Vanuatu to be very important or important, were (in descending order) going to church, respect for family and respect for chiefs.

In recent surveys, Vanuatu has come out near the top of international rankings of happiness. Can it continue? The country now has three times as many people as it did at independence four decades ago, and the present growth rate would nearly double the population to some 560,000 by mid-century. The urban populations of Port Vila and Luganville are growing faster still. As the population grows, self-sufficiency will decline, and reliance on the cash economy will rise. Already Port Vila is seeing violent attacks on wealthy households, murders and sexual assaults that were almost unknown before.

The 2010–11 survey showed a sense of declining knowledge of traditional arts and legends. The penetration of conventional media, such as television, radio and newspapers, is sketchy outside the main towns. Social media, with its fake news and malicious information, is filling the void.[5]

There have been other changes to tradition. While people show strong faith in *kastom*, money is coming to replace traditional wealth in paying for brides or even for *nimangki* status upgrades. Kava used to be drunk sparingly by chiefs and high-ranking people at the end of meetings. Now it is gulped down like any beverage by all and sundry, including women. Kava bars have sprung up all over the islands, fuelling demand, as evidenced by the plants being loaded along the Pentecost coast. "It makes your brain work slower," lamented Sethla Amil at Losinwei in Malekula, echoing Ratu Tevita in Fiji. "You become weak, it makes you lazy. You tend to sleep through the day, neglect the kids, can't pay school fees." Another view is that kava is at least better than alcohol – its drinkers are much less likely to end up brawling in the streets – and healthier than the betel nut chewed north of Vanuatu.

The dream at independence of becoming economic masters in their own country is still a distant mirage. Selling Vanuatuan passports to foreign citizens at US$150,000 each has become a mainstay of government finances. Some 1800 were sold in 2018, most to mainland Chinese, even though Beijing bans dual citizenship for its nationals.

Local and Australianised Cantonese and Tonkinese business families are being pressured by arrivals from the pushy new China. It started in the mid-1990s, when the Chinese government built a new foreign ministry building in Port Vila. Many of the workers who helped construct the new building managed to stay on. Word spread, and Mandarin-speaking entrepreneurs started to arrive, opening all kinds of small and medium businesses. "The 5-million- or 10-million-vatu fee for a business investment is nothing to them," Richard Lo told me at his family's LCM supermarket.

The main street of Luganville is now lined with mainland Chinese stores, distinguished by racks of cheap garments and goods out on the pavement. "After competing with Burns Philp, we are now facing competition from these new Chinese arrivals," Lo said. He can't compete with them on price for the old range of canned food, clothing, utensils and tools. "We can't even get it at that price if we go to China," he said. The pressure has pushed LCM upmarket, investing in a wall of cabinet fridges for pricey imported foods and wines.

The older Chinese families are beset with worries about the future. How long will they be welcome? Anne Lew, eighty-three when I met her, was born in Port Vila to a family from Fukien who ran a bakery, moving to Santo when she married. Her seven children are scattered. Only two remain in Vanuatu. The others, thanks to their Francophone education at the Santo Lycée, are in New Caledonia, Tahiti and France. Vanuatu has become less friendly. "It used to be so simple. Now people are crazy, not the same mentality," she told me at her home behind the Nambawan garage and store. "They swear at us: 'You bastard Chinese.' They want everything free."

Others wonder whether their children, educated at private schools and at university in Sydney, and getting jobs in global investment banks, will want to come back and run a business here. Might it be best to float their business and issue shares to the public instead?

*

In Espíritu Santo I met two people who had decided this island was the safest place in the world to be. Steve Quinto, an American pioneer in the low-cost aviation industry, and his South African–born wife, Ruth, came to Santo in 2006 and decided this was where they would get away from a civilisation that was bent on destroying itself and much of the planet's population. In 2010 they gained the lease of a thousand hectares of forest high in the mountains above the west coast of the island. Their largely self-sufficient settlement, Edenhope, houses themselves and four others and is accessible only by boat, followed by a track of 9 kilometres. When I met them, the Quintos were negotiating a lease over another wilderness tract near the island's Big Bay, where Quirós had tried to build a settlement.

"We are in the middle of a mass extinction event," Quinto said. "That's homo sapiens." Bushfires were raging across vast swathes of Australia at the time. To some at least, these islands, once regarded as too hostile and unhealthy for civilised man, with a native population seeming to be on the path to extinction, are now the region's conscience and hope for survival.

*

What do the indigenous bush communities now make of the world? How reconciled are they to being citizens of Vanuatu? In Luganville, I hired a vehicle to go up to Vanafo. We drove on a sealed road through lightly forested country up to the plateau, between fenced paddocks with scattered trees and grazing light-brown cattle.

We passed a sign in French for a school visible to the left, went up a rise and turned along a rougher road overhung with trees and vines. A man was walking along, dressed only in a small square lap-lap tucked into his belt. We bumped down a side track, past gardens and exotic bushes with flowers like red plastic mesh. The driver said they were "ice-cream plants".

At a house of pandanus thatch, a heavily pregnant young woman in a floral dress came out. We parked in a clearing nearby. A middle-aged man with bushy greying hair and a thick beard emerged, dressed in an All Blacks rugby shirt, green board shorts and white socks under his rubber flip flops. This was Lotty Stevens, one of Jimmy's many sons, born in 1961.

Lotty took us up a rise to a large building constructed in A-frame style of rough timber and pandanus thatch, in the style of longhouses I was to see all over Melanesia. Black tree-fern trunks, carved into emblematic shapes, stood around the entrance. In front was a large round stone, surrounded by a circle of smaller stones.

"It's a *navota*," explained Lotty. A holy stone, which acted like a pathway for communicating with the ancient gods.

Inside, the earth floor was bare, strewn in parts with ashes from a cooking fire. A long table on one side was for mixing up kava. At the far end was a walled-off side room for brides and grooms to get changed in at weddings. Another room was a "holy of holies" where only the most initiated men could enter. I asked Lotty about the beliefs underpinning these arrangements.

"It's a long story," he said. "If I told you, it would be a big surprise."

Down another bush track, a thatch canopy sheltered the grave of Jimmy Stevens, marked by a square of river stones decorated with palm fronds and fresh flowers. A framed portrait of Jimmy hung over the entrance, showing him dressed in a beret and a shirt with a design of leaves, boar's tusks and starry skies and the motto "Nagriamel, Man Kastom."

Children were streaming up the road from the local French-language school to have lunch at home. Back in Luganville, we looked for Fabiano Stevens, the forty-four-year-old son of another of Jimmy's sons. We found him in the one-room cabin where he ran his construction business.

Fabiano was standing in upcoming national elections under a Vemerana banner. The group had recently won two seats in the provincial council covering Santo. (When the votes were counted some weeks later, Fabiano was successful.) He was ready to work with a national government that was to "rebalance" Vanuatu to rebuild *kastom* and traditional culture, Fabiano said. "Our God is real and he will bless our land."

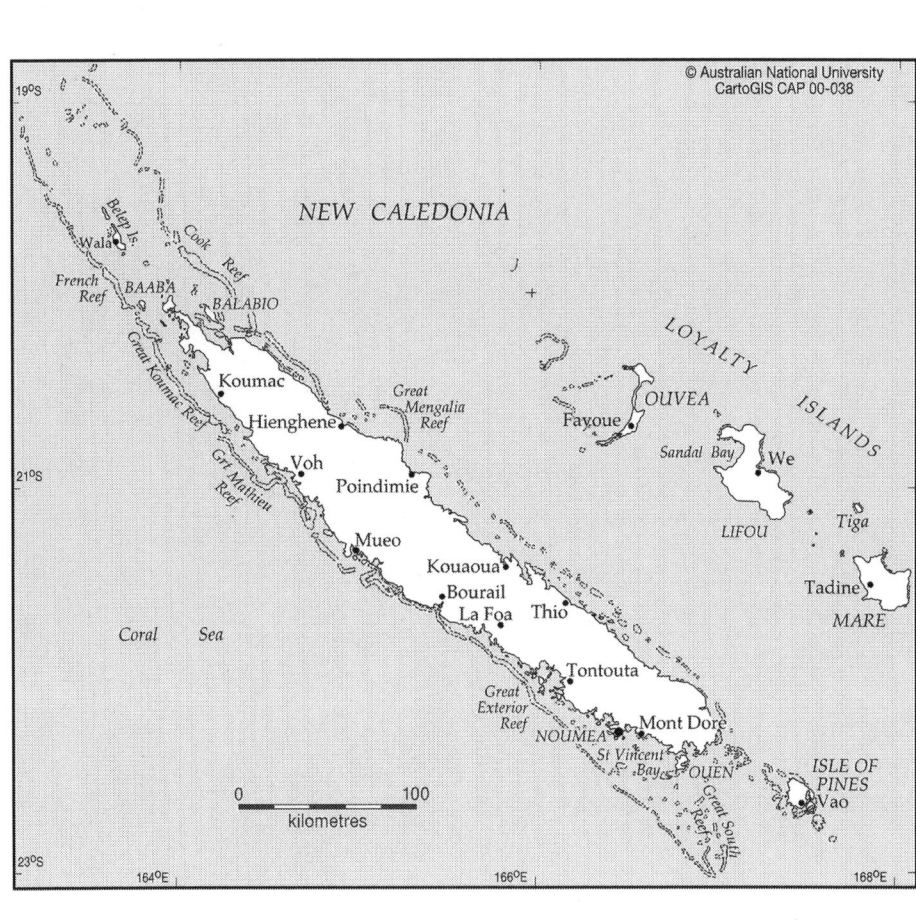

5

NEW CALEDONIA

Events in Kanaky

AT NOUMÉA'S DOMESTIC AIRPORT, Magenta, light was breaking ahead of the 7 am flight. Across the runway, a row of trees began to stand out against the sea. By happy coincidence, a fellow passenger was Charles Wea, one of New Caledonia's Melanesian people known as the Kanaks. He was the foreign affairs advisor to Louis Mapou, the *indépendantiste* Kanak president of the partially autonomous government of New Caledonia. Not only that, he came from the very spot I wished to visit and was related to people involved in the tragic events that took place there.

Charles had studied abroad, most recently a diplomacy course in Melbourne. But this weekend he was engaged in traditional duties. It was the time of year to dig up his small patch of land back in his *tribu* (village) and plant yams to be ready as offerings in ceremonial gatherings later in the year.

We boarded the Air Calédonie turboprop aircraft. It headed away from the mountains of Grande Terre, the main island, and across the sea to the northeast. Our descent through clouds half an hour later revealed a narrow island with waves breaking against low cliffs on one side and a wide expense of shallow lagoon on the other, circled in the distance by islets.

On landing, Charles was greeted by his brother, nephew and niece. We got into his brother's four-wheel drive pickup, which had a clutch of brightly dressed Kanak women sitting in the tray. They agreed to drop me at the *gite* where I would be staying, and they advised against renting a car. "Just stand by the road and hitch. You'll always get a lift," Charles said.

The next morning was a Sunday, and I did just that to get to his village. The island had only 3000 regular inhabitants and one main road along its length. I walked beyond the big shed that housed a small supermarket and put my thumb out. Several cars passed, mostly full of people who'd just done some shopping. One was a small Peugeot containing a Kanak family. It too passed me by. But a few minutes later, it came back empty of most its passengers, turned around and pulled up beside me. The father, a young, bearded man in work clothes, leaned over and asked where I wanted to go.

"Gossanah," I said. I sensed he was a bit taken aback. It was the northernmost *tribu* on the island, a good distance. But André, which I would learn was his name, braced himself and took the task on cheerfully. He knew and respected Charles.

We chatted, me in the back seat, while his young son in front made toys out of plastic objects from the glove box. The road led along a narrow stretch of the island, then into a thicker part near the northern end where we diverted to a winding side road between bush and gardens. We got to Gossanah and saw a wide expanse of buffalo grass, a small church with patchy cement rendering, soaked by the rain, and houses scattered on the far side. None of the instruments on the car's dashboard were working, but André's generosity would have cost him in petrol. After initial protestations, he accepted a contribution for that.

It was just after 10 am and the sound of a service was coming from the church. Charles had told me he'd be there, so I went in and took a back pew. The litany was in French, with one passage in the local Iaai language. The pastor was a handsome, light-skinned young man in a beige jacket and tie. But for the languages and the vigorous singing in harmonies, the service was quite familiar to an Anglophone visitor. Most of the first whites to come to the Loyalties had been English speakers. Some sandalwood gatherers had used this island of Ouvéa as a base for their perilous voyages into the New Hebrides. Then the London Missionary Society had sent in its evangelists. Although in 1853 the island had been annexed by the French, who promoted Catholicism, some English and protestant influence lingered.

Afterwards, Charles and I waited for a rain shower to pass, then walked across the field under a light drizzle. He was aching a bit from digging and planting the previous afternoon. There were too many tree roots in his patch to use any kind of machine, so it was all spadework. We walked past a half-finished house of concrete blocks and corrugated iron that Charles was building for his eventual retirement, a couple of traditional huts with thatch conical roofs, and some poultry coops.

His father's home was another cement-block house, but its centre of activity was a long table outside under an extended shelter of corrugated iron, screened by plants and an old fishing net. Charles' widowed aunt was busy in the kitchen just inside the house. Soon the table was spread with dishes: rice cooked with coconut, chicken in gravy, meat, salad, and small grilled fish that Charles' father had netted that morning. We ate and talked. At one point Charles got me to look at a bird in a nearby tree: one of Ouvéa's unique and rare green parrots.

Then they told me about the events that had unfolded around Gossanah over two weeks in 1988, when the whole modern history of New Caledonia's colonisation exploded in dreadful violence.

That history began when James Cook, on his second voyage in 1774, landed on a large island that he thought looked like Scotland – hence the name. Cook found his reception ashore, near the present-day town of Balade, quite friendly. But subsequent European callers, who included sandalwood traders and beachcombers from Port Jackson, were met with hostility.

The islanders' resentment was entirely explicable. By then, the impact of European invasion had indeed been fatal, hence the title of Alan Moorehead's book about the "discovery" of the Pacific, *The Fatal Impact*.[1]

New Caledonia had been the healthiest place to live in Melanesia when the sea-faring Austronesians, sailing down the island chain from the northwest, settled it between 1050 and 850 BC, according to carbon-dating of their Lapita pottery found by archaeologists. The southernmost island group of Melanesia, New Caledonia is outside the zone of malaria, which suppressed population growth elsewhere. The population stress on food supplies led to two responses over the next millennium. The Melanesians moved into more intensive agriculture, constructing terraces for their yams and other tubers, which in some places were irrigated by water channels, like the rice terraces of Southeast Asia. With this fixed-location farming, villages became more established in one spot. Wider political alliances formed, both to carry out the extensive work required and to protect the food supply, with stone markers delineating different territories. The scholars Bronwen Douglas and Christophe Sand think that New Caledonians were well on the way to "state formation" before Europeans arrived and had shifted from nature worship to ancestor veneration. The usual estimate of the pre-contact population, about 50,000, could be far too low.

But by the time a French admiral landed at Balade in 1853 with twenty sailors and marines to annex New Caledonia for Emperor Napoleon III, visitors saw a sparse, scattered and weakly organised population. What had happened? Sand and his colleagues postulate that in the eight decades following Cook's landing, the diseases his crew and later European visitors introduced – tuberculosis, smallpox, influenza, syphilis, measles – had led to a massive population collapse and a profound change in the organisation of indigenous society.[2]

Then followed a smaller-scale version of the colonisation of Australia. White settlers seized the best sweeps of level land, on the west side of the Grande Terre. A prospector from Australia started what would later grow into the mining giant Société Le Nickel. The Melanesians were pushed into reserves in the mountains and the rugged east coast, forbidden to leave these areas without permission. Gendarmes patrolled the land to protect the settlers. Restive chiefs were exiled to Tahiti. Persistent rebels were guillotined. The Kanaks got together for two big rebellions, the first under a chief named Ataï in 1878, and the second under chief Noël in 1917. Ataï's head ended up in a museum in Paris. Noël's was displayed on a pole in Nouméa.

The Kanak population reached a low of 27,000 in 1921. As in the New Hebrides and Australia, many Europeans expected that the indigenous people were destined for extinction. In the meantime, they were objects of curiosity. In 1931, a "Colonial Exposition" in Paris put naked Kanaks on display, presenting them to the French public as cannibals.

With the fall of France to Nazi Germany in 1940, Nouméa officials were inclined to obey French prime minister Phillipe Pétain's capitulation. However, some 3000 supporters of General Charles de Gaulle, including well-armed *broussards* (bush settlers), occupied the city. The Australian cruiser HMAS *Adelaide* clinched the decision. It installed the French high commissioner in the New Hebrides as the Free French governor. Pétainist officials were allowed to decamp to Indo-China aboard a French navy sloop.

When France was liberated, the "winds of change" began blowing through the European empires. In New Caledonia, the *indigénat* system that had restricted the Kanaks to reserves ended in 1946. In theory they could now go anywhere. In practice, they could perform folkloric dances at hotels in Nouméa; it would be decades before they could enter those hotels as guests.

Political activity flourished in a cautious way. Well-meaning French, Kanak and Polynesian migrants formed the multiracial Union Calédonienne (UC) to pursue the social-economic advancement of a population with vast inequalities, and to take up the opportunities of local government. By 1958, the UC and its leader, Maurice Lenormand, held a majority of seats in the General Council, the locally elected advisory body. They were getting too popular and influential for the comfort of diehard French loyalists, who were uneasily watching what was happening in Africa. In Algiers, army general Raoul Salan worked with the 1.5 million *pieds-noirs* French settlers to resist the Algerian nationalists. In Corsica, French paratroopers seized control. Now, in New Caledonia, army major Henri Loustau conspired with *broussards* to mount a coup against the "communists" of the UC. The governor wilted under the pressure and dissolved the General Council. Then vigilantes hunted down and roughed up UC cabinet members.

In France, the postwar Fourth Republic fell. In January 1959, de Gaulle came out of retirement to install the Fifth Republic. Overseas territories were offered the choice of remaining French territories or becoming independent "with all the consequences". Only Guinea, in West Africa, chose the latter. The departing French ransacked it for anything they could take with them. In New Caledonia, both the UC and the loyalist groups opted to remain part of France.

Once installed in power, de Gaulle bowed to the inevitable and moved towards a referendum in Algeria in the face of bombings and assassinations. Algeria became independent in 1962, along with other African colonies, and hundreds of thousands of *pieds-noirs* moved to metropolitan France or to French overseas territories. Those who came to New Caledonia added a hard new element to the loyalists.

In New Caledonia and France's other realms in the Pacific, de Gaulle took the opposite path. Paris seized back powers previously given to local representatives. Bogus charges deprived the UC's Lenormand of his civil rights for five years, effectively ending his political career.

The governor's 1958 surrender to Major Loustau's show of force helped set "a tradition of extra-constitutional action", according to scholar Stephen Henningham, while the subsequent removal of New Caledonia's limited postwar autonomy showed that nothing given by Paris could be taken as permanent.³ "In sum, de Gaulle's betrayal of New Caledonia was the opposition of his betrayal of the *pieds-noirs*," wrote David Chappell in his political history of the territory, "but it was still a betrayal."⁴

De Gaulle was driven by his goal of creating an independent nuclear *force de frappe* (strike power) for France. His country would never again be overrun from the east. With the loss of bomb-testing sites in the Sahara, the Pacific was the alternative. To the Tahitians, he promised lavish spending as a reward for accepting nuclear testing at Mururoa Atoll, which he went to witness in 1966. New Caledonia was a stepping stone to Tahiti, and a source of a strategic mineral as well. At the peak of America's war in Vietnam, the price of nickel was sky high: exports from New Caledonia were worth five times what Paris was spending in the territory

The French government set up an agency to recruit migrants to the territory, partly to supply labour for the nickel boom, but also explicitly to build up a settler majority to counter the Kanaks. In 1972, French premier Pierre Messmer called it "the last chance to create an additional Francophone country" and avoid indigenous people taking over with support from other Pacific peoples. Between 1969 and 1971, some 15,000 migrants arrived from France and the Polynesian islands, increasing the population by 20 per cent.

Some Kanaks had been to university in France, where they had been exposed to writings about liberation and black consciousness. Nidoïsh Naisseline, son of a high chief on Maré in the Loyalty Islands, was at the Sorbonne studying sociology when he and others got swept up in the May 1968 student uprising in Paris. Naisseline wrote that Kanaks were in an impossible position: expected to assimilate on one hand, while being blocked from doing so by racial discrimination on the other. Now, he wrote, "We don't want to copy anyone. We want to become ourselves again."

On return to New Caledonia, the students began questioning the gradualist policies of the UC. They adopted the *foulard rouge* (red scarf) of the 1871 Paris Communards, some of whom had been exiled to New Caledonia (the island was used as a penal colony in the late nineteenth and early twentieth centuries). New Caledonia's politics became more fragmented, as newer liberationists nudged the UC out of its integrationist ideas. What became known as the *Réveille Canaque* – the Kanak re-awakening – had begun.

At the same time, as in many other places in the Pacific, the churches were anxious to indigenise. They kept an eye out for bright boys who, with steady tutelage, might develop into the priests and bishops of the future. In the northeast of the Grande Terre, one such boy was Jean-Marie Tjibaou, born in 1936 in the tiny village of Tiendanite, a collection of traditional conical thatch-roofed huts and ramshackle corrugated iron cottages in a valley near Hienghène. French troops had stormed up the valley in 1917 when quelling Chief Noël's uprising against conscription. They burnt the villages and shot at fleeing Kanaks. Tjibaou's grandmother, attempting to escape with her four-year-old son, Wenceslas – Tjibaou's father – was fatally shot. Her sister snatched the child and evaded the soldiers.

In 1945, at age nine, Tjibaou left Tiendanite for a succession of Catholic schools and seminaries, entering the priesthood in 1965 and becoming "second vicar" of the big cathedral looking down on the centre of Nouméa from a hill. One of his duties was going around Nouméa at night and taking drunk

Kanaks back to their homes. In their rantings, he heard all their bottled-up feelings about becoming a derided underclass in their own homeland, and about being reduced from the positions of respect they had held in the villages. He came across a copy of a thesis by an older Kanak priest, Apollinaire Anova-Ataba, titled "From Ataï to Independence". Ataba argued that independence was the answer to the anomie of the Kanaks. After his death from leukemia aged thirty-seven in 1966, the church had suppressed the thesis for many years.

In 1968, Tjibaou went to France for further studies. There he read the sympathetic writings about Kanak culture of Maurice Leenhardt, a missionary in New Caledonia in the early twentieth century, and heard lectures by Roger Bastide and Jean Guiart, who downplayed cultural hierarchies and explored syncretic theologies in Africa and South America. Tjibaou left before finishing his thesis in ethnology about the spiritual ties of the Kanaks to their land, returning to Hienghène in 1971. Feeling he could be both a Christian and an animist, he left the priesthood and found work in welfare services, trying to deal with the country's widespread alcoholism and to support women and young people. Delving back into the culture from which he'd been distanced for the previous quarter century, he organised a festival called Melanesia 2000. Held at the Magenta beach in Nouméa in 1975, it drew over 50,000 visitors to see displays of traditional and contemporary arts and historical dramas about colonisation.

It met cynicism from many old white Caldoches, the descendants of early French settlers. Some ex-students of the Paris uprising worried it represented the "folklorisation" of Kanak culture. But younger temporary French residents, known as *les métros*, flocked to see it. Kanaks reported that following the festival, they were more frequently addressed by the respectful *vous* rather than the *tu* used to address children.

During this period, the territory was heading into bitter ferment. Riot squads flown in from France put down protests around Bastille Day in 1974. When de Gaulle's successor, Georges Pompidou, died in office that year, he was replaced by another Gaullist, Valery Giscard d'Estaing, who declined to meet a Kanak delegation seeking expanded autonomy.

The Kanaks formed new political parties that for the first time included the word "liberation" in their names. They spoke of reviving and adapting Kanak custom and nationalising the nickel industry. In parts of the northern Grande Terre, their followers squatted on alienated traditional lands. Loyalists formed vigilante groups and backed a new party formed by businessman Jacques Lafleur.

In 1981, the Socialist Party's François Mitterrand began his fourteen-year presidency of France. Although he continued the main elements of Gaullist foreign policy (and was to approve the bombing of the Greenpeace anti-nuclear protest vessel in Auckland harbour in 1985), he was more conciliatory towards the Kanaks. Four months after taking office, he met Tjibaou and the UC leader, Pierre Declercq, a former schoolteacher from France.

Two months after this meeting, Declercq was murdered in his home, a case that has never been solved. The territory slid into a decade of violence and counter-violence, now referred to obliquely as *les èvènements* (the events). When the Territorial Assembly discussed land reform in 1982, masked and helmeted settlers burst in and beat up pro-independence deputies. Out in the bush, Kanaks stepped up their occupations and sent "eviction notices" to white settlers.

Tjibaou by then had moved from cultural promotion to politics, becoming mayor of his home community around Hienghène. He coined the name Kanaky for the envisaged nation, a wry take on both Kanaka, a word borrowed from Hawai'ian by Australian sugar planters to describe their indentured Melanesian labourers, and the name of the mythical ancestor of the Kanaks, Téâ Kanaké. The *indépendantistes* formed themselves into a new alliance with the provocative name Front de Libération Nationale Kanak et Socialiste, or FLNKS. It adopted a new flag, with blue, red and green horizontal bands behind an emblem featuring the wooden arrowhead carving that traditionally tops the homes of chiefs.

As Territorial Assembly elections approached in November 1984, Tjibaou became the leader of this new alliance. It took a militant approach. A dozen young activists went off to Colonel Gaddafi's Libya for training. The

FLNKS decided not only to boycott the elections but to disrupt them. Its supporters shut down about 40 per cent of polling booths. Settler homes and shops went up in flames. Roads were blockaded. Whites and allied Polynesians attacked the roadblocks with guns and dynamite. The government sent in 4000 soldiers, gendarmes and black-uniformed riot troops. Tear gas and baton charges prevailed. In the elections, Jacques Lafleur's loyalists won a majority, but Tjibaou declared a provisional government.

Mitterrand sent in a new high commissioner to take over, an intellectual politician named Edgard Pisani. Raised in Tunisia, of Maltese descent and with a doctorate in political science, Pisani began knocking heads together and within a few months came up with a pathway that seemed to meet the concerns of both camps: independence in association with France, with foreign affairs, defence and security still delegated to the French government, to be submitted to a vote by those with at least three years of residence. It was the only time such a hybrid option has been put forward by Paris, even tentatively. It still remains an option that might break the deadlock: independence with a lot of ongoing support and involvement by France.

Tjibaou agreed to lift roadblocks and occupations. But more violence rendered the Pisani plan dead on arrival. Within a month of the election, settlers ambushed two truckloads of FLNKS members near Hienghène, killing ten of them and wounding several others. Among the dead were two of Tjibaou's brothers. The main intended target was Tjibaou himself: he would have been in the little convoy but had been held back in Nouméa.

In their frustration, the killers went on to Tiendanite and burnt down Tjibaou's house. They were the remnants of the poor white and *métis* (mixed race) settlers in the region's narrow valleys. Most had been evacuated to Nouméa, their homes torched either by the Kanaks, or by the settlers themselves, in order to leave nothing for the Kanaks. The Kanaks had said they could stay if they joined the boycott. Most, however, voted for Lafleur's loyalist party.

Tiendanite had lost ten of its twenty-six men in one strike. Halfway up the road to the village is one of the monuments to Kanak victims seen across the territory. A plaque with their names, between the burnt-out wrecks of their two pickup trucks, says: *Fils de Kanaky, souviens-toi* (sons of Kanaky, remember).

In response to the attack, Eloi Machoro – also an ex-cleric, trained at a Protestant college in Suva – and three dozen supporters invaded a police station and houses in the white-settled region of La Foa, seizing weapons and declaring the start of a guerrilla campaign to control the hinterland before advancing on the south. They were soon surrounded by 300 gendarmes. At dawn one morning, Machoro told his comrades: "We will show them that Kanaks know how to die." He and another Kanak came out of the house, rifles on their shoulders, and were immediately shot by gendarme snipers. Riots continued. Mitterrand visited briefly. He wrote later that he told Tjibaou: "Let us imagine that I am capable of granting you independence ... with what army will you take Nouméa?"

In 1986, the French socialists lost control of parliament. An ambitious conservative named Jacques Chirac became premier, entering two years of political "cohabitation" with President Mitterrand. He halted land redistribution and resumed authorities previously delegated to the regions. The French government declared that under French law, "*il n'y a pas de peuple Kanak*" (There is not a Kanak people) – only French citizens. The Kanaks successfully lobbied Melanesia's new states and the non-aligned world to have New Caledonia returned to the United Nations' list of territories still to be decolonised, much to the chagrin of the loyalists. It remains on the list today.

The next year, Chirac and his territories minister, Bernard Pons, held a referendum giving the residents of New Caledonia a stark choice: a bit more autonomy, or independence with no further aid from France (similar to de Gaulle's blunt offer in 1958). Now there were 8000 French troops and police in the territory, about one soldier for every twenty-five inhabitants. Troops were detached into small groups and sent to roam the countryside, a strategy from the Algerian war known as *nomadisation*.

The French far-right-wing politician Jean-Marie Le Pen, leader of the Front Nationale, flew in to rally loyalists. Their supporters harassed journalists and observers from English-speaking countries, assumed always to be conspiring to push the French and their glorious language out of the Pacific. The Australian consul-general, John Dauth, was expelled for alleged interference in local affairs. The referendum was boycotted by Kanaks, and the result was a 98 per cent vote to stay with France. No one but the loyalists believed it proved anything.

In October 1987, the seven accused over the December 1984 Hienghène massacre that had killed Tjibaou's brothers went on trial. The judge accepted their argument that the attack was "anticipated self-defence" and acquitted them. The verdict threw Tjibaou into deep despair. "The hunting of the Kanak is permitted," he said. He wrote personal letters to Mitterrand. But even this sympathetic president could not shake himself away from the mythology of the French republic or put himself in the mind of a different people who saw themselves as subjects, not citizens.

Now we come to the bloody events of 1988.

Despite the rising tensions, the French government had decided to hold elections for New Caledonia's Territorial Assembly on 24 April, the same day as the first round of presidential elections across France and all its possessions. Jacques Chirac, the premier, was standing against Mitterrand, with Le Pen the third main contestant.

The FLNKS decided it was time for a major disruption and seizure of power. On 22 April, blockades were to go up all over the Grande Terre while militants would seize the gendarmeries in the Loyalty Islands. On Ouvéa, the *indépendantiste* raiding group was headed by Alphonse Dianou, a graduate of a protestant seminary in Suva. On his return he had joined the UC and initially advocated non-violent action. But recent events had turned him to a belief that only force could achieve any advance.

On the appointed day, he and some two dozen others attacked the gendarmerie at Fayaoue, in the middle of Ouvéa. Today, it is a deserted-looking compound of single-storey buildings and whitewashed stones behind a barbed-wire fence, with a couple of old cannon barrels pointing out to the lagoon. Across the road are memorials listing the locals who died in the two world wars and in a shipping disaster in the 1950s.

When Dianou and his group attacked, police officers resisted. In the ensuing fight, the Kanaks shot dead four gendarmes before being able to grab guns from the armoury. Then, as Fayaoue was exposed and close to the airport, they decided to decamp rather than stay, taking fourteen surviving officers as hostages. They retreated to a safer redoubt: Gossanah and the rocky landscape in the bush to its east, which hid a number of legend-shrouded caves. Holed up in one of these, surviving on food sent in from the village, they got word of mouth that was more and more ominous.

The attacks that were supposed to happen simultaneously in Lifou and Maré had not occurred. The blockades on Grande Terre were a shambles. The unplanned deaths at Fayaoue had set off an outcry, and French authorities were promising a stern response. Dianou and the eighteen other Kanaks in the cave were now the targets.

In the first round of the French presidential election, Mitterand received the most votes but was short of an overall majority, so it went to a second round between him and Chirac, scheduled for 8 May. To win, Chirac needed most of the 20 per cent of voters who had supported Le Pen in the first round. To do that, he had to show even more toughness against outsiders and the enemies of France.

French soldiers and special police took control of Gossanah and banned the media from entering. Soon, the grassy field filled with 300 troops and their tents, trucks and helicopters. Keen for intelligence about the location of the cave, army officers detained villagers and pressured them. Some were stripped and bashed, including Charles Wea's elderly grandfather and uncle Djubelly Wea. Charles' father, Maki Wea, was flown to Fayaoue and put on the radio to try to get the FLNKS leadership to negotiate. Eight soldiers and a magistrate were led up to the cave for possible negotiations, but were taken hostage as well. The Kanaks did not trust the French, and it seemed the French were impatient for talks to fail.

As the siege dragged on, with Dianou repeating his demand for a timetable for independence in return for releasing the hostages, Chirac was anxious for action. He said he would not negotiate with "terrorists" carrying out acts of "barbarity" and guerrilla warfare. Bernard Pons, his interior and territories minister, flew to Ouvéa. On 5 May, three days before the second presidential election round, the army and police attacked. Helicopters fired incendiary rockets around the cave entrance to clear the bush. Next came fusillades of bullets, tear gas and grenades. Somehow, all twenty-three hostages emerged alive, but sixteen of their captors were shot dead in the fighting, along with two soldiers. Two Kanaks captured alive were executed on the spot. Dianou was badly wounded and left to die without any attempt to get him medical attention.

Of the army's captives in Gossanah village, twenty-nine were flown to France and placed in prisons around Paris. They included Charles' uncle, Djubelly Wea. Medical examination showed that eight had been beaten, with signs of cigarette burns and long periods in tight constraints. Three days later, Wea's grandfather, badly shaken by his ordeal, died.

Chirac lost the presidential election to Mitterrand anyway, and then in the legislature elections in June lost to the Socialist Party. Cohabitation was over, for the time being. Michel Rocard became premier, promising to make calming New Caledonia a top priority. Within days of taking office, he invited the two sides to a conference in an old palace, Matignon, and told them they were not leaving or allowed to communicate with the outside until they had come up with a consensus to avoid civil war. The plan they agreed to, refined a few weeks later, was for a ten-year period of economic development, focused on Kanak-populated regions, along with intensive training of Kanaks for higher offices and a referendum on independence at the end of the decade. An amnesty would be granted for the deaths of Declercq, Machoro, Dianou and the Ouvéa gendarmes.

Amazingly, both Tjibaou and Lafleur, who had not met in five years, agreed to this "Matignon Accord" and were pictured shaking hands.

For Lafleur, agreeing to the proposal was comparatively easy. The independence question was kicked into the future, by which time a Kanak leadership and middle class might be happy enough with a version of the status quo. For Tjibaou, however, it was a huge gamble. He had gone to Paris with instructions from his movement to listen and report back, but not to agree to anything. The decision to sign the accord was his alone.

It met bitter criticism from many Kanak figures. "The slave agreed to shake hands with his master in order to reconcile the French," said Léopold Jorédie. But the plan was approved by the FLNKS in July, and later in a low-turnout French referendum (though not in New Caledonia) that gave it political force in France. Tjibaou harboured doubts. Over the following months, he wondered if he had been trapped and tricked. He had sleepless nights. But what was the alternative? The Kanaks were too few and too weak for guerrilla war. The accord at least gave them the chance to prepare to run their own country.

Gossanah nursed its anger and grief. It went into the customary year-long period of mourning. It had been left to carry the weight of the French counterattack. If everyone had done what Dianou and his Ouvéa comrades had done, Kanaky might already have emerged. The villagers of Gossanah declared their rejection of the Matignon Accord.

At the end of the mourning year, the people of Ouvéa gathered for the consecration of the monument and final place of interment for the nineteen Kanaks killed in the cave, on the shore of the lagoon at Hwaadrila in the middle of the island. Tjibaou and his devoted deputy from the Loyalty Islands, Yeiwéne Yeiwéne, came to honour them. They offered the traditional gifts of cloth, shell money and yams. "We rush forward because this blood of the dead is living, it calls out to us, it is our blood," Tjibaou said. "It is the blood of those who demand freedom for our people."

Charles' uncle Djubelly Wea, back from prison in France, walked up to Tjibaou as if to shake hands. Then he produced a pistol and shot both Tjibaou and Yeiwéne dead. Immediately, Tjibaou's bodyguard, Daniel Fisdiepas, shot and killed Wea.

The shock went around the Pacific. Ministers from many of the region's governments attended the funeral held for the two FLNKS leaders in Nouméa's cathedral. Michel Rocard gave a fine speech that showed great sympathy and understanding of Tjibaou's intellectual journey. He recalled that at Matignon, he overheard Tjibaou say to Yeiwéne: "Watch out for the big black hole." Yeiwéne had replied: "Whatever happens, we are there together." About 20,000 people gathered in the streets outside the cathedral, mostly Kanak but also a fair number of Caldoches, *métros* and Polynesians from Wallis Island. They watched the funeral cortege take the two bodies out to Magenta to be flown out for burial in their home villages, Tjibaou to Hienghène, Yeiwéne to Maré.

At Gossanah, after lunch and before my lift back to the *gite*, Charles Wea walked me across to the grave of his uncle Djubelly and his grandfather. It was marked by a small, square terraced garden, its levels contained by rough walls of coral. Djubelly's traditional house was preserved nearby.

In front of the grave was a marble plaque with gilt lettering: *A toutes les générations à venir, Souvenez-vous: en la nuit de 4 Mai 1989 le sang fut versé à Ouvéa*: To all the generations to come, remember: on the night of 4 May 1989, blood was shed at Ouvéa. The next line said simply *Pardon*, followed by the Aiai translation: *Haiömonu me ûsoköu*. The last line was hopeful: *Que se lève une Aurore nouvelle*. Let a new dawn rise. The date was 2004 – fifteen years after the Hwaadrila shootings.

I asked Charles Wea what reputation his uncle Djubelly now had among Kanaks, and his answer surprised me. "A lot of people think he was right," Charles said. "After more than thirty years [since the Matignon Accord], where are we now?"

Indeed, thirty-five years since the accord, the territory was again at a political impasse. In the decade after Matignon, development stepped up in New Caledonia. Kanaks got special training and their regions received more funding. The government bought Jacques Lafleur out of his nickel mine, Société Minière du Sud Pacifique, and transferred ownership to the northern and island provinces. A new nickel refinery was built, in partnership with international mining company Xstrata.

A new centre of Melanesian culture was commissioned and built on the same shore at Magenta where Tjibaou had held his cultural festival in 1975. The fine building, designed by Renzo Piano and incorporating elements of Kanak architecture, is indeed a marvel. To some it symbolises the re-entry of Kanaks to the city from which they were barred until 1946. To some, it is emblematic of a "cult of Tjibaou", masterminded by France, sanctifying his willingness to compromise and put aside independence in exchange for tangible uplift.

In 1997, Premier Lionel Jospin's government proposed a new accord to replace Matignon. It recognised that New Caledonia had been taken without consultation or consent, and that there had been "shadows" as well as light since 1853. Kanak custom was to have equal status with French civil law, and experts on custom would advise judges, magistrates and police, with a Customary Senate advising the government as a whole. There would be more Kanak place names and work would begin on new emblems. The territory's future would be decided in a series of three referendums, fifteen to twenty years in the future, with the electoral roll "frozen" to include only those who were resident in 1998, plus their children. There was talk of "shared sovereignty", and New Caledonia was to become a *pays d'outre mer* (an overseas country), although no one was too sure what these terms meant or if they would change much in practice.

No charismatic leader had emerged to replace Tjibaou. The remaining Kanak leaders were experiencing the actual problems of running the regional and territorial governments, and realising that independence would not be as easy as they might once have imagined. Many settlers hoped that by postponing the question, by the time the referendums rolled around, Kanak leaders might be content with their perks, and the cultural ties of the Kanak population might have loosened.

The Nouméa Accord, as it became known, was signed on 5 May 1998. Passed by a territorial referendum by a 72 per cent majority on a 74 per cent turnout, it was enacted into the French constitution in 1999 by the required joint sitting of the National Assembly and the Senate with a 60 per cent majority.

The territory's politicians continued to jostle for elected positions, both locally and in Paris, where New Caledonia has two seats in each house. At times, there were hopes that a sense of "common destiny" was developing. When Nouméa hosted the Pacific Games in 2011, it was agreed that both the Kanaky flag and the French tricolour would fly side by side, and that arrangement has more or less continued. For a while, the UC cooperated with a new moderate faction of loyalists.

But the demographics held when it came time for the referendums. By then, the French president was the breezy young conservative Emmanuel

Macron. In the first referendum, held in 2018, the vote for independence was 43 per cent. In the second, in 2020, it had grown to 47 per cent. The "yes" vote was concentrated in the central and northern parts of the Grande Terre, while the "no" vote was strongest in the southern region, around Nouméa. The two main racial groups were divided on their "common destiny".

Some detected in the drift to the "yes" vote a steady movement of Pacific Islander and other minorities towards the Kanak cause, maybe a sense of Oceanic identity taking hold. Intermarriage between the races was rising. Roestam, a taxi-driver of Javanese descent, told me he was married to a Polynesian woman. "There is a lot of *métissage*," he said with a smile.

The third vote loomed at the end of 2021. Then, in September that year, the Delta variant of the Covid-19 virus swept New Caledonia, quickly infecting over 13,000 of its 270,000 people. More than 280 of them died, one of the world's highest mortality rates, and of them about 60 per cent were Kanak. The Kanak parties begged for the referendum to be postponed a year. Its communities had embarked on the traditional year of mourning, when activity is subdued until the dead are placed in permanent graves. In addition, quarantine restrictions limited movement, putting the Kanak parties at a disadvantage, as they normally campaigned by meetings of voters scattered in small villages and the islands, while the more urbanised loyalists enjoyed good internet connectivity.

Macron and his territories minister, Sébastien Lecornu, insisted on the vote going ahead. The president was facing his first re-election test in April 2022. Macron's competition now came from the right, notably from Le Pen's daughter Marine.

The loyalist campaign warned of a geostrategic threat and the importance of French power to ward it off. "France's presence will protect us from China's appetite and efforts to take control of the region," said "no" campaigner Christopher Gygès, who said the vote was a choice between France and China. Even the relatively moderate politician Philippe Gomès warned of automatic "recolonisation" by China if New Caledonians voted "yes" to independence.

The loyalists were campaigning in a vacuum. As they had in 1987, the Kanak parties decided to boycott the December referendum. Participation fell from around 86 per cent in the first two polls to 43.9 per cent, with those abstaining mostly in the Kanak regions. Of those who voted, 96.5 per cent voted "no". In thirty-four years, New Caledonia had completed a full circle.

The result was immediately declared null and void by the Melanesian Spearhead Group, a forum of Vanuatu, Fiji, Solomon Islands and Papua New Guinea. The Pacific Islands Forum – a wider regional grouping that includes Melanesian, Polynesian and Micronesian states as well as Australia and New Zealand – was more diplomatic: the boycott needed to be taken "into the contextual consideration and analysis of the result".

Unfazed, Macron declared that "France is more beautiful because New Caledonia decided to stay". The other conservative candidates for president also applauded the result. Local opponents of independence were also jubilant. "Tonight we are French and we will stay that way. It's no longer negotiable," said Sonia Backès, president of the Assembly of South Province and a fervent loyalist. To her, the Nouméa Accord was now defunct, allowing the electoral rolls to be thrown open to more recent arrivals and putting an end to special economic support for Kanak-dominated regions.

In July 2023, Macron arrived in New Caledonia, accompanied by a demonstration of French ability to swing military power into the Pacific: a squadron of Rafale fighters flown out from France. New Caledonia was French because it had chosen to be French in three referendums, he told a crowd of 10,000 Europeans and Polynesians in Nouméa's Place des Cocotiers. Now the priorities would be transforming the nickel industry into a low-cost green-energy industry and expanding agriculture. The voice of France would resonate in the Indo-Pacific, helped by a new military academy in New Caledonia for the region's armed forces: "If independence is to choose tomorrow to have a Chinese base here, or be dependent on other fleets, good luck!"

But to less partisan analysts, the boycott had also been a show of force by the Kanak parties. Their call to stay away from the polls had been almost universally observed by the Kanaks. In addition, Kanaks had shown their ability to mount significant street power. During 2020 and 2021, rioting and blockades gripped the south of Grande Terre and Nouméa itself, after authorities aided the Brazilian mining giant Vale to sell its nickel mines and refinery to other foreign interests, rather than considering local bidders. The protests pressured the eventual buyer to allocate equity to a Kanak institution.

Since the referendum, Macron's vision of New Caledonia's future has been crumbling. Indonesia's promotion of its nickel industry saw world prices for the metal tumble. Two of the three nickel smelters in New Caledonia shut down in 2023, with their mines reverting to exporting unprocessed ore. Few saw any prospect of a green energy revolution coming to save the industry. New Caledonia would have to fall back on agriculture and tourism. With nickel previously providing some 25 per cent of private-sector employment, the flow of Europeans and other non-Kanaks away from the country seemed likely to grow. Even before the nickel crisis, about 2000 residents, most of them white, were leaving New Caledonia each year. And while Macron won re-election in 2022, his supporters in the national assembly went into minority government. Widening the territory's electoral franchise was possibly unattainable without the unsavoury support of the far right led by Marine Le Pen.

Even then, it was a fantasy to think Paris could get New Caledonia removed from the United Nations' list of colonised countries, as was pointed out to me by Mathias Chauchat, professor of public law at the University of New Caledonia in Nouméa . For the United Nations, colonised people have the right of self-determination. "In essence, opening the electoral roll would give power to the whites. It would revert to the colony like before, with the French in power and the Kanaks like an aboriginal minority. They would be left with their customs on the margin, all the while saying that their identity was recognised. It would be a system of apartheid that doesn't say its name," Chauchat told me over coffee on Nouméa's seafront.

When Chauchat said the same things on Nouméa television panels, loyalists circulated a petition asking the French government to deport him. The descendants of transported convicts and political prisoners were now calling for an effective critic of their politics, happily settled in New Caledonia for several decades, to be exiled – to France!

A return to violent protest could happen without much warning, one regional official told me. I met another academic, Patrice Godin, an anthropologist also resident in New Caledonia for decades, and recounted what Charles Wea had told me at the grave of his uncle Djubelly. "When political negotiations fail, it is not the most open and moderate leaders who prevail, but the most radical," Godin said. "One wonders whether the French government is aware of this. I am currently sensing great concern among Kanak elected representatives and political decision-makers. If they fail to change the government's policy, they know that their activists, their voters and the majority of the Kanak population will withdraw their support. They are already facing a great deal of criticism. If the government does not listen to them, it will contribute to the rise of a new generation of Kanak politicians who will be less conciliatory than those they are discussing with today. This may take time, but it is inevitable. Kanak demands are too far advanced for the movement to die out."

In Koné, the centre of the northern region, I met Patricia Goa, a member of its assembly, who spoke of the anomie, particularly among the men who used to be the providers and protectors of their *tribus* and families. Changes, including to gender roles, had left them adrift. Figures like herself, benefiting from the 50 per cent female representation set in the accords, reinforced this feeling. "Now I am seeing that sometimes for a man in front of me, I am a threat," she said. Another sign of a people adrift was the proliferation of new religions, evangelistic and Pentecostal churches founded by pastors from Australia, New Zealand and Vanuatu.

Yes, Godin said, the thirty-five years since the Matignon Accord had changed the Kanak people and their way of life, producing more graduates, managers, intellectuals. "But this evolution has in no way altered the Kanak desire for decolonisation," he said. "Quite the contrary, as shown by the results of the three referendums ... We might even say that this desire is more considered, and it is a result of the changes that have taken place."

Developments under the accords had deepened the nationalist idea among young and old Kanaks alike. "This is why the Kanak people are now capable of imagining new forms of independence, inspired by those implemented in Oceania," Godin said, referring to models of "independence in association" like the relationship between the Cook Islands and New Zealand, or the Marianas and the United States. "But unfortunately we do not get the impression that the French government has made much progress on this subject. The document on '*le oui et le non*', drawn up by the French government to inform the vote in the third referendum, was revealing from this point of view. It borders on caricature. To read it, New Caledonians had nothing to gain from independence, whatever the terms."

At Koné, I sat down to a lunch of tuna tartare and white wine in a smart café with Magalie Tingal-Lémé, who was about to head off to the UN General Assembly's opening session as an FLNKS representative, working from a Melanesian Spearhead Group office housed in its member states' missions. She expressed disappointment with Macron, who had seemed at first to bring a new kind of thinking to Paris. Yes, the Kanak parties were willing to discuss a form of association with France, which they called "interdependence", but only after independence and transfer of sovereignty was conceded, Tingal Lémé said. And it could not be exclusive. "We don't need France to protect us, because we are not in a war," she said.

So far, the French government has refused to pick up overtures offering this pathway from figures such as Daniel Goa, the leader of the UC. Chauchat, the constitutional law professor, and Godin, the social anthropologist who has studied the Kanaks for decades, are baffled. "There is no other solution, and definitely no solution in France," Chauchat said, adding that full independence was "fool's gold". The best immediate solution for the Kanaks would be for nothing to happen, to keep the dream of independence alive and prevent the opening of the electoral roll, he said. "We have to wait."

And so the dire predictions came to pass. In May 2024, Macron pressed on, putting forward legislation to widen the local franchise to anyone resident in the territory for ten years or more. When it was approved in Paris by both the National Assembly and the Senate – preparatory to a joint sitting to give it constitutional force – New Caledonia erupted into a new civil war. Mass protests called by Kanak parties turned into burning and looting of French-run businesses around Nouméa, and road blocks. Settler neighbourhoods barricaded themselves in, protected by vigilantes. With an estimated 100,000 firearms in private hands, the potential for armed conflict was, and remains, high. Macron flew in thousands of soldiers and police, who restored a precarious calm, interrupted by sporadic arson attacks and blockades. Thirteen people were shot: two gendarmes, the rest Kanaks. Within weeks, police arrested 2343 people, nearly all Kanaks. About 700 businesses were destroyed by arson and looting, according to the Industries Federation of New Caledonia, with total damage estimated at €2.2 billion (A$3.55 billion). Although Macron's ministers called for calm and dialogue, their actions further inflamed Kanak anger. Police arrested five young members of a committee that had organised the initial protests against the voting changes. They were charged with criminal incitement and flown to France the same day, where they were locked up in widely dispersed jails. The echoes of the nineteenth-century colonial practice of political exile were noted.

A possible way out of the deadlock emerged soon afterwards, when snap National Assembly elections in France called by Macron resulted in a split parliament, with the leftish New Popular Front emerging as the largest bloc, ahead of Macron's centrist-right Ensemble and the far-right National Rally of Marine le Pen (Jean-Marie's daughter), but still short of a majority. Many members of the New Popular Front had voted against Macron's electoral changes for New Caledonia. The leader of its largest Socialist component, Jean-Luc Mélenchon, had been scathing about the violent outcome. "One hundred and seventy years of relentlessness were not enough to defeat the Kanak will to once again become sovereign over their destiny, and no one will ever succeed," he said. "There is no way out of a colonial situation other than decolonisation, and everything else is a waste of time." But Macron was intent on shutting such voices out of government. He appointed Michel Barnier, a veteran politician from the conservative Republicans and a former foreign minister under Chirac, as prime minister, with a nod from Le Pen that her National Rally could work with him. That lasted only three months:

her party voted with the left to bring Barnier down. Macron tried again with a more centrist veteran, François Bayrou.

For their part, the die-hard loyalists in Nouméa were having none of the message about decolonisation. Sonia Backès called for the territory to be partitioned between the affluent, white-dominated region around Nouméa and the Kanak-populated north of the Grande Terre and Loyalty Islands. "Oil and water don't mix," she said on Bastille Day. "The Nouméa Accord [of 1998] wanted to impose a fusion or an assimilation. It has only generated an implosion. This common destiny has failed ... [and] the project of an institutionally united New Caledonia, based on a living together, one with the other, is over and done with."

Partition is not without precedent in the French realm. In the 1970s, the loyalist island of Mayotte was excluded from the newly independent Comoro Islands in the Indian Ocean. In the same era, as we've seen, French agencies supported nativist movements on the islands of Espíritu Santo and Tanna in their attempts to secede from the emerging state of Vanuatu.

But in New Caledonia it was not entirely a picture of separation. In the hinterlands outside Nouméa, during May 2024, Kanak, Caldoche and Islander leaders organised night patrols to keep the towns secure.[5]

Contained within the National Assembly election was another sign of possible convergence. One of the two seats for New Caledonia, covering the rural areas of the Grande Terre, was won by Emmanuel Tjibaou, a son of the assassinated Jean-Marie Tjibaou and in France a recognised expert on Oceanic cultures. He became the Assembly's first pro-independence member for thirty-eight years, overcoming a 1988 gerrymander intended to keep Kanaks out of parliament by adding settler-majority suburbs of Nouméa to the mainly rural island. In November 2024, Tjibaou was elected head of the largest pro-independence party, the Union Calédonienne, and announced the goal of reaching a "Kanaky Agreement" by 24 September 2025, the anniversary of New Caledonia's annexation in 1853. This would begin a five-year "transition period" concluded by New Caledonia's accession to full sovereignty, under a status yet to be defined. The other seat, covering urban Nouméa and the outlying Loyalty Islands, predictably went to a loyalist,

Nicolas Metzdorf. But this electorate produced its own surprise. The losing candidate, Omayra Naisseline, the pro-independence daughter-in-law of the *foulard rouge* leader of the early independence fight, won a sizable 48 per cent of the vote. Combined, Tjibaou and Naisseline won 53 per cent of the 156,000 valid votes cast across New Caledonia. The electoral rolls had been open to all French citizens, including the short-term *métros*, unlike the local assembly and referendum rolls, which were restricted to long-term residents under the 1998 agreement. And the question of New Caledonia's future was not posed directly on the ballot papers. But they were still "sobering results" for loyalists.[6] The result could indicate a widening acceptance of independence, or at least of its inevitability in some form. A growing number of the Polynesians from the French-held islands scattered to the east, about 10 per cent of the population, are drawn to a movement called L'Éveil Océanien (The Oceanic Awakening) and seem to be wavering. Another 11.3 per cent say they belong to more than one ethnic group.

Then there is another 7.5 per cent, thought to mostly be whites, who simply call themselves "Caledonian". They probably include many Caldoches, who sometimes liken themselves to the Niaouli, a hardy form of eucalypt found across New Caledonia, and see themselves staying whatever happens. Like their counterparts in Australasia, they nurse their bush legend, even though fewer than a thousand *broussards* now live in rural areas. Nicolas Kurtovitch, a poet and writer descended from a prisoner deported over 150 years ago, has said he feels "Oceanian" by identity.[7] If forced out, most Caldoches would move to Australia or New Zealand if they could, predicted the anthropologist Paul de Deckker nearly thirty years ago. "A Caledonian of today is most certainly closer to an Australian by cultural reference or mental space than he is to a French metropolitan."[8] But it need not come to that.

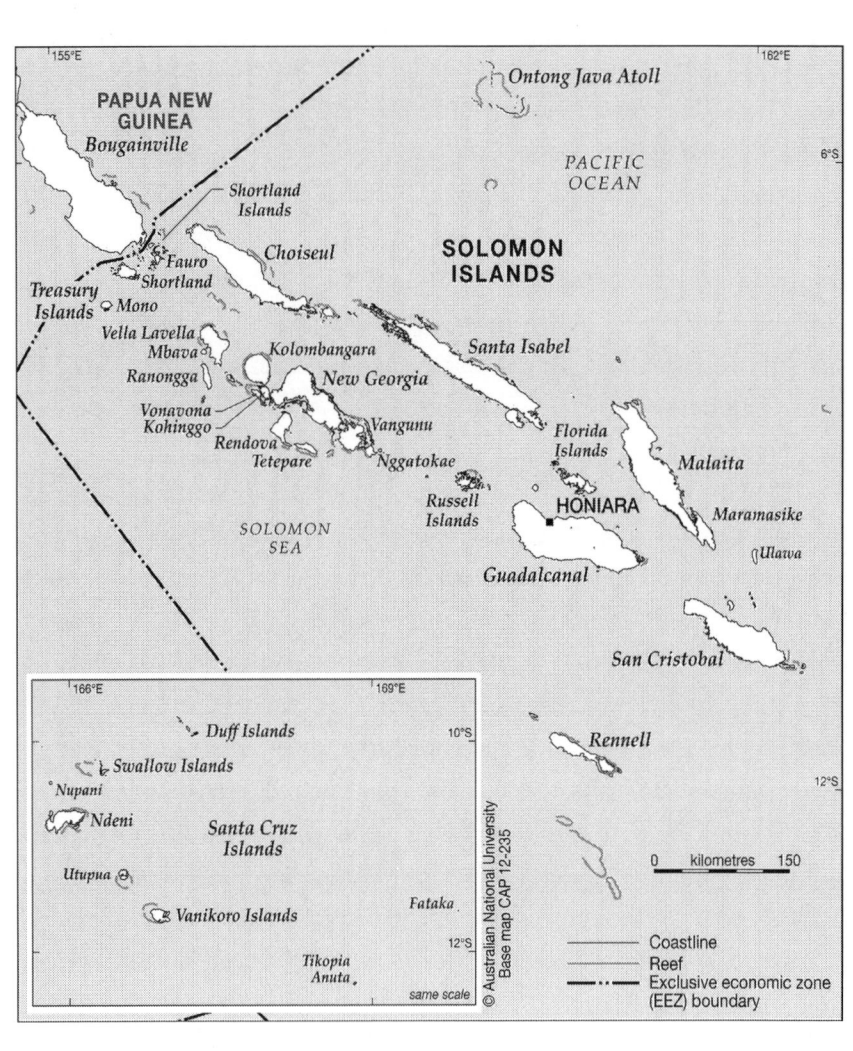

6

SOLOMON ISLANDS

Colonial Afterthought, Strategic Pivot

WIDE SEA GAPS SEPARATE Vanuatu and New Caledonia from their nearest Melanesian neighbour to the north, the Solomon Islands, and no ferries run. I saw the chance of a passage when the Anglican bishop James Tama told me in Luganville that he was expecting a visit by his prelate, who was based in the Solomon's capital, Honiara.

The Anglican archdiocese of Melanesia does not match the boundaries set by European empires. As well as the Solomon Islands, it encompasses the northern part of Vanuatu, which was the most French part of the former New Hebrides condominium, and the Loyalty Islands of New Caledonia. It is yet more testimony to the arbitrariness of the frontiers left by the European powers.

The archbishop ministers to his scattered flock from a small ship, the *Southern Cross*. This ship, the seventh of that name, would soon be coming to collect priests for a synod with the archbishop, before sailing back to Honiara, Tama told me. He seemed optimistic I could get a berth.

Then came the Covid pandemic, and the huge Cyclone Harold that devastated Vanuatu's northern islands. The archbishop's mission was called off, and the church took the opportunity of the two-year Covid disruption to retire the ageing *Southern Cross* and, with the help of Anglicans in New Zealand, order a new vessel from South Korea, bigger and sturdier to handle the wilder weather expected with climate change.

It was a while before I could get into the Solomons, and when I did it was, more prosaically, by plane from Brisbane. In the crowded centre of Honiara, there was a sense of hidden contest. The islanders bustled along, dressed in casual cast-offs from Australian charity bins or local floral prints, shod in rubber flip-flops, dodging rain puddles between Chinese general stores and the big vegetable and fish market. The scene was peaceful and unthreatening. Down one end of the single main street, however, were the outsized Chinese embassy and Australian high commission, with forbidding high-security frontages. Once again, this ramshackle collection of islands had become a pivot in strategic contest.

Named in 1568 by the Spanish explorer Álvaro de Mendaña y Neira for the purported source of King Solomon's gold, these islands initially had little to attract the Europeans. They were unhealthy places, rife with deadly malaria and skin infections. The islanders were fierce, head-hunters in some places, who killed some of the early missionaries. So the Solomons escaped the early race for colonial possessions.

But in 1886, Britain and Germany agreed to divide the Solomon Islands between them: Germany taking the islands of Buka, Bougainville, the Shortland Islands, Choiseul and Isabel – inhabited mostly by peoples of quite dark skin – and Britain exerting control over the island chain southwards, populated by lighter-skinned peoples. For both countries, it was more a case of keeping the other power out than of actually wanting the Solomons. When London declared the British Protectorate of the Solomon Islands in 1893, the title showed limited ambition to change anything. HMS *Curacoa*, the warship that had earlier shelled Port Resolution in Tanna, sailed around, notifying islanders of their new status. The governor of Fiji sent a resident commissioner in 1896, reporting back to Suva. He set up a base at Tulagi, on the central island of Nggela, an island that, being lightly populated and far from any dense hinterland, was easily defensible. In 1899, a further adjustment saw Germany cede the Shortlands, Choiseul and Isabel to Britain in return for Western Samoa and certain African territories. The islanders concerned were probably unaware of the notional switch from Iron Cross to Union Jack.

Life continued to be brutal, on both sides of the encounter. The islanders pursued their feuds and raids. Even after the abolition of "blackbirding" to Australia, labour recruiting for other places, including a string of new coconut plantations in Guadalcanal and Isabel, was risky and violent. When there was serious trouble, the usual British response was a naval bombardment.

The American author Jack London gives a vivid glimpse into this period. In 1907 he built a ketch in San Francisco, named the *Snark* after Lewis Carroll's fictional elusive animal, and sailed westwards, eventually reaching the Solomons. On the coast of Guadalcanal, London and his wife, Charmian, stayed at the Pendyffryn plantation, enjoying days filled with games, music and horseback rides, evenings of poker and billiards, and nights with a loaded rifle in every bedroom. They carried pistols at all times. It provided the locale for London's novel *Adventure*, rated by many as his least impressive book.

London was invited to travel aboard a recruiting boat to Malaita, a more heavily populated but untamed island and the plantations' main source of labour. The journey promised excitement and danger. His Japanese crewman reminded London that the *Minota* "had been captured six months before on the Malaita coast, that her captain had been chopped to pieces with tomahawks, and that, according to the barbarian sense of equity on that sweet isle, she owed two more heads."[1] An elegant ketch that had once cruised Sydney Harbour, the *Minota* was now prepared for action. Around its sides, its crew strung lines of barbed wire to protect against boarders. Pistols and rifles were kept ready and the crew practised shooting, partly to intimidate the score of "return boys" they were taking back to Malaita from Guadalcanal plantations.

They put into Su'u, a bay midway along Malaita's west coast, but no recruits appeared to sign up for three years' work at £6 a year. They ran up the coast to the Langa Langa Lagoon, passing Binu, where the *Minota* had been ransacked and its captain killed six months earlier. A missionary informed them that a British warship sent from Fiji had just left after a belated punitive expedition; its landing party had burnt three villages and killed thirty pigs as punishment. All the islanders had fled into the bush, save for a baby dropped into the sea in the rush and drowned. At Malu'u, in Malaita's north, the *Minota* ran aground on a reef. A strenuous salvage effort got it off, while another missionary persuaded local islanders not to plunder it.

London's health eventually collapsed from tropical ulcers and a mysterious syndrome later thought to come from excessive ultraviolet exposure. The couple took a steamer to Sydney, where he recuperated in hospital before returning to San Francisco. The *Snark* was brought to Australia and sold to an English syndicate for recruiting and trading around the New Hebrides.

Twenty years later, in 1927, British control was still tenuous. There were only about forty government officials among the 650 whites and Asians in the Solomons. The rest were missionaries, traders and planters. "It was a Gilbert and Sullivan world in miniature, a world of caricature colonialists, of whisky, quinine and coconuts," wrote Roger Keesing and Peter Corris.[2] Caroline Mytinger, a glamourous American artist who came up to the Solomons on the Burns Philp steamer *Mataram* in 1927, later wrote of a visit to the plantation Jack London had visited, by then renamed Berande and taken over by a big copra processing company. It was still a Maughamesque world. A planter whom London had met was said to have shot himself after his wife, a Spanish "countess", had run off with a recruiter. French missionaries had opened a school for girls. A mission schooner, the *Ark of God*, had brought measles with it, reducing the population to eighty in Ruavatu, down from 115. Before the 1919 flu pandemic, it had been 300.

At the western end of Guadalcanal, Mytinger stayed on Tanakombo plantation, which a widow with three children struggled to keep running after the death of her husband from "blackwater fever" (a severe form of malaria) three years earlier. The estate was mortgaged to the "Octopus of the Pacific" – presumably one of the Australian trading firms Burns Philp and W.R. Carpenter. Death came quickly and easily in the islands. Vivian Nankervis, a young cadet planter who'd come up from Sydney with Mytinger and her companion Margaret Warner, died one month after landing, from dysentery and malaria and "attack by boys". Other fellow passengers included two planters' wives, one recovered from blackwater fever who "looked more like a medical school cadaver".[3]

Malaita remained resistant, especially the large group of bush people across a central belt of the island called the Kwaio. The evangelist Florence Young had established the Queensland Kanaka Mission in 1886 on her brother's plantation near Bundaberg and converted about 2500 islanders there. Seeing the imminent deportation of the islanders under the White Australia policy, including about 3000 Malaitans, she decided to move with them. In 1906, she came to a small built-up island off Malaita's east coast, Ngongosila, and established the South Seas Evangelical Church. It was a perilous undertaking. Further round the coast, a missionary was killed in 1911, prompting another punitive raid from Fiji that saw villages burnt and five Kwaio killed.

The Kwaio had also lost young men to the blackbirding trade. One in four did not return, and in local minds this put a blood bounty on any white man who turned up. Those young Kwaio men who did come back brought with them flintlock rifles and steel tools, giving them power and prestige that upset the traditional order. A cult of warriors known as *ramo* emerged.

The British administration set up a district office for Malaita in 1909 and in 1915 an Australian named William Bell became the district officer. From a settler family in East Gippsland, he had gone off to the Boer War and then to the Solomons as a recruiter before joining the administration. A bachelor and non-drinker who liked music and Shakespeare, he stayed aloof from the hard-drinking planters and traders. Although he was sceptical of some of the missionaries for destroying local culture, he was a stern enforcer of British law. He intervened in the blood feuds that kept Malaita in a cycle of violence, but he took a nuanced approach: killing a person who had killed your relative was more excusable than killing the killer's relatives and was punished comparatively lightly, with a bond. Nonetheless, Bell built up a stock of bounties on his head by sending some assassins off for judgement in Tulagi followed by hanging in Fiji. For protection, he was surrounded by a squad of armed native police.

In 1920, the administration applied a 5-shilling-a-year tax on all adult islanders, a standard measure around the empire designed to increase the supply of labour by forcing people into paid work. Most of the Malaitans who complied found the money by indenturing young men and collecting "beach payments" from recruiters. "The recruiting ships followed the tax-collecting party like vultures," explain Keesing and Corris. "The head tax, forcing Malaitans into a cash economy, forcing them to export the muscle-power of their young men for low wages, had come to stay."[4] Alternatively, they could sell their traditional shell money to the native constables guarding the tax collector, who could sell it at a profit elsewhere.

The tax built up huge resentment among a people who saw little return from the government, especially after beach payments were officially banned, forcing families to sell more of their shell money and pigs. It was effectively a tax used to deprive people of liberties, Mytinger wrote, thinking of the customary practices the administration declared illegal. "The villagers do not know what the government is going to disapprove of and punish next. It is better to tell nothing to the white men, explain nothing, and offer nothing; just say 'yes' to every question – that, at least, will keep the men in good humour."[5]

As he aged, Bell became less tolerant. He swore and lashed out. His nickname was "Koburu", meaning a strong west wind or cyclone. In 1926 he led a raid inland from Gwee'abe to arrest twelve tax defaulters. There were clashes, and Bell's police guard carried off pigs. A powerful *ramo* named Basiana, then aged about forty-five, ground down an ancestral shell pendant to make his fifth "shilling". Bell accepted it, called him a "bastard" and warned he would not accept such a substitute again.

The next year, with another round of tax collection imminent, the seething Basiana began planning an attack on Bell, dismissing those who warned about the likely retribution. The plotters sacrificed pigs at traditional stone altars. Word spread, even reaching Bell as his launch, *Auki*, approached. On 2 October 1927, *Auki* entered Sinalagu Bay. A shelter for tax collection was built on a clearing atop the little promontory at Gwee'abe. Rumours spread, erroneously, that as well as the head tax, Bell would be confiscating firearms.

Everyone sensed trouble. A recruiting ship, the *Wheatsheaf*, was anchored for business in the bay. A launch run by the Seventh-day Adventists was also there. Their crews retreated to their vessels. The Adventist pastor,

John Anderson, later wrote that local headmen were urging Bell to go back to the *Auki* and receive taxpayers two by two in a dinghy. Bell refused, saying he could bluff any objectors.

At dawn on 4 October, Basiana and his followers came down. Basiana approached Bell, grabbed a rifle and clubbed Bell over the head. Another man brained Bell's cadet, Kenneth Lillies. The police guard fought back, killing several of the attackers, but thirteen police were killed before the rest fled to the beach and made it back to the launch. The Adventists patched up the wounded. The *Auki*'s bosun, with the help of local Christian converts, went ashore and recovered the bodies of Bell and Lillies. The launch set off north to Ngongosila, where the two dead officials were buried on the shore near Florence Young's mission.

The next day, the *Auki* and the *Wheatsheaf* reached Tulagi. Morse code signals flashed the news to Fiji: Malaita was in revolt. The British governor called for help from the Admiralty; it passed the request to the Royal Australian Navy. The cruiser HMAS *Adelaide* set sail on 10 October, trailed by its collier. The Australian prime minister, Stanley Bruce, rejected backbench suggestions that this was colonial toadying: Bell's brother George (later Sir George and speaker of the House of Representatives) was a member of the Australian parliament. The press said the *Adelaide*'s captain, G.C. Harrison, was "the right man to put Fuzzy Wuzzy in his place".

At Tulagi, planters and missionaries streamed in from their outposts. White residents volunteered to join the retribution. Mytinger records that when the *Mataram* pulled in, planters swarmed on board to hit the ship's bar. They had been drilling in the sun and had a thirst, despite their rations already including a quart of whisky per week "to fight malaria". She met two women who had been "run off" Malaita, one the wife of a missionary who had been at Su'u for fifteen years who complained the Malaitans were "insolent, untrustworthy, filthy, stupid, lazy, cunning, ungrateful".

The *Adelaide* arrived at Sinalagu on 16 October, twelve days after the massacre. Government launches brought around twenty-four civilian volunteers and some forty native police. Expatriates were living on their boats. Work had stopped in the plantations. Lines of volunteers, police and navy bluejackets climbed paths into the mountains, carrying rifles and three Lewis machine guns. Many of the white men collapsed and had to be carried back to the *Adelaide* by stretcher. Others were portered up the hills. The volunteers, who came to be known as the "whisky army" or the "breathless army", were especially useless; each needed two bearers to carry their kit. They acted as though they had been given open slather to shoot any Kwaio on sight. By mid-November, all the volunteers had been pulled out. The *Adelaide*'s Captain Harrison said they were a "useless and undisciplined crowd who ought never to have been sent on the Expedition at all".[6]

The cruiser returned to Sydney on 18 November, neither it nor its sailors having fired a shot. A fifth of its crew were hospitalised with malaria, dysentery and tropical sores. By then it was clear that Malaita was not in a state of rebellion. In Auki, some 480 non-Kwaio had actually volunteered to help hunt down Basiana. Nearly all were turned away to avoid it turning into tribal war.

The civilian and police action was less commendable. While the white civilians were no threat to Basiana or other Kwaio warriors, the native police set up camp in his village, taking actions calculated to insult and hurt. They smashed ancestral skulls and scattered the fragments inside the hut where women confined themselves during menstruation. They burnt drums and carvings, shot pigs and sprayed taro gardens with weedkiller. They gang-raped female relatives of the rebels. Some thirteen women and girls were shot, and male prisoners were executed before they could be taken to a stockade put up at Gwee'abe. Keesing and Corris write that at least fifty-five Kwaio died in total, their deaths blamed on self-defence, resisting arrest or the "innate savagery" of native police avenging colleagues killed at Gwee'abe.

Eventually, Basiana gave himself up to avoid further retribution, having seen his wife and children safe and made sacrifices to his ancestors. He and some 200 others were taken to Tulagi. He was among eleven charged with murder. He and five others were given the death sentence.

On 29 June 1928, Basiana was hanged. His sons Anifelo, fourteen, and Laefi, seven, had been brought to Tulagi and were made to watch – sixty years after the last public execution in Britain. Before he mounted the scaffold, Basiana uttered a curse on Tulagi.

He and his comrades had taken "a final and desperate stand against the subjugation of their way of life by an alien power", write Keesing and Corris. "For the colonialists to have recognised that their adversaries were struggling to preserve their sovereignty ... [they] would have had to attribute to them a humanity, a cultural heritage, a political legitimacy that was in those days unimaginable for black savages and lowly natives."[7]

But it was unwise to take "too romantic a view of the past", the authors note. "The Kwaio were not noble savages. Their social system was flawed by endemic blood feuding; and those who resisted colonial hegemony were those who had most to gain by preserving the old ways." Kwaio society had two strands – men of war and men of peace. "The reckless men of violence left the men of peace to rebuild the shattered homeland. But while fighting rear-guard for old ways, they were also forerunners in a struggle to achieve humanity and dignity as equals in the community of nations."

The 1930s saw the British Solomons continue as a picture of neglect. Government-appointed headmen were often venal and mostly disrespected. The price of copra collapsed in the Great Depression. The plantations laid off workers. With little cash in the villages, Australian and Chinese trading boats stopped travelling around to sell manufactured goods. There was a widely held view that the Solomon Islanders were dying out. The eminent Queensland doctor Raphael Cilento voiced a theory that melancholia was "diminishing the activity of the seminal glands" in the islanders. The medical campaigns that did happen, against yaws and hookworm, were funded by the Lever Brothers plantations and the Rockefeller Foundation.

From their experiences on the plantations in Queensland and Fiji, the islanders drew their own conclusions. They saw indigenous populations pushed aside if the colonists saw any value in their lands. The administrators were there to keep them down. White men got off lightly for crimes against natives. While abroad the islanders put aside some traditional *tabu* and formed friendships outside their own groups, leading to a new sense of shared identity. "What is certain is that in both Queensland and Fiji, Islanders forged new, broader ethnic identities as Malaitans, Solomon Islanders, and Melanesians," writes historian David Akin.[8]

Some realised they would have to work together back home to protect and empower themselves. On Isabel, Anglican priest Richard Fallowes set up a kind of civil administration, with headmen having the power to impose small punishments. Fallowes came back as a layman in 1938 and organised assemblies of headmen from the islands of Isabel, Savo and Nggela. They asked what they were getting in the way of medical services, technical education and higher pay from the government after eighteen years of the head tax and seventy-eight years of church collections. The alarmed resident commissioner and Anglican bishops combined to get Fallowes deported in 1939, painting his movement as a cult – the standard way of disparaging indigenous initiatives.

As had happened in Tanna with John Frum, word spread that Americans were different from the stand-offish British. In central Malaita in 1939, a traditional priest named Noto'l predicted a US invasion would kill all government officials and bring money and goods. He had stockades built, pigs dedicated and calico flags hung on the long houses where adult men gathered. The idea seems to have sprung from a six-week visit to the Kwaio several years earlier by ornithologists Walter Eyerdam and William Coultas from New York's American Museum of Natural History. They had shared food and blankets with their local helpers. "Without realizing it, Eyerdam and Coultas managed to lay waste to some of the basic rules of colonial white-black relations," writes Akin.[9] But the Americans did not immediately come, Noto'l got arrested, and his movement dissipated.

Then, Basiana's curse came true.

After taking Rabaul and Bougainville, Japanese imperial forces pushed south into the Solomons in May and June 1942, driving the British from Tulagi and grabbing a stretch of Guadalcanal where they began work on a strategic air base.

The United States readied to meet them. US marines moved up through New Zealand and the New Hebrides to land on Guadalcanal in August. There began the much-storied battle to push the Japanese off the airfield and hold them back while it was completed for Americans to use. Between the islands, naval and air battles raged for months.

Although the British "protectorate" had completely failed, some white men took to the jungles to run the coast-watching network, reporting Japanese air and ship movements. This won local assistance and regained some British prestige. The Anglican archbishop, Walter Baddeley, also stayed on, hiding out in Malaita and Nggela. He would later re-emerge and attach himself as chaplain to the Fijian battalion when it landed on Guadalcanal.

The Americans sent a ship over to Malaita, which had been left alone by the Japanese, to engage labour for the airfield and other works on Guadalcanal. About 2700 islanders signed up. As Akin observes, nothing could have prepared Malaitans for the high-intensity modern warfare on Guadalcanal. They were put to work building camps, roads and the airfield, and planting gardens, burying the dead, and loading and unloading cargo. They were bombed and shelled by the Japanese, with eleven men killed in one attack in January 1943.

The scale of the US forces and their abundant supplies were astonishing. The American soldiers casually gave them clothing, tools, food, stretcher beds, mosquito nets and even weapons. The skills and literacy of African American soldiers particularly impressed the islanders. Some Americans asked them why they were not rising up for independence. British officials running the Solomon Islands Labour Corps tried to counteract this influence, by restricting pay to £1 a month, banning trousers and shirts (instead of shorts and bare chests), and seizing the American gifts as "loot". But the islanders could earn £15 a month doing cooking, laundry and other chores for the Americans, or by selling curios. When unrest developed in response to the British approach, the US command assigned its own officers to the labour force.

As the fighting moved away to the north, ferment grew within the labour corps. In 1944, the idea of Maasina Ruru, a "Law of Brotherhood", gained many followers. When the war ended in 1945, many workers returned to their villages and spread the notion. A man from Are'are in Malaita's south, Nori, emerged as its main apostle. He was an orator who, as one official noted, "could charm the birds out of the trees for a Melanesian audience".

Travelling around by canoe, he told large crowds that they had been let down by the government and must take their future into their own hands. Drawing partly on the thwarted efforts of Fallowes, he urged cooperative development through bigger villages and gardens, the reform of customs, and population growth. Maasina Ruru also had other, more educated and worldly leaders who had been to Australia and New Zealand and seen their labour movements. Another leader was Anifelo, son of Basiana, who as a fourteen-year-old had watched his father being hanged at Tulagi. He had been a police drummer, then an evangelist and lastly an anti-colonial leader who helped bring many other Kwaio into Maasina Ruru.

By 1946, the movement divided Malaita into nine districts, mainly along language lines, and had created a shadow administration with its own police force and courts, which imposed fines or community labour. By early 1947, new towns established by the movement circled Malaita's coast, with several thousand people living in them. Some were highly regulated, with bells announcing times for work, lights out and sleep, and passes required for movement in and out. The leaders drafted codes of customary law, worked out ways to ease tabus and compiled genealogies to help settle landownership disputes. Most South Seas Evangelicals joined the movement, along with most lay Anglicans and a few indigenous priests. The Catholics were sympathetic. By 1947 it was an organised and powerful force across Malaita, Nggela, parts of Isabel and the island of Makira to the south.

The district officer based in Auki, Eustace Sandars, had been in Malaita for twenty years and was sympathetic to the movement. He spoke on platforms alongside Nori. But in July 1947 he was replaced by a new district officer, Roy Davies, who was keen to restore government authority. Heated radio signals from Auki to Tulagi, Tulagi to Suva, suggested Malaita was once against on the brink of revolt.

Expat circles distorted the name of the movement to "Marching Rule" to suggest it was a paramilitary organisation, drilling its followers to prepare for violent overthrow of British rule. There had been some drills, with white uniforms and fake wooden weapons. But as Akin notes, military-style drills were common on plantations and mission schools around the Pacific, used as a way to manage workers.

In 1947 the British launched "Operation Delouse" against the leaders of the movement. A legal officer drew up a public order regulation, authorising preventive action. In a radio broadcast, the resident commissioner accused the Maasina Ruru leaders of engineering terrorism and robbery, running a network of illegal spies and courts, and threatening death to those who resisted. The liberty of the native peoples was being endangered by a "military despotism" comparable to that of Nazi Germany and Japan. People should not listen to rumours, but should consult their local district officer, missionary or plantation owner. "Your welfare and their welfare are one." All three pillars of authority – the colonial government, the church and the planters – opposed Maasina Ruru for self-interested reasons. Government officials wanted to be in charge again. Planters wanted the old indentured labour system restored. Churches wanted their congregations back.

At the end of August 1947, three police raiding parties landed at northern Malaita. They arrested movement leaders, then moved to Auki and further south, while other raids arrested movement members on the other islands. No shots were fired, and the movement leaders surrendered peacefully. They urged their followers to remain calm. Many movement members turned up at police compounds to ask if they could be arrested too. In the background, the empire exercised its naval might. The Australian warships *Warramunga*, *Contest* and *Shoalhaven* hovered off Malaita in September. The British aircraft carrier *Theseus*, escorted by destroyers *Cockade* and *Aeneas*, flew a formation of fighters over the island.

The administration congratulated itself on a great success. Maasina Ruru had been a cult, a mass delusion of the native mind, went the official line. But then the legal tangles intensified. Where were the islanders to testify that they had been oppressed into joining and obeying the movement? There were none, and so the charges had to be changed to conspiracy to set up illegal courts, although there was also a shortage of evidence for this in most cases. The terms of conspiracy were so vague, any Malaitan could have been convicted.

The district officer, Roy Davies, doubled as magistrate, passing judgement on the people he had rounded up. Requests for defence lawyers were refused on the grounds the accused would not be facing a legally qualified prosecutor! Akin documents that the thirty-three accused chiefs had little chance of acquittal in the trials that took place between November 1947 and February 1948. Nori and some other leaders got six years' jail. Most of the 3000 other arrestees spent a year or two working on roads. In 1950, all were released.

Quietly, the administration moved to address the issues raised by the movement. In 1947, it appointed the first director of education. In late 1952, it set up a Malaita Council as the first stage of self-government, which turned out to be Maasina Ruru in disguise: its first president and many of its members had been leading figures in the movement. By the end of 1953, tranquillity was restored on Malaita.

Nearly all of Maasina Ruru's aims had been met, aside from independence and a lift in the basic wage, writes Akin. Government officials had tried to portray the movement as a retreat to "old" custom, a reaction against the modern world, rather than a pathway to it. On Malaita, it had forced a change in the government's approach, replacing force with persuasion. "Maasina Ruru did not win Malaitans control over the government, but it did cast off a good measure of the government's control over Malaitans."[10]

Soon the "winds of change", as British prime minister Harold Macmillan called the decolonisation of India, Africa and Malaya, were wafting into the Pacific. The Solomon Islanders did not press for the independence that came in 1978, after a hurried quarter century of development. Instead, the pressure came from London, where the UK government was anxious to offload colonial responsibilities, especially those east of the Suez Canal. As historian Michael Wesley has written, "no-one questioned that a Westminster-style sovereign state, complete with Constitution, capital city and national borders, would replace the British Protectorate."[11]

Perhaps it might have been better if political systems had been allowed to grow organically from indigenous initiatives such as Maasina Ruru. The result might have been messier – a federation, a confederation or a constellation of small states – but it might also have entailed a happier synthesis of custom and modernity. Perhaps it might have avoided the inherent conflict that Gregoire Nimbtik, over in Vanuatu, identified between the Westminster system and *kastom*.

After 1978, Solomons politics involved a sweeping turnover of members of parliament every election, giving MPs an incentive to make the most of the term they had. Governments formed and fell as MPs shifted their support in return for payments or promises of ministerial posts. As in the other Melanesian states, a growing proportion of government expenditure passed through electorate "development funds" dispensed by MPs, often to local interests in exchange for a promise of blocks of votes at the next election.

To feed this appetite for government revenue and to get the foreign exchange for imports, a prime minister in the early 1990s removed restrictions on the logging of fine hardwood. Timber companies, many from Malaysia, were soon harvesting at an unsustainable rate. Government revenues surged, but little of this money found its way beyond Honiara. The budget deficit and public debt still grew, and medical services, schools and policing still lacked funds. Rivers of cash flowed to politicians who approved logging concessions and export clearances.

As the money flowed in Honiara, the city drew more migrants, particularly from Malaita. Malaitans soon formed half the capital's residents, spilling out to the city fringes and building settlements on the lands of the island's indigenous Guale people. The Guale had already seen much of their land alienated under British rule for coconut, cocoa and palm-oil plantations. Loggers were operating in their remote forests. A big goldmine had opened in the centre of the island.

The Guale had a similar movement to Maasina Ruru, distantly influenced by it and flourishing a few years later. More deeply mystical than Maasina Ruru, it began in about 1956 when Pelise Moro, a young man from the Weather Coast (as the southwest-facing side of Guadalcanal is called), fell ill and had visions. He wrote his version of the origins of the island, using its pre-Spanish name of Isatabu, and preached a message of self-help through a structure of district leaders, population registries and tax collection. As Moro aged (he died in 2006), the movement faded. But some of its ideas fomented among younger people on the Weather Coast in the 1990s. In 1998, the provincial premier of Guadalcanal, Ezekiel Alebua, demanded huge state compensation for lands taken for the national capital, Honiara.

Young Guale hotheads, led by Harold Keke, formed fighting groups and armed themselves with weapons seized from police stations. From the Weather Coast they waged attacks on Malaitan settlers.

In response, Andrew Nori, a son of the Maasina Ruru founder, encouraged a new "Malaita Eagle Force". In June 2000, helped by the many Malaitans in the Royal Solomon Islands Police, the Eagle Force took over the main police armoury in Honiara, seized police patrol boats and blocked roads in and out of the capital. Fighting and assassinations raged across Guadalcanal. Tens of thousands of residents fled to safe areas or to other islands. Honiara's airport closed. Fuel and other supplies dried up.

It was a war of guns and customary beliefs. Australian photojournalist Ben Bohane captured the fighting spirit of the young Isatabu warriors on the Weather Coast and in the central mountains. The Malaitan Eagle Force, meanwhile, drew on workers in the modern economy. One afternoon, correspondent Craig Skehan rang *The Sydney Morning Herald*'s foreign desk to tell me of a slaughter he had just witnessed near Honiara. Near-naked Isatabu warriors, believing they had been conferred invulnerability by spells, had tried to attack Malaitans firing automatic weapons from a bulldozer armoured with steel plate.

Bizarrely, the parliament and government continued to operate through all this mayhem. The treasury continued to issue cheques, some for hazy compensation claims, including a very large one for police who asked the finance minister at gunpoint for "unpaid salaries". The government ran out of money and had its electricity cut off. But it was still, theoretically at least, wielding sovereign power. In April 2003, Prime Minister Allan Kemakeza asked the Australian prime minister, John Howard, for help in preventing Solomon Islands from sliding into "anarchy".

At the end of July 2003, a force of nearly 2000 soldiers and 253 police arrived, including personnel from Papua New Guinea, Fiji and several other Pacific states alongside its Australian and New Zealand core. This force, the Regional Assistance Mission to the Solomon Islands (RAMSI), worked, sometimes uneasily, alongside the elected national government and its changing prime ministers. Peace and disarmament soon followed, helped by Harold Keke's early surrender in August 2003, before the longer task of rebuilding governance, state finances and the police. The intervention didn't end until 2017, by which time nearly A$3 billion had been spent.[12]

It almost came unstuck in April 2006, after elections installed a new parliament but with many of its notorious characters returned and several reformers ousted. Its vote trading resulted in street protests marshalled by supporters of the loser, who accused the winner of having had backing from Chinese commercial interests. This developed into rioting focused on Honiara's Chinatown. Australian and other police and soldiers were again on the streets to restore order. A new prime minister, Manasseh Sogavare, emerged after switching sides.

Despite the shocks of 1998–2003, nothing much had changed in the mindset of elected members of parliament when I visited after these troubles settled down. People still regarded their local MP as a walking ATM, there to help in times of sickness or other need, said Sogavare's private secretary, retired priest John Roughan. Unsustainable logging was in full swing, long-resident economist Tony Hughes said, even around places like the Marovo Lagoon that should be kept pristine for tourism. At the central bank, its governor, Rick Houenipwela, pointed out that the population was meanwhile growing 3 per cent a year. "People call it a time bomb," he told me. "At the moment, the subsistence economy is postponing the explosion. But it's under a lot of stress. The village system can't sustain these population pressures." Sue Ingram, an anthropologist then directing the government reform arm of the regional mission, told me: "There is an utter disconnect between the village, which is the natural, organic institution of traditional society, and the nation-state, which stays in Honiara."

The RAMSI exercise turned out to be a bandaid rather than a cure for all these problems, which returned and worsened with the injection of a new destabilising ingredient, great power competition.

7

MALAITA

Sharks, Crocodiles and Other Ancestors

IT WAS DÉJÀ VU IN HONIARA seventeen years later. Manasseh Sogavare was back as prime minister, for the fourth time. The fundamental dilemmas of politics, constitutionality and economics were much the same. Timber was still being ripped out of islands like Choiseul, Sogavare's home, at double the sustainable rate. Honiara itself had recently been torn by rioting, the results visible in the charred ruins of the old Chinatown and some of the newer Chinese investments such as a hotel-casino.

Fingers were again pointed at the Malaitans as the main troublemakers. But there was ambivalence in the perception this time. The Western powers around the Pacific had cheered the Malaitans on for their opposition to Sogavare's closer links with China after he switched diplomatic recognition from Taipei to Beijing soon after regaining office in 2019. But at the same time, their violence required yet another military and police intervention from Australia, New Zealand, Fiji and Papua New Guinea to stop the destruction and shore up constitutional government, less than five years after the costly and prolonged RAMSI mission wound up. And while Sogavare was grateful to them for saving his government and perhaps his skin, he was inclined to salve his humiliation by seeking more security aid from China.

What was it about Malaita, this perennial source of resistance and human energy? Early in my visit, I was again at sea. A taxi took me down to the Point Cruz inter-island shipping jetties. The new fast ferry to Auki, the main town on Malaita, had just departed. That left the MV *Taimareho I*, a white-painted ship of about 500 tons. Built some decades earlier, it had served in South Korea before being sold to a church-run shipping line in the Solomons.

In April 2020, this ship had had a brush with Cyclone Harold before the eye of the storm moved south to devastate Vanuatu's north and lash Fiji. Laden with 738 people, many travelling to their home villages amid the new pandemic lockdowns, the *Taimareho* set out for Malaita despite cyclone warnings. Between Guadalcanal and Malaita, three massive waves battered the ship, washing twenty-seven passengers overboard to drown. The captain was prosecuted for manslaughter; when I visited, the case was still running.

Three and a half years after this disaster, ticketless passengers were trooping up the gangway and staking out seat and deck space. Boxes of cargo and heavier baggage were passed over the rails for crew to stow. With the cyclone in mind, I made my way to the upper deck, well above the waves. A Malaitan family made space for me on a seat. As night fell, the ship backed out from the wharf and headed east at a steady 12 knots. Crewmen came around to sell tickets and take down names, but by then of course it was too late to exercise any loading limits. The trip was a rollicking five hours, with sheets of spray and rain squalls sometimes hitting the canvas weather-shields even up on the top deck, making sleep near impossible. A betel-nut seller plied his wares. The family sitting in front shared some deep-fried taro and other snacks, most welcome since I'd had no food since the small airline meals served on the flights from Sydney to Brisbane, and then to Honiara, much earlier in the day.

Sometime towards midnight, the sea suddenly went calm: we were inside the wide Langa-Langa Lagoon around Auki. Red and green channel lights flashed in the darkness. The *Taimareho* edged alongside a floodlit jetty. Passengers swarmed ashore. Boxes of cargo, rolled up mats, eskies of produce piled up on the dock. The family who had shared their food went off to find a truck that would take them up a coastal road to their village, many more hours of arduous travel later.

Being the only white man on the ship, I was easy enough for my local guide, Silas Malai, to spot. We walked through the silent town of low buildings, navigating water-filled potholes, to the hotel he'd found for me.

At seven the next morning I walked out to the nearby covered market, which was already lively with women selling fruit, vegetables and fish. Out across the pale blue lagoon, houses crowded a small island with a seawall of coral rock. Silas and another man emerged, having just had a standing breakfast at a market stall. Both were dressed in shorts and rubber flip-flops. Silas had mentioned his companion as an important interlocutor for the place I wanted to visit on the eastern coast of Malaita. This was Ronnie Jethro Butala, the local member of the Malaita provincial assembly and the assembly's widely respected speaker.

We walked down to a Chinese-run store where four-wheel drive vehicles and trucks were pulled up. A heavy rainstorm swept in. The expanding puddle in the street had us edging into the store until the storm passed and the water receded. Ronnie took me up to the town's top hotel for an English-style breakfast of egg, bacon, sausage and toast. I queued at the Bank South Pacific to withdraw cash for what was going to be an expensive trip, off the grid.

Mid-morning, our driver, a young, bearded islander named Thomson, said his LandCruiser was ready to go. Silas, Ronnie's son, Junior, and I sat in the cabin, while other passengers crouched in the tray with a tarp for protection. The first two hours were easy enough, on a wide road of pressed gravel. Malaita is a long island of mountains that rise steeply from narrow coastal fringes. We were going across the range. About midway, we stopped at a strip of stalls made of timber and corrugated iron. I bought a fresh coconut and drank the milk from the rough hole dug by the vendor with his parang, some of it splashing down my chin.

This, it soon emerged, was as far as road improvement had got.

Mobile phone coverage faded as we reached the eastern descent, a series of bogs with deep wheel ruts. The LandCruiser lurched through them, wheels spinning, engine racing. On either side was a riot of jungle. A prolific bush – fellow passenger Francis Sia, a high school teacher, told me it was called the *falotha* – had long wide leaves like a banana and multi-petalled blooms of rich ivory the size of magnolias, ringed by smaller pink flowers. We came to a river ford. Thomson turned the vehicle around and backed across to avoid water getting into the air intake. The road ended at a causeway of coral rocks, pushing out from a gap in the mangroves into a wide lagoon.

In a timber shack, teenage boys played cards for small coins. A fibreglass dinghy with a powerful outboard motor waited. We passed over the jerry cans of fuel we'd brought from Auki to the dinghy's owner, along with a wad of dollars, then distributed ourselves to balance the boat. It headed out to the south, riding over and sometimes crashing down from the swells. We got soaked by rain showers, then dried out in the rush of speed. Moss-green hills rose steeply from the shore of low white limestone cliffs, glimpsed between the rise and fall of the waves. Behind the cliffs were dark mountains.

After an hour and a half, we rounded a jagged point and entered a wide inlet of deep, calm water. Once called Port Diamond, it was now known by its original name, Sinalagu. Our boat pulled into a small settlement called Takwasi, nestled among trees on a beach of coral pebbles and broken shell. We waded ashore, installing ourselves in a roughly built guesthouse of four rooms and a wide verandah. The dinghy went off with the other passenger from Auki, a young woman with sun-bleached hair named Cyreen who had introduced herself as the local nurse, taking supplies from Auki back to her clinic further around the bay.

Our small party sprawled around the verandah. Silas and I walked along the rocky shore to the next cluster of houses, which had a standpipe and shower plugged into the groundwater gushing out of the hillside behind. Stripped to our shorts, we had a public shower.

Back at the guesthouse, the village women had been busy in the cookhouse, which had an open fire and a sow and her piglets in a poke alongside. Older pigs and chickens foraged the beach. Dinner came: boiled rice with a mix of tinned tuna and instant noodles, and hot tea. A small solar panel provided a dim light and some power to recharge our phones – useful for taking pictures but nothing else. The mobile tower just up the coast was powered by a solar array that only worked in prolonged sunlight. It was now the rainy season.

In the morning, we secured two narrow dugout canoes and got ourselves paddled around the jade-green water of the bay. In the distance we could see other people out in similar canoes. Fish jumped nearby as we passed. We came to the place called Gwee'abe, a few simple houses by the side of a wooded promontory, with a steep mountain behind.

It was hard to believe that an incident here, just out of living memory, had caused a crisis of the British Empire. It was here that in 1927 an Australian cruiser, belching coal smoke from its four funnels and bristling with 6-inch guns, had anchored for a month, sending armed parties ashore to find, kill or capture district officer William Bell's attackers.

All this history and the subsequent rebellion were still alive to everyone around Sinalagu Bay, and wherever I stopped on Malaita.

Across from Gwee'abe was a blue-painted house that had been built by Jonathan Fifi'i, who had been in the wartime labour corps in Guadalcanal with Nori and talked to American soldiers. Aged about twenty-four, he returned in 1945 and with Nori held a meeting here to explain Maasina Ruru to people who came down from the bush. Fifi'i became the movement's chief for the Kwaio and was eventually imprisoned with Nori. On release, he was active in politics, in the new Malaita Council and then in the Solomon Islands Legislative Assembly at the time of independence.

At the guesthouse in Takwasi, we were joined by Ronnie Butala's cousin, Paul Ladoa, who was forty-five years of age. We sat around as Paul, Silas and Junior cut up strips of black tobacco and rolled them in pieces of notepaper to smoke. Paul's grand-uncle had been with Basiana in the attack on Bell and was hanged at Tulagi. Paul's grandfather had been wounded and also taken to Tulagi. "They thought he would die, so he was released," Paul said.

Paul's father had been a *fata'abe*, a priest of traditional spirit worship. Aged about ten, Paul had gone with his father to a stone altar where a pig was sacrificed to allay the spirits over a breach of tabu: a woman had urinated in the wrong place in a village. He recalls his father cutting up the pig, keeping the organs and head for himself, and saving the meat for the villagers. "He burned the pig's hair in a fire and talked to the ancestor's god: 'This is for you,'" Paul said. I asked the name of the god. "We can't utter the name of the god, just talk about him in another way. Only the priest can say. To know the name, you have to be a priest and use it the right way."

"There are *hiki*, a word you use to talk to the ancestors," Paul recalled. "When they say it, things happen." There were *hiki* for plants, for gardens, for fishing, for war." Silas added: "When I speak a *hiki*, I am no longer Silas, I am speaking directly to the ancestors."

But in his twenties, Paul had decided it was time to give up traditional law. It was so burdensome, always sacrificing pigs to apologise. People who stayed up in the bush to observe the old ways were getting no education or other help. You got more help if you converted to Christianity.

Up in the mountains of Malaita there were still communities following custom, reachable only by arduous bush trails, Paul said. Later I read accounts by scientists at the Australian Museum in Sydney of recent expeditions into this deep interior to meet these peoples. The interlopers were sometimes required to remove most of their clothes, out of tact.

But bush people were increasingly moving down to the coast, Paul said, and traditional practices were loosening in some ways. Before, a man had to show he could build a house, make things and earn money before he could marry. Now, courting started early. I mentioned seeing written in charcoal, in good English, on the side of a village house: "Your face is breaking my heart." There were wry smiles. It was evidence of the education being provided at the school around the bay, but also of how custom was fading even before it had been fully documented for future generations. "I am the last one to attend the sacrifice of the pigs," Paul said. "This may be the last ending of the customary life."

He mentioned that Roger Keesing, the American anthropologist who had spent decades among the Kwaio and co-written the definitive account of the "Malaita Incident" of 1927 (and had also helped Fifi'i write his autobiography), was buried in the hills above Sinalagu after his death in 1993. So too were Basiana and the others executed on Tulagi.

On the way back to the Auki Road landing, our dinghy was to call in at Ngongosila Island, where we saw the graves of William Bell and Kenneth Lillies, well looked after in a patch of ground near the South Seas Evangelical Church started by Florence Young. Talking to locals at Sinalagu, I got the feeling that Bell, for all his irascibility, was appreciated by Malaitans – even the Kwaio – as someone who had begun to understand them. There was sorrow for him too.

"There is still much to talk about, to write about the coming of Christianity to the Kwaio," Paul said. "We need a new anthropologist to come."

It was the same road, but worse going back to Auki. After the call at Ngongosila, we landed at the jetty in Atori. Thomson and his LandCruiser had already departed. But there was an Isuzu 3-tonne truck ready to go, and we joined its passengers. The haul up the eastern side of the ranges was a lot harder than when we had slid down it the other way. All on board frequently had to dismount and join a tug o' war line to help haul the truck through the bogs. The trip out had taken five hours; the return took ten.

In Auki, the history of the Kwaio resistance and Maasina Ruru was also alive. I met Samson and Rocky Gaa, whose father, Salathiel Salana Gaa, had been the son of a customary priest, picked out for education by a Catholic priest, and then worked for Bell's successor and the wartime coast-watchers, before becoming one of Maasina Ruru's founders. "They were asking for their own government, for actual power," said Samson, a schoolteacher. "We are already civilised people. We have our own laws, our own way of life." When the protectorate formed the Malaita Council to replace Maasina Ruru, the movement effectively transferred to the council. Samson's father was its president for two terms.

Other Maasina Ruru members were among the early cohort of national parliamentarians. I met Allan Taki, who had been an MP for three terms in Honiara. His family had come down from the bush to a Maasina Ruru settlement. Now aged ninety and living in a simple house with his family, he recalled arriving at parliament to be sworn in. He dressed traditionally: a lavalava around his waist; bare chest and feet; body ornaments; a war club in his belt and a spear in his hand. The attendants refused to let him in until he returned in trousers, shirt and shoes.

I travelled back to Honiara from Auki on the twin-hulled vessel I had missed on the way over. All the passengers sat inside the air-conditioned cabin while the ship bashed at high-speed through the waves of the Indispensable Strait, taking only two hours.

Once I settled into a small guesthouse and had a look around town, two aspects of the new interest in the Solomons by outside powers came into focus. One was the infusion of cash from the thousands of Solomon Islanders who were going to Australia and New Zealand each year for spells of seasonal agricultural work and other short-term employment. About 7000 were already away, and another 15,000 had lodged applications. Paul Ladoa, the traditional priest's son I had met with in Sinalagu, had a son working at a meatworks in Perth. David, the driver of the shuttle bus to my lodge on its ridge above Honiara, told me he had signed up and was awaiting the call.

The other change was highly visible: a newly built 12,000-seat stadium, surrounded by clustered pools, basketball and other courts and martial arts rings. Teams of workmen were planting palm plants on median strips and verges. Honiara was in the final stages of preparing to host the Pacific Games, with several thousand athletes from twenty-four island nations and territories competing. The stadium and other facilities were a gift of the People's Republic of China.

The gift was a reward for Sogavare's diplomatic switch from Taiwan to China, and for his perseverance through the political heat that followed. He had faced down a revolt inspired by the newly elected provincial premier of Malaita, Daniel Suidani, who emphasised his claim to political descent from Maasina Ruruu by putting up monuments to the movement around Auki. Taiwan's aid program had been helping agriculture in Malaita for many years. In a region pervaded by foreign and local Christian preachers, it was not hard to portray the officially atheist People's Republic as sinister.

In the 2006 riots, the long-established stores run by older Chinese migrants largely survived. Their owners had arrived in colonial times, before communist rule in China. They had loyal islander staff, who stood outside during the riots and talked the mobs out of looting and burning. But by 2021, most stores had been leased to newcomers from the People's Republic. Many of the original owners had moved to Queensland or were now pursuing less conspicuous businesses. The mob attacked them all, reducing Chinatown to burnt-out walls and frameworks.

The rioting was speedily quelled by another rushed insertion of Australian and other regional forces, but Sogavare was not happy. Within a month of his rescue, he was talking to the Chinese embassy about security aid. In March 2022, a draft security pact between China and the Solomons was leaked, probably through Suidani's circle. In its English wording it said that "China may, according to its own needs", replenish and transition military forces through Solomon Islands "to protect the safety of Chinese personnel and major projects in Solomon Islands". The following month, the Chinese foreign minister, Wang Yi, arrived in Honiara and signed the agreement with Sogavare. The final text has still not been published, and it is unclear what ratification processes have been followed.

Wang Yi went on, much less successfully, to a meeting of the Pacific Islands Forum in Fiji, a grouping of the independent island nations as well as Australia and New Zealand in which China and other outside powers have observer status. There, Wang circulated a draft regional agreement on security cooperation with members of the forum that recognised Beijing. It was an unexpected gambit and he met a wall of suspicion, forcing him to drop the proposal.

All this had been causing uproar in Australia and the United States. Suidani became a hero of China hawks in both countries. After the security pact was signed, he and his adviser Celsus Talifilu were sponsored by a Seattle-based non-profit foundation supporting indigenous rights, Nia Tero, for appearances in Washington and New York, with additional crowd-funding supported by media outlets associated with Falun Gong, the strongly anti-communist spiritual movement suppressed in China but a flourishing anti-Beijing critic elsewhere. Sogavare meanwhile worked to bring Malaita into line by cutting off the flow of aid into the province. In a perhaps ill-judged move, the US government had announced a US$25 million aid program for Malaita, focused on sustainable village and forestry development. Honiara insisted such aid programs had to come through the central government, rather than going directly to the provinces. When the US tried to use a civil contractor, Winrock, to come in as a non-government organisation to undertake sustainable forestry and other development schemes, under legislation governing charitable activity, hoping this less-official status would pass, Honiara delayed work permits for its foreign managers and experts. A proposal from Washington in 2019 to resume sending Peace Corps volunteers to the Solomons, after a twenty-five-year absence, still awaits approval.

In the Malaitan provincial assembly, Sogavare's supporters put up three motions of no confidence in Suidani as governor. The first failed. Street protests in Auki prevented the second from getting to a vote. In January 2023, the third was passed. Soon after, the national government used its supervisory powers to disqualify Suidani from the provincial assembly.[1]

Although accusations of bribery flew thick and fast around the no-confidence votes, Ronnie Jethro Butala, the speaker of the Malaitan assembly (and my introduction to Sinalagu), says he saw no evidence of it. It was just that Malaitans could see they were losing out. "A lot of the Malaita public were getting tired of geopolitics," Butala told me. "No more funding was coming from the national government, and also the national government diverted all the projects from Malaita to other provinces."

Sogavare looked on with relief and satisfaction as the Pacific Games proceeded without disruption in November 2023. "Sports is the glue that holds the nation together," he told local reporters. "It binds and unites us. It brings out the best out of us, as individuals and collectively as a nation." Veteran Honiara journalist Dorothy Wickham, descended from an English trader on Bougainville and his islander wife, backed Sogavare's assessment of the games and their nation-building significance. "The only time you see Solomon Islanders proud of their own country is when there are things like this," she told me.

How was the switch to Beijing now seen, I asked her. "I see some benefits in it," Wickham said. "The best thing is the Americans have come back in, and the Australians are making more effort now. They are falling over themselves." Indeed, Honiara's harbour was experiencing a flurry of Australian and US Navy ships bringing in support for the games.

The Westminster system sits lightly on these islands, whose people still largely have to fend for themselves. Before leaving, I took another small ship, the MV *Fairlady*, sharing benches and deck space with people returning home to the islands of the north. The ship's previous identity in Japan as the *Hahajima Maru* was painted over on the white hull. It chugged across the Savo Sea, scene of epic naval battles, and across the Tryon-Hackman Line, the boundary between northern and southern languages, named after its academic proponents. Through the evening and night, we pulled into floodlit jetties around the Marovo Lagoon and New Georgia Island.

On board, I tiptoed over fellow passengers sleeping on mats on the crowded decks to reach the canteen hatch, which dispensed cup-noodles and instant coffee, and gradually got into conversation with the people around me, who told me of lives between the modern world of mobile phones and semi-subsistence village life.

Seventh-day Adventist pastor Craig Mathias had been down in Honiara to stock up on supplies and see his daughter, who was enrolled as a nursing student at the national university. Now he was heading back to his parish on Kolombangara Island. Belief in local spirits – big and little ones – persisted there, he said. In his preaching he did not oppose all aspects of *kastom*, he told me, just the bad, violent parts. China was even reaching into Kolombangara, with a proposed takeover of a large timber plantation. The Chinese buyer's plans for a new port had instantly raised suspicions among Australia's febrile media that it was a secret naval base. Mathias shrugged: it was all above the island people's heads.

A woman in her twenties, Sima Angolo, was meeting her family at Munda to go back by dinghy to their home island in Roviana Lagoon, further round the coast of New Georgia. She told me of talking to the crocodiles in her river. "When I go in the river they float alongside," she said. "They slide off logs when others come by, but I tell them not to when I am there. They understand." Her great-grandmother's sister had been expelled from the village for committing adultery. She had turned into a crocodile, but a good one.

By then I understood why the official coat of arms of the Solomon Islands has a shark on one side and a crocodile on the other. In the Langa Langa Lagoon and other places, saltwater people were still paddling out to summon and feed sharks. In the National Museum in Honiara, there is a funeral casket from Santa Ana Island, a black shark shape with a compartment carved out to house the skull and jawbone of the deceased. The sharks and crocodiles are the ancestors, spirits of a nation still forming.

In April 2024, Sogavare's government held the elections that had been postponed because of the Pacific Games the previous year, and his party gained only twenty-two of the fifty seats in the parliament. When a governing coalition formed over the following weeks, Sogavare stepped back to become finance minister. The foreign minister who had negotiated the diplomatic switch and the 2022 security agreement, Jeremiah Manele, became the new prime minister. Manele, originally from the island of Santa Isabel, had done postgraduate study at Oxford before representing the Solomons at the United Nations and with RAMSI. He provided continuity from Sogavare, without the truculence.

In the simultaneous provincial elections, Suidani was re-elected to the Malaitan assembly but did not contest the premiership. Malaita's new premier, Elijah Asilaua, said partnership between the provincial and national governments was important for the delivery of essential services and development projects. Asilaua said he was determined to avoid a repeat of past tensions and was eager to work closely with the Manele government.

Although the heat has gone out of the switch, the "geopolitics" continues. There was talk of the Solomons forming its own army instead of relying on outside intervention. Australia was quick to step up, sending its defence minister to Honiara to offer assistance if the idea went ahead.

Despite the big splashes of aid from China such as the stadium, local feeling was not friendly towards China and the Chinese, Dorothy Wickham told me. "But ... they see [that] provinces like Western [Province] that have allowed Chinese investment and Chinese money in have taken leaps and bounds, and they compare it to say Malaita, where the roads are just terrible ... It's like throwing a coconut in the sea – it will roll with the waves."

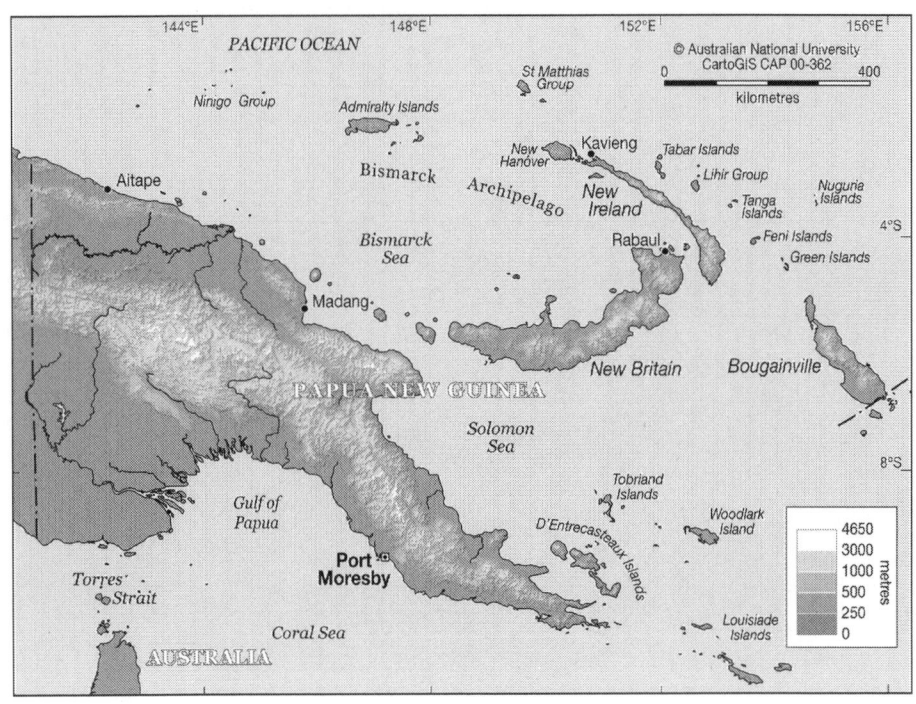

8

BOUGAINVILLE

The Promised Land

AT THE NORTHERN END of the Solomons, regular ferries like the MV *Fairlady* turn around at Gizo, an island township from which divers set out to explore wartime wrecks in the nearby lagoon. To go further, there are intermittent passenger boats or rusting cargo ships and barges, or an air service if you have the money.

The main centre is Taro, a town of timber and corrugated iron houses sprawling among palms and fruit trees on a small flat island just off the large island of Choiseul. There I stayed in a simple wooden guesthouse on a sandy lane that ran down to the pale-green water of the channel between Taro and the long green line of Choiseul. The continual rumbling of heavy trucks hauling newly cut hardwood logs away for shipment to China could be heard drifting across from the larger island. A food stall sold some deliciously greasy battered fish, with slices of taro pudding instead of chips. In the evening, a provincial assembly member joined me for rounds of beer, until the nearby stall put down its grill and closed for the night. Like Suidani in Malaita, he was fed up with distant Honiara, and thought Choiseul Province could join Bougainville, a few hours away by outboard dinghy, if it got independence.

Should you be allowed to make the short sea transit from the Solomon Islands to Bougainville, you would travel on one of the ubiquitous fibreglass dinghies known as banana boats. The skipper guns the big outboard out through a reef entrance, then bashes through the waves of a sea alternately blue and grey as you get doused by spray and rainstorms. You pass small islands, some just sand spits with a clutch of palms, like the castaway's islands in cartoons, until a few hours later, an immense mountainous island looms to the northwest.

This is Bougainville, its people separated from their cultural brothers on Taro and Choiseul by the imperial Monopoly games of the European powers. You have crossed the border between the Solomon Islands and Papua New Guinea, normally open only to "traditional" crossings by local people for small-scale commerce and social meetings. Outsiders can only make the crossing with special permission from both governments. One day, perhaps, it will be an interesting tourism route with larger and safer boats, sustaining small eco-resorts and other ventures. For now, authorities are more concerned about the possible misuse of the crossing by smugglers of drugs and guns, or by criminals and illegal migrants. Only two decades ago, banana boats like this evaded Papua New Guinean patrols to take weapons and supplies to rebels on Bougainville, and to take out their wounded.

People making the crossing from Taro usually head for Kieta, past the seaside airport at Aropa, where a windsock flies at the end of a long clearing. On landing at a nearby coral-pebble beach, they walk up to the road and wait for a minibus into the township of Arawa. On the way is the port of Kieta, with a large steel warehouse, some containers and a grader to shovel copra into cargo-bags. Tucked next to the road is a Mitsubishi "Zero" fighter plane on a plinth, relic of the mighty war that once raged here.

I had come along this road nearly four decades ago, after landing at Aropa in a small turboprop aircraft from the Japanese-built airstrip at Munda, on New Georgia Island in the Solomons, now a defunct air route. A similar bus had carried me into Kieta. Then, the township still held a few buildings from its time as an administrative centre for central and southern Bougainville under German and then Australian colonial rule.

In those colonial days, patrol officers known as kiaps went out on foot or by boat to issue government orders and try to collect taxes. In the early days, the job was perilous. When the schooner carrying Caroline Mytinger stopped in Kieta on the way to Rabaul in New Guinea in the late 1920s, it picked up a young Australian kiap named in her diary only as Sammy. He needed treatment for a wound in his foot caused by an arrow tipped with flying-fox teeth. He had been attacked as payback for an offence committed by an unconnected white man who had previously visited the area.

In 1987 the Kieta Hotel, overlooking the port and scenic Pokpok Island, was still in business. I was one of the few guests and was soon sinking can after can of South Pacific beer with the publican, a genial middle-aged Australian named Barry Walker. He was known as the Phantom, after the hero of the Lee Falk comic serialised in the Papua New Guinea *Post-Courier*, and his bar was known as the Skull Cave. A radio droned with the call of horse races on Australian tracks. Walker was frequently on the phone: he was a bookie for punters all over Papua New Guinea.

While staying there, I went out to look around Arawa, a few kilometres north. It had been laid out on a cleared coconut plantation and, but for the Bougainvilleans and other islanders, had the appearance of a town in Queensland. The paved streets had neat gutters and footpaths. The banks and offices carried familiar Australian names. The residential areas had rows of Queenslander-style bungalows raised on stilts, with space beneath them to park cars and boats. Young white women in frocks and tennis outfits pushed infants in strollers around supermarkets and clinics. I was invited to lunch by some expat business executives at their club. They wore tailored shorts and long white socks. They spoke dismissively about the efforts of local entrepreneurs to open small shops around the town: these always failed, it seemed, because the owners could not refuse credit to their relatives.

It was all financed by a huge hole being gouged out of the mountain spine to the west, at a place called Panguna. Bougainville Copper Ltd, a subsidiary of the Rio Tinto mining giant run out of Melbourne, was grinding the copper-infused rock into a slurry, which was sent past Arawa by pipeline to a nearby dock. A power plant there provided electricity for the mine and the town.

When I returned to Arawa in 2006, the town looked like a post-apocalyptic movie set. Decaying buildings lined the streets. The expats were gone. The electricity lines had long gone, salvaged for scrap. Vines hung from the pylons. Supersized ore trucks rusted by the roadside, slumped on deflated tyres. Islander families camped in the abandoned Queenslander houses. As twilight fell, they cooked on open fires in the gardens.

The road up to the mine site at Panguna was closed. The mine was a no-go area, placed under tabu by rebels who had proclaimed Bougainville independent. They called the island Me'ekamui, the "Promised Land". Their leader, Francis Ona, had proclaimed himself king before his death in 2005, the year before my visit.

At that time, and for many years later, down at the far south of Bougainville, a man from the fractious Siwai people held out in a different way. In the late 1990s, Noah Musingku had set up a group that soon morphed from Pentecostal sect into a pyramid scheme called U-Vistract, taking some $200 million from tens of thousands of trusting savers, mainly in Papua New Guinea. Authorities ran Musingku out of Australia, then Port Moresby, then the Solomon Islands. In 2003 he came back to Bougainville and set up his bank under Ona's patronage, equipped with computers and satellite links. He hired a squad of former Fiji Army soldiers as guards. When his pyramid scheme went bust, he tried placating his clients with "Jesus money" and other fake currency, produced by a Brisbane printing business.

On my 2006 visit to Arawa, there was a small guesthouse run by UN relief agencies amid all the dereliction. From there, I went to see two actors who had moved back to Bougainville in the wake of conflict. In a long career with the National Theatre Company in Port Moresby, actor and playwright William Takaku had played Man Friday to Pierce Brosnan's Robinson Crusoe in a 1997 film of Daniel Defoe's classic, shot near Madang. Earlier, he'd played an edgier Friday in a play in Port Moresby, in which Crusoe eventually begs to be initiated into Friday's tribe rather than be repatriated. He'd also written an opera, *Erberia*, based on the creation legends of Bougainville.

Takaku was a big, muscular, handsome man in late middle age. His friend and fellow actor from their Moresby days, Nick Gioni, was slight and Puckish, with an endearing smile and bright eyes. He had been to the Edinburgh Festival and found Edinburgh "a very cultured place". We sat on a woven palm mat. Both men were bare-chested. Takaku talked and talked, mostly about the environment of the islands being ripped apart by logging and mining, and about the dependency on imported foods, which he blamed for all the new ills in the Pacific – correctly in the case of diabetes, wrongly in the case of HIV. A young woman, slim and dark, sat in the background. She snorted with amusement, or perhaps derision, when Takaku expounded his view that the foreskin augmented female satisfaction during sexual intercourse. She disappeared out to the fireplace, and came back with a soup of smoked fish and bush spinach.

The next day, we met up again. I had provided money for fuel and the hire of a vehicle to drop us at the path leading to Takaku's home village, Pidia, and to pick us up again in the afternoon. The track started off the rise in the main road close to Kieta. We walked along it, following the spine of the peninsula jutting eastwards. We quickly passed the remains of the Kieta Hotel, a concrete slab grown over with vines and weeds, and along a trail through a botanic garden of exotic trees and bushes. After a couple of hours the trail turned down the slope to the peninsula's north side, and we reached the shore at Pidia. Somewhere on this slope was a rock-shelter where archaeologists had found pottery dating back 1500 years. Calm green shallows washed under overhanging trees. A rope hung from a branch, and we swung out into the tepid water. We lounged and talked, then walked up to the village, where we sat at the front of a house on stilts and a woman brought us some rice and tinned fish before we set off back to the road.

Around this time, the New Zealand writer Lloyd Jones published his novel *Mister Pip*, about the dreadful conflict that had occurred between my visits. Some years later, Pidia was a locale for a film adaptation of the book. When I returned to Bougainville recently, I found some people who still could not steel themselves to watch the film; they knew the village mother raped and murdered by Papua New Guinean soldiers whom it portrays.

William Takaku was not there when I returned again: he had died suddenly of a heart attack in 2011, on his way to see a doctor in Port Moresby about chest pains. I found Nick Gioni in his village on the south side of Kieta, a dispersed collection of small huts. A woman was having her hair tended by a girl. Boys with rapper-style haircuts jostled on a bench. Smoke wafted fragrantly from the cooking hut. Nick's son Allan, an alert man of around thirty, went off to find his father. Nick appeared, thin and leathery-skinned now, with red eyes. I guessed he'd been asleep. He remembered my visit and spoke wistfully of his times with Takaku. "He always enjoyed the situation," Nick said.

I travelled to Panguna with Joyce Ampa'oi, who had grown up in Arawa and Panguna. She was back visiting from the Gold Coast in Queensland, where she lived with her Australian husband, whom she'd met during a career in hotel management. We hired a vehicle for the forty-minute drive up the highway, initially through plantations and gardens, then up through jungle covered hills. We reached a mountain saddle dotted with ruined sheds and building foundation slabs.

"Here was a shipping office, a bank, the Kawerong coffee shop run by my mother. The supermarket over there, the church, the mess, the ladies' accommodation, the hospital, the kindergarten," Joyce said. "The expat executives lived up there, the managing director's residence up on top – you can see the rubble." A gateway in a low wall opened to a tangle of vines: "That was the 50-metre swimming pool." Four rusting light towers marked out a playing field, now scrub. A flight of steps led up to a concrete slab. "That was the cricket club. There was an indoor sports centre over there." She recalled a big boxing match between world featherweight champion Eusebio Pedroza of Panama and local hero Johnny Aba.

Then we came to the big hole, a vast empty quarry where a mountain peak had once jutted. We stood on the edge and peered down its terraced sides. A pool of cuprous-green water was down in the centre, below the tunnel that drained away most of the rainwater. A few tiny figures moved on the quarry's floor. "They live down there, sluicing for gold," Joyce said.

No matter how much one has read about the mine and the conflict it caused, the scene is stunning. This had been a slice of Australia, inserted in the late 1960s into a Pacific island whose disparate peoples had lived by age-old custom until, starting less than a century before, they were invaded successively by German colonisers, labour recruiters, European missionaries, Australian patrol officers and the armies of Japan and the Allies, before returning to civilian colonial rule from distant Port Moresby and Canberra.

The motivation for the mine had been the huge deposit of copper and gold underneath the mountain. It worked well, it seemed, for nearly twenty years. Once it began production in 1969, Bougainville Copper's mine provided 17 per cent of Papua New Guinea's internal revenue and 12 per cent of its gross domestic product, underwriting the transition to independence in September 1975.

Joyce's late father, Severinus, was one of a number of Bougainvilleans who joined this enclave. He had been educated and trained as a teacher by Marist fathers and was hired as a community liaison officer by Bougainville Copper. Later, he became a successful small businessman, running a fleet of Australian-made Ford Falcon taxis in Arawa. The family lived in a house built for them by the company on their traditional land, close to the mine. Joyce went to the schools in Arawa and Panguna. "It was a beautiful life, from my recollection," she said. "I had white friends. We mixed and hung about. Your next-door neighbours were Australian or Swedish or whatever. You talk to a lot of the kids that grew up there, they still have their friends from that whole collage of cultures."

Yet the huge mine never sat well with other Bougainvilleans. How could it? Right from the start, villagers refused to accept the British model of crown ownership of underground resources, whereby the village might own the surface of the land, but what was beneath belonged to the government.

Until the early 1960s, Bougainville had been a quiet backwater in the Australian-run territories of Papua and New Guinea. A Catalina flying boat came in from Rabaul every two weeks, landing in the calm water between Kieta and Pokpok Island, dropping off frozen meat, mail and the occasional passenger. A Burns Philp ship, the *Tulagi*, came every six weeks to load copra and deliver more supplies.

Then in 1963, a geologist with Conzinc Riotinto Australia (CRA) read reports from government geologists dating back to 1936 about indications of copper and gold in Bougainville's mountains. A prospecting team arrived in 1964 and headed inland, accompanied by a policeman: an early sign of the official backing the company would get. From the start, villagers objected to the intrusion into their land, sometimes chasing off surveyors and pulling out their pegs.

The government patrol officers told to help the mineral exploration did so uneasily. "Like all kiaps, we had been taught that native land was sacrosanct and that landowners could transfer land only by native custom," recalled Bill Brown, a kiap assigned to Bougainville around this time. "Accordingly, we had always told the people that nobody could take their land from them. Now we were being told that those rules applied only to the surface of the land and not what lay beneath. The land laws that we had administered and upheld did not apply to mining. We did not – we could not – like the mining legislation."[1]

Trying to allay these concerns, the administration brought five men from Bougainville, including Joyce's father, Severinus, to Australia in September 1965, accompanied by a patrol officer and travelling at CRA's expense. In Canberra, this group suggested that a share of royalties should go to landowners, a share of the mine's profits should go to Bougainville and the territory administration should devote more revenue to the island's development. "Nobody said no and they returned home satisfied," Brown remembered.

Some five months later, in February 1966, the Australian minister for territories, Charles Barnes, came to Kieta for a two-day inspection of the site. A politician from the Country Party, part of the ruling conservative coalition in Canberra, Barnes was already widely seen as a diehard defender of patronising racial views at a time when Australia's Aboriginal rights movement was stirring. As recounted to Brown by another kiap who attended a public meeting with him, Barnes was asked by one local elder: "The mine may not be of benefit to us old guys, but what about our children and our children's children? What is it going to do for them?"

Barnes replied: "It is not going to do anything for you, for your children or for your grandchildren, but it is going to do wonders for the people of Papua and New Guinea as a whole."

As one official reported a month later:

> The effects [of Barnes' remark] on CRA's activities were dramatic. Three days later, trees were felled ... two days after that, surveyors met opposition in cutting lines west of the area being drilled ... The geologist in charge was told by the landowners that they wished to see mining activity confined to the area of present activities (about one-mile square) until they had the opportunity to see the effects of mining on the land, and also what they would get out of it. A few days later our present area of activities was surrounded by *tambu* (keep out) signs.

The administration and the company pressed on, with more and more police sent into Bougainville to overawe opposition to prospecting and roadbuilding. Brown and his fellow kiaps went out on patrols to try to talk people around. The mining law had been changed to pay landowners occupation fees and compensate them for damage. "Their response was vitriolic," Brown wrote.

> The people were not interested in financial compensation. They were dismissive of the changes to the law. They repudiated the right of the House of Assembly to make laws about mining or ownership of minerals on their land. And they totally rejected the notion that CRA prospectors, or anybody else, had the right to enter their land.

In Port Moresby, this was seen as unreasonably selfish. The landowners were trying to deprive Papua New Guinea of the massive revenues from the mine and its economic side benefits, said the lands secretary. Sure, some areas would be made useless for a time by open-cut mining and by the dumping of overburden and tailings, but compensation would be paid for this, plus 5 per cent of copper royalties. Meanwhile locals would have job opportunities and see the value of their land rising.

"Maybe he [Barnes] did not foresee that the sloping hillsides covered by ancient forest, sacred trees and stones, and mountain streams and pools, would be destroyed," Brown commented. "The people's precious land and the heritage it held would be replaced by barren rock at the bottom of a 2000-foot-deep hole. He certainly did not mention the miserliness of the $2 per acre ($4.94 per hectare) per annum prescribed occupation fee."

In early 1967, Brown himself was called down to Canberra to explain this strange selfishness to a meeting of high-level officials. As he wrote:

> The group was not interested in my opinion or anything I had to say about Bougainville. They did not seem to understand or care that 21 different languages were spoken on Bougainville ... that those different languages and different beliefs affected Bougainvillean attitudes to the Administration, to Australia and to CRA. Astoundingly, they did not even seem interested in murmurs of secession. One of the top brass, presumably drawing on his Malaysian Insurgency experience, suggested that when I returned to Bougainville, I should, in the appropriate circumstances, establish crowd control – roll a plastic streamer out along the ground and tell people it would be curtains if they stepped over it.

Barnes got the approval of prime minister Harold Holt's cabinet in April 1967 for mine development to go ahead, and in August that year the enabling legislation was passed by the House of Assembly in Port Moresby, then still dominated by nominated officials and expats. It provided for compulsory acquisition of land needed for mining, treatment plants, town sites, ports, wharves, power stations, dams, roads, railways, tunnels, pipelines and transmission lines, and for the disposal of overburden and tailings. Bougainville Copper gained a forty-two-year mining lease, with provision for two extensions of twenty-one years.

It was always highly unlikely that the Bougainville people, especially the Nasioi, the largest language group whose land straddled the centre of the island including Panguna and Kieta, would harken to appeals to the greater good of Papua New Guinea.

The islanders had much in common with Melanesians elsewhere. They lived in small settlements, subsisting on root crops and pigs; there was a division between "bush" and "saltwater" people; and they believed in ancestral spirits. But except for some groups on the outer islands and coastal fringes who intermarried with people from other parts of the Pacific, they had been isolated until recent times. Warfare and fear of evil forest spirits discouraged people from venturing far.

The Nasioi and others have a matrilineal descent system, distinct from many other parts of Papua New Guinea. The Bougainvilleans are also very black. Scientists who ran a "derma-spectrometer" over a sample group found them blacker than most Africans, quite unlike the "redskins", as they called the light brown people found elsewhere in the country, but similar to the skin colour typical of the northern Solomon Islands.

Bougainvilleans had no particular reason to trust white men. The Germans had done nothing much for them from their enclave on the Buka Passage at the north of the main island. The Germans found recruits for their police and military mostly on Buka Island, across the channel. (Some Melanesian troops had even been sent to quell a rebellion in Tanganyika.) The first German government station opened in Kieta only in 1905, and the first doctor arrived in 1913. The Marists came and opened churches and schools, but the other European faces were the "recruiters" for plantation labour elsewhere in German New Guinea, young men ordered into money-earning contracts by their elders. Many of these latter-day blackbirders were from Australia. One was "Peanuts" McConville. When he was killed during a landing for recruits, a punitive expedition from the Germans followed.

The Australian administration that came after the seizure of German New Guinea in 1914, for the first few years a military one, was also harsh. Although officially banned, flogging continued. When villagers refused to pay their head tax, their houses were burnt down. Here, as elsewhere, cronyism and corruption marked the expropriation of German property. The

Australians forcibly repressed a long-running conflict between two groups near Buin in 1920. They took the leader of one side, Babala, and two others to Rabaul for trial, then brought them back to Buin for execution by firing squad.

Pacification continued "with conspicuous brutality", according to historian Peter Elder.[2] In 1932–35 a cargo cult spread across Buka, led by a man named Pako who predicted the usual mix of wealth arriving by sea, if people got ready by abandoning traditional wealth and social hierarchies. It was suppressed by arrests and deportation to other islands.

When the Japanese arrived in 1942, the small Australian garrison at Kieta had already fled. This was wise enough but did little to assure the people that Australia was looking after them. By contrast, the Marist fathers stayed, and twelve of them lost their lives.

Bougainville gave the Japanese a cautious welcome, wanting to believe their assurances of co-prosperity and anti-colonialism. Pako's followers on Buka assumed there had been a mistake: the Japanese – not the returning Germans as Pako had predicted – were bringing the cargo. Villagers joined Japanese food-growing projects, but the demands on their labour and food stocks were increasingly harsh and were accompanied by cruel punishments for defiance. Some villagers started sheltering the Australian Coastwatchers, military intelligence operatives who observed Japanese movements and radioed reports back to the Allied forces.

When US marines landed at Torokina on the west coast of Bougainville in late 1944 and then handed fighting over to Australian and New Zealand forces, a man named Mesiamo, from the Nagovisi group, organised local men into an irregular force to harass the Japanese. The "Black Brigadier" was claimed by both church and state. The administration rewarded him by appointing him "No. 1 Boy" on the island. The Catholics had another view. "Misiamo [sic] did not fight for Australia – he fought for the 'Lotu' (Church Faith)," said an account in a Catholic mission journal in 1946. The man had not been entirely devout (another history points out his five wives), but when the Japanese came and burnt down the churches, he and the Nagovisi declared war.

The Australian administration returned in 1945, isolating itself on the island of Sohano in the Buka Passage, with not much cash to rebuild the devastated modern elements of the economy. The first government high school opened only in 1964, so the Marists remained the main educators, their seminary turning out the first young people in the colony with any sort of tertiary education. Some, such as John Momis and Leo Hannet, later moved into politics.

The patronising attitudes I found later among expats in Arawa had been shown in the early 1960s, when two young Buka men, John Teosin and Francis Hagai, set up the Hahalis Welfare Society in the north of Bougainville with cooperative operations in agriculture and trade, perhaps similar to the Malekula Native Company in the New Hebrides. It grew to have some 5000 members, eight stores, its own trucks and electric generators, and vocational classes.

The social side of Hahalis drew it into conflict with the church. It was said to run "baby gardens" where young unmarried women were visited by male society members. Scandalised critics called these brothels. The society called them "matrimonial clubs" and a rational system of trial marriage. When the Catholics excommunicated society leaders, they responded by setting up their own form of Christian worship, incorporating ancestral spirits.

While the churches were losing parishioners, the administration was losing money. In 1962, the society advised its members to stop paying the annual head tax, on the grounds that the government was doing nothing for them. Larger and larger government contingents were sent to enforce the tax, meeting stiff resistance. Finally, a force of 400 police, drawn from all over the territory, quelled the movement by making hundreds of arrests. The movement simmered on, but it was another example of a worthy entrepreneurial effort being pulled down under the guise of sexual immorality, when the objection to paying the tax might have been countered by more deft and inclusive politics.

This was tacitly admitted. As with Maasina Ruru in the Solomons, the Hahalis affair had the effect of galvanising the administration into more active development, through new schools and a highly successful malaria eradication effort. The Marists also saw the importance of meeting their flock's hunger for economic improvement and undertook projects in timber milling, road construction and coconut planting.

Even so, when the copper project confronted the Bougainvilleans only a few years later, it was no wonder they feared the worst. As the kiap Bill Brown told a newspaper in 1967:

> Their isolation complex and their deep but understandable preoccupation with their land has created a situation where they refuse to believe anything we tell them, or in fact anything which another Papuan or New Guinean tells them.

So the project went ahead, without consent and without much understanding of who had the traditional authority to decide questions of land use. In some places, men with an eye on money usurped the matrilineal system of the local Nasioi people. When women lay down in front of bulldozers, police hauled them away. The company men were baffled. The mine's first managing director, Don Vernon, would later write that the land had seemed largely empty of habitation and agriculture: "Yet we were to learn that every square metre of the apparent wilderness belonged to someone under customary land law."[3]

In 1975, as Papua New Guinea moved into independence from Australian rule, many people in Bougainville supported a move for a separate statehood.

In its seventeen years of operation, Bougainville extracted 3 million tonnes of copper, along with associated gold and silver. That this came from rock with an average copper content of 0.34 per cent gives an idea of the volume of rock dug up and discarded. The landscape disappeared, becoming a huge hole surrounded by dumps of overburden, while ground-up rock washed down a river to the west coast, coating the banks with verdigris-like residue, raising the riverbed so that surrounding land became swamp, and extending silt out into the coastal fishing grounds.

It all started unravelling in 1988. The murder of a local nurse led to a rampage by Bougainvilleans against migrants from the Papua New Guinea highlands living in squatter settlements around Arawa, who were blamed for crime. A younger group challenged established Panguna landowners over the distribution of the 5 per cent of copper royalties conceded by Port Moresby. To make their point, they cut the power line to the mine. Port Moresby sent in the notoriously rough police mobile squad, whose rampages led to armed rebellion by a newly formed Bougainville Revolutionary Army (BRA).

In July 1989, Joyce Ampa'oi flew back one Friday for the mid-year college break; she was studying in Madang, on Papua New Guinea's mainland. Her father collected her from the airport. Around 10 pm that night, the family heard an explosion in the distance and the power went off. Through the night and the next morning, they heard the popping of distant gunshots. The BRA had blown down another of the pylons carrying power to Panguna.

About midday on the Saturday, soldiers from the PNG Defence Force emerged from the bush around the family's house. "They called us out, and made us lie face down in the yard, with guns to our heads," Joyce told me. "They asked us: 'Do you have any BRA people come through?' We said we had no idea." Severinus Ampa'oi told the soldiers he was under police protection, as someone previously connected with the mine, and had the police commissioner's phone number.

The soldiers withdrew, one of them gratuitously firing a bullet through the windscreen of the family's car.

Later that afternoon, Joyce was playing with her young nieces and nephews in the garden. "Then one coconut fell, then another," she said. "Then it hit me: someone was shooting across the treetops, from one ridge to another. I grabbed the kids and ran inside. Then a helicopter came in low overhead and fired rockets into the hillside."

The family packed up and moved down to Arawa that Saturday. They never saw their house again. The next Tuesday it burnt down. The following month, the family moved to Port Moresby. In November that year,

Bougainville Copper declared the mine closed and paid out its staff. "It was all such a shock," Joyce said. "We thought it would be sorted out. Nobody expected this place to blow up just like that."

But it did, evolving into a civil war on this lovely, remote island. The PNG Defence Force, with just two under-equipped battalions of infantry, had little hope of a decisive blow. The political head of the BRA was a former mine worker, Francis Ona, from the breakaway group of Panguna landowners. But its military commander was a young Bougainvillean, Sam Kauona, who had graduated from the Australian Army's officer training school at Portsea, near Melbourne, with a specialisation in explosives, before becoming a captain in the PNG Defence Force. When he learned his own army was being sent into Bougainville, he deserted.

Kauona's young volunteers seized weapons from soldiers and police or made crude pipe-guns. Dominic Babatani, who commanded a BRA company operating around Arawa, told me how they'd gone to Torokina, where the departing US and Australian forces had buried dumps of weapons in 1945. His group found a heavy machine gun in working condition, retrieved belts of ammunition, and made a mount for it in an abandoned mine workshop. He showed me where his men had used it to drive off a PNG patrol boat trying to land soldiers on Arawa's beach.

The fighting became a three-way conflict between the government forces, the BRA rebels and largely non-Nasioi islanders in militia groups known as the Resistance, who had been antagonised by the BRA's depredations. Villages emptied around Panguna. "All the mothers and families moved into the refuge centres, but the boys were holding the fort up in the jungle," said Alphons Tavore, a former BRA fighter whom I encountered up at Panguna, where he managed a cooperative that fostered chicken raising. "In 1990 there was a ceasefire, but it broke down the following year. The care-centres closed and everyone went back into the mountains until 1997," Tavore said. "We survived on wild yams, choko vines, possums, crabs, fish."

Up to 20,000 of Bougainville's then 200,000 people are estimated to have died, some from direct conflict and violence, most from sickness due to exposure to the elements and the collapse of medical services.

It came to a head in 1996 and 1997. The BRA used young women to lure government soldiers and police into an ambush, where twelve were slaughtered. The military operation collapsed. PNG prime minister Sir Julius Chan's attempts to negotiate with the BRA were not reciprocated. Then his soldiers assassinated the premier of a transitional government Chan had set up in Bougainville. Chan's cabinet turned to an African mercenary force, formed by Sandline International, a gun-for-hire company run by a suave ex–British Army officer. It readied an operation to clear out the BRA using a Mi-24 helicopter gunship and other heavy weapons, then to reopen the Panguna mine in return for a share of the revenue.

Disclosure of this plan led to a mutiny by the PNG Defence Force in Port Moresby and the fall of Chan's government. The new government and the nominal Bougainville premier worked out a ceasefire agreement with Kauona's forces. An international monitoring group moved in and talks for a permanent settlement began under New Zealand auspices – Australia being suspect in local eyes. In 2001, the attending parties signed the Bougainville Peace Agreement setting up a new Autonomous Bougainville Government, with a referendum on independence to be held by June 2020.

Francis Ona never joined the process and, as we have seen, before he died in 2005, he proclaimed himself king of a state he declared was already independent, Me'ekamui.

The political and diplomatic can had been kicked far down the road when the referendum came in November 2019. Port Moresby had squandered the eighteen years it was given to build the case for Bougainville remaining in Papua New Guinea. Starved of funds, the autonomous government, based on Buka Island and headed since 2010 by the Catholic priest turned veteran politico John Momis, was not an advertisement for the status quo or anything like it.

Six months before the referendum, the replacement of Papua New Guinea's prime minister of the previous eight years, Peter O'Neill, amid various fiscal scandals, had jolted Port Moresby into belated action. His replacement,

James Marape, finally disbursed the 30 million Kina (AU$14 million) allocated to a referendum commission to be chaired by the former Irish prime minister Bertie Ahern.

But government efforts to win over Bougainvilleans with promises of better services and Melanesian brotherhood fell on deaf ears. Marape took his cabinet to the island and promised a billion Kina for development over ten years – not long after his government had asked Australia for 300 million Kina just to balance that year's budget.

At referendum rallies there was hardly a PNG flag in sight. Most people wore shirts and vests adorned with the Bougainville flag, its design based on a headdress worn by young boys approaching traditional initiation ceremonies. Many garments carried the slogans "Black is beautiful" or "Kawas Pawa" (Black Power).

When I drove with Dominic Babatani down to meet the former BRA commander Sam Kauona, he also talked of a broad consensus. Now living at a sprawling family compound on the coast south of Kieta, where his cattle wandered between coconut groves and the beach, he said firmly: "Bougainville's intention is to go for full independence."

On the ground, Kauona had welded his former fighters and their opponents in the Resistance into a powerful island-wide movement, known as the Bougainville Ex-Combatants Core Group. It operated as a kind of home guard in normal times, helping to quell disturbances. It had helped to maintain security around the referendum, but not in a neutral way. It told people to enrol and to vote for independence.

I also met Genevieve Korokoro, who studied at the Queensland University of Technology and had returned to become Arawa's deputy mayor. "This is your chance," she said she tells people. "You suffered for it. It is your only chance to decide on the political future of Bougainville." She had her own mindset. "I'm for independence," she said. "I want to put this thing to a stop somewhere. It's been from our forefathers, from colonial times. So let us go for this chance and see what happens. But we have to work on it: it's not going to be easy."

In the November 2019 poll, the Bougainvilleans voted 98 per cent for independence. There were no significant reports of any wrongdoing in the polling or counting.

The most obvious challenge for an independent state would be financial. Over 90 per cent of the present autonomous government annual budget of about 300 million kina has been funded by transfers from the central government and foreign aid. "An independent Bougainville would require two to three times more," estimated economist Satish Chand. Carving out a notional share of PNG's licence fees for tuna fishing would bring perhaps 100 million kina. The remaining funding gap is still wide.[4]

For this reason, the autonomous government has been "hell-bent" – as one foreign adviser put it in Buka – on getting at least one big copper-gold mine operating, either the old Panguna site or a new project, or both. In 2015, it enacted a new mining law, giving ownership of mineral resources to landowners rather than the state. Miners now have to wrangle deals with the villagers sitting on top of the resource.

With the mountainous spine of the island fused with copper and its streambeds flecked with gold, would-be mine operators had been arriving since the conflict ended to take Rio Tinto's place, from the United States, Canada and Australia. But Rio Tinto decided not to stick around. It got out of Bougainville Copper Ltd in mid-2016, leaving the PNG and Bougainville governments each holding 36.4 per cent equity, and various investors the rest. In 2012, the company had said that a bare-bones reopening of the mine would take five years and cost US$5.2 billion.

For a lot of ordinary Bougainville people, however, worries about the money are for later. Funding for what? The highway down the island is still only paved in patches near Buka. Japanese aid got some bridges rebuilt, but vehicles still need to ford one big river across submerged rocks and pebbles. The clinic in Arawa, financed by Australian aid, is barely coping with the community's needs. A large coconut oil refinery, built in Arawa by an earlier mining hopeful, is locked up.

Schools have reopened. Bougainville has one of the fastest growing populations in the world, already estimated at over 300,000, but a generation now grown to adulthood missed out on education during the conflict.

"Young people have grown up displaced in care-centres," said Korokoro, the Arawa deputy mayor. "In the villages they had some sort of authority from the chiefs and parents. Now the parents don't have control over them. We need to get the sixteen- to twenty-year-olds into technical training and apprenticeships." The Arawa Technical College, opened during the mining years, is abandoned. A drug culture had sprung up. Cannabis was being grown all over the island. People were drinking a home-brew liquor known as *wara* (water) made from coconut or pineapple juice. "It's an awful taste," she said. "You feel you are getting drunk just from sniffing it or the person who has been drinking it."

Most Bougainvilleans have got used to looking after themselves, growing, gathering or catching their own food, with cash coming from small businesses such as transport and shops, selling *buai* (betel nut) or panning for gold in streams. Every evening, the hills around Arawa show pinpricks of light from household hydroelectric plants, fashioned from rewired generators and alternators salvaged from mining vehicles. "We don't really need the mine to reopen," Korokoro said. "We have enough natural resources: tuna, coconuts, vanilla, tourism. If there is to be mining, maybe later. Why waste time when people are not ready for it?"

But a more immediate obstacle to independence is the need for the referendum outcome to be ratified by the PNG parliament. This proviso was included in the peace agreement to break a deadlock, at the suggestion of the then Australian foreign minister, Alexander Downer. It enabled the agreement to be sold in two different ways. In Port Moresby, it allowed leaders to stress that they had the ultimate say over the outcome. Elsewhere, Downer and others could say that ignoring a strong vote for independence would be unthinkable.

Marape had promised that the decision would be enacted in the parliament's five-year term, which began in 2022. When I met him during the 2022 election campaign, Marape said he wished the issue had not landed on his plate as prime minister. He said his officials were investigating a compromise, such as an "associated nation" status for Bougainville, like the Cook Islands have with New Zealand. For their part, the Bougainville leaders in

Buka floated the idea of engaging an independent facilitator to help secure a post-referendum agreement.

Nearly five years since the referendum, the sweeping pro-independence result was put to the PNG parliament to ratify or reject in June 2024. Marape was reluctant to let Bougainville go. Instead, PNG defence forces could be banned from entering the province, he suggested. The conciliatory governor and MP for the PNG East Sepik province, Allan Bird, said proper funding could help a "way forward". When I'd met with him in 2019, ahead of the referendum, he'd said ratification should be based on the voting outcome.

The three MPs from Bougainville were adamant. "We have decided," said one of them, Peter Tsiamalili. "Release us. We were able to survive on our own for ten years. No money will solve anything." Another, Francesca Semoso, shed tears as she spoke. Papua New Guinea had committed "an unforgiveable sin" by sending its soldiers to kill. "The way to say sorry is to give Bougainville independence. You don't feel what we feel every day." Bougainville had lost more than 25,000 people as a result of the conflict, she said; it was second only to the Second World War in casualties for the country. "How do you expect me to feel? I have not recovered any of my grandchildren. I don't even know where they are." The debate was suspended, and as of this book going to press the ratification had still not been put to a vote. The PNG and Bougainville governments enlisted a former New Zealand governor-general and defence chief who had led peacekeepers after the 1997 ceasefire, Sir Jerry Mateparae, as a "moderator" to help bring about an agreed settlement.

For Canberra, the question is excruciating. Before the vote, the easy diplomatic line had been to express support for a "peaceful resolution" of the Bougainville conflict. Senior officials had spent their careers patching up fraying states in the region. "Will we actually come out and say that we think Bougainville should be independent?" asks James Batley, who as a diplomat was involved in the island's peace process and later the Solomon Islands regional mission.

No other governments in the region have been barracking for Bougainville's secession, either. The issue has been studiously avoided in the Pacific

Islands Forum and the Melanesian Spearhead Group. Honiara was particularly sensitive. "Solomons leaders are terrified about what could happen in Bougainville," said Batley. "Partly because of [the possibility of] violence breaking out again and how it could spill over, and partly because it poses an existential question about the Solomons' future."

Yet Canberra would risk deepening existing distrust from Bougainvilleans if it were seen to be holding things back. Although Australia perceives itself as a benevolent power, its record in Bougainville is not so benign. "It was Bougainville Copper Ltd, which is an Australian company, which dictated the war in Bougainville and subsequently supported it in terms of finance [for the] military," Sam Kauona told me. "It was like an Australian proxy war in Bougainville."

Kauona, for one, saw the island forging ahead with independence regardless of what Port Moresby does, and building ties with its neighbours – including reconciling with Australia. "We will go ahead from our position of victory," he told me. "Papua New Guinea would be making a big mistake if some advisors tell them not to ratify. Their country will go down, their country will collapse."

As part of a pre-referendum clean-up, a little over a hundred firearms were surrendered. It can be presumed that many more have been stashed away, along with buried US and Japanese arms. Attempting to extend PNG rule by force could lead to another war, not one that would be relished by the PNG Defence Force. "We defeated them, humiliated them," Kauona said. "But we don't talk about it and rub it in."

Batley wondered if he was "thinking like a white man" in seeing the referendum outcome as a point of no return; perhaps that underestimated the Melanesians' capacity to keep talking. But he also thought it a mistake to assume national boundaries in the southwest Pacific are fixed: "Why should we assume that the independence settlement is permanent?"

Bougainville was an unprecedented challenge. "It's just a situation that we cannot ultimately control and shape," Batley said. Applying the tacit version of the Monroe Doctrine that Australia has adopted towards Melanesia could well mean supporting a new and currently cashless nation of

300,000 people. "It would cost us an absolute fortune," Batley said. "RAMSI was near enough to $3 billion over fourteen years. It would be easily of the same magnitude."

The costs of Australia's colonial and attempted nation-building ventures in the southwest Pacific were only just starting to come due.

9

PAPUA NEW GUINEA

The Island Pearls

MY VISA RAN OUT BEFORE I could make the only sea connection for the next stage of my journey through Melanesia: aboard the MV *Chebu*, a stubby European-style ferry part owned by Bougainville's autonomous government that ran between Buka, Rabaul, Kimbe and Lae. By the time I got back to Papua New Guinea more than two years later, the *Chebu* had been withdrawn from service, coronavirus travel restrictions having made it uneconomical. So I flew to Rabaul to pick up the track.

From the Kokopo airport, you drive into Rabaul between warehouses and boatyards, Chinese-owned trading stores and clusters of brightly dressed people, mostly women, waiting for minibuses outside a covered market. Along an improbably grand avenue – two lanes in each direction, divided by a tree-studded median strip – we turned into the Rabaul Hotel.

I'd stayed here more than fifteen years earlier, and nothing much had changed. A central building with a lobby decorated with photographs of old Rabaul; a Chinese-style dining room; a largely deserted bar; a conference room; and, across a grassy central square, two-storey wings of guest rooms. A shed housed a diesel generator, which sprang to use whenever the local grid was down, and nearby a concrete staircase led underground. When I later found that its iron grille was unlocked, I went down to find a rusted anti-aircraft cannon and steps leading further underground. During the Japanese occupation of 1942–45, the hotel's original buildings had been taken over, and this had been the bomb shelter.

Susie Alexander, whose Australian parents had bought the hotel after the war ended, was still in charge. On my first visit, she'd organised a meeting with some senior men from Tolai villages around Rabaul, and I'd been impressed by their willingness to learn from the wider world and yet uphold their own culture.

Numbering about 200,000 people, the Tolai are one of Papua New Guinea's largest language groups, surpassed in numbers only by the Engans in the New Guinea highlands. Some centuries back, they migrated across from New Ireland, the long, skinny island to the northeast, and occupied the gently undulating, highly fertile Gazelle Peninsula as well as the Duke of York Islands, displacing the first settlers, the easternmost Papuans now known as the Bainings, to mountains further south in New Britain.

Although New Britain had been added to European charts as early as 1699 by William Dampier, and other navigators sailed around it later, it was not until the 1870s that Europeans began close contact with the islanders. German traders arrived in 1872 and set up stations in the Duke of York Islands, as did the first missionary, Dr George Brown, a Methodist, in 1875. The four Fijian catechists of his advance party were killed and eaten by the Tolai. Brown organised a punitive expedition in response.

Fantasies about a life of bounty under a tropical sun, combined with utter ignorance of local conditions, led to the next European incursion. In France, Charles Bonaventure du Breil, Marquis de Rays, had returned from failed ventures in the American West, Senegal, Madagascar and Indochina, and needed money. Then he read of a French sea captain's visit to a bay at the southern end of New Ireland, described as a paradise. The marquis took out an advertisement in a Paris newspaper, offering land at low prices in the "free colony of Port Breton", which would be part of a realm called La Nouvelle France. Within two years he had 3000 volunteer settlers who between them had subscribed a half million francs. He bought a three-masted ship, the *Chandernagore*, for the first voyage out, but French authorities were dubious about its seaworthiness and he had to embark his passengers at a Dutch port.

Finally arriving in 1880, the settlers found Port Breton to be hemmed in by steep, jungle-clad hills, with only a narrow strip of flat land, and perpetually doused by heavy rain. Three more shiploads of would-be settlers set sail from European ports, the last in 1881, even as survivors of earlier groups, ravaged by malaria and malnutrition, were arriving in the French penal colony of New Caledonia. When their ship was again declared unseaworthy, they were stranded in Nouméa until the premier of New South Wales, Sir Henry Parkes, sent a rescue vessel. Most settled in Australia, including a group of Italians who formed a small colony within a colony on the Richmond River.

Another of the Marquis de Rays' vessels, a small steamship called the *Génil*, added an extra touch of infamy to his project. On an island called Mioko, in the Duke of York group, a German naturalist was killed during an argument with islanders. German traders organised a plan for collective punishment. They landed on one side of Mioko and drove its people towards the opposite coast, where the Mioko people expected to be able to escape in their canoes. There they were met by the *Génil*, its crew shooting them with a Gatling gun (an early type of machine gun).

The marquis was convicted for fraud in France and spent six years in jail. His victims were Europeans desperate for a new life. If anyone thought of punishing the *Génil*'s captain for the massacre of the Mioko men, women and children, it would have been too late, as he died soon afterwards in Manila.

There were many more punitive expeditions to come across Melanesia, and the Tolai were soon to get an exacting new master. Keen to capture more of the value from the copra so eagerly sought by European soap manufacturers, in 1883 a German acquired land by barter for the first expatriate coconut plantation. The next year, Germany declared a protectorate over much of the north coast of the island of New Guinea to the east of the Dutch domain, to be known as Kaiser-Wilhelmsland. In 1885, another protectorate was declared over the islands to the northeast of New Guinea, including New Britain – renamed Neu-Pommern (New Pomerania). At first, the imperially chartered New Guinea Company ran the string of settlements, until a government administration took over in 1889. From the treaty port now known as Qingdao in eastern China, the German East Asiatic Fleet of heavy and light cruisers enforced the Kaiser's control over this new domain.

The Tolai were tricked by early planters, who acquired some 40 per cent of the Gazelle Peninsula in little-understood barters with local men for axes, guns and tobacco – transactions recognised by the German authorities but meaningless under customary matrilineal ownership. However, the Tolai quickly adapted and took advantage of the new regime. First, they traded produce and land for manufactured tools and goods. Then, as German plantations opened, rather than supplying labour, the Tolai traded the food they grew to feed workers imported from further afield, including Bougainville and the Solomons.

They already had a highly developed semi-cash economy, in the form of shell money or *tambu* – the strings of tiny cowrie-like shells fetched, at some risk, from Nakanai, a bay held by another people some 200 miles down New Britain Island. The Tolai were not unique in using shells as currency, but they had perhaps the most highly developed system. Tolai farmers specialised in particular crops and sold them for shell money to buy other things they needed. They had no central authority, just scattered matrilineal groups that occasionally came into conflict. But a "peace of the market" governed their traditional economy. Goods, even human flesh, were valued in strings of shell money. Families saved in shell money and vested their savings in the storehouses of local big men, who in turn became bankers, lending shell money for a set premium on repayment, effectively a form of interest. Some of these big men combined both wealth and traditional elder status and became government authorities, organising secret men's societies known as *duk-duk* that sent out enforcers dressed as *tubuan* (spirits) to collect fines for misbehaviour. Banking scandals happened, usually on the death of a big man when gaps in his assets were revealed. This "primitive capitalism" had its limits. Rather than investing in larger-scale productive assets, the Tolai saved shell money chiefly to pay for their own funeral rites, to ensure a comfortable afterlife rather than the grim wasteland that awaited those not seen out of this world properly. Consumption, beyond daily necessities, was low.

But it meant the Tolai were familiar with the concepts of currency, saving and interest. And initially the Germans were happy to accept payment of taxes in shell money, as they could pay Tolai workers in that currency. As the economy of German New Guinea developed, however, they began to insist on cash. The Tolai then started accumulating Deutschemarks for certain things, while saving their *tambu* for traditional rituals such as funerals and weddings.[1]

By the time war broke out in distant Europe in 1914, Rabaul was the capital of a network of thriving, firmly disciplined settlements across the north coast of New Guinea through the Bismarck Archipelago, down to Buka and Bougainville. A school opened in Rabaul in 1906 for bright young Tolai, who were employed as office auxiliaries and medical orderlies. A wireless station linked Rabaul to other German possessions across the western Pacific and to the base of the East Asiatic Fleet in China. The town itself had been laid out in a grand pattern of tree-lined avenues, with a fine mansion for the governor.

Within two days of war being declared on 4 August 1914, Britain's war office asked Australia and New Zealand to take control of German possessions in the Pacific, with priority given to shutting down the German wireless stations. An expeditionary force set sail from Sydney thirteen days later. Backed by cruisers, destroyers and a submarine of the Royal Australian Navy – a fleet only delivered from Britain in 1911 – soldiers and sailors landed at Kokopo on 11 September and advanced towards the wireless station. This and other positions were taken with the loss of six Australian lives, the first Australian battle casualties of the First World War, while the Australian submarine disappeared with the loss of all its crew, its wreckage only discovered more than a century later. One German was killed, along with some thirty native policemen.

The Australians hoisted the flag – British, of course – in Rabaul on 13 September and issued a proclamation in English and a rough Pidjin: *New feller master, he strong feller too much*. The German acting governor emerged from the jungle on 17 September and signed a conditional surrender of all the German colonies. The Australians went on to occupy other settlements, such as Madang, later in September. Those Germans allowed to stay on, under parole, were kept in their place by public canings for infractions of the military order.[2]

London had stipulated that the German possessions were to be occupied, not annexed, so throughout the war the New Guinea settlements were run by the Australian military, with German companies and plantations continuing to operate. The Versailles Treaty of 1919 eventually gave the victors their spoils, conditionally in the form of League of Nations mandates, with German New Guinea going to Australia.

And what a prize it was – a string of largely undamaged ports and towns, thriving plantations and Rabaul itself, dubbed "the pearl of the Pacific". A new Australian governor moved into the German residence on Numanala Hill in Rabaul. An Expropriation Board confiscated all German property and assets, passing them out to Australian firms, with established trading houses Burns Philp and W.R. Carpenter building on their dominance elsewhere in the Pacific. The Commonwealth Bank of Australia had opened a branch in Rabaul in 1916 to serve the military administration. It was now joined by other Australian commercial banks.

A scheme to divide up German plantations and parcel them out to Australian war veterans became mired in scandal. W.R. Carpenter signed up returned diggers as dummy settlers to take initial ownership of German plantation land, on the understanding they would be bought out at a modest profit so the land parcels could be amalgamated back into large estates. (Among the willing dummies in this scheme was Stan Howard, father of the Australian prime minister John Howard, who gained and on-sold a choice bit of plantation land on Kar Kar Island, near Madang.)[3]

Two threads of expatriate influence continued from the earlier regime. German missionaries from the Catholic Church's Sacred Heart Society had come to the region as part of the Marquis de Rays expedition and stayed on, joined by the Methodists and, in 1929, the Seventh-day Adventists. The missions continued to provide all primary education and in the 1930s had opened high schools and technical colleges, all using the Tolai language for teaching.

Chinese small businessmen had begun arriving from their turbulent homeland late in the nineteenth century, and continued to arrive. They opened trading stores, restaurants and hotels. Following an older brother, Chin Pak arrived about 1920 aged twenty-two or so, from Taishan in Guangdong, via Macau and Hong Kong. He started out as a tailor, then got invited over to New Ireland to help another Chinese man clear a plantation. Before long he was starting his own plantation and building a small trading ship.

The Chinese slotted in between the whites at the top and islanders below, living separately and socialising in their own clubs and venues such as the Kuomintang Hall but mixing with both of the other groups in everyday business. However, on assuming the League of Nations mandate, the Australians applied a local version of the White Australia policy – ludicrously, in a territory populated mostly by Melanesians – and restricted the entry of Asians from 1921, meaning Chinese pioneers such as Chin Pak found their matrimonial choices limited to candidates already in New Guinea. He married a New Ireland woman, Miriam Tinkoria, with whom he went on to have seven children. The sixth, Julius Chan (using a Cantonese form of the family name), born in August 1939, would later become prime minister of an independent Papua New Guinea.

Rabaul, with its pleasant climate, well laid-out streets and utilities, peaceful ambiance and links by Burns Philp steamer to Australia and Manila, became a base for exploration and development of the New Guinea main island and the other Pacific Islands, especially when gold was discovered in the Wau Valley, inland from Salamaua, on the eastern end of the main New Guinea island.

A colourful, if not reliably accurate, account of this period can be found in the autobiography of Errol Flynn. Aged seventeen, Flynn fled scandal in Sydney in 1927 to Rabaul, where he was taken on as a probationary cadet officer, with the task of advising villagers on the use of soap, latrines and other sanitation measures. After an entanglement with the wife of an Australian official, which ended with Flynn beating up the husband, Flynn was given a "second chance" and ordered to accompany a patrol officer, named in Flynn's memoir as Taylor, and ten native police by schooner to Madang, on a punitive expedition to catch the killers of some expatriate gold prospectors. They found the bloated bodies of the prospectors, but nearby villages were deserted. Other police parties brought in half a dozen captives to Madang. According to Flynn, Taylor had gallows built, handed out rice and calico to some 2000 local people attending and hanged the captives, to the great amusement of the unrelated crowd.

On returning to Rabaul, Flynn found he had been sacked anyway, and hung out at a Chinese-run hotel, Ah Sim's. There he met a man who had acquired a German plantation on New Ireland, and Flynn found himself appointed its manager, in charge of 120 indentured labourers drawn from two tribes of traditional enemies. With no knowledge of coconut growing, he found his daily routine was to instruct his native foreman: "Carry on, Boss Boy."

Further adventures included buying a share in a trading schooner, a spell in jail for punching a Chinese man who failed to show respect – the Chinese were supposed to step aside, tip their hats and say *gude masta* (good day, sir) on passing a white man – and joining a prospecting trek inland from Salamaua into the new Edie Creek goldfield. Almost daily, coastal men were dying of pneumonia on the arduous haul across 8000-foot mountain ridges. A capsize on the Sepik, a clash with tribesmen that almost got him convicted of murder, a tobacco farm near Port Moresby and numerous romantic encounters followed, until Flynn was spotted to play Fletcher Christian in the first film about the *Bounty* mutiny. Some years later, when Flynn was a famous Hollywood star, a Rabaul dentist and other local creditors wrote to ask if he was now in a position to settle his outstanding bills. Flynn posted back a signed photograph of himself, with a note that this would be valuable enough to cover the debts.[4]

A more trustworthy memoir comes from Caroline Mytinger, who noted that the more respectable expatriates – government officers, lawyers, doctors, and bank, shipping and trading managers – went to the Rabaul Hotel. The "riffraff" still went to Ah Chee's in Chinatown, which is no doubt the "Ah Sim's" recalled by Flynn. She and her companion Margaret Warner took rooms at Ah Chee's that had no doors, only curtains, while their servants slept on the balcony floor outside. On Saturday nights there was always a poker game, noisy with the clink of bottles, music from wind-up gramophones, shouts of "Boy!" and raucous laughter, the air heavy with beer fumes and cigarette smoke.

Mytinger recounted the scandals among the expats. When a planter was poisoned, his wife and the overseer were tried for his murder. They were acquitted, but the overseer suicided. Then the woman's daughter eloped with a married man, whose wife subsequently suicided. An expat's unmarried daughter, back from school in Australia, got pregnant, and another did something even more unthinkable by getting pregnant to an islander, who narrowly avoided lynching.

The Tolai and other islanders mostly appear in the background of these expat tales, although they were very much part of urban and plantation life, working as stevedores, porters, drivers, police and junior functionaries. The women came into Rabaul to sell produce, putting on colourful loose blouses as bare breasts were banned in town. By 1929, the islanders had had enough of their low wages and some 3200 walked off their jobs, including most of the local policemen, assembling at Catholic and Methodist mission stations. Australian officials and other expats had had no inkling of the strike before it happened. It petered out with little achieved, but indignant expats railed against the leniency of the administration. A board of inquiry dismissed the suggestion that wages were too low and recommended moving native labour quarters further out of town and imposing a night-time curfew.

By then, the Tolai had moved up the rungs of capitalism. They started accumulating shillings, although trading them for more easily portable bank notes had its obstacles – Chinese traders demanded 22 shillings for a £1 note, rather than the official twenty. Kin groups pooled their savings to buy productive assets. As the economic anthropologist Scarlett Epstein noted, at first contact with Europeans, the Tolai still used stone axes, knives made of bamboo, and pointed sticks. Only fifty years later they owned trucks, copra driers and cocoa fermenters. There was still some ambiguity about ownership of these assets, but young men started in 1934 to discuss whether matrilineage really suited these modern things.

This phase of Rabaul came to a crashing finale. After a night of earthquake tremors on 29 May 1937, the townspeople noticed the sea boiling around a low island called Vulcan that had a shallow water-filled crater. Shoals of dead fish floated in the bay. Mid-afternoon, Vulcan exploded with a roar, sending a column of fumes, ash and rock thousands of metres into the air. Whites, Chinese and local people ran for higher ground around the governor's residence, fearing a tsunami. On 30 May, Matupit also erupted violently, adding to the deluge of volcanic ash and rocks over the town. That night came lightning and thunder, then a rainstorm that washed avalanches of ash into the town. The sea was covered with floating pumice. Townspeople trekked over to the western coast, where an American freighter began ferrying them to safety at Kokopo. Rabaul lay in ruins, its famous trees stripped of leaves, buildings collapsed under the weight of ash, and 507 people killed.

The headquarters of the trust territory of New Guinea moved to Lae, the port on the mainland. Rabaul and the Gazelle Peninsula had not quite five years before the next catastrophe.

In 1941, with the Japanese threat building, Australia sent 1400 soldiers to defend Rabaul and its environs. After the attack on Pearl Harbor, this "Lark Force" gained an air wing of ten Wirraway trainers and four Hudson bombers. Ships arrived to evacuate white women and children, but not Chinese or mixed-race dependants.

Lark Force was consciously sacrificed by the Australian command in the hope it would delay the Japanese advance southwards. It hardly did. Air raids began early in January, with the Wirraways no match for Japanese aircraft – even lumbering reconnaissance flying boats could out-speed them. On 20 January 1942 a fleet of four aircraft carriers plus cruisers and transports arrived just to the north. Between 21 and 23 January, landings seized Rabaul and the nearby coast.

The Lark Force commander gave the order "Every man for himself"; his soldiers scattered in small groups to the east and south in New Britain. About 600 of them were eventually taken off the coast by small ships. Scores died of dysentery and malaria in the jungles. Some 150 surrendered at the

Tol Plantation and were shot or bayoneted; one, feigning death, escaped and revealed the atrocity. Mid that year, the Japanese embarked 1054 Australian and other prisoners on the cargo ship *Montevideo Maru* to labour camps in Japan. An American submarine torpedoed the ship; it went down with all the prisoners locked in its holds.

In the space of twenty-eight years, the Tolai had seen two lots of white masters vanquished and humiliated in a matter of days. They and other islanders made themselves scarce, and the Japanese initially left them alone. Youngsters cadged cigarettes from the soldiers by saying "Japan Boy number one, Australia Boy number ten."

The invading soldiers spread themselves out in abandoned houses and other buildings and looted the Burns Philp stores of food and drink. Hundreds of Korean, Okinawan and Taiwanese women had travelled with the invasion force, and were installed as "comfort women" in official brothels – soldiers were given a "thirty-minute ticket" every fortnight to avail themselves of this facility. It spared the island's women from sexual slavery and, largely, from rape.[5]

Japan's front line soon moved further south to the Solomon Islands, so Rabaul was an easy berth in 1942. As the Japanese novelist Morio Kita wrote:

> The troops at the front line [on Guadalcanal] were living through hell, but here the officers enjoyed a style of life suitable to a large rear-guard base, drinking beer in huts where the lampshades were made tastefully out of palm leaves, while for the lower ranks there were even women, mostly brought in from Korea and Okinawa. They formed long queues outside a wretched, bleak building, the "rest and recreation centre" where these women were available, like people waiting to use a public toilet.[6]

After the tide of war turned, the occupation became harsher. Powerful American aircraft were bombing freely. The Japanese conscripted local men to dig tunnels into the cliffs around Blanche Bay and sent thousands to work as carriers. Villagers had to grow rice and other food for the army;

any objections were met with instant beheading. The Kempeitai (military police) ranged the island looking for Australian Coastwatchers, and later Australian commando units landed by small ships. Julius Chan's family and other Chinese were moved into internment settlements.

Cut off from replenishment, the 89,000 strong Japanese garrison focused on growing food, while their officers struggled to maintain the warrior code. Later famous as a *manga* artist, Shigeru Mizuki was among them. He suffered from malaria and lost an arm from a bomb blast but was tempted to stay on when the war ended. In 1973 he drew a searing sequence of *manga* strips about Rabaul, showing soldiers being blasted and strafed by US planes and brutalised by their own officers to prepare them for suicide attacks.[7]

In September 1945, Australian forces came back, and it was the turn of the Japanese to be humiliated. They were put to work clearing up rubble and rehabilitating gardens and plantations, jeered at by islanders who now called out "Australia Boy number one, Japan Boy number ten". Military authority transferred to the returning civil administration. Rabaul was no longer the capital of New Guinea. The former League of Nations mandate was replaced by a UN trusteeship, merging Papua and New Guinea into a single territory, and Australia was charged with developing it towards self-government and self-determination. Port Moresby became the capital, and Rabaul district headquarters for East New Britain.

Although greatly damaged by bombing, the Gazelle Peninsula and New Ireland were the most accessible for government services, with a road network putting most villages in relatively easy reach. It was still a "dual economy", with whites and Chinese running most of the modern sector activity. But the Tolai were thriving too. Visiting in 1951, the British anthropologist Raymond Firth observed a vigorous economy, with markets operating in three currencies: shell, shillings and tobacco. Scarlett Epstein, doing her fieldwork in 1959–60, saw Tolai operating transport and large-scale cocoa fermentaries. Kin group ownership meant many were used to the idea of holding small equity in large enterprises, and some elders had put their shillings into Australian shares and investment trusts.

A racial hierarchy persisted, as Harry West, who arrived in Rabaul as a district commissioner in late 1959, recalled:

> At the time there was a 9 o'clock curfew. No New Guinea national could be at large inside the town boundary between 9 pm and 6 am unless holding a "pass" from an employer. Everything was divided on a racial basis. Separate schools, hospitals, clubs and cemeteries for whites, blacks, Chinese and mixed-race. Even separate spaces in churches. The swimming pool was for white only. Burns Philp and Colyer Watson would only serve "natives" if they had a "pass" from "master".[8]

Schools had reopened, still run by missions, but with English on the curriculum. Some of the more prosperous Chinese began sending their sons and daughters to schools in Australia, mostly in the Catholic system. Julius Chan went from the Sacred Heart school in Rabaul to Marist College Ashgrove in Brisbane, graduating to the University of Queensland where he studied agricultural science until a motorbike accident forced his return to Papua New Guinea, where he took a job as a trainee government auditor in Port Moresby.

Those coming up from islander communities, such as John Kaputin among the Tolai and John Momis down in Bougainville, often found their path to higher education through Catholic seminaries, later dropping their priestly vocation in favour of politics.

One of the Tolai men I'd met in 2006, Kolis Babate, had gone down to Bougainville as a young man in the 1970s and been trained as a boilermaker and welder by the copper mining company. He spoke warmly of his mentoring by its Australian, New Zealand, British and Yugoslav tradesmen. He was back in the village now, one of its elders, and running his own workshop. The most precious currency in the village was still shell money, saved by families for marriages and funeral rites.

Not surprisingly, in retrospect, the first organised stirrings against Australian rule began among the Tolai, in response to plans for multiracial councils. "With more than 100 years of white domination, it was evident that they had gained little and lost a lot," recalled Harry West, who remained district commissioner through the 1960s.

> Many of them were landless through the virtual stealing of vast areas of land by the Germans, that had not been rectified, and pressures were rising through the demands of cash cropping as well as subsistence farming and rapid population growth, related to excellent medical services. Having lost their land, economically they saw the central government's move towards multi-racial councils as strangling them politically and socially.

The movement they formed, known as the Mataungans, held mass meetings and opposed the district council elections. Clashes broke out in December 1969, with jail sentences for those who assaulted council supporters. The uprising became a political issue in Australia too. Leftists marched in Sydney with "Free the Tolai 16" placards. The federal opposition leader, Gough Whitlam, visited Rabaul in January 1970 and expressed sympathy for the Mataungan aims and accused the conservative Coalition government of dragging its feet on preparing Papua New Guinea for independence.

John Gorton, the prime minister, came to address the Tolai in July that year. A thousand police stood by in Rabaul, a third of the entire PNG police force. A navy patrol boat was ready to evacuate Gorton if necessary. He stepped off the plane with a pistol in his pocket, given to him by an official as a precaution. Some 10,000 Mataungan supporters had gathered at the airport, whipped up by their leaders. Undercover police cut the wires to their loudspeakers, which deflated the tense atmosphere. Gorton, standing on a set of aeroplane boarding stairs, invited Mataungan leaders Kaputin and Oscar Tammur to stand alongside him, which also helped. Gorton got out of the airport safely and was driven to Queen Elizabeth Park, where he addressed a large crowd of council supporters.

The police reinforcements stayed on after he left, and later in July, Gorton's cabinet authorised the administrator of Papua New Guinea to deploy the Pacific Islands Regiment, the two-battalion army, in support of the police if necessary. It would have been a disastrous move, wrote military historian Robert O'Neill, given the soldiers had no riot-control training and would almost certainly have used greater force than the police.

Fortunately, the step was not taken, not even a year later, when West's successor as district commissioner, Jack Emanuel, went out to a plantation the Mataungans had occupied and was stabbed to death with a rusty Japanese bayonet while trying to negotiate.

But soon afterwards the Mataungan grievance was subsumed by quickening political developments in the whole territory. Three of their leaders were elected to the new House of Assembly in Port Moresby in 1972 and joined Michael Somare's new government, which was given control of most domestic affairs. Kaputin and others went on to play important roles in national politics before and after independence in September 1975.

The Tolai remained somewhat ambivalent about their place in Papua New Guinea. The uprising in Bougainville resonated. In 2006, Kolis Babate was expecting the island to break away at some point. "I think the country would be better broken up," he told me. "People are so different, between the islands."

In this part of New Britain, there is a feeling that previous exploitative masters had just been replaced by another one. I couldn't find Kolis Babate, the man who had gained his trade skills working for Bougainville Copper, on my most recent visit, but Albert Konie expressed similar sentiments. Just turned fifty-one, he was born in the Gazelle Peninsula to parents who had migrated from Maprik in East Sepik Province.

The referendum in Bougainville, with its decisive result, had been held two years before we spoke, and I asked him his feelings about that. "People in Bougainville are more advanced in their thinking," Konie said. "They are setting a pathway for us as indigenous people, that we cannot be manipulated by outsiders. What we have on the land belongs to us. We need to be economically re-empowered. This is our land, our blood lines, everything belongs to us. Bougainville is setting a pathway for all of Papua New Guinea. They just see and embrace the changes. We cannot just sit down."

"Before independence we had only one copper mine, Bougainville Copper Ltd," Konie went on. "Now we have a lot of copper and gold mines, but our people are not economically empowered. Mothers are dying in the rural hospitals, there are no proper roads, hospitals. Forty years of independence! Papua New Guinea is not advancing – it's going down. Now we have the influence of the Chinese, invading our country. We are selling our birthrights to the red army, the red ants. And we have signed an agreement with ExxonMobil for our oil. Every shipment going out is 800 million kina. We are not seeing the impact of that 800 million. Who is benefitting? If we want to secure our land, our future, we must be economically empowered … Why are kids wearing torn trousers? Why are some of the kids not having breakfast? I don't think we are independent. We are like puppets. The government going and signing agreements with other countries: we are signing our death warrants. We are dying. Mothers are dying. People are using all our resources: the cocoa beans, the coffee beans, the coconuts. Then there is palm oil – the economy is okay, but the land is barren forever. We are sweating our guts [out], the product is going out. The product coming back to us, we pay much more money [for it]. It's not working for us. For me, I support Bougainville gaining independence. They are setting the pathway for all of us. They are fighting for their rights on the land."

Indeed, land alienation had not ended with colonial rule. In 1964, the World Bank noted vast potential for a sustainable timber industry. Across the islands and the mainland north coast, logging stepped up. Domestic construction used some of the lesser grades of timber, but the best went overseas as logs. As well as a vast swathe of jungle inland from Vanimo in the West Sepik, three areas in New Britain became centres for logging. The widest swathes were in West New Britain, on the flat lands of the coast around its main town, Kimbe. Another was at Open Bay, at the neck of the Gazelle Peninsula.

As soon as the tall timber disappeared, the Australian administration backed the clearing of the land for palm oil plantations. Nearly half the land was to be reserved for smallholders, but the rest would be turned over to expatriate "nucleus estates" that would provide a reliable supply to nearby factories. Increasingly, planting oil palm has become a second-stage commercial activity for loggers after they have reaped a fortune from cutting ancient hardwood trees and shipping them off to ports in eastern China, where they are turned into prestige flooring for homes in the rich world.

Among these companies is the Rimbunan Hijau group, founded in 1975 by a reclusive businessman named Tiong Hiew King and headquartered in the Sarawak River town of Sibu, in Malaysia. After the clearing of Sarawak's forests became an issue of national and international concern, it registered in Papua New Guinea and was soon buying up forestry leases from smaller players.

Logging quickly became a contentious industry. A decade after independence, the government appointed a judicial commission of inquiry. The commissioner, Justice T.E. "Tos" Barnett, found widespread corruption and mismanagement in his final report in 1989. Foreign logging companies were "roaming the countryside with the self-assurance of robber barons; bribing politicians and leaders, creating social disharmony and ignoring laws and policy in order to gain access to, rip out, and export ... valuable timber".

But the lessons of the Barnett Report were soon forgotten, and Michael Somare's government stepped up the issuing of forestry leases from 2002. By the time Peter O'Neill forced Somare out of power in 2011, some 52,000 square kilometres, or 11 per cent of Papua New Guinea's land area, had been turned over to foreign and national enterprises, in most cases for the maximum ninety-nine years, with the state forestry authority rubber-stamping licences to clear the rainforests and export the timber.

On coming to office, O'Neill set up another commission of inquiry, focused on the controversial "special leases". In the majority of cases for which findings were published, the commission found that leaseholders broke the law, usually by disregarding the rights and involvement of traditional landowning communities, after obtaining their initial consent through fraud. No findings were published for any of the leases reviewed in East New Britain Province.[9]

Rimbunan Hijau secured leases over three land tracts in the Pomio area, in the far southwest corner of the province, in 2010, and a subsidiary gained licences to clear the forest in them the following year. By 2017, the group had cleared about 210 square kilometres of rainforest and exported

US$122 million worth of timber, according to estimates by the activist group Global Witness, based on satellite imagery and other metrics. Planting of oil palm and construction of a mill followed, in what is called the Sigete/Mukus Integrated Rural Development Project. Rimbunan Hijau says all is well, with some 4000 local people "directly employed" and "millions" of dollars in royalties going to local communities, who also benefited from a new network of roads and airstrips.

A counter-narrative, taken up by the Catholic bishopric in Rabaul, is put by a women's movement in Pomio: that companies secured agreement to their leases by bribing local men – men who under matrilineal *kastom* had no right to broker land. Loss of access to foraging sites in the rainforest has had a drastic effect on village food supplies, while the presence of outside workers has put women at greater risk when foraging away from their homes.[10]

Having made his point about Somare's tolerance of an abused system, O'Neill was not about to interfere with a lucrative agribusiness. By this time, Rimbunan Hijau had become a sprawling presence in Papua New Guinea, owning *The National* – one of the two daily newspapers – and building the Vision City shopping mall and a plush new Port Moresby hotel, the Stanley, in time for the 2018 Asia Pacific Leaders Summit in the capital.

In June 2016, two immigration officers flew from Port Moresby to Rabaul and served a deportation notice on Doug Tennent, a New Zealander who had been a lecturer in law at the University of Papua New Guinea and had then become a lay missionary with the Rabaul diocese, specifically trying to negotiate on behalf of the Pomio people for a more equitable agreement with Rimbunan Hijau. He was accused of violating the terms of his visa by "engaging in sensitive landowner issues in the East New Britain Province".

After strenuous support from his bishop, Francesco Panfilo, who said that all of Tennent's activity had been done on the bishop's behalf and under his instruction, Tennent returned in August 2017, but he was warned "not to get involved in activist activities which creates tension amongst land owners".

The landowner issues did not go away. They also dogged the other big palm oil presence in the province, the East New Britain Resources Group, controlled by another Malaysian, Tan Eng Kwee. It entered the province about the same time as Rimbunan Hijau in 2010, gaining leases and sites for palm oil mills. This company attracted similar local resistance and government support, including punitive police raids when locals cut down palm plants.

According to Global Witness, one of its investigators posed as a plantation investor at a meeting in a Kokopo restaurant with executives of a group subsidiary, Tzen Niugini, seeking advice on how to deal with troublesome community resistance to a plantation in Thailand. The executives admitted giving favours to government officials to get approval, such as payment of school fees or "tokens" like a new Toyota LandCruiser. There were gifts to the forestry minister, to his departmental secretary, to members of the National Forestry Board. "Roughly, sometimes the minister needs about a hundred thousand, fifty thousand [kina]," one of the executives is reported to have said.[11]

In response to the crescendo of reports about malpractice, the Hershey Company, the American confectionery giant that is a major user of palm oil, put East New Britain Resources on its "no buy" list in August 2021, followed by Rimbunan Hijau in February 2022.

*

Living next door to an active volcano creates unease. On the island of New Britain, near Rabaul, Tavurvur had erupted again in 1994, massively, after lying dormant for more than half a century. This time, modern vulcanology gave warnings in time for evacuation, and only five people were killed. But the showers of ash piled up, burying the small airfield on the flat land between the port and the volcano. All the houses on this side collapsed under the weight of accumulated ash. Susie Alexander, who had just had her first child, stayed with staff at the Rabaul Hotel as they shovelled ash off its roofs and saved the structures. Today, what was previously a suburb of expat bungalows is scrubland, intersected by a grid of roads dug out of ash at least a metre deep.

There was a minor eruption in 2014, and Tavurvur still rumbles and spits smoke occasionally. On holidays, townsfolk and tourists drive out to a bayside stretch of dark grey ash, intersected by a stream of hot, sulphur-laden water, to look across to its peak, with vendors selling cold drinks and souvenir artefacts.

There are still fragments of old times. One such is the Rabaul Yacht Club. Susie had urged me to be in town for a Friday night. "You'll meet everyone and find out everything you need to know," she said. The club is on the waterfront at one end of the port, a sturdy open-ended barn decorated with a ship's wheel and other nautical paraphernalia. I recalled it from my first visit, when it was patronised by a few expats. Among them had been a man who hitched his horse inside at one end of the clubhouse, told his Doberman dogs to sit, and took himself to the bar. This time, the expats were greatly outnumbered by local men and women. A new fixture was a giant TV screen, on which an Australian rugby league game was playing. Children worked their mobile phones: the club was the only place in Rabaul with free wi-fi.

In the hubbub, stubbies of brown-labelled South Pacific beer kept coming. I met: Julius Chan's brother Michael; the club's commodore; Mate Litric, the Croatian priest at the Catholic church; his Panamanian seminarian, Pablo; a New Zealand couple ferrying a yacht back to Australia for its owner. It was a long night of "just one mores". Amid my blurry recollections the next day, I recalled agreeing to meet with Sean, who was big in road transport on New Britain, and found a beer coaster with his phone number on it.

As part of my Melanesian journey, I wanted to traverse the island by land, at least as far as Kimbe, the West New Britain capital. Sean assured me he had vehicles running the route all the time. The palm oil industry had made extensive inroads in West New Britain, meaning its stock of areca palms had dwindled, displaced by oil palm plantations. Meanwhile the influx of workers for the plantations had increased demand for *buai*, or betel nut, the seed of the areca palm. Cut and chewed with slaked lime, *buai* produces a mild stimulant effect, a mouthful of vivid red spit – and, in the longer term, discoloured teeth and the risk of mouth cancer. Meeting demand for *buai* was keeping Sean's trucking business busy.

A driver called Conrad would be taking the next trip, Sean told me on Saturday. As soon as a load was assured, we would set off. On Sunday I went to mass at Father Litric's church. On Monday morning, I checked out of the hotel to stand by, and on Monday evening I checked back in again. At 8 pm came a phone call. It was Conrad, parked out the front: "Come immediately." I checked out again.

A LandCruiser utility waited in the hotel driveway, and I could make out some shadowy figures sitting in the tray. I threw my bag in next to them and took the front passenger seat beside Conrad. We drove out of Rabaul along a broad road, rendezvoused with an Isuzu truck, and at about midnight diverted to a side track. As the track became steeper, it seemed more like a creek bed than a road. Lurching and brushing aside bushes, our convoy pulled up in a place called Vunapalading. We parked in a compound edged by a house of corrugated iron, a shed, stacks of white polythene sacks, and thick plantations of the elegant areca or betel palm. An extended family stood watching our arrival, under a solar-powered light.

While the crews loaded sixty-seven sacks of *buai*, each weighing about 20 kilograms, into the vehicles, I spoke to the family member who I assumed would be most likely to speak English, a slight young woman. At first I thought she might be still in high school, but Sarah Leo turned out to be a mother of three and a *buai* trader. She climbed into the tray and came with us to Kimbe, with ten bags of *buai* she had acquired for 50 kina each. Her husband stayed behind to mind the children.

At about 1.30 am, we lurched back down the track to the highway. The night was a jolting trundle along a potholed road through the forest. At a broad clearing, under tall trees lit by lamps, we stopped and bought hot drinks from a stall. By daybreak, we were descending into a valley, and at 8 am we rolled into a dazzling stretch of coast with views to distant volcanoes near Kimbe. We stopped for breakfast at a row of food stalls facing the beach. Boiled saveloys seemed to be a popular German legacy, here and elsewhere in Papua New Guinea. With a hardboiled egg and two donuts, it filled the gap.

The travellers in the tray of the LandCruiser now included some passengers transferred from other vehicles at the middle-of-the-night rest stop: a mother and her small child, and a slim young woman, Ruth Wartuam, who turned out to be highly educated and who spoke perfect English. Ruth was working in the law courts in Kokopo while pursuing a law degree at the University of Papua New Guinea. She was also supporting her younger siblings by trading *buai*, as their parents had died. She had recently had tuberculosis, and after six months of successful treatment was working on gaining back her lost weight. It was a humbling story.

Our journey, or the worst of it, seemed for a moment to be over. But in fact it would be another four hours before we even left East New Britain: we did not arrive at the provincial border, the Pandi River, until about 1 pm.

The 100-metre-wide waterway rippled over a bed of stones. The Isuzu truck could not cross, so its cargo was loaded into a flat-bottomed boat. But Conrad drove the LandCruiser into the water, its wheels juddering on the stones. I put my feet up on the dashboard as the cabin flooded. A wave washed over the bonnet when we got to the middle. It seemed likely the motor would conk out any moment, but then the front wheels gripped an incline and we were out on a dry ramp up to the other bank.

We lingered as the crew unloaded the sacks of *buai* from the boat into a stack by the roadside. Ruth and the other women who owned them intended to leave us here and settled down to await a truck promised from Kimbe. Conrad was unwilling to go further while the women were still sitting out in the open by the riverbank, unprotected. He drove the utility a short distance from the river into a sombre stretch of silent dark-green palms, in rows like pillars of some vast temple – a mature oil-palm plantation. We parked at a crossroad where women were selling snacks and drinks. The afternoon wore on. Dump trucks laden with bunches of oil-palm fruit roared up and down a nearby road. The promised truck from Kimbe never came. Finally, a local driver was found who was willing to take the women into Kimbe, but first he had to finish another job. By dusk, we saw him picking up Ruth and the other women and their *buai*, and we took off for Kimbe.

A few hours later, Conrad noticed a knocking sound coming from the left-hand front wheel. On the roadside, he and a crewman jacked up the heavily laden vehicle and removed the wheel. The young crewman then stripped the wheel hub expertly. I never knew wheels had so many parts. The fault was revealed to be a broken bearing. Conrad had a spare, and once it was fitted, the wheel hub rebuilt and the wheel reattached, we resumed our ride. The young mechanic was entirely self-taught through observation, Conrad told me.

On through the night, the LandCruiser whizzed through oil-palm plantations and sleeping villages, crossing bridges with a *bang-bang-bang* of metal deck-plates, like the defiant stamp of the goats crossing the troll's bridge in the Norwegian fairy tale. We got into Kimbe at 3 am, thirty-one hours after setting off from Rabaul.

In the morning, before heading out to Hoskins airfield for my flight to Port Moresby, I took a look around Kimbe. I found Conrad parked outside the market, his cargo unloaded. The women were inside negotiating sales with dealers. Then they would all board the LandCruiser and travel home without resting. Conrad would need to chew a fair bit of *buai* to stay awake.

From Port Moresby, I got a call through to Sarah Leo, who was now back home in Vunapalading. Yes, she had sold her ten bags of *buai* for 250 kina apiece. After paying 100 kina per bag to Conrad for transport, and the 50 kina she had paid for the *buai* in East New Britain, she had made a net profit of 1000 kina. After resting for a day or two, she would start preparing for another trip. I asked what she would do with her earnings. "I want to go to school, to the training centre in Kokopo," she said. "I will pay the school fees myself. To do a six-month course as a crane operator. Then I will be looking for a job."

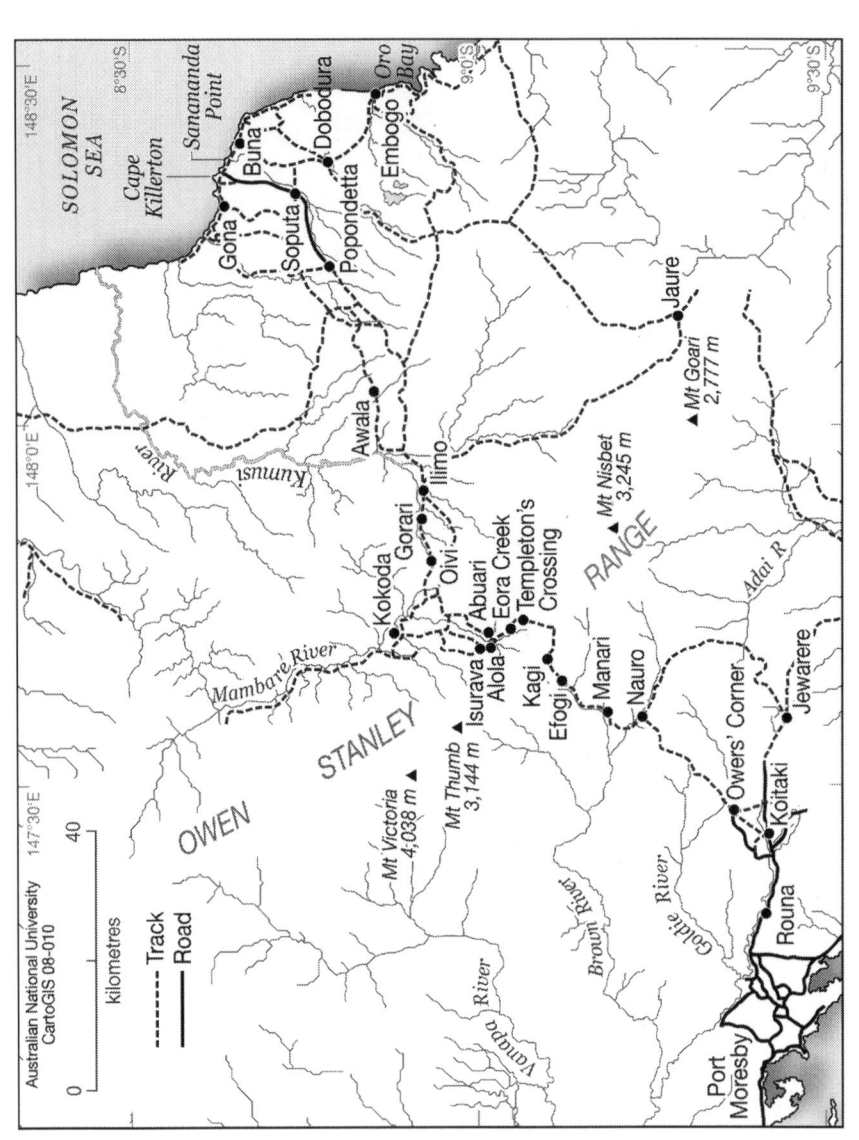

10

PORT MORESBY

A Capital City Unto Itself

ALL ROADS MAY LEAD TO ROME, but hardly any roads lead to Port Moresby. From the east, there is a paved road from Sogeri, only 46 kilometres long. From the west, a road runs nearly 300 kilometres through low-lying coastal country from Kerema, a town of a few thousand people at the head of the Papuan Gulf.

Beyond these places, the road connections peter out into a few muddy tracks, then into jungle and mountains. Few countries have a capital so inaccessible to the majority of its citizens. People with the funds to buy an air ticket may choose to fly, but at times even the air connections stop, when suppliers cannot get the foreign exchange from the central bank to import fuel.

You can walk in, as I once did along the famous Kokoda Track from the north side of the Owen Stanley Range. It is only 96 kilometres long, but it took our group of parents and sons nine days up and down the ridges and valleys, even with fit young porters from the Moresby squatter settlements carrying our backpacks, tents and food supplies. Yet the jungles and mountains were a strangely hospitable temporary home. The long dark-green corridors of the track itself provided shade after the hot, acid-green clearings. Beside the track were trees with pale salmon trunks, trees that soared straight up into the canopy, vines that had become trees themselves and bushes with big purple and red berries like Tibetan rosary beads.

We camped in grass clearings, bathed in delicious fast-flowing streams, watched the Southern Cross wheel round the edge of the blazing sky. We saw Papuan village life close up: houses of roughly sawn bush timber with tin or thatch roofs, sunlight slanting through the cookhouse smoke, cheerful kids, teenage mothers and old folk – the young men were mostly away for cash-paying work. On the track, family groups would pass us – mostly women in faded print dresses and rubber flip flops, hung with string bags full of bedding, food or a baby, bigger kids helping with a small load – effortlessly walking past as we trudged.

The designer hiking gear on just one of us – the $420 Gore-Tex boots, damp-dispersal socks, quick-dry shirt and shorts, fancy waterbags in fancier backpacks – in addition to our antimalarials, insect repellents and anti-inflammatory pills, probably added up to more than the tangible assets of any of the households we passed. At Efogi, one of the bigger villages with a grass airstrip and a health clinic, we met the district nurse, Anne, who described her work attending to minor injuries and administering inoculations. We asked what transport she had to reach the outlying places. She laughed, looking down at her feet. "I have someone to carry the vaccines" she said.

About halfway up the long climb out of the Goldie River Valley, a steep hillside devoid of jungle shade, the unexpectedly gruelling finale to our southwards journey, a butterfly kept coming back to settle on my arm. It was a lustrous thing about 8 centimetres across, with velvety wings of purple and brown, one of the hundreds of wonderful species found in Papua New Guinea. It seemed a blessing and a farewell. Up at the top, at the terminus of the road to Owers' Corner, I looked back. The Owen Stanley Range receded: fold upon fold of deep green mountain, not a sign of human settlement. The first clouds of the afternoon bank-up were still wispy; later they'd be a lowering, inky mass. The mountains and their hidden people were withdrawing into themselves.

It was once, briefly, possible to drive out of Port Moresby through the mountains and reach the island's north. When the Japanese attacked in early 1942, they bombed and strafed the goldfields towns of Wau and Bulolo across the ranges, and Australian army engineers blew up what was left. With air evacuation no longer possible, the remaining 200 civilians set off southwards by foot to an even more remote small mining site called Bulldog – terrain the Australian war correspondent Peter Ryan called "longer, higher, steeper, wetter, colder and rougher" than Kokoda, and inhabited by the fierce Kukukuku tribe. Crossing the watershed, they reached south-flowing rivers and floated down to the Gulf coast on bamboo rafts. They walked east along the beach to a mission station at Yule Island, and from there reached Moresby aboard big Papuan double canoes with "crab-claw" woven-fibre sails. Army engineers then carved out a road, employing hundreds of conscripted Papuan men along the Bulldog Track, just over 3000 metres above sea level at its highest point. Trucks and jeeps ground up this road for two years, supplying the army units harassing the Japanese along the eastern and northern coasts. Then it fell into disuse, and the wilderness took it back.[1]

After the war, when Papua and New Guinea were merged, it was briefly canvassed that the joint capital should be Lae, the base of inter-island shipping and the terminus of a nascent road system into the highlands. But the familiarity of Port Moresby, its dry climate and its orientation south towards Australia saw that idea dissipate.

Since then, the idea has periodically surfaced of reopening a road connection to the highlands and north coast. It makes a lot of economic sense. Instead of transporting produce by road down to Lae and from there by sea, a twelve-day process, the highlands food bowl would be connected by relatively cheap and fast transport to the consumers of Port Moresby, replacing shipments of chilled and frozen foods coming by sea up from Australia and New Zealand. The latest iteration of this idea, initiated in 2019, is a World Bank study of a land route down from Mendi, in the southern highlands, to the Papuan Gulf at Kikori. From Kikori, ferries would take the trucks into Port Moresby. The transit time would be two days.

Perhaps this plan will lapse for lack of political drive too. As well as vegetables and meat, the trans-island highway would bring people. Port Moresby is already a seething, unplanned city of peoples thrown into close proximity and economic competition, and highlander migrants dominate some sectors, such as the minibuses that provide the main form of public transport. Their crews sometimes get into ethnic fights that can shut down the city and have left people dead. Behind the flat areas with their orderly housing, office and stores, migrants crowd into shanty settlements running up small valleys. The original Papuan habitants cling to a few seashore areas. They maintain their own vigilante groups, ready to restrict access and fight off any criminal intruders.

It's not hard to see why you feel safer out in the jungle than in Port Moresby. On the Kokoda Track, I slept alone in a tent next to Papuan villages. The capital is another world. For well-off expats like me, accommodation is a hotel with hot showers, cold beer, buffet dinners and soft beds, barricaded against the city's poor and *raskol* gangs by razor wire, armed guards and Dobermans. Outside, residents move from settlements to workplaces and markets, constantly alert to possible theft and assault. Bags, phones and watches get snatched. Sometimes the robbers use pipe-guns to relieve office workers of the few kina in their wallets; sometimes they even steal their shoes. With 80,000 school-leavers seeking work every year and only 5000 new formal-sector jobs created annually, even in good times, towns are filling up with idle young people, who often turn to theft and prostitution.

After numerous home invasions by gangs of young *raskols* swarming over security fences to rob and rape, expats have tended to move from bungalows into heavily protected condominium blocks. Drawing on surveys of a well-off, cosmopolitan sample, the Economist Intelligence Unit regularly ranks Port Moresby as one of the "least liveable" cities in the world. At least it has lost the title of the world's least liveable city, which it won in 2004; in recent years it has been ranked sixth from the bottom of the list.

It is nevertheless a very attractive city. The sea front is narrow, backed by a low range of bare hills, facing a turquoise expanse of reef and the blue of the open sea beyond. The villages of the original Papuan people are built on stilts over the water in several places, with lively produce markets close by. On the hills, upmarket condominiums are replacing colonial bungalows on winding roads. Up and over one steep hill is the main business district, where multi-storey offices crowd out the surviving weatherboard and brick buildings of the Australian era. On the pavements below, small traders sell betel nut and newspapers. Parking touts offer guidance and protection. Beyond, the coast loops into the port, where big cargo ships tie up after navigating past wartime wrecks and coral shoals. Another road loops over to a valley that holds the main military barracks, named after Lieutenant-Governor Hubert Murray, past markets and shopping centres protected by security fences. In a square at Four Mile Market, women sit and crochet *bilums* (string bags) and *biwas* (body ornaments) for sale. Further out, in the flat Waigani District, are government offices and the spectacular parliament building, modelled after a Sepik *haus tambaran* – a traditional spirit house – with a new national museum alongside. Beyond are the campus of the University of Papua New Guinea and the airport. It's busy, colourful and friendly, if you watch your belongings. In the late afternoons and early evenings, people gather on Ela Beach and parks in the golden light for touch rugby, soccer and walks. Then the city goes silent, as most residents go home.

A high level of crime can't be denied, and in recent years more serious criminals have used modern guns. Some weapons are imported across the land border from Indonesia, some bought with ganja from Australian motorbike gangs. Other illegal guns come from police and military arsenals, some of them lost in the field during the Bougainville conflict and others simply sold or hired out. Gangs target banks, fuel stations and government payrolls, often with inside knowledge from *wantoks*, or people of the same ethnic group.

In one of Port Moresby's squatter settlements, two former convicts talked to me some years back about their lives. Both had fathers in government jobs but started stealing at an early age before graduating to bigger things. "Government payrolls – that was our speciality," said one, who asked to be known as "Ken Sain". "That's what we did for survival. Most of them were inside jobs – they would tell us when they [would be] moving the money." The pair were eventually caught and did time in Port Moresby's Bomana Jail. Since then, one got a clerical job that allowed him to save enough to set up a small stall selling cold drinks, cigarettes and betel nut. The other moved into the fringes of politics, organising muscle and shows of support for politicians.

With little prompting, as we sat on broken furniture in Ken Sain's yard, one of the teenage boys hanging around ran off and reappeared, showing us a homemade .22 pistol under his t-shirt, which sported the words "Western Union Money Transfer". The bullets, Ken Sain said, came from the police. "Only about 10 per cent of the young boys here have jobs," said Ken Sain. "The rest hang around drinking beer, smoking marijuana and committing robberies, thefts, bag snatching. When the government leaders steal millions, nothing happens. When we steal 5 kina, we get ten years in Bomana."

He had a dim view of the unfairness of it all. The two former gangsters said they would welcome the return of Australian police, an idea floated every time there's an upsurge in crime. "Our police shoot us first before they do anything; the Australian police ask us questions," Ken Sain said. "The PNG police harass the informal sector, scatter the goods at the roadside market, chase the women away. They're expecting bribes, very corrupt. When they check our pockets, they take anything in them, plus our watches. They are worse than us."

Police admit they are hardly coping. "We are one against a thousand, with their guns and drugs," one senior policeman in Mount Hagen told me. The police drove around in uninsured vehicles – when they had vehicles at all. At one low point Port Moresby's detective squads for general offences, stolen cars, armed robbery, homicide and sexual offences shared one car. "If you get shot, you get taken to Port Moresby General Hospital and you probably die," said one inspector. "Your family get nothing." Overtime pay had stopped in the 1980s. Much policing work was carried out by unpaid and untrained reservists, who provided their own equipment. At this time, the sole police helicopter in the country was out of service for want of funds for repairs.

An ordinary policeman on about 400 kina per month before tax, living in barracks that have not been repaired since 1975, needs little inducement to abandon standard operating procedures. "People go into the station and say: 'If you grab this guy, I'll give you 200 bucks or a case of beer,' and the officer just goes and makes the arrest," the inspector told me. "The case fails in court, and the criminal then sues the government for wrongful arrest."

(In 2004 outstanding legal claims against the state arising from unlawful police actions amounted to more than double the total police budget for that year.)

Shootouts between police patrols and gangs were common, especially when the criminals were Goilalas, members of a tribe from the mountains northwest of Port Moresby noted for their aggressiveness. "The point when you start shooting is when your life is in danger," the inspector said. "Once a Goilala starts shooting, that's it. In other parts of the world, like Australia, when you are chasing suspects, they will try to run away or hide. Here, if they have an opportunity, they will shoot at you, or go at you with a bush knife or a stick."

He told of being accompanied by an Australian Federal Police officer during an operation when police opened fire on suspects and hit one. "She [the AFP officer] proceeded to give him first aid. We had to intervene – if we take a person and he dies, the family will ask us for compensation. If he dies in the ambulance or at the hospital, it's OK. If he dies with us, we killed him," he said. Sometimes police get fed up with the justice system, he said. "We catch suspects in the act, and they get off. Why do these guys who've raped a woman or stolen a car keep getting off? We might as well put him out of circulation. When he comes out of Bomana and he does the same thing, he gets shot. He dies."

The police inspector said his patrols faced gangs armed with M16 and FN assault rifles, grenades and pistols. "The gangs are now cooperating. One will supply the weapons, the other the cars, the other the safe house to divide up the takings. The gangs are not working in isolation anymore. They all work together." Newcomers from mainland China are introducing more sophisticated crime. "They use PNG nationals to carry out extortion, drugs like *shabu-shabu* [amphetamines], money laundering and people smuggling," the officer said. "But someone upstairs has been paid off. You take the case to them, and he's saying it's rubbish, it's not true."

When I reached Port Moresby from Kimbe this time, the atmosphere had eased. There were numerous taxis that were safe to use, their drivers contactable by mobile phone. But it was still advisable to lock your car doors while driving and not to rest your arm on the open window, lest your watch be snatched off. There was still an unofficial night-time curfew for most inhabitants, with the streets quiet after 7 pm and few taxis about after this hour.

Mobs can form in a flash. In January 2024, what has been called a payroll glitch resulted in sharp cuts to many public servants' fortnightly pay, including cuts of around 50 per cent for low-ranking staff in the police, prison service and other agencies. Victims of the error in Port Moresby walked off the job and besieged the national parliament. After word spread by mobile phone, mobs took the opportunity to plunder shops, some of which were set on fire. Extra police were flown in and a call-out of the battalion at Port Moresby's Murray Barracks restored order. A two-week state of emergency was declared. The damage was estimated at almost 1 billion kina (A$406 million) and the bodies of twenty-two victims were found, some presumed killed by store owners and their security guards, others trapped in buildings set on fire.

The Royal Papua New Guinea Constabulary still numbered only about 7300 for the entire country, about 2000 more than at independence in 1975. The national population, now estimated at 9 million, 10 million or 11 million, is three times what it then was. The police now have more vehicles, and cell phones enable people to call for help and record evidence, but that's not enough. "If you need the police and you want them to come to your village or wherever, you've got a real problem," says Sinclair Dinnen, a specialist in Pacific crime and security at the Australian National University. "The first thing they will ask for is a payment, ostensibly to pay for fuel. They do need fuel, but there's quite a lot of rent-seeking behaviour across the police force – given the fact they can get away with it and people expect to pay the police to assist them, particularly if it involves travelling."

A vast army of at least 30,000 private security guards meanwhile provide a static and mobile protection for institutions, companies and work sites. That's the figure for employees of registered security firms, far outnumbering the police, military and correctional services combined. An unknown number work for unregistered security groups.

Out in the villages, communities rely on semi-formal village courts, or restitutions arranged by elders and priests. Engaging with the police and the district courts means long delays, expensive trips and waiting in the towns. The very old, who remember pre-independence times, regret the passing of the kiap system, whereby a patrol officer backed by a small squad of constables roamed his district as both investigator and magistrate, encouraged settlement of disputes, and ordered punishment and compensation for small crimes.

In the urban settlements, local committees often play a similar role to the village courts. "Most people do not rely on the uniformed police for their policing needs," Dinnen told me on one of his periodic visits to Port Moresby. "If something goes missing, you go to your local networks, the committees. Sometimes for a small fee, they will eventually find out who stole your radio and maybe arrange for it to be returned. The police would not be interested in that kind of stuff."

Away from the big towns, police are stuck in rundown buildings and housing, surrounded by people they cannot quell. "They have guns, but they are always going to be outnumbered, and there are a lot of guns out there," Dinnen said. "So they have to police by consent, which is a kind of irony, because the police shoot a lot of people." It means not a lot of conventional crime detection gets done.

The last census was in 2011, and it was badly run, partly because the computers at the central tally office were stolen at a crucial point. The coronavirus epidemic meant the planned 2021 census had to be rescheduled to mid-2024. A UN agency had a shot at estimating the population from satellite imagery of human settlements, and came up with a figure of 17 million. It was regarded with scepticism by the government and foreign agencies, but few were ready to categorically rule out the discovery of a million or two unsuspected citizens. The estimate was later amended to about 11 million.

Even in Port Moresby, many thousands of eligible voters found their names not on the electoral rolls for the national elections of 2022. Officials cited lack of funds to update the rolls. When voting day came, citizens queued for hours. When some crowded around officials to seek a reason for the delay, police opened fire at one point, killing a young mother holding her baby. At the end of the year, the city's main hospital was found to be storing bodies of deceased patients in an open shed, as the refrigerated morgue was full. It hastily organised a mass burial in the hospital grounds. The hospital was designed for the current official population of Port Moresby, about 400,000. The head of the PNG doctors' association, James Naipao, said the population was really 1.3 million, which makes it Melanesia's first million-plus city.

Most of those residents live in settlements, which a UN Habitat report in 2010 said were "characterised by a lack of planning, poor infrastructure and a lack of urban services". In part, that lack of support is due to a widespread feeling that these people should not be there – that living in a city is somehow un-Melanesian. PNG's first prime minister, Michael Somare, argued against urbanisation in the 1970s, and academics wrote of the country's "ambivalent townsmen".[2]

Sometimes city authorities have attempted to clear out squatters, without plans for rehousing them. No doubt the authorities expected the ousted people to realise it was time to return to the village. The violent resistance belies this.

Many city residents do think of returning to their rural places of origin on retirement. Air travellers to small towns will often see coffins being loaded into the cargo hold – people who did not live to return "home" but wanted at least to be buried there. However, as a recent Australian National University study reports, "new generations of people who have grown up in towns and who are not familiar with the day-to-day rhythms of village life are now growing in number. These people have made cities their permanent homes."[3] Yet the same study felt obliged to note that "in some ways, the legitimacy of Melanesian urbanism is yet to be established", more than four decades after Somare expressed concern about developing cities and the academics wrote of the ambivalence of Papua New Guinea's townspeople.

After the January 2024 rioting, the same attitudes resurfaced. James Marape, the prime minister, said he and the National Capital District governor,

Powes Parkop, would look at applying a vagrancy law to restrict "unnecessary" movement into Port Moresby. "People have proven they are not fit to live in the city," he said.

The same ANU study said urban investment often worsens inequalities, because the elite define the investment priorities and government funds are "co-opted by political patronage". The elite wanted to position Port Moresby as a global city, and Papua New Guinea as a middle power in the region. So money went into the international airport, new roads connecting it to the top hotels, facilities to host regional games, and the shorefront pavilion built to host the 2018 Asia-Pacific Economic Cooperation (APEC) summit (the summit also saw the baffling purchase of forty Maserati and three Bentley luxury cars). Funds are spent on iconic projects rather than housing, water supply and sanitation where it is most needed, especially in the settlements. While the settlements have a reputation for poverty and crime, this stereotype ignores the strong communities found in them, and the increasing number of salaried wage earners who cannot afford to live elsewhere and who may have made substantial investment in their homes, even without secure land tenure.

International events directed at a global audience also often result in "intensified policing of marginal groups seen as undermining the modernist aesthetics of orderliness and prosperity". In some cases, this includes forcible relocation.

The informal economy is also targeted. In New Britain, I encountered the extensive networks of the betel nut trade. This trade has drawn criticism from Port Moresby elites. As the ANU study notes:

> Betel nut vendors sell a national commodity that represents Melanesian solidarity and sociality, yet they are also spoken of in popular debate as a criminal underclass whose activities undermine law and order and public health and have even been the target of the notorious "*buai* ban".

There is incremental and patchy progress in turning "settlements to suburbs", as a city hall catchcry goes. Rebecca Kuku, a reporter with *The National* newspaper, told me her parents have lived in their home in a settlement since the 1960s, on a fairly secure leasehold. Her father is an accountant and her mother a homemaker. Her grandparents had come from the Gulf, and the family still speaks Tairuma, their language of origin, as well as Tok Pisin and English. They go back to the ancestral village at Christmas. A couple of years ago, their neighbourhood got electricity and running water, although there is not yet sewerage, so pit toilets are used. A driveable road came up the hill, police patrols are more common and the incidence of robberies and burglaries has fallen. Fights tend to break out among young people after drinking sessions on public holidays. Even for graduates like Rebecca, the 800 kina average fortnightly rent of a room in a suburban house would take more than half a typical 1500 kina fortnightly pay packet. The cheap alternative would be 50 kina per fortnight for a cubicle in a settlement shanty, with pit toilet, a water tap some distance away and a long and risky walk to the nearest public minibus route. So she stays with her parents. She walks twenty minutes down the hill to get a minibus to work in the morning. The new road means a company shuttle bus can drop her at her door when the news shift ends after dark.

While ordinary residents and small-scale entrepreneurs struggle to survive, the big end of town in Port Moresby receives lavish bank funding, favourable land leases and ready planning approvals. The construction of liquified natural gas projects saw previously modest hotels – comparable to Australian motor-lodges – upgraded to the kind of luxury found in upscale Southeast Asian resorts, and new ones built. The political and big business class meet and plot in their bars and conference rooms.

In 2022, newly re-elected prime minister James Marape and city governor Powes Parkop turned up for the launch of a subdevelopment on a site fronting the turquoise Coral Sea. This was a twenty-two-storey apartment building on reclaimed foreshore land, part of the Paga Hill project. The squatters who had been living on the state-owned land had been evicted and dumped on the city's outskirts. The developer turned out to be a Malaysian entrepreneur who had taken over the site for an annual fee of 8400 kina (US$2400), with the lease running for ninety-three years. Parkop thanked him for having trust in the capital city and for building modern accommodation. The city government had devised its "Amazing Port Moresby" global branding campaign to promote the capital as a liveable city, he said, "but the government can't do it alone". Parkop launched several initiatives to improve the livelihoods of ordinary residents: as well as "Settlements into Suburbs" there was a "*Yumi Lukautim Mosbi*" (Let's all look after Moresby) community awareness drive. But as Paga Hill shows, it is the wealthy sector that gets the breaks.

To come back to Port Moresby periodically is to plunge back into its semi-underground rumour mill, with its gossip about the latest scandals involving top politicians and their allies. Civil disturbances and political intrigue feed into each other. The January 2024 riots came just before the end of the eighteen-month "grace period" following an election, during which no-confidence motions against the government are not permitted. As soon as the period ended, several MPs left James Marape's ruling coalition, blaming him for the payroll glitch, and filed no-confidence motions. Marape supporters managed to disqualify these motions on technical grounds and by adjourning parliament. But clearly, it was open season.

Scandals are generally forgiven within a few years. The biggest scandal of the early independence years came during the prime ministership of Paias Wingti, who called a commission of inquiry into the forestry industry, chaired by the Supreme Court justice T.E. "Tos" Barnett. The move was inspired by the awarding of a large timber concession in the mid-1980s by the then forestry minister, Ted Diro, who turned out to have been given an interest in the project through concealed trust arrangements. The disclosure forced Diro out of politics in 1991, but he was elected back into parliament six years later. In 2019, the defence force named the first of a new class of patrol ship donated by Australia as HMPNGS *Diro* (before entering parliament, Diro had been chief of the defence force).

Barnett's report showed a pilot light of integrity still burning. But nothing much changed in Port Moresby politics. In 2002, Barnett – by then retired from the judiciary – was called back to inquire into corruption, along with another retired judge, Don Sawong. They looked into the role of a rising young accountant, Peter O'Neill, son of an Australian district magistrate and his Southern Highlands wife, who had been appointed to run state enterprises and statutory bodies. Their report dealt with O'Neill's role at the National Provident Fund, a compulsory pension fund set up in 1995 for all companies with twenty or more staff. Sawong looked into O'Neill's connections at the Investment Corporation of Papua New Guinea (ICPNG), and the Investment Corporation Fund of Papua New Guinea, an investment fund managed by the ICPNG.[4] The bodies were set up in 1971 to build up local equity in economic activity. The two judges reported a pattern of milking funds from the state bodies, through undervaluations in the sale of assets and large transaction fees awarded to O'Neill's associates.

Although the report was tabled in parliament, it remained unavailable to the public for more than a decade until posted on the internet by an anti-corruption group, PNGi Portal. O'Neill by then was well entrenched in parliament, having been elected in 2002 to represent his mother's home region. He faced court on one charge relating to an alleged illegal payment in a high-rise building deal for the pension fund, but the charge was dropped in 2006 for "insufficient evidence". Delays and prosecutorial errors got most of his alleged associates off.

More than a decade later, the local branch of the anti-corruption watchdog Transparency International put out a report, *Lest We Forget: A Review of 20 Unresolved Issues of National Concern, 2007–2017*, that covered murky construction projects, state-sanctioned landgrabs, state agencies resisting accountability, state abuse of assets and funds, state laxness towards critical bills, and state travesties of justice. It was another forlorn attempt to keep accountability alive, as unresolved old scandals got buried under new ones. By the time the report came out, O'Neill had been prime minister since 2011, after successfully presenting himself as a cleaner alternative to the tarnished Somare government that had been in power since 2002 (the beginning of Somare's third stint in office).

O'Neill promised a new independent commission against corruption, but what was delivered was a more temporary "Task Force Sweep" under a resolute official named Sam Koim. After two years it turned its attention to O'Neill, who was consequently arrested over allegedly excessive fees paid to a big law firm by the finance department when he was its minister. The case went nowhere. Funding for the task force was cut and it folded.

When James Marape finally rolled Peter O'Neill in a no-confidence motion in 2019, he brought over Bryan Kramer from the opposition benches. Member for an electorate in Madang, raised in a missionary family and educated in Queensland, Kramer had been a strident critic of O'Neill and his alleged corruption. He joined the Marape government on condition of being given the police portfolio. Once he was police minister, he and police commissioner David Manning (also appointed by Marape) had a first look. "We lifted the floorboards up and saw just how bad it was … it is extremely bad," Kramer told me in 2022. "Corruption is essentially imbedded into every segment of government. People are stealing at an accelerating rate because they can. The biggest challenge you had in addressing corruption is first the police making an arrest. The police aren't making arrests because most of them are following politicians around. And their boss is the commissioner of police, who is appointed by corrupt politicians, and they're directed not to make arrests."

"The police have to be reformed – if there are no arrests, there's no deterrence," Kramer insisted. Then he added, in a wry echo of what the professional *raskol* and payroll robber "Ken Sain" had said to me: "Stealing from a bank, you get shot. Stealing public money, no one will touch you." I put to Kramer the widespread suspicion that prosecutors can be bribed to throw cases against well-resourced defendants. He didn't entirely disagree. "But there's a degree of incompetence. Like police not getting proper warrants," he said. "Over the years the standards have dropped. No one's been doing their job for so long."

In cases of "grand corruption", which often include international conspirators, the poorly resourced agencies are up against law firms with skilled expatriate partners, Kramer said. He noted that there were risks at every stage of the legal process. "If the prosecutor doesn't present the file the case is dismissed. The next risk stage is the magistrate, then the public prosecutor who can withdraw the charge, then next is your national court judge. Then the Supreme Court, which is a bit more difficult because you need a bench of three."

Kramer went after O'Neill, trying to pin him for irregularities in the purchases of electrical generators from Israel ahead of the APEC summit. O'Neill in turn tried to nobble Kramer, seeking a court injunction on the basis that Kramer was interfering with the work of the police by pushing for the arrest. An obliging supreme court justice awarded the injunction, effectively barring the minister from taking complaints from the public and passing them on, writing about cases online or allowing comments on his website. Kramer got a five-member bench to overturn this injunction. O'Neill was taken to court, but the judge found no criminal intent behind the generator purchase.

Marape later moved Kramer into the justice and immigration portfolios, with the work of reforming the police barely started. Kramer was drummed out of parliament in 2023 after a panel of judges found him guilty of "scandalising the judiciary" with disparaging social media comments. His attempts at prosecution over grand corruption were nearly all dismissed on technical grounds or for "lack of evidence".

Australia had been trying to assist the police since the late 1980s, mostly focusing on the training of command echelons and specialist units. The vexed issue of resources was largely untouched. "Arguably the most realistic assessment of Australian support is that it has helped the RPNGC [Royal Papua New Guinea Constabulary] maintain a semblance of organisational functionality, rather than making a major difference to police effectiveness or improved security in the wider PNG community," wrote Sinclair Dinnen and his ANU colleague Grant Walton. A study by consultancy firm Deloitte in 2020 said the force needed an extra 126 million kina a year to cover its funding gap, and a one-off capital injection of about 3.9 billion kina to deliver its service mandate. There was also a suggestion that police numbers needed to be at least doubled.[5] It looked an impossible suggestion, but in December 2023, Marape announced he would do just that, in five years. The Australian government pledged to fund a new police academy.

Dinnen agreed with these policies, up to a point. "There is a need for more police," he told me. And he acknowledged the law-enforcement challenges facing the country: "there are guns everywhere, a lot of discontent, a lot of grievance, a lot of anger in the community. The towns are growing rapidly, with massive settlements with a lot of issues and violence, and the police simply can't cope."

But he was not sure that doubling police numbers was the answer. "The police have to be better looked after," he said. "And in some ways, there's an argument for having a small, well-looked-after professional force who have enough fuel and access to transport, who are skilled up in investigations and doing the policing kind of thing." This force would be the nucleus of a hybrid policing arrangement like the one being developed in Bougainville. There, helped by advice from New Zealand police over the last twenty years, the autonomous island had developed a tiny force of regular police in just three police stations, backed up by a larger number of "community auxiliary police" who deal with local disputes, sorcery allegations and domestic violence.

Dinnen observed that after the civil war, Bougainvilleans had a deep appreciation of peace, which was not always the case in the rest of the country. "In many parts of Papua New Guinea it would work very well, but there are other parts that are so ridden with conflict – the obvious ones like Hela, Jiwaka and parts of Enga – places where often there is resource development and very clear winners and lots of very clear losers. There you get what are in effect low levels of insurgency, and no police force should be expected to deal with that." In 2022, Marape announced plans for a third army battalion to be raised and based in Hela. No follow-up on this announcement has so far been apparent.

Regulators are meanwhile wrestling to get control of the big new player in Papua New Guinea: China. As we saw in Honiara in 2023, when Port Moresby hosted the 2015 Pacific Games, Chinese construction companies came in for quick builds of sporting facilities using Chinese workers and stayed on, undercutting their competitors. Business and aid agreements with China abounded, helped by two Chinese migrant businesswomen, Ni Yumei and Ru "Dora" Lu, who had developed a close rapport with then prime minister O'Neill and his ministers and become investment promoters in Port Moresby. Lady Ni, as she is now known, thanks to her marriage to Italian-Australian builder Sir Luciano Cragnolini, also helped found a new secondary school in Port Moresby, the Butuka Academy, modelled on Chinese schools and aimed at cultivating a new elite.

As well as these high-level newcomers, a wave of Chinese small entrepreneurs has arrived from the coastal Fujian Province in the last three decades, whether by overstaying tourist and business visas, or smuggled aboard logging ships or fishing boats – no one can be sure how. Washing out from Port Moresby to the further corners of Papua New Guinea, they have established hundreds of general stores and *kai* (fast food) bars across towns big and small.

Operating purely with cash, ignoring company tax and GST obligations and importing goods through sometimes unorthodox channels, at times sourcing them directly from factories and wholesalers in China, the Fujian businesses have been unbeatable competition at the bottom end of the consumer market.

As we saw in Rabaul, there had been two earlier waves of Chinese migration. The first came between the late nineteenth century and the Second World War. Because of the White Australia policy, the entry of Chinese women was made difficult. Many Chinese men married local women, often sending their children to Catholic boarding schools in Queensland. The second wave arrived between 1945 and the 1960s, in many cases via Malaya and Singapore. They spoke the dialects of southern China at home and English and Tok Pisin for business. Unless they had already moved up into specialised trading, light manufacturing or food processing – like Malaysian-born Sandra Lau's Tropicana group – they too found the third wave from Fujian taking their business from under them.

Paul Barker, director of Port Moresby's Institute of National Affairs, recalled one member of a long-established Chinese business family explaining why she had closed what had previously been the biggest supermarket in Madang. "There are two major problems for business in Madang," she told him. "One is the *raskols*, two is the new Chinese. The new Chinese have only two words of English: 'How much?' It applies to anyone who arrives on their doorsteps, whether it's the *raskol* gangs, or the customs officers, or the police."

Their doggedness has attracted a qualified admiration. "The one thing I'll say about the Chinese is that they work hard," said Cameron Mackellar, chief executive of the Brian Bell Group in Port Moresby, the biggest remaining Australian-founded trading house in Papua New Guinea, spanning trade electricals, homewares, chemicals and property. The company sells wholesale to some of the new Chinese stores in remote centres. "They come out here and they go to places that quite frankly you and I would never go. And they live there, and they set up a little Chinese store, and they probably don't pay tax, or duty or GST or any of those things. But that's an obligation for the government to monitor and manage. But they are ruthless when it comes to surviving. That's what they do. On one hand, I tip my hat to them. On the other, I wish it was a fairer playing field."

O'Neill visited China frequently. "Peter O'Neill could not resist red carpets, and the Chinese rolled them out for him," said Barker. In June 2018 O'Neill signed up to Xi Jinping's signature Belt and Road Initiative. Over the following year, the number of Chinese state-owned enterprises operating in Papua New Guinea jumped from twenty-one to at least thirty-nine, according to a tally by the ANU scholar Peter Connolly, and around seventy-nine if Chinese provincial enterprises were counted. Connolly says these enterprises are effectively a "fourth wave" from China – speaking Mandarin, employing a Chinese workforce as much as possible, segregated from PNG society and, as one executive of a state-owned enterprise (SOE) admitted to him, pursuing Chinese state interests over commercial interests when required, even if it means making a loss.

Hence some of the more fanciful business ventures, including a multi-billion-dollar free-trade zone on Papua New Guinea's swampy, sparsely populated south coast facing the Torres Strait, complete with a naval base and an airport, pictured in promotional materials with fighter aircraft taking off. As another ANU analyst, Graeme Smith, has noted, it was the executive of an SOE based in Vanuatu who approached the Solomons government with the offer of US$500 million in grants and loans from the Chinese state if it switched diplomatic recognition from Taipei to Beijing. The link between diplomatic support and aid and investment is crude.

MELANESIA

Ahead of the November 2018 summit of the APEC grouping, held in Port Moresby for the first time, a Chinese SOE jumped in to help O'Neill's government prepare, laying out 10 kilometres of four-lane ceremonial roads and a waterfront convention hall in 200 days. Xi Jinping was a triumphant figure at that APEC, particularly as Donald Trump was absent and his vice-president, Mike Pence, flew in daily from Cairns rather than risk staying in Port Moresby. It was the high point of Chinese influence so far, and Australia, the United States, Japan and New Zealand hurriedly tried to compete with Xi's infrastructure offers. The four allies declared a US$1.7 billion "PNG Electrification Partnership" to bring electricity to 70 per cent of PNG's population by 2030, up from the 10 to 15 per cent then connected to the grid.

Like a lot of big announcements by outsiders, the devil was in the practical detail. It relied heavily on the domestic electricity authority, which, like most PNG public enterprises, is poorly run. And the country's topography of mountains and islands suggests dispersed networks, rather than an integrated grid, which was another aspect breezily ignored. About 70 per cent of people already have some electricity from solar or micro-hydro generation. Not that China's plans in the power sector were advancing either. A proposed US$800 million hydro scheme on the northern Ramu River and a US$145 million transmission and substation project met political controversy over alleged improper tendering and doubts about Port Moresby's ability to meet "take or pay" obligations to buy the power output over fifty years.

Under Marape, Chinese business interests came under increased scrutiny from authorities. Immigration officers raided the Ramu Nickel project near Madang and hauled up numerous Chinese workers for violations of their work permits. He shut down the huge Porgera gold mine in the Enga highlands, partly owned by a Chinese company, for over two years when its operating contract came up for renewal, to get more royalties and equity for surrounding communities as the price of reopening. A flagship building put up in Port Moresby's central business district by the state-owned China Railway Construction Engineering Group became an unintended symbol of Chinese shoddiness. The twenty-three-storey Noble Centre was denied an occupancy certificate by the city building authority because of some seventy-five electrical, fire safety and structural faults. It remains unoccupied.

In an office just down the street from the Noble Centre, the former corruption-hunter Sam Koim had a new role as chief of the Internal Revenue Commission. The stocky lawyer told me part of his mission was to level the playing field complained about by Mackellar. Previous tax inspections and attempted audits had made little progress. "Sending teams down on the ground has a lot of risks," he said. "You get the classic example of a Chinese not knowing any Tok Pisin or English, or trying to bribe us, sometimes successfully." Instead, the revenue service was using a "net worth" approach to build up a model of each business's operation, from things such as vehicles purchased and containers cleared through customs, and then comparing that with any declared income. Then would follow a swoop by a joint task force of tax inspectors, immigration officials and police fraud detectives. So far, the amount of tax being evaded was unclear. "I can't quantify it, but it's substantial," Koim said. "I think you could double or triple the GST collection."

And so Port Moresby muddles along. A place so cut off from its hinterland that even the Japanese Imperial Army, which had captured the supposedly impregnable Port Arthur from the Russians in 1904 and Singapore from the British in 1942, could not reach it. A capital that sucks up the revenue from vast petroleum and mineral projects and spends it almost entirely on its own sustenance, with some siphoned off into Cairns real estate and the region's casinos.

Yet it is also a city with an emerging consciousness, with journalists empowered by the internet to break out of the timid self-censorship of its two newspapers, young people with skills to penetrate corporate registers and balance sheets, academics to critique state budgets, students to come out and protest, and second- and third-generation residents who feel they belong to Moresby more than to the villages of their ancestors, and are asserting their citizenship.

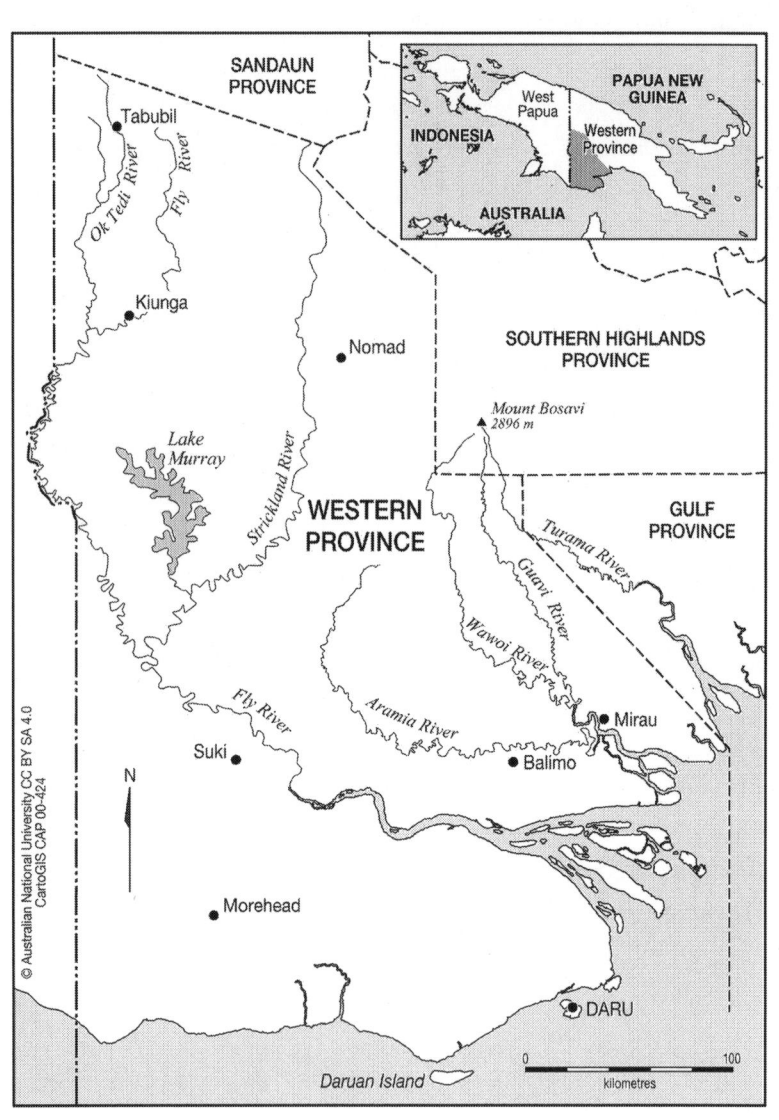

11

WESTERN PROVINCE

Jungle and Water

A MUDBANK IN A SMALL TOWNSHIP called Kiunga is Grand Central Station for the widest administrative expanse of Papua New Guinea: the wetlands of Western Province. The twisting Fly River and its tributaries are the roads and railways. The vehicles are dugout canoes, hollowed out from tree trunks 12 or 15 metres long, or fibreglass dinghies, all with an outboard clamped to the end. The province sprawls to the south, ending only 4 kilometres from the nearest part of Australia in the Torres Strait. Its 200,000 people are Australia's nearest neighbours.

Sometimes, when it's been raining up in the headwaters in the Star Mountains and the Tari and Enga highlands, the mudbank is narrow, a ledge under the tree line. On this trip, there was a drought up there, and the bank was 100 metres of sloping hard mud. Groups of Papuans waited beside piles of bags and *bilums* bulging with things they'd bought at the Chinese stores up along the single paved road of the town. Others passed belongings down into the boats, before arranging themselves aboard and settling in for a long transit up or down the Fly.

It is 458 nautical miles from the sea, nearly 850 kilometres, but just downriver from the mudbank are ocean-going ships. Here copper concentrate from the Ok Tedi mine up at Tabubil in the Star Mountains comes as slurry in a pipeline, is dried out and loaded into a bulk carrier for export. A fully laden ore ship was tied up, stranded by the low river level. A small oil tanker was readying to leave; having pumped out its fuel for the mine and the town's generator, it was drawing less water.

Anchored out in the channel was the *Kuku*, a 166-ton little coaster of a bygone age: white, with a splash of pink undercoat on a ding, and the superstructure dark grey. Built in South Australia circa 1953, it eventually passed into service supplying mine sites in Lihir Island, off New Ireland, and other places, until North Fly Rubber Ltd bought it in 1983 for $150,000. That day, it was going downriver and I had a passage on it.

But as always with transport in Papua New Guinea, you had to wait for the cargo to fill up. The *Kuku* might be coming back with rubber from smallholders along the river system, but it would help profitability if it could earn something going on the way out. For three days, the ship's crew waited. Then a truck lurched down the track onto the mudbank and levered its container onto the ground. A chain of labourers carried lengths of timber, sheets of corrugated iron, sacks of cement and a spindly steel cabinet, all to be loaded onto dinghies and ferried out to the *Kuku*, which was moored mid-stream.

When I went out in a dinghy, the *Kuku*'s captain, Stonewig Ame, a stocky man in his sixties from Kerema in the Gulf, was leaning over the handrail outside the wheelhouse, supervising the last of the cargo being swung up in a rope sling and over into the hold by ship's derrick. The *Kuku*'s mechanic, Max Wabadala, a lanky young man with aviator sunglasses, was working its levers and pumping its donkey engine.

I explored the ship. Behind the high bow was an enclosed forecastle with cabins for crew, the derrick, a long welldeck with a hold covered by timber planks and tarpaulins, and a two-deck wheelhouse and aftercastle above the engine room. Behind the wheelhouse was my tiny cabin, with space for a single berth. The deck below held a galley with a gas stove and a trade store, opened by a flap on the lower port side, stocked with simple items such as dried noodles, tinned fish, packets of rice and, naturally enough, *kuku* for smokes. The ship's name, I was told, came from the word in Police Motu (the vernacular of Australian-ruled Papua, now displaced by

Tok Pisin) for the raw black tobacco strips that I'd seen rolled and smoked in Bougainville and the Solomons.

Three times the "last boat" came with more cargo. At 8 pm, the light fading, crewmen Frank Someke, Kevin Mala and Anselom Nelson put on the hatch-covers. Down in the galley, coxswain and cook Gagole Aika served up dinner of chicken, rice and spinach, passed around on plates and eaten on deck. Then a power-winch clanked the anchor and its chain aboard. Stonewig swung the huge old wooden wheel, and the *Kuku* turned into the stream. We passed the streetlights of Kiunga town, the floodlit rampart of the Ok Tedi wharf, the ore carrier waiting for the river to rise, the tanker discharging its fuel.

And then darkness.

Dim tree lines on either side, a floodlight in the bow showing brown, rippling water. In the wheelhouse, Stonewig watched a small radar monitor hung from the cabinet roof. It showed the banks ahead in acid green. A bronze voice-pipe, with its whistle to alert the engineer, was still in place but now redundant, as the helmsman controlled the engine directly with a throttle. On a tiny chart table on one side, the first page of a chart-book was open, showing the sinuous course of the Fly. It was surveyed in 1981, for Ok Tedi. Watching Stonewig, I could see that his tactic was to hug the outer curves, where the water could be assumed to run deepest.

After a couple of hours, I decided to turn in and went to my cabin. It had a narrow bunk with an old sprung mattress, shelves and a cabinet looming over it at the foot, and a narrow strip of floor. At one end, a door led into a cubicle with a porcelain toilet and a handbasin. To my gratitude, a tiny air-conditioner had been put through the bulkhead, and the crew had left an electric jug and a handful of tea bags and coffee sachets. After a spray of insecticide, I turned off the strip light, and settled down to sleep.

Drowsily, I heard the ship's bell at midnight for a change of watch and drifted back into sleep. Sometime later, the ship heaved underneath me. The engine stopped, then went into reverse. I looked at my watch, it was 1.30 am. On opening the cabin door, I could see only sheets of rain and flashes of lightning. The *Kuku* drifted in a circle. Then the engine went slow ahead.

I looked in the wheelhouse. "Sandbank," said Gagole, now at the helm. "It's all right."

About 5 am, another jolt, and slow ahead. This time, something underwater. At 6.45 am, Redentor Caggauan, the supercargo running the rubber-buying side of the expedition, came to tell me that breakfast was ready. A jolly Filipino who first came to Papua New Guinea to teach in a Catholic high school, he preferred the river life while his Filipina wife ran the rubber factory back in Kiunga.

Breakfast was two warmed sandwiches of tinned spam splattered with peanut butter and a mug of "three-in-one", made from a sachet containing coffee, sugar and milk powder.

By now, the *Kuku* had reached the bulge in the Fly where it, and the national border, crossed the 141st meridian of longitude that long-ago European statesmen had agreed would separate their realms. My mobile phone no longer had a signal, but its global positioning system showed where we were and had adjusted its time an hour back to Eastern Indonesian Time.

The banks beyond the dark brown mud were capped by flat country of low scrub and tall grass, with scattered tall trees. Some had bare trunks up to a topknot of leaves. Some were completely dressed in vines. On the Indonesian bank was a cluster of thatch huts and some floats marking out a fish net. Redentor pointed out a clearing where helicopters occasionally landed, bringing soldiers to camp. Across the river on the PNG side was a small grass shack on stilts and some people sitting near a canoe. The villagers crisscrossed the border at will.

Back in Kiunga, I'd gone to the edge of the town to see the simple camp where the PNG Defence Force rotates a company of soldiers, just 100 men, to go out on patrol and maintain a semblance of border security. In 1986, I'd taken a boat up the Ok Tedi tributary of the Fly to visit a camp where several hundred people had fled from an army sweep in West Papua. They had been reluctant to talk to someone who spoke Indonesian, regarding me as a spy who would pass details back to Jakarta through intelligence exchanges. This had rankled a bit, as I was then persona non grata in Indonesia from my time as a correspondent.

WESTERN PROVINCE

That morning, aboard the *Kuku*, we learned from the 9 am radio sked that last night's rainstorm had dumped 444 millimetres in just a few hours, which would be good for the water level in the river. We moved out of the border bulge and my mobile automatically set time ahead an hour. We chugged on. I thought of the first outsiders who came up here, with the flamboyant Italian naturalist and explorer Luigi Maria D'Albertis in 1876. A veteran of Garibaldi's unification of Italy, he had collected specimens in the Arfak Mountains of Dutch New Guinea and on Yule Island in Papua. This record persuaded the New South Wales government to provide him with a steam launch to explore the Fly.

The 9-ton, 52-foot open vessel, the *Neva*, with only 6 inches of freeboard, crammed with an eleven-member multiracial crew, flying the Italian tricolour and the NSW blue ensign, chuffed its way upriver, with stops to cut firewood for its boiler and to shoot and skin exotic birds and animals. D'Albertis came prepared for trouble with local people. He had a stock of fire-rockets tipped with small amounts of explosive fused to go off close to land. These, warning shots from revolvers and operatic arias from D'Albertis, were enough to scatter the bands of warriors who came to meet the invaders with their bows and arrows. In the deserted villages he helped himself to human heads and other sacred objects.

He got beyond present-day Kiunga before low water and a mutinous crew forced him to turn back. D'Albertis returned to general acclaim, although some critics accused him of "buccaneering" and intimidation. He returned on the *Neva* the next year, but didn't get as far and found the villages ready to deal with him. The *Neva* had to fight its way through flotillas of war canoes. D'Albertis had narrow escapes from accurate volleys of arrows. Frightened crewmen took off in the dinghy, never to be seen again. This time, the gunshots were not fired in the air – if indeed they had been on the first expedition – and they killed at least one Papuan, whose head was taken by a Fijian crewman. To his regret, D'Albertis's life of exploration ended here. Retired in Rome, he built himself a Papuan-style house on stilts in the Pontine Marshes, where he would retire to dream about his adventures on the Fly.[1]

The *Kuku* motored southwards. After lunch of tinned tuna, rice, a green vegetable and two smoked saveloys, Redentor spotted a tarpaulin tent and canoe on the bank. Gagole swung the ship into the stream and hovered nearly. A woman with stringy muscles and grey-black hair paddled the canoe alongside and held up a 60-centimetre barramundi she had just netted.

Two small bags of rice, two tins of spam, three packets of instant noodles, a tin of mackerel and two plastic scrubbers went into her canoe, and the *Kuku* moved on. Redentor and his assistant Samson worked on the fish, scraping off scales the size of ten-cent coins, then cutting it into steaks. Some went into the oven that evening, baked with soy sauce, vinegar and curry spices. The rest went into the freezer.

It was late afternoon, and the anxiety among the crew was whether we'd get to our first stop, the government wharf at Aiambak, in time to watch the first game of the State of Origin, the annual rugby league tournament between New South Wales and Queensland. All of Papua New Guinea stops to watch this fast and muscular event, which usually includes some of its own sons on either side.

That it could be watched in this extremely remote little settlement was a benefit extracted from a fight over the money flowing from the giant Ok Tedi mine.

This project was opened by Australia's BHP in 1981 first getting at the gold in the mountainous cap, then digging a vast open-cut pit for the copper, along with a 140-kilometre highway and the slurry pipeline down to Kiunga, a hydroelectric plant, and a township called Tabubil with its own hotel, school and airport.

But in a region of high rainfall and frequent earthquakes, disaster was not far off. In 1984, a landslide destroyed the half-built tailings dam holding back millions of tonnes of silt. The chemical-laced tailings flooded over the gardens along the rivers. Trees died. Fish stocks dropped. In the 1990s, the region's Yonggom and other language groups started a class action against BHP, eventually getting a US$29 million out-of-court settlement.

BHP wanted to close the mine, but with Bougainville Copper shut down, Port Moresby needed Ok Tedi to save its external accounts and fiscal balances. In 2002 BHP handed its 52 per cent stake to a new trustee, the PNG Sustainable Development Program, with indemnity from future claims.

Fortunately, the trustee company retained two-thirds of its dividends in a Singapore fund to provide an income stream after the mine closed, with the rest devoted to development projects across Western Province. By 2012, the long-term fund amounted to US$1.4 billion. It was a tempting target for Peter O'Neill, after he tipped out Michael Somare in 2011. In 2012, he demanded that BHP renegotiate its divestment to PNG Sustainable Development and declared persona non grata the Ok Tedi chairman Ross Garnaut, the Australian economist who had devised PNG's resource tax system around the time of independence, forcing him to resign. It was effectively nationalisation. In September 2013, bills were passed declaring Sustainable Development's equity – by then 63 per cent following the exit of a minor shareholder – transferred to the government, and the amount of any compensation to be set by the government. BHP's immunity was removed, and it was told by O'Neill it would get no other resource leases in the country until it transferred control of PNG Sustainable Development.

Mekere Morauta, a former head of the central bank who as prime minister in 1999–2002 had attempted deep economic reform only to see it unwound after Somare's return, stepped in as the new chairman of PNG Sustainable Development. He shaped up to fight O'Neill. The Sustainable Development Program had been registered, wisely, as a company in Singapore. As prime minister, Morauta said, he had structured it this way because "I feared in the future that sticky, gluey hands would try to penetrate it". While it failed to get back control of the mine, Sustainable Development retained control over the trust funds.

One of the benefits of this was a chain of mobile phone towers at settlements along the Fly River and its main tributaries. Aiambak has one of them, and through it the State of Origin rugby league game played in Brisbane the night we were due could be linked to a big-screen TV. We tied up in time, and the crew climbed onto the wharf and disappeared to watch.

Next morning, when they reassembled for the peanut butter and spam breakfast, we heard disturbing news. Some months back, the owner of

Aiambak's Chinese store had got into a dispute with a group of young Papuans who claimed he owed them compensation for some work. He refused. The young men returned with bush knives. In a melee, one of them hacked the Chinese storekeeper. He died of the wound. The five Papuans grabbed what they could and fled up country, into the Awin tribal lands to the north. But word got out where they were hiding. Chinese business owners along the Fly chartered a helicopter for a squad of police to catch them. The five were surprised and cornered. All were killed.

Unloading started at 7.30 am and finished at 9.30: bundles of timber, slings of cement bags, boxes of building stuff. The *Kuku* headed down river, and at 1 pm nudged alongside a steep bank of red clay, with barely enough water underneath the hull. On the grass above the embankment were containers and a two-storey steel building, set in a garden featuring delicate palm trees. The garden was surrounded by a security fence of sharp steel spikes. This was the riverside part of a large settlement called Obo.

The hatch-covers came off, the donkey engine clattered into life and Max swung the remaining cargo out of the hold. This time it was PVC pipes, the mysterious steel cabinet, and other things destined for a pilot rice-growing project. A rice expert from Vietnam was watching. We walked into the settlement.

A razor-wire enclosure was going up in front of a corrugated-iron trade store. Inside, racks of brightly patterned clothing were hung up overhead. Young Papuan staff sold packaged food, tools and utensils from behind a grill. A thin Chinese man of about forty was standing by the entrance, dressed in shorts, t-shirt, flip flops and a baseball cap pulled low. He reluctantly engaged in conversation. He came from Fujian, on the east coast of China, eight years ago, leaving his family there.

We walked around the back of a two-storey building, the ground floor an open workshop, the top floor a guesthouse. The workshop had a bench for gutting barramundi and four large freezers. David, an Australian man in shorts and t-shirt, told us he sold the frozen fish to ships going up to Ok Tedi, or sometimes to Bob Bates, an Australian who ran a small chain of luxury wilderness resorts, including one further down the Fly and one in Lake

Murray. Bates flew his own small aircraft to bring down his guests from Mount Hagen, his base, and often took barramundi as a backload.

On one table was a contraption of glass and spiral tubes. David and his Papuan colleague offered me a plastic bottle filled with what the machine made: a clear, filmy liquid.

"It's 95 per cent proof," David said. "Sugar, yeast, water."

"No fruit?"

"We've tried banana, pineapple. But why spoil the flavour? Why bring in beer, that's only 5 per cent alcohol, and have to pay the transport for the rest?"

We declined the drink and went back to the boat. A dinghy loaded with people from Lake Murray was alongside. Redentor sold them two drums of fuel for a bit less than the store was charging. A man on the boat said that everyone in the region was desperate to get their rubber sold. "It's our only cash," he said.

In the morning, a pair of dinghies arrived, flying large national flags. Manesa Kambong came on board to introduce himself. He had just quit his job in the Department of Works to run as a candidate for provincial governor in the upcoming elections. He said he was spending between 150,000 and 200,000 kina on his campaign, a modest amount compared to the millions being splashed in the highlands. "A thousand here and there," he said. His campaign was a long shot, as Kambong was up against forty other candidates. (He was to miss out.)

The *Kuku* backed out of the mooring, its propellor stirring up mud from the shallow bottom. Many pages had been turned in the chart book. Twenty minutes later, at 214 nautical miles from the Fly's mouth, Stonewig turned the *Kuku* left into the Strickland River and we headed northeast. The Strickland was as wide as the Fly down here, its calm surface belying a strong current. Coming down the Fly, the satnav reader showed us making 10 knots. Going upstream in the Strickland, our speed was down to 5.

At 11 am, Stonewig dropped back on the throttle and steered the *Kuku* close to the left bank, where a thatch house was glimpsed through thick palms and low bush. The *Kuku* lay alongside the bank, and the crew tied a rope to an overhanging branch. This was where the loading of the return cargo started.

The *Kuku*'s mission went back to 1967. A young Australian, Warren Dutton, had been in Kiunga four years then, initially as a kiap for the Australian administration at a time when he and other patrol officers were still making first contact with remote groups, dealing occasionally with tribal fights and cannibalism, and the average life expectancy at birth of the Awin and Yonggom people of the upper Fly was estimated at twenty-nine for males and sixteen for females. Just across the watershed of the range, on the Sepik side, at a place called Telefomin, the last fatal clash for a patrol had occurred only ten years earlier, in 1953, with kiap Gerald Szarka, cadet Geoff Harris and constables Buritori and Furari killed by arrows.

Then, in 1967, Dutton resigned to contest the first elections for the new legislative assembly, a successful start to a political career that saw him become a government minister in the early decades of independence. To keep himself employed in the meantime, he agreed to help a syndicate of crocodile skin traders in Lake Murray, the vast lake to the east of the Fly River. Since the 1920s, the administration had been pushing rubber as a cash crop, especially in the wetter parts of Papua. During the Second World War, Papua had kept sending thousands of tonnes of rubber each year to Australia, helping the war effort. The crocodile dealers had some money saved, and Dutton suggested they form a company and try to build up rubber production. "*Tryim thasol*" was the response: "Give it a go."

So the North Fly Rubber Company was born, with Dutton putting in money of his own, although not much happened until the high-yield seeds they ordered sprouted into producing trees some years later. Now a rubber factory ran near the guesthouse and transport enterprise run by Dutton and his wife, Joy, fed by latex collected from hundreds of small holders along the rivers and tracks of Western Province, and even from across the Indonesian border.

At this stop on the Strickland, canoes appeared and tied up alongside. The hatches were opened, and the derrick got into action, swinging aboard cylindrical blocks of latex the size of Turkish poufs. A crewman read the weight from a scale inserted between the cargo hook and the rope sling.

Then the latex was dumped into the hold, which soon emanated a sour, vinegary stink. The sellers climbed up to the deck in front of the wheelhouse. The chart table had now become the counter for purchase, payment doled out through an open window. They were shy, thin people, like Jerry and Koleni Uriba, who got 224 kina for their 160 kilograms, and Gib and Sadawa Jamai, who got 456 kina for their 326 kilograms. Both couples said most of the cash would go towards school fees for their children.

The *Kuku* untied and motored on up the Strickland. At dusk, we came to a high embankment, above which a single light was gleaming. Stonewig put the ship slowly alongside the bank. A crewman secured a bow line to a coconut tree. A crowd of men slowly gathered to look. A separate group of women and small children also watched. Egege village was a seasonal camp, Redentor told me. People come from Lake Murray in the dry months and hunt in the bushland nearby for deer, cassowary and pigs with their dogs and bows and arrows.

Egege was close to the junction of the Herbert River, which brings water from Lake Murray into the Strickland and was the way into the lake. Stonewig asked the onlookers about the level of water in the Herbert. "Very brown," they said.

We had our evening meal of fish and rice. Around the outside lights on the ship were blizzards of insects.

After breakfast, the *Kuku* set off. Watching the depth sounder, hand on the throttle for sudden engine reversal if necessary, Stonewig eased the *Kuku* into the Herbert. Slowly we motored up its twisting course. About 9 am, women paddling a flock of small dugout canoes beckoned us. They traded three large catfish for packets of rice, tins of Besta-brand mackerel in tomato sauce and packets of Maggi noodles. The largest of the catfish was chosen for lunch. Gagole cut off its tail, provoking a wiggle, then proceeded to other cuts before finishing by severing the head. The other two catfish, on the deck close to this exercise, were put into the freezer alive. At least they were eased into death.

Just before 10 am, the *Kuku* reached the southernmost edge of Lake Murray. But what the GPS map on my mobile phone said should be expanses of water were now vast banks of mud, some already capped by grasses and reeds. Stonewig decided not to enter the lake any further. Two years earlier, the *Kuku* was stranded in the lake for two months by falling water. He nosed the ship into one mud bank, tying up to a log from the bow and keeping the stern out in the deepest water with an anchor.

There was a mobile signal here, from a tower at Miwa village. The message went out that rubber tappers will have to bring their latex down to the *Kuku* if they want to sell it. Canoes gathered around the ship, some paddled, some with outboards, and some with tiny Kubota petrol motors attached to a long propellor shaft that doubled as rudder. These motors came from over the Indonesian border, in exchange for fragrant eaglewood, much used in Asian incense, and fish "maw", the dried flotation bladders of large fish like the barramundi that, for some reason, are a prized ingredient in Chinese traditional medicine.

At 1 pm, Redentor rang the ship's bell, and the loading, weighing and paying for the latex in the canoes began. But the need to spend fuel to get across the lake must have deterred many tappers. At the end of the day, the load was only 7 tonnes, a fraction of the *Kuku*'s capacity. Redentor was talking by phone with Warren Dutton about whether to turn back and abandon this buying trip. The cargo taken down to Aiambak and Obo, along with the 7 tonnes of latex, had already taken the voyage above the break-even point.

But my hopes of looking around Lake Murray were not lost. Among the boats gathered around the *Kuku* was an outboard dinghy with North Fly Rubber's local agent, Clarence Jambura, who had come down from the government station at Boboa Island. Not only that, he was connected to the village of Usakof, which I dearly wanted to see. He agreed to take me to Usakof the next morning. Another man selling his rubber, Samson Doa, was down from Usakof and was going back that night. He would tell people I was coming.

The reason for my interest was that a hundred years earlier, in November 1922, the Australian photographer Frank Hurley, along with Allan Riverstone McCulloch, an expert on fish and insects at the Australian Museum in Sydney, had ventured into the lake. It was only the fourth time that white men had gone there, the first group having arrived only nine years earlier.

For many villagers it was their first contact with white men.

Already famous from Ernest Shackleton expedition to the Antarctic and the Western Front, Hurley had been in Papua before, in 1920–21 under the auspices of the Anglican Board of Missions. As well as a treasure-house of black-and-white stills, he had movie footage and sound recordings he was shaping into a silent movie titled *Pearls and Savages*. But he felt it needed more "savagery" – specifically, visuals of head-hunting, cannibalism and strange rituals.

So, with sponsorship by the Hordern department store family, other business figures and the racy Sydney newspaper *The Sun*, and with the imprimatur of the Australian Museum helping him to get permission from the territory administration, Hurley ventured into one of the least explored parts of Australia's territory of Papua, in a locally acquired motorised ketch he renamed the *Eureka*.

Hurley and McCulloch took the *Eureka* up the Fly, Strickland and Herbert rivers into Lake Murray and went ashore, guarded by four crew members armed with pistols and rifles. They came across a skull and arrows placed on their path but replaced this warning with "peace offerings" of cloth and empty tins, and continued towards a village on a rise above the lake, which seems to have been Usakof.

They found no one around and entered a ceremonial longhouse in search of "ethnological" specimens. As Hurley noted:

> In the cause of Science, McCulloch allows that even unfair exchange is no robbery; so we collected and exchanged to the great advantage of the owners and to our complete satisfaction. Skulls, human bits, and tit-bits filled our bone-bag; whilst axes, knives, and fabrics were substituted ... Human heads! Stuffed heads! ... Had we raided a bank and carried off the bullion we could scarcely have been more pleased with such desirable objects.

A week later, a group of men, probably from Usakof, ventured out to the *Eureka* in their long dugout canoes. Some climbed onboard the ketch and were shown its marvels of equipment and machines. They tasted salt and sugar. Hurley persuaded one striking-looking warrior named Muji to sit for a photograph, one of the fine portraits that are perhaps his best legacy from his Papuan expeditions. Then they returned to Port Moresby.

In the early morning, I set off for Usakof with Clarence Jambura in his dinghy, the little *Kuku* receding in the vast scape of water, mudflats and cloudy sky. (On its next rubber-buying trip it went right down to the delta of the Fly. Traversing the Tirere Passage eastwards to get to the Bamu River, it anchored for the night. Redentor radioed that at 5 am several dinghies swarmed the *Kuku*. Men armed with bush knives claimed the ship had cut Damera village's fishing nets, and in compensation demanded fuel, replacement nets and money. Redentor wisely gave the "pirates" some of what they demanded, and the *Kuku* was allowed to proceed.)

After about ninety minutes crossing the lake, seeing clumps of trees on islands and promontories, beds of lotus, and occasional canoes, we came to Usakof. A row of elevated houses of rough timber and thatch fronted the beach, where dinghies and canoes were pulled up. As Clarence cut the motor and we drifted in, Samson Doa walked down. He guided us through a village of similar houses, open on the ground where cooking fires smouldered in beds of stones, with ladders leading up to a single room above.

It was a Sunday, and across a grassy square with football posts the village's churches – Catholic, Seventh-day Adventist and at least two other denominations – were ringing bells and wooden gongs. But they were ignored by a crowd of about a hundred men, young to middle-aged, waiting in a longhouse of timber and thatch.

Inside, with Doa translating from the local Kuni language and Tok Pisin as required, Usakof's senior men asked me about my purpose. I explained that it was the centenary of the Hurley-McCulloch expedition, and I wanted to know their collective memory of it.

I had some of Hurley's photographs on my mobile phone, including a famous one of McCulloch sitting with a spread of their collected skulls and artefacts, and showed them around.

Unanimously, they wanted the "powerful things" that Hurley and McCulloch had stolen to be restored somehow to Usakof. "Those things are still powerful," said Amsida Dili, fifty-three. Could they hurt people? "Yes." Could they save people? "Yes."

Many said that the warrior-chief Muji whom Hurley had photographed (wrongly transcribing his name as Hamuji) had disappeared when the *Eureka* left the lake. They wanted him accounted for. "Frank Hurley took Muji, and all those powerful things," said one man. "We are looking for him. How can we get our powerful things back? We are looking: maybe he had children, grandchildren in Sydney."

"Before, our grandfathers were relying on these things," said Akana Malo, fifty-four. "Then the white men came and took these things from us, along with the chief Muji. They were our belief, until we were civilised, until the missionaries – from them we knew God and we started worshipping. Those things were powerful, and today these things are still powerful.

"Our grandfathers were fighting with six other tribes, and they were using these powerful things. Frank Hurley came in the middle of a fight. Our people were not very strong after that."

Adrian Umaka, who told me he was a great-grandson of Muji, was a pastor with one of the churches in the village and was translating the Bible into Kuni. But he also thought the objects still had power. "There are two special things, a jawbone and a skull," he said. "They can talk, they can tell. They can make the enemy weak. They can tell us when they come."

On their return to Port Moresby before heading home, Hurley and McCulloch ran into problems with the haul they had collected from Lake Murray and from other places along the rivers. The magistrate in Daru, the government station at the mouth of the Fly, had registered a complaint of theft, menacing behaviour and "unethical collecting" against them. On their way down the Fly, Hurley and McCulloch had been less than discreet about their collecting methods when talking to a missionary. The administration impounded their entire collection, pending an inquiry. Hubert Murray, the still-revered lieutenant-governor of Papua from 1908 until his death in 1940, was highly protective of his native charges.

An allegation that Papuans had been forced to hand over items at gunpoint was found to be untrue, and it was accepted that some had been traded for modern utensils. However, Hurley and McCulloch were found at fault in a visit to the village of Kaimari, in the Purari River estuary before they entered Lake Murray. After taking magnificent pictures of warriors sitting at the entrance to a cathedral-like longhouse hung with carved and painted boards depicting ancestor stories, the pair had sneaked into the longhouse while Kaimari's men were away at a mourning ceremony. Penetrating its holy of holies, hidden behind a screen, they found crocodile-like figures woven from cane strips. Hurley used a flash to take pictures. Beneath the figures were several bull-roarers, small boards whirled at the end of strings that made an ominous sound striking fear of the monster-god into the villagers. The pair helped themselves to some of these bull-roarers. Then, with suspicious men returning, they replaced the screen and retreated, setting off firecrackers to cause confusion.

In *The Sun* and in letters to the prime minister, Billy Hughes, and other ministers, Hurley railed against what he claimed was unfair and hypocritical treatment by the administration of Papua. Confiscation and return of a storyboard and several bull-roarers to Kaimari eventually resolved the dispute. The rest of the collection was released and deposited with the Australian Museum. Nothing was returned to Usakof.

As for the fate of Muji, there is nothing in the diaries of Hurley or McCulloch, or the records of the Papuan administration, to suggest he might have been taken away on the *Eureka*. It seems likely to remain a mystery for Usakof's people.

For Hurley, the controversy about unethical collecting was "water off a duck's back", says Tim Griffiths, a Sydney lawyer who has written about Hurley and visited Lake Murray. Allan McCulloch, who came back from Papua in poor health from dysentery and malaria, felt it deeply. He was the "fall guy", says Brendan Atkins, author of a recent biography of McCulloch, *The Naturalist*. In 1924, the museum's trustees refused to approve him attending a scientific conference in Hawai'i, triggering a mental breakdown. On a year's leave on half pay, he found another sponsor for an anticipated fisheries symposium to Hawai'i the next year. He wrote a far-sighted paper about conserving the Pacific's fish stocks. But before he delivered it, McCulloch's depression deepened. He wangled papers to buy a pistol and shot himself. He was only forty.

The Hurley-McCulloch expedition remains a matter of embarrassment to the Australian Museum, custodian of the collected material and images. Museums in Germany, France and Britain are now returning artefacts pillaged from former colonial possessions, notably the famous Benin Bronzes of West Africa. In Australia, campaigns have been mounted for the return of Aboriginal artefacts taken by explorers and Aboriginal human remains taken as ethnological specimens by nineteenth-century scientists and lodged in museums overseas. Less publicised are the extensive collections of Indigenous and Oceanic artefacts and human remains – mostly in the form of trophy skulls and preserved heads – lodged in the country's own museums.

The Australian Museum holds the Hurley-McCulloch collection and some 1300 photographic images taken by Hurley in Papua. Murray, the governor, also built up the Papuan Official Collection – he ordered his patrol officers to bring back samples acquired voluntarily and forbad personal collecting – to record native culture before it was changed by European contact or the people themselves died out. The collection is now at the National Museum of Australia in Canberra, but only parts of it are ever exhibited. The MacGregor Collection, named for an earlier governor, when Papua was under British rule, is in the Queensland Museum. Both these collections are now essentially held in trust for the successor state, Papua New Guinea, as both MacGregor and Murray stipulated.

The moment has now arrived for the Australian Museum to restore the stolen items to Usakof, it seems. But if so, how? In Usakof, I canvassed with the senior men some of the options. Return them to Usakof? But if so, how would they be secured and preserved? Lodge them in Papua New Guinea's new National Museum in Port Moresby? Or could they be given some special recognition at the Australian Museum?

There are precedents for return. The Australian Museum has been turning over objects to Australian Indigenous communities for nearly fifty years, and more recently to New Zealand and Pacific nations as well. At Vanuatu's independence in 1980, the museum returned a large slit-drum, collected on Efate and donated by a Burns Philp trader in the 1890s. As for the MacGregor collection, ANU scholar Anna Edmundson has written that the Queensland Museum reached an agreement with prime minister Michael Somare after Papua New Guinea's independence in 1975 to return 60 per cent of it to Port Moresby, retaining the rest as a mark of shared history. But these official collections contained very little of the "inalienable patrimony" of Papuan tribes such as ancestor figures, bull-roarers and sacred flutes which simply would not have been traded voluntarily at any price. Most items were the everyday weapons and utensils of the time, easily replaceable, and not necessarily the result of unequal barter. Papuans and others often astutely traded them to get the manufactured items they wanted.

The Hurley-McCulloch collection seems different. That the administration confiscated and returned two of its sacred bull-roarers suggests, in retrospect, the entire collection was suspect. As Atkins found in a note by McCulloch to his museum about his negotiations at Kaimari, where, as well as the two bull-roarers stolen on a first visit, they persuaded reluctant men to hand over several more of the instruments:

> All the time there was the feeling that I was violating the genuine beliefs and fears of a large crowd who would certainly have refused permission to even see these things had it not been for the fear in which white men are held in villages "under control" of the government.[2]

When repatriations do happen, most transfers are to national museums. To send the items to an isolated community, where most buildings are made from bush materials and the only electricity comes from small solar panels, would risk rapid deterioration, or possibly theft and sale on the market for "primitive art" in Europe and North America.

The Australian Museum's list of objects from the Hurley-McCulloch expedition includes some 845 from Western Province, including five "human skulls" and one "human cranial", which could fit the collective memory in Usakof of what was taken. These "skulls" could possibly be the distinctive heads kept at Lake Murray, where the skin and neck are retained, stuffed with clay and plant material. Such "over-model skulls" were unlikely to have been willingly traded.

Handling them is a delicate matter. "These objects hold great power to this day, especially for people from those cultures," says Atkins, who keeps open in his book the idea that in some kind of "karmic trouble" they might have affected McCulloch's health. Across Melanesia, from Fiji to New Guinea, fear of sorcery runs deep. Tim Griffiths says he can't persuade some Papua New Guineans to come with him to the lovely new National Museum in Port Moresby, for fear they might see or touch some object with bad powers.

Some scholars think sacred objects such as the heads have no place in a foreign museum anyway. "The best place for them is to be returned," Edmundson said. "There's no point keeping things in storage that can never be displayed, and ethically cannot be used as teaching aids or be researched."

I left in Clarence Jambura's dinghy to overnight on Boboa Island, location of the government station at Lake Murray. I thought about the yearning for recognition I'd felt among Usakof's people, members of a language group with only about 6000 people. It was expressed in a wistful remark made by Adrian Umaka, Muji's great-grandson and translator of the Bible into Kuni, as he showed me around Usakof.

"The world does not know us," he said.

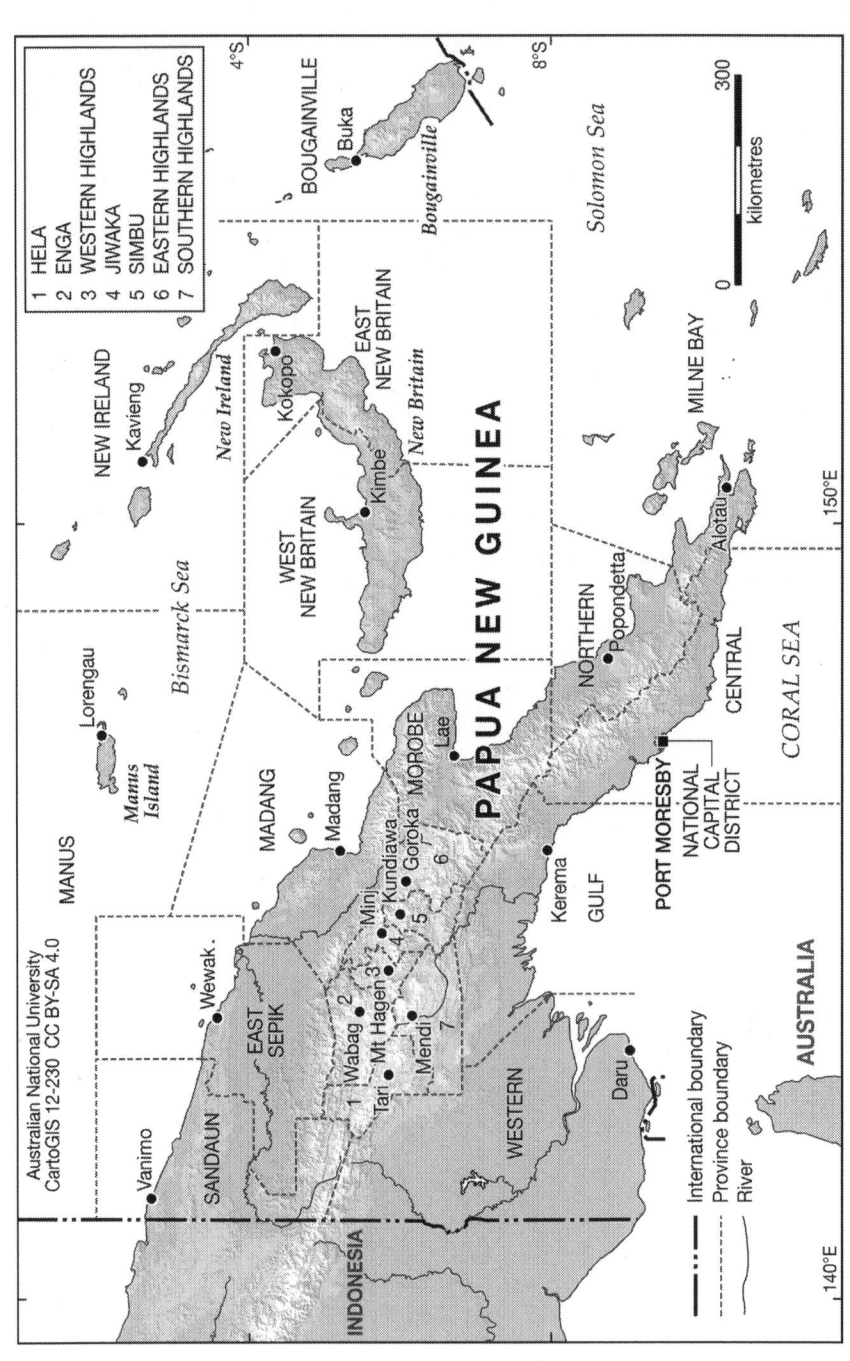

12

THE HIGHLANDS

The Third Realm

DOWN THE BUMPY GRASS AIRSTRIP on Boboa Island, Bob Bates gunned his single-engine turboprop and climbed away from Lake Murray towards Mount Hagen. Steep ridges and deep valleys replaced the undulating jungle below. Tiny villages and isolated houses sat in clearings on the valley floors and hillsides, some with narrow roads snaking up to them, some not. Then the green-black bulk of Mount Giluwe loomed above us on the right, its crater of old lava and ash, scored by rain, more than 3000 feet above our 11,000-foot cruise level.

The first white men to see this mountain were the Australian gold prospector Mick Leahy and the assistant district officer Jim Taylor in 1933. The aeroplane had been indirectly responsible for this opening to the world. Four years after the 1926 rush into the tropical Klondike of Wau, Bulolo and Edie Creek at the eastern end of New Guinea island, individual gold prospectors were being pushed aside by bigger money raised on the stock exchanges of Australia and Canada. Sluices and pans were replaced by massive dredges, floating in ponds on the riverbeds, sucking up gravel.

A new aircraft made this possible. The Junkers G31 was ugly – a monster with a corrugated aluminium fuselage and three motors, one in front of the open cockpit – but it could carry over 3 tonnes of cargo, loaded by crane through a big hatch in the cabin roof. This was just enough for the largest component of the gold dredges that could not be disassembled further, a tumbler shaft, to be flown in from Lae on the coast – with only sixty minutes of fuel for the forty-five-minute flight and the copilot left behind.

Some prospectors signed up to work for the big companies, housed in Australian-style townships with clubs, sporting tournaments and dances. "But for others, the lifestyle of the independent miner continued to exert a strong pull," writes Michael Waterhouse in his history of this gold rush. "With little mining possible around Edie Creek, many miners began to look further afield – in the process exploring country never before visited by Europeans."[1]

Mick Leahy had been a railway clerk and timber cutter in Townsville before joining the rush in 1926, along with three of his brothers. In 1930, aged twenty-nine, he and another prospector, Michael Dwyer, searched rivers northwest of the known goldfields and came within sight of the Goroka Valley, in what is now the Eastern Highlands Province. They went south and found the Wahgi River, encountering large, previously unknown groups of people who thought the foreigners were ancestors and tried to rub off their white skins. They kept going southwards through the cordillera, using canoes when the river widened, and reached the Gulf of Papua, becoming the first white men to cross the New Guinea mainland.

Back in the goldfields, Mick and his brother Paddy prospected in closer but more deadly areas, in the Watut River domain of the fierce Kukukuku tribe. In 1931, with only a few seconds' warning from one of their carriers, they woke to a pre-dawn attack. Mick was clubbed on the head and Paddy hit with arrows, but they blazed back with their guns, killing several warriors. The New Guinea administration mounted punitive expeditions, randomly arresting men who might possibly have been in the area of the attacks on the prospectors and killing many Kukukuku who fought back.

Unable to stop the miners and missionaries from spreading out, the administration extended its network of patrol posts, clearing landing strips for them to be supplied by light aircraft. The furthest out was near the present-day town of Kainantu, where mountains start to rise to the west, established in 1932.

THE HIGHLANDS

Aviation and pacification went together from that point, with aerial reconnaissance a precursor to patrols out into "uncontrolled" areas.

Leahy was undeterred from exploration, but he was now more wary and ready to kill at the first sign of hostility. In 1933, he and others entered the densely populated Wahgi Valley. Along with the administration's Jim Taylor, he crossed the territory of the Chimbu people to present-day Mount Hagen. In 1934, an expedition took them west into the land of the Enga, to a point 32 kilometres beyond the present-day provincial capital, Wabag. "The Highlands were now open: aerodromes were enthusiastically stamped out by myriad bare feet and villagers sent to the coast to bring back amazing tales of white men's cargo," writes historian James Griffin.[2]

Up until these explorations, the administration had comfortably assumed that the interior of New Guinea was a mass of impossible mountains, lightly populated. This myth was exploded when Leahy and Taylor went far beyond Kainantu. On his return, Taylor reported finding of a region inhabited by an estimated 200,000 people, which he called the "Middle Kingdom".

Taylor found his account scarcely believed by his superiors, who until then thought the 38,000 Tolai people of the Gazelle Peninsula were the largest local group. Actually, projecting back from early postwar census numbers, the population would have been more like 500,000. "In the space of one month, in 1933, the government of the then Mandated Territory of New Guinea had its administrative responsibility for people doubled," wrote Ian Downs, prewar kiap and postwar coffee planter in the highlands.[3]

A rush of gold miners and missionaries followed, many getting into violent clashes with local people. The administration promptly declared the whole region "uncontrolled" and closed it to all Europeans, with the Leahy brothers and a few missionaries of established churches excepted. Patrol posts with small detachments of police opened in several centres and extended a tenuous peace.

This ban on entry, and then the Pacific War – when the highlands became forward bases for air and commando harassment of the Japanese in Lae and the northern coast – kept the middle kingdom from becoming "another Kenya", where a fertile valley, hard-working people and pleasant climate drew in white settlers. When civil administration returned, there were many ex-officials and others seeking mining licences in places such as the Porgera River and land allocations around Goroka. But this form of colonisation was deliberately prevented by Canberra, which allowed only a few expatriates to settle outside the towns and began encouraging the local people to plant coffee and other cash crops. The new peace, although broken by occasional eruptions of tribal fighting, allowed the highlanders to stop their previous migration up into the mountain sides for safety and re-occupy the valley floors.

As some of the privileged pioneers were allowed to stay, the Leahy brothers moved into agriculture. Mick gained a lease on land between Wau and Lae. He married an Australian woman and had five children with her, but never acknowledged the three children he had with Mount Hagen women who had "unabashedly" volunteered to test his humanity in the exploration days – they were raised by his brother Danny. Another brother, Jim Leahy, was a pioneer in coffee, founding the trading firm Collins and Leahy.

Jim Taylor, along with kiap John Black, undertook an even more arduous exploration in 1938, striking out westwards from Mount Hagen through the upper Sepik region to the Netherlands East Indies border. It took fifteen months to cover 3000 kilometres, with his train of 300 carriers and police resupplied by air drops. In the process he discovered the Porgera goldfield, recently established by Canada's Barrick Gold as a huge open-cut mine. When war came, he went to Angoram on the Sepik to relieve a district officer. In a Conradian episode, the officer refused to hand over his authority and ambushed Taylor's party, wounding Taylor before shooting himself. Taylor stayed in the Sepik, harassing Japanese patrols and rescuing Allied airmen. He left the colonial service in 1949, married a Wahgi Valley woman, Yerima Manamp, and settled near Goroka to raise a family and grow coffee and peanuts.

Flying into the highlands today, the aircraft breaking through clouds above wide green valleys patched with brown squares of well-weeded vegetable gardens and scattered with clusters of houses roofed with corrugated iron or thatch, smoke rising from cooking fires and burn-offs, you share some of the wonderment felt by the earlier arrivals from the outside world.

The local men now wear football shirts emblazoned with the sponsors of rugby league teams in far off New South Wales and Queensland, and the women loose floral tops over plain skirts or leggings. They consult their mobile phones and queue at ATMs outside the Bank South Pacific branches. They wait for rides in pickup trucks and minibuses back to their settlements. Less than a hundred years after "first contact", the speed with which the highlanders adapted is still astonishing.

They threw themselves out into the wider world with gusto once peace and civil administration returned at the end of 1945. Their young men joined a highland labour scheme run by the newly combined government of Papua and New Guinea, taking them to plantations and work sites across the country and exposing them to modern ways.

Pressure built in Australia for European settlement, causing the government to consider applications for blocks of no more than 200 acres from willing lessors. A flood of applicants included officials, real estate promoters and even Australian members of parliament. Most were rejected, and a compromise saw a very limited number approved for people such as the Leahy brothers and Taylor, who had existing local relationships. The blocks offered to them were sited in land previously used as battlegrounds. Dispersed along feeder roads to Goroka and Mount Hagen, they acted as buffers between traditional enemies and as pilot coffee plantations for local people to study and emulate.

The high-grown Arabica coffee that resulted became an important cash crop and export. The need to get it to market impelled the construction of a highway into the highlands. First came the relatively easy stretch up the Markham River Valley from Lae, across low-lying grassland for about 160 kilometres to Kainantu. A second stretch from Goroka took six months, with gangs of workers paid in cash and coffee seedlings. They were fed with produce from gardens planted in advance. Using hand tools, they excavated cuttings through the hillsides, cambered the road, laid gravel and felled huge trees to support dozens of bridges. Another workforce of up to 10,000 carved out a similar road west from Goroka to Mount Hagen. The labourers worked without protective clothing in cold and rainy conditions, over mountain passes up to 2500 metres above sea level.

By the end of 1953, cars and light trucks could drive up from the Markham Valley to Mount Hagen, along much the same route walked by Mick Leahy and Jim Taylor in 1933. Further roadwork extended the highway west to Wabag and Laiagam in the Enga lands, and a spur highway south from near Mount Hagen down to Mendi in the southern highlands. By the time the coffee seedlings grew into productive bushes, the highway was ready to take the beans down to Lae. Highlanders who had seen aircraft years before any vehicles considered cars more modern. By 1955 some were driving their own trucks down to Lae.

It was a fine day as Bob Bates levelled his little plane down onto the runway at Mount Hagen and taxied to a collection of parked aircraft along from the main passenger terminal. After climbing over the back of the copilot's seat and the cargo in the cabin, I got out into the warm dry heat of the highlands.

We watched the unloading of bags and consignments, and Bob oversaw the placement of polystyrene boxes of frozen barramundi into the back of his ute. He drove me into town, several kilometres along a road that had more businesses and fast-food shops than I remembered, plus traffic lights at a big intersection that few drivers seemed to be obeying. Bob point out two funeral parlours facing each other across the highway, one called Paradise, the other Serenity, both run by Filipinos who'd started out as partners then become competitors.

Bob dropped me at the Missionary House, a guesthouse that according to my guidebook offered a cheaper but still central alternative to the main hotel, the Highlander. It was close to the Mount Hagen Club, which I remembered from previous trips as the place to meet local oldtimers: expats working in the coffee industry, first- or second-wave Chinese businessmen, some high-ranking Papua New Guineans. I walked around at dusk, had a solitary meal and a couple of beers, then made to walk back to the guesthouse. It was dark now, and the barkeeper, a Southern Highlander named Christine, was appalled. She called in one of the security guards to escort me. Holding a sword-length bush knife at his side, he walked me the 300 metres back.

THE HIGHLANDS

In Mount Hagen, I'd hoped to meet again with the local politician who was one of the most impressive of the Melanesian big-men of his generation. Paias Wingti had grown up in a nearby village as a member of the Jiga tribe and the son of a notable big man. His father, Wingti Wimb, had gone to work for Danny Leahy on his Kuta alluvial gold lease in the 1930s, becoming "boss boi" or foreman and then, in 1946, was appointed a *luluai* (village official) by the administration. He had the prosperity and status to marry six wives, and he fathered thirty-one children – although this was no barrier to him getting baptised as a Catholic aged fifty-nine and receiving communion from the hands of the visiting Pope John Paul II in 1982.

Paias Wingti, born in 1951, did not start school until age ten, but he quickly caught up at a high school in Mount Hagen. He entered the University of Papua New Guinea to do an economics degree, became active in student politics and travelled to Australia. In his final year he dropped out to run in the 1977 elections, the first after independence, and won a seat in the Western Highlands.

Ten years after independence, in 1985, I made my first visit to Papua New Guinea to interview the prime minister, Michael Somare. The gloss had come off his promises for nationhood. The economy had slowed, and unemployment and crime were rampant in the main towns. But the coffee industry was thriving. I met a young German technician in one of the factories: he told me there was not a more equitable industry structure for growers anywhere in the world.

Soon after that visit, Wingti led other "young Turks" in a vote of no confidence that ousted Somare. I visited again, and found a leader more attuned to the deregulated, pro-market thinking of the time, a reserved personality who occasionally broke out in an impish smile.

Julius Chan, who was then his deputy and finance minister, gave him high marks in his 2014 autobiography. Chan found Wingti different from other highlanders.

> He did not carry that heavy Highlander 'bang' type of impulsive decision making, although when it was required he would do it. Otherwise

he was good to work with, a very smart man who had some good advisors around him and friends in the business world. He was able to assess the presentation of a subject and then make a decision without having to think much about it. He was really astute.[4]

While Wingti certainly would have soaked up many lessons about leadership from his father, his own authority was by no means hereditary. Unlike the pyramid of chiefly power found in Polynesian societies such as Hawai'i and Tonga, and transplanted to Fiji by the Tongan invasions, Papua New Guinea's leaders had to make their own way, in smaller, fragmented societies. They had to build up obligations, usually by calculated displays of munificence and charity. Wealth was accumulated to be given away, in the right doses to the right people. Big men such as Wingti had to show themselves as humble and modest.

In 2006, I encountered Wingti again in Mount Hagen. He was then the governor of the Western Highlands, a position that gave him both a seat in the national parliament and supervision of government activity and spending across the whole province. Wingti was sitting at a table in the garden of the Highlander Hotel, an imposing figure in a wide-brimmed felt hat surrounded by deferential men. I went up and reintroduced myself. He remembered me from the 1980s and invited me to join him on a drive out to an important peace ceremony.

We climbed into his LandCruiser and as we drove we chatted about his efforts to promote the coffee industry. I gathered he had some investments in it himself. I thought PNG coffee had lost its distinction in the market, thinking of how Timor-Leste had promoted its coffee by association with its independence struggle. There should be stories attached to PNG coffee, I said. He liked that.

We went along narrow roads between small plantations, up into hills where immense eucalypts and *klinki* pines waved in a cool breeze above Kelua, a village of low houses built variously of corrugated iron and thatch. On a grassy, shaded field, no less than 240 large pigs were pegged to stakes. Semi-naked people adorned with multicoloured feathers and face paint danced. It was a gathering of the Yamuga tribe, Wingti explained. They were about to hand over these pigs to other tribes who had helped them in a huge tribal war that had erupted in 1975.

A pastor, George Joshua Aki, got up to read a lesson from the Book of Judges, about the Ammonites being delivered into the hands of the Israelites. Local leaders harangued the crowd. Wingti lectured them about the need to work hard in their village plantations and become more self-reliant. "Unemployment is the biggest problem and it's going to get worse unless we can get some economic activity going," he said. The provincial treasury chief, Nathan Wantepe, who had travelled up with us, stepped up to hand over an 80,000 kina cheque for new village classrooms.

We got back in the vehicle and went back to Mount Hagen before the clubbing and cooking of the pigs. Wingti was ousted in the elections the following year, but voted back in for two more terms in 2012.

This visit, Wingti was out of town in Port Moresby, and I never did catch up with him on his campaign for re-election, which failed. I took a minibus down the highway, crammed among extended highlander families and sacks of yams, to Goroka, where the current prime minister was due to campaign. At the town's airport, I waited among a clutch of heavily armed police and local candidates also wearing the kind of Australian bush felt hat favoured by Wingti. James Marape ambled across the tarmac from his chartered aircraft, smiling as young men dressed as the region's famous "mud men" warriors danced around him. At fifty-one, he was twenty years younger than Wingti, and although also a highlander – a Huli tribesman from Mendi in the Southern Highlands, in his case – he had a grounding across Papua New Guinea. His father had been a Seventh-day Adventist pastor; Marape had spent his childhood in various parishes, from Ningerum in the upper Fly River country to Buin in the south of Bougainville. He'd gone to the church's high school in Goroka and then the university in Port Moresby. Later he married Rachael, a Sepik woman raised in Madang. All these places claimed him to some extent as their own.

On splitting with Peter O'Neill in 2019, Marape had joined the vestiges of the Pangu Party that Somare and others had founded in the run-up to independence and rebuilt it into a strong electoral force (Pangu is an acronym for "Papua and New Guinea United"). Throughout the day, I travelled in a police vehicle to crowded election gatherings on village greens to hear Marape promising, in Tok Pisin, that his government would back indigenous enterprise.

Back in Goroka that evening, the party had taken over most of the main hotel, the Bird of Paradise, with candidates and campaign workers gathered in the big dining room that evening. Marape had promised to come and give us travelling reporters one-on-one interviews. He arrived and worked the room, greeting people as he moved from table to table.

We journalists staked out an area on the open patio next to the dining room to allow natural light for the video camera set up by the ABC's Natalie Whiting. But there was an awkward presence. A heavily intoxicated highland man was hanging around our group, trying to tell us something. As Marape came over, hotel security guards and burly police officers moved in for what was going to be a rough eviction. But then Marape spotted the situation and walked closer. To our astonishment he embraced the man and got him to sit quietly in a corner. We found out later the man had been his high-school classmate. He was now somewhat lapsed by Seventh-day Adventist standards, but still not cast into darkness by Marape.

Before my encounter with Marape that day, I'd been trying to fathom this politician. Although steeped in Biblical teaching, he had joined politics in his place of tribal origin among the Huli, who were exponents of political clientelism par excellence. It was a region where candidates amassed vast amounts of money, which they then dispensed to create obligations among local opinion leaders, and to hand out largesse such as slabs of South Pacific beer to ordinary voters.

In previous election campaigns I'd seen rival groups of political musclemen on the brink of violence with makeshift weapons. This time it was widely reported they had assault rifles, and the demand for guns was so high, the black-market price had risen sharply. In the years up to 2014, ExxonMobil and its partners had spent US$19 billion tapping into natural gas deposits tucked in the folds of the cordillera, building liquefaction plants and facilities to load the liquified gas into cryogenic tankers for export to Asia. For years, convoys of heavy trucks had rumbled day and night up the highway from Lae to bring the components of the wells and processing plant up for fabrication. In an echo of the early 1930s experience bringing gold dredges bit by bit into Bulolo and Wau by air, the largest parts of the LNG plant were simply too big to be hauled by road. The consortium carved a long, paved airstrip out of the hills. A giant Antonov jet transport played the same role as the Junkers trimotors eight decades earlier.

A small fraction of this money got splashed around the Southern Highlands in provincial and community royalties. Some was spent on public facilities. A lot went to village leaders, men who sat around in all-day card games, sending out for *buai* and cigarettes. How could Marape – who had come to power three years earlier proclaiming he wanted Papua New Guinea to be the world's "richest Black Christian nation" – not be steeped in this clientelism if he wanted to stay on top?

Academics told me that in this election, would-be candidates in the highlands should not bother unless they had at least 2 million kina ($800,000) to spend. At places like Mount Hagen, locals scoffed and said a winning budget would be more like 20 million kina. With an average of thirty candidates vying for each seat, the region was awash with voter bribery. Some candidates were running to lose, selling their second and third preferences to others.

Marape was up against a main rival universally acknowledged to be a moneybags and master of political intrigue, and to have a vendetta against Marape himself. Peter O'Neill had been educated in Australia as an accountant and built up a sizable business operation, before, as we have seen, getting into some legal difficulties in the late 1990s over his running of the state pension and investment funds. But he won a seat in parliament, and in 2011 was able to take advantage of an absence due to illness by the ageing Michael Somare to seize the prime ministership.

At the time, O'Neill had been hailed by some as representing a chance to clean up the laxities of Somare's second and longest stretch in power, marked by a free-for-all for Malaysia's loggers, an open door for Chinese small traders, collapsing health and education services and falling efficiency in state-run infrastructure. Despite the earlier scandals, many had cautiously welcomed O'Neill as someone who might bring private-sector efficiency into government.

These hopes were dashed. "There was no such thing as conflict of interest," says Paul Barker. "His business enterprises were burgeoning. He was clearly spending a lot of his working hours advancing his business interests, rather than the government's interests." Ministers were irked at being pushed out of decisions made by a circle of associates around the prime minister, and department chiefs appointed over their heads. His ordinary MPs were also becoming unhappy. Early on, O'Neill had increased the electorate fund put at the discretion of local MPs to 10 million kina a year. Ostensibly meant to support government services such as clinics, schools and roads, the funds are often deployed to attach the MP's name to high-profile projects, or for electioneering. "It's pork-barrelling," Governor Allan Bird told me. "It's not a recent phenomenon, it's just become more pronounced."

A tightening of this funding contributed to O'Neill's downfall. When he came into office, the economy was booming, thanks largely to the ExxonMobil gas project. But soon after the gas came on stream in 2014, global oil and gas prices crashed. O'Neill's government had borrowed A$1.3 billion from the Union Bank of Switzerland (UBS) to buy 10.1 per cent of the Australian company Oil Search, a partner with ExxonMobil. When its share price fell, a put option forced O'Neill's government to sell the shareholding and repay the loan, at a loss of $340 million. When gas revenue streams dropped because of the lower prices, O'Neill resorted to commercial loans and high-interest bond sales to domestic institutions to finance the government. The government interest bill soared from about 5 per cent of domestic revenue to about 20 per cent by the time he left office.

O'Neill's treasury now had less money to hand out to the MPs' slush funds for their local projects. "I guess that's where the economy intersects with politics," explained Maholopa Laveil, an economics lecturer at the University of Papua New Guinea. "If you have government revenue falling, you can't keep governing coalitions together. That's when you lose power."

There were other casualties. The 20 percent of MPs' electoral funds supposed to be spent on health was the first to be cut back. Vaccination rates for infants fell from 70–80 per cent to 30 per cent by 2018, contributing to outbreaks of polio and tuberculosis. At the best of times, the delivery of essential services had been falling behind population growth, which at 3 per cent a year meant the population would double in about twenty-four years. To cap it all off, a severe earthquake hit the Southern Highlands in 2018, causing widespread damage and casualties, with emergency operations further draining government revenues. It was also seen as symbolic of things going wrong in Port Moresby. The highlands are normally much less geologically active than the volcanic "ring of fire" around the north coast and eastern islands.

In early 2019, Marape was able to pull the rug from under O'Neill in a vote of confidence. As we've seen, he then brought in Bryan Kramer as police minister to go after O'Neill. Not surprisingly, this gave an edge to O'Neill's anxiety to get the prime ministership back, or at least to be the power behind the throne. In this election, O'Neill's People's National Congress had endorsed no less than ninety-four candidates for the 118 seats, and none seemed to be lacking funding. O'Neill also received conspicuously favourable coverage in the strongest newspaper, the *Post-Courier*, whose journalists and senior executives had been entertained in an all-night drinking session at O'Neill's brewery at the start of the campaign.

Marape's first three years as prime minister were not easy. The Covid-19 pandemic put the country into isolation and hampered vital supplies, although the mass casualties many feared did not eventuate despite a vaccination rate of only a few per cent. Then, just before the elections in 2022, fuel prices jumped because of the Ukraine crisis. Those higher petroleum prices would show up in increased government revenue months later, but the effect on costs was immediate.

Then, having jumped from O'Neill's party to Pangu – which clings somewhat to its 1960s liberation-theory origins with a policy of "economic independence" – Marape put the squeeze on the country's biggest gold producer, the Canadian and Chinese-owned Porgera mine, after its operating lease expired. He demanded and eventually got a higher equity share for surrounding Enga Province and landowners, with more to be acquired in another ten years. This involved a two-year shutdown at a time of high gold prices, with a loss of about 2 billion kina in revenue. O'Neill made much of this in the campaign.

And after three years, there were still some wondering how different James Marape was from Peter O'Neill. "He's an enigma," said Paul Barker. Marape engaged well with everyone, referred often to his Christian faith, and did not hold back on delivering hard news if required. "But others say: Yes, but he's the Christian, sweet face of Peter O'Neill. He learnt his tricks with Peter O'Neill, he was part of his cabinet [as finance minister], he knew what was going on, he wasn't blowing whistles."

Allan Bird, the East Sepik governor, found Marape to be sincere in what he said and promised. "He wants the right thing, and then he has to balance it among all the conflicting interests" Bird said. "That can't be easy. We're on the same WhatsApp group and the guy goes to bed at 3 am every night."

But there were some who said Marape was just as bad as O'Neill. One was Father Jan Czuba, a Polish-born priest and former rector of the Catholic-founded Divine Word University in Madang, who had been secretary of the government's higher education department. He told me of a brush with Marape over a demand for diversion of funds from the department's budget for political purposes.

In Goroka, I asked Marape how he was different from O'Neill. He demurred at saying he was a better man. "Every man has his good side," Marape said. "But as time progressed, power got into [O'Neill's] head, and his heart shifted away from the main goalpost, which is to say equally to all parts of the country and do it right for everyone. The decisions made must be collective decisions, instead of one-man decisions. We come from a Melanesian society where it's more democratic in every sense, where you make decisions collectively. You take the blame together. But if you make one-man decisions, you must take the blame with you. Some of us reached the tolerance rate where we can't be part of that sort of regime where you make a call and you expect everyone else to follow."

I asked Marape what drove him, which is a softish question to toss to a politician, but sometimes gets them to think beyond their current talking points. Marape said it was his rural upbringing. "I come from a place where they've been harvesting oil and gas, and even up to the date I took office there was no electricity, no sealed road," he said "That is my mind space. At independence I was at a place called Nomad River. If I were to take you back there today, that place is as it was in 1975. Yet only thirty minutes by road you have a world-class gold and copper mine, Ok Tedi. So this kind of thing drives me. I feel the unfairness of distribution of the benefits to all parts of the country."

After a visit to his old Seventh-day Adventist school, Marape was flying back to Port Moresby the next day. I decided to stay in the highlands and head back to Mount Hagen. I went out early to the bus stop on the edge of the marketplace and found my way to the westbound buses. There were none. I got into conversation with a group of young men and women who were also waiting with their bags. They were students from the University of Goroka, all from Mendi, heading home for their vacation. The problem was that political candidates had hired huge fleets of buses, trucks and other vehicles to shunt their supporters around, leaving regular commuters stranded.

We waited. The least shy of the students was Natasha Mawe, about to turn twenty, who was in her second year studying biology and agricultural science and aiming to work in some kind of agribusiness if possible. In Goroka they all lived in student dorms on campus. The mixed group of young men and women were friends, no more than that. "If I had a boyfriend and they learned about it at home, I would be beaten with a broomstick," Natasha said. Parents of daughters in Mendi held out for a bride price, she told me, which could run to 100,000 kina or more, plus pigs.

I went back to wait in the hotel lobby. If they found transport, they would come and collect me. It did not seem at all hopeful. The alternative was to check into the hotel again and wait or fly back to Port Moresby, then up to Mount Hagen. But a couple of hours later, I had a call. It was Natasha. "Come down to the front entrance, we are waiting." I went out with my bags and found an early-model LandCruiser. I was ushered into the front seat.

The students were in the back on bench seats.

The driver was a bespectacled man who looked to be around fifty and introduced himself as John Kiap. He was a doctor, specialising in anaesthesia, who had driven down from Mount Hagen for a job interview at the Goroka hospital. He had swung by the bus stop in the hope of finding some passengers to defray his fuel costs on the trip back. An engaging conversationalist, he told me how fake news on Facebook had completely stymied the government's attempts to vaccinate the population against Covid-19. Facebook posts said the vaccine would cause sterility, it would insert a tracking device, and so on. The result was only six per cent coverage. Yet Papua New Guinea seemed largely unscathed. Kiap could only conjecture that herd immunity was achieved in the very young population.

He kept a steady, safe pace, and stopped for relief and snacks. Driving through towns was the main obstacle. Police roadblocks set up to check against transfer of weapons were occasions for shakedowns. Twenty-kina notes were passed to officers half-stoned on *buai*.

We got into Mount Hagen after dark. The buses for Mendi had all gone. It was especially dangerous for southern highlanders. Just recently, a bus from the southern highlands had pulled into Mount Hagen early one morning after an overnight trip. A gang of local *raskols* jumped the sleepy passengers and robbed them of all valuables. But the passengers had managed to grab one of the gang. They put him on the bus, drove it back to Mendi and beheaded him. It resulted in a wave of attacks against southern highlanders in Mount Hagen.

Kiap knew of a cheap but safe guesthouse close to the centre of town, and we paid for a large family room for the students to doss down in. The next day, I learned, Kiap had driven them down to Mendi himself. He and his wife came round to my hotel for coffee, and I was able to persuade him to accept some money for his fuel costs.

Three months after I returned to Sydney, Goroka was hit by a strong earthquake, damaging many buildings and causing some fatalities. I was in touch with these travel companions again through WhatsApp. Kiap had got the job and was in Goroka. The female dormitory at the university had been thrown off its foundations and was unsafe to occupy. Natasha and her friends had had to find places to stay in settlements around the town. We organised some assistance to help them through to the end of the year.

Observing the PNG election in 2017, an Australian National University team found that cheating and money politics were "more widespread and more brazen than ever before" while violence had exploded with 204 people killed, mostly in the highland provinces. Among the vignettes: supporters of one candidate commandeering voting booths and filling in ballot papers; a proportion of voters in one district voting an average eighteen times each; one group of eight young men filling in the ballots for 3000 people; boxes of ballot papers stolen and destroyed.

The 2022 election had not shaped up any better. The Covid epidemic caused the 2021 census to be postponed three years, so the electoral roll was guesswork based on flawed assumptions. A survey had found 97 percent of Papua New Guinea's 930,000 mobile phone users active on Facebook. Numerous fake Facebook accounts were purporting to belong to leading politicians – over twenty claimed to be Marape – mostly for phishing scams, but many to spread false rumours.

Yet for all the flaws in the electoral roll and attempts at voting irregularity, the result was generally accepted and a new government formed, led by Marape's Pangu Party, which won fifty-nine seats. The political miracle repeated every five years in Papua New Guinea had occurred again, not least in the unruly "middle kingdom" that had been the last main region opened to the modern world less than a century earlier.

13

THE SEPIK

Sacred River

IT FLOWS OUT OF THE LITTLE EXPLORED limestone gorges and high mountains of the Victor Emanuel Range, crosses an international border, then meanders eastwards, parallel to the north coast of New Guinea, half a kilometre wide much of the way, feeding lakes and wetlands, until, 1146 kilometres from its source, it disgorges a vast plume of muddy water into the Bismarck Sea.

The Sepik River captures the imagination like the Congo of Joseph Conrad, although naturally in different ways for expatriates and for Papua New Guineans.

Seaforth Mackenzie, judge and acting administrator for Australia in the newly seized German New Guinea, painted a distinctly Conradian picture in his official history of the First World War: "there clings about the Sepik the mystery of unknown and unguessed things – the secrets of its far-flung hinterland, of its sullen, crocodile-haunted waters, of the tribes that dwell by its banks, practice strange rites, and hold dark beliefs".[1]

People could disappear up this river. After taking the string of German settlements along the New Guinea coast and the islands in 1914, the Australian navy sent two of its destroyers, the *Parramatta* and the *Warrego*, into the Sepik, searching for a German gunboat rumoured to be hiding out. These 500-ton ships got some 360 kilometres upriver before giving up the search.

Even in the 1950s, nearly all the jungle and wetlands from the south bank of the Sepik to the central mountain spine were declared a "restricted area" by the Australian administration, meaning access was barred to most outsiders.

Decades later, in 2020, a young Papua New Guinean environmentalist, Duncan Gabi, saw hope and strength among the Sepik's people rather than "strange rites" and "dark beliefs". His group had arrived one afternoon by canoe at the village of Korogu, in the middle Sepik region. Korogu is one of the villages that still maintains and respects its *haus tambaran*, or spirit house, a structure seen in several parts of the country but noted for its boldness of design in East Sepik. A soaring façade is adorned with elliptical shields or panels bearing carvings of ancestor figures and totems, coloured with ochre, red clay and blacking. It has a narrow entrance reserved for initiated men and youths beginning initiation. Inside, the thatch-roofed chamber slopes to a sanctum at the rear. In Korogu, the initiation still includes scarification of the young men's backs, leaving rows of bumpy scars resembling the scales of the crocodiles found in the river.

Although Gabi is from another region and tribe and does not know the Niyaura language spoken in Korogu, his work trying to protect the river ecology had gained him respect and acceptance that other outsiders might not get. On arrival, he found the village in turmoil and the *haus tambaran* fenced off. Village elders told them the spirit house had been desecrated by two young men, who, drunk, had gone in and removed the sticks used to beat the big *garamut* drum, a hollowed-out tree trunk. The drum's "tongue" had been removed, meaning it could no longer speak to the people.

To restore the drum, the elders had resolved to summon the river god, Sukundimi, to walk through the village. This would take four calls from within the *haus tambaran*, but the dreaded arrival of the god could be avoided if the desecraters provided a pig to be slaughtered as an appeasement of divine anger. Apparently the malefactors had been given ample time to arrange this. But Gabi heard the first call going out. "The elders said it was the call of the crocodile," he later wrote. "It was like nothing I have ever heard, not even a foreigner with his complex and high-tech audio devices could duplicate that sound ... The sound was out of this world. It gave me goosebumps and made my skin crawl."

Two further calls were made. Gabi and other uninitiated people retreated inside houses, forbidden to look out. But then, before the final call that would unleash the crocodile god and require all the village's valuables to be sequestered inside the *haus tambaran* forever, they heard the squealing of a pig. Divine retribution was avoided, and later Gabi and his friends were invited to see the pig being consumed inside the spirit house by the elders. It was an epiphany for Gabi:

> All I know is that I was a proud Melanesian that afternoon, to see gods and men holding rogues accountable for breaking the ancient laws of the land," he wrote. "The laws of Melanesia are not written on paper and passed by parliament. They are not written in ink. They are written in the hearts and minds of the people. Melanesian laws are carved on totem poles and sung in poetic songs. Without documentation, these laws have survived because of the sacred *haus tambaran*, the gods and the men who stand to enforce the laws and so maintain order in society. The *haus tambaran* is not just a spirit house, it is a system of government. It is older than the Western systems. It is the place where ancient laws were enacted, issues debated and problems resolved. The *haus tambaran* is the place where young men are brought to learn the ways of their fathers and where they are taught philosophy. The *haus tambaran* is a place of worship, a governing body and a school. It houses the ancient gods, it is the three arms of government, it is a library and a university of Melanesian wisdom – politics, philosophy, wizardry and magic, and fine art ... The colonisers came and told us we had no proper systems of governance and laws. They imposed on us their systems of government and laws which only benefited them and the elites. They imposed their Christian religion on us and cursed and doomed our traditional religions. They told us to abandon our gods and deities and embrace a Jewish god who looks like an American. White Jesus, the powerful image of white superiority; the image of colonisation and subordination.[2]

All over Melanesia, you will find villages like this turning to *kastom* to assure their security and wellbeing but struggling to keep their young observant in the face of home-brew alcohol and social media.

On the Sepik, I was exploring the second part of Duncan Gabi's conclusions. Did the people see Christianity as an alien creed imposed by force, and had it doomed traditional religions? For a long time, I'd been captivated by a photograph of the Catholic church at Ambunti, a government station since German times on the middle reaches of the Sepik. It showed a nave with wooden columns deeply carved with human faces, a ceiling painted with writhing figures and emblems, panels of painted spirits behind the altar.

In Wewak, the provincial governor's staff connected me with a visiting official who wanted to inspect this part of the river and worked out a deal to share the costs of fuel and canoe hire. A staffer and his son came along, and we piled into the back of a newish government LandCruiser one morning. A heavily built man in police fatigues sat in the front passenger seat. The driver was a younger man in khaki cotton-drill clothes, somewhere between civilian dress and uniform; when he turned in greeting, I saw a neat, military-style moustache. Over the next two days I learned he was the government's security supervisor for the northwest of the country, stationed in Vanimo close to the Indonesian border crossing. The policeman was his bodyguard, nursing an assault rifle with a fold-up stock at his feet.

After driving for some hours through low mountains, skirting the town of Maprik and running through open areas of spiky *kunai* grass, we came down to the Sepik at a small collection of houses, a store and a workshop on a high bank. Long dugout canoes nosed into the mudflat below, a single-file row of passengers sitting in each. We stocked up on instant noodles and tins at the store, then watched as our fuel containers were filled by hand-pump from a drum. A white fibreglass dinghy with an orange strake was waiting. We arranged ourselves aboard, and the outboard gunned us upriver.

Two hours later, we pulled into Ambunti, a clutch of small corrugated-iron buildings on a green river flat backed by high forested hills. The church had been built in the 1970s, with two German priests encouraging elders to contribute to its construction. The result was a church whose pillar carvings told the story of creation, and whose ceiling panels told the stories of the people, the crocodiles and fish, the river, the mountains. Some of the imagery was highly sexual, said Polish-born Jan Czuba, who was the priest at Ambunti in between 1985 and 1995. What he learned to admire in the local culture, not so far removed from Christianity, still had him shaking his head at the arrogant assumptions of the German and Australian administrators. "We took for granted they had nothing," he told me, adding: "The word 'primitive' is a scandal."

The experience of the Catholic priests in Ambunti was part of a developing belief within the Vatican that the Christian faith had to be integrated into local cultures. An even more colourful expression of this was taking place in the Torricelli Mountains, which lie between the upper Sepik and the coastal town of Aitape. At a mission station called Fatima, a priest named Patrick McGeaver had set himself to reverse the destruction of the local culture attempted by the first missionaries in the 1930s. An Irishman whose first language was Gaelic, he had a keen sense of how language and culture can be diminished by an invader.

As witnessed by the zoologist Tim Flannery in the late 1980s, McGeaver delivered the mass in the local Olo language, while wearing a headdress of *cus-cus* (possum) fur and amulets of bird of paradise plumes. Parish women sang and danced bare-breasted for the visiting bishop from Vanimo. The priest had interviewed the old men about pre-Christian customs and incorporated traditional words from birth and initiation rituals into baptisms and confirmations. He organised the building of a *haus tambaran* for the first time in decades, adorned with spirit masks, some of them 5 metres tall.[3]

This movement came as the church was grappling with the realisation that Christianity had been delivered to the non-European world alongside colonial exploitation and slavery. Then-cardinal Joseph Ratzinger (later Pope Benedict XVI) held a series of "continental synods" in Rome, at which bishops from these realms gave thoughts on the way forward for the then pope, John Paul II.

The synod for Oceania, held in 1998, gave a cautious nod to concepts of natural spirits, ancestral veneration and tabu as religious precursors, in the findings pronounced by Pope John Paul:

MELANESIA

When the missionaries first brought the Gospel to Aboriginal or Maori people, or to the island nations, they found peoples who already possessed an ancient and profound sense of the sacred. Religious practices and rituals were very much part of their daily lives and thoroughly permeated their cultures. The missionaries brought the truth of the Gospel which is foreign to no one; but at times some sought to impose elements which were culturally alien to the people. There is a need now for careful discernment to see what is of the Gospel and what is not, what is essential and what is less so. Such a task, it must be said, is made more difficult because of the process of colonization and modernization, which has blurred the line between the indigenous and the imported. One of the most notable features of the peoples of Oceania is their powerful sense of community and solidarity in family and tribe, village or neighbourhood. This means that decisions are reached by consensus achieved through an often long and complex process of dialogue. Touched by the grace of God, the peoples' natural sense of community made them receptive to the mystery of *communion* offered in Christ. The Church in Oceania demonstrates a real spirit of cooperation, extending to the various Christian communities and to all people of good will. Deep respect for tradition and authority is also part of the traditional cultures of Oceania. Hence the present generation's sense of solidarity with those who went before them, and the exceptional authority accorded to parents and traditional leaders.

The way forward was therefore "inculturation" for the church, the Pope agreed. "On the one hand, certain cultural values must be transformed and purified, if they are to find a place in a genuinely Christian culture. On the other hand, in various cultures Christian values readily take root. Inculturation is born out of respect for both the Gospel and the culture in which it is proclaimed and welcomed."[4]

Finding common beliefs among the hundreds of language groups, many cut off from their neighbours, was always going to be hard. But scholars who persisted found many cases where religious concepts were far more advanced than the low place in the hierarchy of religious development assigned to the Melanesians by nineteenth-century evolutionists. Some indeed had a belief in a supreme being of creation, one who would punish wrongdoers in the spirit world. The cathedral-like sacred spaces of the *haus tambaran* in Sepik, the *eravo* of the Papuan coast, the initiations, the incantations for continued supply of crops and pigs, the veneration for inherited wisdom could all be seen as deserving of respect – and as precursors for the Christian faith.

The Catholics and to an extent the Anglicans had, and have, more scope to accommodate this. Their churches house the tombs of warriors, artists and kings. Masses are said for the souls of the departed. Holy communion, the symbolic sharing of the body and blood of Jesus, could be seen as a twist on the ritual cannibalism of the Melanesians to imbibe the spirit and strength of the great enemy.

To be sure, the missionaries had a battle explaining the notion of forgiveness as a virtue in itself, as opposed to settlement of disputes by payback calculations. Nor was peace always a goal. As a leading scholar of comparative religion, Garry Trompf of the University of Sydney, wrote in his major study of Melanesian beliefs: "Groups who were traditional enemies and whose cultures actually depended on head-hunting and ambush as an impetus to group esteem, planting, building, even their art, had every reason to keep on fighting."[5]

There was a widespread belief in the power of sorcery, something to be feared and to be used. As we have seen, it continues, along with the belief in the power of sacred traditional objects. But the Melanesians are not alone in this. The Europeans over the centuries have been gripped periodically by panics about witchcraft and the power of the devil. Folk myths about goblins, trolls and fairies persisted until recent times. Priests are called in to exorcise bad spirits.

Father Litric, the priest in Rabaul, said many of his parishioners still believed in witchcraft but were too ashamed to talk about it with him. He takes this as an acknowledgement that it is bad, and as the start of waning power for such beliefs, as happened in Europe. "By stopping the belief, these things lost their power, their grip on people," he told me. It would be unrealistic to expect it to disappear in just 150 years since the first Christian missionaries arrived on the fringes of New Guinea, and much less time since they penetrated its interior. "To expect them to have a change of heart that took Europeans two thousand years – it doesn't work like this in 150 years," Litric said. "It's like water that drips on stone. Nothing happens for hundreds of years, then you can see a hole in the stone."

In several places, I encountered Christians who also held to spiritual elements of *kastom*. There was the pastor Adrian Umaka in Lake Murray, who spoke of the "powerful objects" stolen a hundred years earlier. In Rabaul, Albert Konie, the son of East Sepik migrants, listed the three grades of spirits seen by the Tolai: the small and most amiable goblin *tambaran*, the tall *itolaraki*, who came out their caves to splash around in the sea at dusk and could cause minor illnesses, and the *kaia*, like big snakes living in volcanoes who got angry when people were bad.

"We have Christianity, but in our subconscious minds, this is taught from childhood," Konie told me. "My father came from Maprik in East Sepik. We share the same type of beliefs. We believe in a place where our ancestral spirits live. Religion is a concept of men, *kastom* is also an ideology of the common man. The Biblical thing is the truth, and *kastom* is fading away because of the churches ... What we are preserving now is our heritage, our identity as Papua New Guinean. We believe in the spirits of the forefathers. We hold on to the religious truth, but we still treasure our forefathers. It's like giving you an identity in society. And if you don't do anything, then people see you as a foreigner. They gossip about you."

The appreciation of indigenous belief systems and push to "inculturate" came well over a century after the first missionaries arrived. And whereas the apostles and their successors spread the Christian message around the Mediterranean world very much as small groups of outsiders, the missionaries to Melanesia came backed by imperial powers. Gabi is right that Christianity was initially imposed, and Melanesians made to feel inferior.

That approach persists among many of the small, new Christian groups evangelising across Melanesia. The opening of the highlands in the 1950s saw dozens of these small evangelic missions setting up in what might be called a "soul rush". In 1962 an Australian official fired a starter gun to open claims to newly gazetted sites at Porgera: missionaries ran off in competition for the best mission sites. "By the early 1970s ... the eastern highlands had all the appearances of being the most missionised province on earth," Trompf noted, with "over 80 Christian denominations and sects of one sort or another being represented there". They tended towards a "conservative" approach to the Christian faith, which Trompf defined as "a literalist or fundamentalist approach to the Bible, a belief that the Scriptures, as the holy word of God, are inerrant, and to be confirmed as faultless by Bible scholars or students". The Protestant striving to strip Christianity of all hints of "idolatry" (such as icons, statues of Jesus, works of art and worship of the Virgin Mary and saints) is often extended in Melanesia to wholesale rejection of traditional ritual and art as the work of the devil. In a further push to convert the Melanesians came the Pentecostals, with their greater emphasis on the powers of the Holy Spirit, as shown in rapturous singing, speaking in tongues, faith healing and prophecy.[6]

Still, for all their lampoonable excesses, the bigger churches provide networks of higher education, medical assistance and a form of community policing – as shown in Rabaul, where when the police proved helpless, Father Litric once brokered a settlement to communal violence that shut down the town.

Here on the Sepik River today, the churches face a deep challenge as big development projects threaten the ecology that is so much part of the traditional cosmic belief system of the people.

Gabi and his environment group were travelling along the Sepik to rally opposition to one giant project that could devastate this immense river system if things went wrong: the Frieda River gold and copper mine, proposed at a site close to Telefomin in the mountains near the Sepik headwaters. The Frieda tumbles out of the central mountain chain then snakes north to join the Sepik. It would be another vast copper-gold open cut, on the scale of Freeport across the border in West Papua, Ok Tedi on the other side of the range, or Bougainville Copper – all of which have been ecological disasters, with waste rock and tailings spilling into the rivers and lowlands below. Various environmental groups say the seismic activity, high rainfall and uncertain geology make the Frieda project essentially unsafe.

The mine's promoter, PanAust, is an Australian-based company controlled by a Chinese state-owned enterprise and calls it a "nation-building project" with wide commercial and socio-economic prospects. The scheme also includes a hydroelectric plant, power grid, and road, airport and seaport upgrades. Groups such as Gabi's Save the Sepik have been rousing the elders in *haus tambaran* up and down the Sepik to call for a ban on the project.

Albert Konie, the East Sepik man raised in Rabaul, was vehement in his opposition to the Frieda River mine. "The river is the final frontier, the last destination. It is the Amazon of the Pacific," he said. "Get the money elsewhere. Tomorrow. They must see that every day of creation was for the foundation of this world. They will say it's safe, but [that's] not true. The money collected will never benefit the Sepik region. People around the world want to see the nature, the culture – for generations, for two thousand years. They will never see. Don't sell it for the mine. Money cannot buy everything. It's just destruction."

Down in Wewak, I had asked Allan Bird about it. The provincial governor and MP was cautious, saying the project would have to show how it would mitigate the risk, but so far it was high-risk. "You can't have another Fly River here," he said. "It would be a massive disaster. Not only that, we would have civil unrest. They've got to figure out how not to get to that point. That's not up to me, that's for whoever wants to develop the thing."

It did not assure him that a Chinese state enterprise was pushing the mine. "Our experience with Chinese companies doesn't give me a lot of confidence," he said. "If they can take a short cut they will. Ramu Nickel is going to look like a cakewalk when Frieda goes wrong, trust me. I'm having to deal with young people in my province who build weapons and fight with them. My young people are not like the young people in Madang. You'll have a full-scale war here. That's what I'm worried about."

Ramu Nickel was not only accused of labour violations that had led to inspectors raiding the project after Marape took office. Developed by the state-owned Metallurgical Corporation of China, its refinery located on the edge of the Bismarck Sea was an environmental worry from the start. A fatal industrial accident in 2016 revealed safety mechanisms had been inactivated to speed production. In 2019, a spill of toxic slurry turned nearby waters bright red, taking locally caught fish off the market in Madang and causing skin rashes on swimmers for months.

After dumping my bag at the guesthouse in Ambunti, I met Johannes Teven, a stocky man of middle age who is a river tourist guide and also a verger at the Ambunti church. We walked along the riverbank, under tall trees, and across the new airstrip that ran up a valley away from the river.

On the edge of the straggling village, we came to a rise, then walked around the neat priest's house and saw a sad sight. The remnants of the famous church were stacked on its former concrete slab. Six months earlier, in December 2021, the church had collapsed in a fierce rainstorm. The famous pillars were stacked in a heap, the carved faces already weathered under the sun and rain. "We are collecting funds to rebuild, we have a bank account open," Teven said. It was hoped the pillars could be incorporated into a more secure structure.

When the church was built, back in the 1970s, the priests had been able to call on the old men from seven villages around Ambunti to decorate it with legends from the river and mountains, the stories of the ancestors, the images of the crocodiles, fish, birds and forest animals.

From the concrete platform, I looked across a vista of river, banana plantations on the far bank, then rolling jungle and distant mountains. I wondered if the stories were still out there.

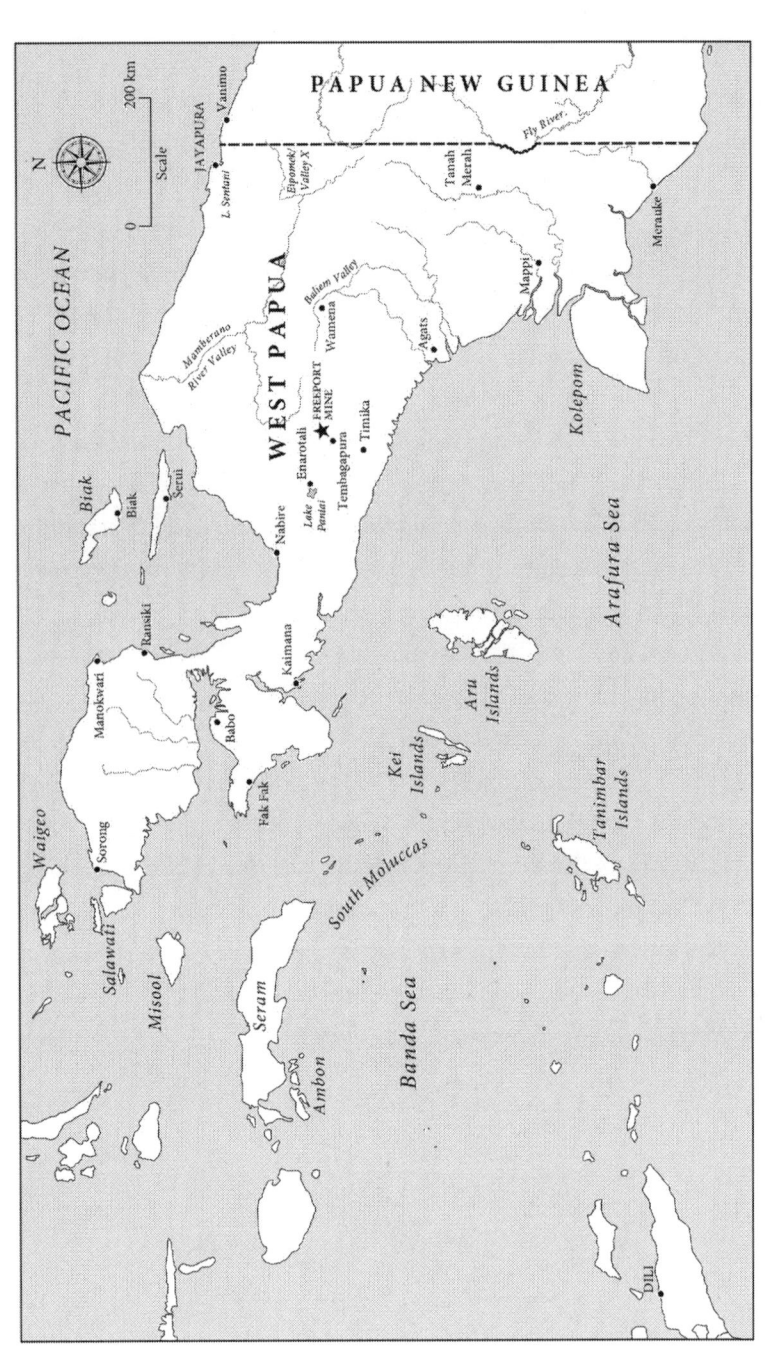

14

WEST PAPUA

The Edge of Time Before

HAD I CONTINUED UP THE SEPIK from Ambunti to a place called Green River – a journey of about three days by canoe, Johannes Teven told me – I would have come to a road that led, after several hours' travel, to the town of Vanimo on the coast. This was the northwestern outpost of administration in Papua New Guinea, the capital of Sandaun (Sundown) Province.

It is little visited except by Malaysian logging ships collecting hardwood trees cut in the interior, by surfers attracted to its reef breaks, and by the very few travellers who obtain a visa at the Indonesian consulate in town and proceed by public minibus to the border.

There you might exit Papua New Guinea via a small immigration shed and a gate in a wire-mesh fence. Overhead are the national flag with its bird of paradise and Southern Cross motifs and the flags of Papua New Guinea's twenty provinces. A billboard facing Indonesia proclaims Papua New Guinea to be a Christian nation, a pointed notice to its mostly Muslim neighbour. A platoon of PNG soldiers might be standing around their battered Toyota LandCruisers.

Ahead is an archway in front of a new white concrete building designed to impress. It has multiple flagpoles too, but all fly the red-and-white Indonesian national flag. Except for the ancient pennants of a few traditional principalities, no regional flag is allowed to fly in what is known – ever more shrilly in recent years – as the *Negara Kesatuan* (Unitary State) of the *Republik Indonesia* – especially not the "Morning Star" flag that Papuans would fly if they were allowed.

The border was closed because of the Covid epidemic when I went up the Sepik, although local householders and traders still went on Tuesdays and Thursdays to the informal market beside the immigration posts to stock up on cheap Indonesian processed foods and utensils, or to tend gardens on traditional lands. If it is now open, I probably would not be allowed in anyway, as my name would come up as a journalist and when I applied recently to Jakarta for a media visa to visit Papua there was no response. So, this chapter draws on two visits long ago.

On my second trip in 2013 I had travelled to this border post from the Indonesian side. From there, it was a two-hour taxi ride around hillsides of green jungle and bays of blue sea into Jayapura, the main city of western New Guinea. As you drive into the centre, the roadside commerce is Southeast Asian – small food stalls, motorcycle workshops, tyre dealers, and fewer Melanesian figures than you see out in the rural fringes.

On that visit I caught up with the sad developments in what is generally known as West Papua. During the Suharto era, Indonesia flooded the region with "transmigrants" from Java, Bali and Sulawesi, so that now the ethnic Papuans were only a narrow majority of the 5.6 million population. As Suharto's rule crumbled in 1998, Papuans came out to demonstrate for a new act of self-determination. In Biak, soldiers massacred hundreds gathered at a raising of the "Morning Star" independence flag. A navy ship took captives out to sea for execution, their bodies dumped overboard. In 2001, special forces soldiers had garrotted the Papuan leader Theys Eluay after inviting him to dinner at their base. This effectively ended prospects raised by the liberal reformist Indonesian president, Abdurrahman Wahid, that Jakarta would loosen its grip. Wahid was engineered out of office soon after by his deputy president, Megawati Sukarnoputri, daughter of Indonesia's first president, Sukarno. She installed as her defence minister the army general who had praised Eluay's assassins as "patriots". The military-nationalist deep state was back in charge.[1] It was around this time that the

"Unitary State" label started being applied routinely to Indonesia's official name, particularly by a military anxious to defend its internal security role and to push back against the post-Suharto devolution of power.

In 2003, Megawati split the single province into two, on the advice of her intelligence service, to weaken the independence movement.[2] In another false dawn, a new president in 2014, Joko Widodo, announced that all of West Papua would be freely accessible to journalists, diplomats and international agencies. He was quickly overruled by the deep state. As his two permitted terms came towards an end, in 2022 Jakarta announced, without local consultation, that three more new provinces would be carved out as well.

I have often thought back to my first visit to Jayapura, in 1976. That was only seven years after the "Act of Free Choice" that delivered Western New Guinea to Indonesia. The US administration of John F. Kennedy had told the Dutch in the early 1960s that their attempt to nurture the territory towards independence from Indonesia was over; the Cold War struggle to stop Southeast Asia turning to communism made cultivating Jakarta more important. A mining company from New Orleans also had its eye on the massive copper and gold deposit discovered in the territory's southern mountains by Dutch geologists in 1936.[3] The Papuans were depicted as savages: the ethnologist Michael Rockefeller, a scion of the great business dynasty, had disappeared in 1961 collecting artefacts on the south coast.[4]

The Papuans I encountered in 1976 were seething, not willing to accept that the gates had closed permanently. Even being allowed to enter what was now known as Irian Jaya – Victorious Irian – had been an unusual break for a young freelance journalist then working in Jakarta. A huge earthquake had struck the high mountains of the interior; reports were coming of possibly thousands of casualties among the Papuans and imminent starvation because food gardens had been swept away by landslides.

At Biak, the island off the north coast, I stayed in a sprawling single-storey hotel of rooms with lengthy verandahs, originally built for General Douglas MacArthur as his temporary forward headquarters on the way to his famous "return" to the Philippines. A small turboprop took me into Sentani, an airstrip on flat country inland from Jayapura.

I carried a letter of introduction from Jusuf Wanandi, one of the young intellectuals grouped around General Ali Murtopo, an intelligence specialist who had helped General Suharto ease out Sukarno a decade earlier. At a guesthouse on a hillside overlooking the port of Jayapura, I was visited by a contact of Wanandi, a young Javanese man with a Catholic first name. The young man was helpful, connecting me with the Missionary Aviation Fellowship, whose light aircraft were the only means of getting to the earthquake zone.

But first I had to get a *surat jalan*, a travel permit, from the military. We took a taxi down to the army headquarters, and I found myself facing the local commander for Kopkamtib – the military's feared Operational Command for the Restoration of Security and Order, set up in 1965 to hunt down and suppress the last remnants of the Indonesian Communist Party, plus any other threats to Suharto's New Order regime. He would have been irked to have a foreign journalist in his bailiwick at the best of times, but earlier in 1976 (unknown to the outside world, bar some friendly intelligence agencies, and certainly to me) the Indonesia army had sent thousands of troops in a sweep southeast of Jayapura to destroy the base camps of the Organisasi Papua Merdeka (Free Papua Movement) that had started an armed insurgency within two years of the Act of Free Choice. To make matters worse, I inadvertently referred to Wanandi by his original Chinese name, Liem Bian Kie, by which most of his Jakarta contacts knew him. We came away without the permit. My guide said I'd put my foot in it: the colonel was an anti-Chinese racist.

That evening, I found a bar on the waterfront full of Papuan beer-drinkers only too eager to tell of their thwarted dreams. It was a strange mix of people. A Scottish telephone engineer installing cables around the city invited a Papuan lady in a slinky dress to dance to the disco music. He came back to his beer in dismay. "It was a bloke!" he said. I had a skinful myself and made it back to the hotel to find reception closed. Each room key was attached to a large wooden globe the size of a doorknob, to prevent guests pocketing them. They were kept in a glass-fronted cabinet behind the counter. I went behind the counter and pulled the glass door open. The cabinet lurched forwards, and multiple wooden globes clattered onto the tiled floor. I got down to replace them, then glanced up. A row of Papuan faces looked down at me in alarm.

Word came next morning that my *surat jalan* had been approved. Soon I was sitting next to the pilot of a Pilatus Porter, a Swiss aircraft built for short take-offs and landings. We headed south, across dark green jungle that morphed into ever more jagged mountains. Eventually the pilot pointed ahead. I could see nothing at first, until I focused on a light-green strip of land on a mountainside. The aircraft headed towards it, heading for the lower margin. As we neared, the grass strip slanted upwards. We touched down, and the slope quickly brought the plane to a halt. The pilot revved up and turned the plane at the top, ready for a downhill take-off.

A small crowd of men wearing penis gourds, some carrying bows and arrows, looked timidly on. There was a small white timber house for a missionary couple from the Unevangelized Fields Mission. The wife, Dina Cole, a Canadian, came and gave me a rundown of the reports that had come in from outlying villages. The death toll might be between 500 and 1000. The immediate threat was the loss of food supplies because of the destroyed gardens.

The missionaries had a small helicopter, a Perspex bubble big enough for two people with an engine and a framework boom behind. The pilot, Geoff Heritage, had been in the US Army somewhere in Indochina. I took the role of loadmaster. The missionaries put bags of sweet potato on the skids on my side. Heritage lifted us off and flew us across a landscape of deep valleys running north from the central spine of snow-topped mountains to the south. We would zoom across razorback ridges that fell sickeningly thousands of feet on either side. In one valley, a landslide blocked a gorge and had created a lake several kilometres long up the valley behind, stagnant lime green in colour and choked with floating trees and debris.

Banking sharply into the mountainside, Heritage would take the helicopter low over tiny jungle clearings with thatch-roofed huts. While he hovered, I kicked the potato sacks free to fall to the ground. Speaking through his microphone to my earphones, Heritage checked that they had avoided hitting any dwelling or the naked tribespeople looking up.

MELANESIA

The food deliveries finished, Heritage flew me into another valley and landed next to a sprawling canvas encampment. Some young Westerners, dressed in bush clothes, many of them bearded, emerged and approached to introduce themselves. They were a multidisciplinary expedition from German universities who had set up their camp the previous year to study the local people and their environment before they were irrevocably changed by contact with the outside world.

I asked the name of the place, and they said it was Valley X.

It was not quite first contact, but close enough. During the Second World War, a joyriding flight by American airmen and nurses had crash-landed in the Baliem Valley, some fifty miles to the northwest. Word of strange people had spread from the limited contact between the Baliem Valley's Dani and Lani people and their neighbours. Then in 1958 the French filmmaker Pierre-Dominique Gaisseau had walked across the country nearby, the result being his documentary *The Sky Above, the Mud Below*. In October 1969, Gaisseau and two others in a film team landed by parachute in a valley that Gaisseau marked on a map with an X. They were received peacefully and stayed some weeks, supplied by air drops, then made their way out by walking down valleys and, where possible, riding down rivers in rubber boats.

One of the scholars introduced himself as Volker Heeschen, a linguist who had already penetrated the Mek dialect spoken in the valley. When a group of young men came up to the helicopter and put their hands behind the perspex in wonder, he was able to translate for me. One of them was a young man called Imser who came close, patting me on the chest with the flat of his hand in what Heeschen said was the friendly greeting of the local people. Imser wore only a penis gourd attached at the top to a woven cane belt, a necklace of dogs' teeth, and a pig tusk through the septum of his nose.

He described the situation since the earthquake. His village had no more sweet potato or bananas and might need to slaughter its pigs because they could not be fed. Six houses had been swept away and three men were dead. "Our world has been destroyed," he summed it up. Another man called Nimde said the earthquake had struck just before dawn, when the people were stirring to stoke their fires and climb the mountainside to their gardens. This enabled them to run to safer ground in the forest. "Even the father of the oldest man in my village had not seen an earthquake as big as this," Nimde said. Thomas Michel, an anthropologist, had been sleeping in a village across the valley. As he struggled out of his sleeping bag, huge boulders whizzed past, striking sparks from other rocks. The villagers headed to the mountain top for safety, but then sent their women back to collect the pigs.

The German expedition had been joined in Valley X only a few months before by a missionary. As I did my interviews, it became clear that a cultural race was on. The missionaries were out to replace the traditional beliefs and much of the lifestyle as fast and as completely as possible. One of the wives was proud that she and her husband had conducted the first "white wedding" among their flock.

From what both missionaries and researchers said, many of the tribespeople saw the earthquake as a supernatural event. Hellfire preaching by the missionaries was at least partly responsible. "Some were very worried because shortly before I had been reading to them the last part of Mark's gospel, which referred to earthquakes and calamities and they feared this was the Day of Judgment," said one missionary, an American from a mission that had been opened eight years earlier at Kiwi, on the eastern side of the earthquake zone. In another village, Omban, the people had recently burnt their fetishes in a public demonstration of turning to Christ. "But like all people, they preferred to hedge their bets and kept some fetishes buried in the ground, just in case. Just after the earthquake they brought in these hidden fetishes and said that maybe God was angry they had kept them. I guess we're lucky they didn't make the alternative deduction that the earthquake occurred because of the original burning."

In another valley, called Fa-Malinkele, the blame was tentatively put on the Indonesians, whom the people had never seen but who were rumoured to be a savage lot, and whose name was close to the word for ghost, *isa*.

The zeal of the missionaries to convert drew a lot of eye-rolling from the young Germans. When I got back to Jayapura, I heard many stories of extreme proselytising, including a German pastor who hovered over villagers in a chartered helicopter, reading passages of the bible through loudspeakers, drawing volleys of arrows in return. A story I wrote about this for *The Washington Post* got syndicated around small-city newspapers in the United States and made me for a while the subject of a public letter campaign, accusing me of succumbing to the poisonous words of Catholic fathers and the wine they served. The attack was led by Don Richardson, a Canadian who had been a missionary among the Asmat and Sawi people of the south coast since 1962. He had written a book called *Peace Child*, based on his discovery of a "redemptive analogy" in his flock's culture that opened a pathway to understanding the Christian message. He postulated that if you looked into any indigenous culture, such an analogy could be found. Up in the Jayawijaya Mountains, there was little sign his colleagues had found one or were looking very hard for it.

The German scholars were well aware that as they recorded and explored the old ways, their presence itself was having a big impact on how the Eipo – as the region's Mek speakers were called – saw themselves and the world. Villagers had seen and touched a helicopter. Some were now asking for old ballpoint pens to stick through their noses instead of pig tusks. Some had eaten rice for the first time. There was apprehension about it all, said Wolfgang Nelke, an anthropologist. "They fear the cultural change of new contacts. The old men sense this could be the beginning of the change."

The results of the German research flowed for decades, in scientific papers and academic theses, in documentary films, and in collections of photographs and artefacts lodged with museums and institutes. The field study was interrupted in 1977–78 when the Germans were told to leave. Down in the Baliem Valley, an Indonesian unit had intervened to stop a tribal fight among the Dani and Lani. Both warring tribes then turned on the Indonesians, in what became a valley-wide insurrection. The Indonesian military responded with strafing and napalm strikes on villages with its new OV-10 ground attack aircraft supplied by the United States. When the uprising was quelled, research visits resumed. Volker Heeschen visited the Eipo more than twenty times between 1981 and 2014.

The collected work is an astonishing, sometimes deeply moving picture of a small world about to be overwhelmed and changed by outside contact.[5]

At the time of the research visits, the Eipo were estimated to number between 26,000 and 31,500, living quite isolated from neighbouring language groups. The name for their language, Mek, means "water" or "river" and is also the name of tree species mentioned in their myths, including as a source from which their ancestors emerged. They were genetically isolated too, and on average were no more than 150 centimetres tall. Dialects of Mek varied from valley to valley, but intermarriage was common. They lived in hamlets of between fifty to 150 people and preferred to be in close physical proximity. Their staple food source was sweet potato, introduced to Asia from South America in the sixteenth century and finding its way to this remote valley in time forgotten. The Eipo cultivated it in clearings that yielded three successive crops before ten years of fallow. On steep slopes, garden beds were planted in timber and branch trusses across the hillside.

The sweet potato also fed the domestic pigs, which were kept in enclosures or tethered. People did not eat their own pigs. They were gifted for ceremonies or traded for utensils. The highlights of village life were the periodic feasts with neighbouring communities, in carefully calibrated rounds of entertainment and gift-giving to maintain peace and friendship. There was pleasure in gift-giving, but it was a form of balanced reciprocity rather than an attempt to achieve big-man status through lavish generosity and the creation of obligations.

In each hamlet was a men's house and a women's house, as well as individual family houses. Women stayed in the women's house while menstruating and around childbirth. The men's houses were the preserve of those males initiated into legend. One was especially holy. It was believed to be the nucleus of an original settlement of the Eipo and housed a sacred digging stick regarded as an instrument of creation. According to legend, the stick had emerged from a mountain in the main divide of New Guinea and had carved out ridges and valleys. It symbolised the people's graduation from hunting and collecting to agriculture. The fame of this men's house had spread beyond the Mek region into the lands of the Ok speakers to the east, straddling the border with Papua New Guinea. When it was rebuilt during the Germans' stay, the local men carried out the job in one day, in a state of "extreme euphoria", with the sacred digging stick wrapped in leaves to shield it from view of the uninitiated. The earthquake destroyed this rebuilt men's house, and many of its sacred objects were swept away and buried.

Living between 1600 and 2000 metres above sea level, the Eipo were the people closest to the mountain tops. They believed they had been there since the beginnings of the human race. Their ancestors had emerged from the mountains in animal bodies, cohabiting with other animals that later became totems for their human descendants. Some villages traced their ancestry to the taro plant, others to a particular tree species, a specific river, rocks from the riverbed, a possum, the sun or the moon. One group claimed ancestry from a pig that had ordered its own death; while dying, it had marked out the locations for men's houses and territorial boundaries. Gradually, humans had changed the land to make it fertile. When these ancestors stopped wandering, they built the men's houses, which became the spiritual centre of each village, securing life and growth. The men's houses contained bodily relics of ancestors. This creation mythology was more interesting and important for the Eipo than any intervening history, which was largely forgotten in any detail. Wars and forced migrations had happened, but these were a part of a chain of similar events stretching back into the past.

The people lived alongside ghosts and spirits, they believed. The dead were placed initially high in a tree or on a forest platform, wrapped in leaves and grasses, then later transferred to a garden house. Their bones would eventually be put into an ossuary in a cave or rock cleft. The skull, the hand or the mummified arm of a famous man might be kept as a relic in the men's house. The ancestors were needed to support the growth of the young and the crops. They were kept happy with gifts and their relics anointed with pig fat. Their spirits haunted different areas, some of which were not cultivated because of this.

Every five to ten years, boys aged between three and ten were taken away from their mothers for initiation. First they spent a night in the men's house, then two months in another house away from the village where they were fed certain food reserved for men, anointed with pig fat and told their secret sacred names. They were then brought back to the village, stepping over the prone bodies of the women. Later, the boys were given their first penis gourds and had their hair woven in a particular way.

Marriage was quite informal. The nuptials involved a modest exchange of gifts by the families of both parties, and the bride then moved in with her husband's household. Only a small number of men had more than one wife. Men usually stayed overnight in the men's house, rarely in the family home, but couples would stay overnight in their garden house if they wanted to be alone. Population was kept in balance with food supplies through infanticide: the newborn would be wrapped in leaves and left to die of exposure. The German team witnessed seven births, one of which was followed by infanticide. It was expected that the earthquake would result in more.

In general men stayed away from women, reflecting an attitude seen across many Melanesian societies. They congregated in the men's houses and were especially fearful of contact with menstrual or childbirth fluids. The women did much or most of the hard routine work of tending the gardens and the household. More women committed suicide than men, and more women were killed after being accused of sorcery.

And yet, the researchers found a measure of female agency. Young women sought out men they fancied, leading to love affairs and marriages. One newly married woman left her husband's village and returned to her home village because she was unhappy. There were many divorces. There was a powerful female spirit in the mountains, called Kerem. And while men organised festivities and took the centre of attention with displays of oratory, the women were the composers of songs. They sang them at feasts and during childbirth. The men were aware that many songs were inspired by love affairs, and that their lyrics often contained metaphors about them. Some songs teased and ridiculed men in general.

Among many songs that Volker Heeschen collected and translated was one by a young Eipo widow named Oleto, which she wrote, composed and sang on farewelling her deceased husband and joining another man. Years later, the Anglo-American poet Frederick Turner reworked Heeschen's translation into a poem:

MELANESIA

By ferny limb, by curly tree
I heard one say, I heard one say,
"What's thine is mine and is not thine",
I heard her say, I heard her say
Lost will I be and far away.
"My curly limb! My ferny-tree!",
I heard her say, I heard her say.
Friends and gossips! Old companions!
Lost will I be and far away.
"Oh curly-heart, o housey-home,"
I hear me say, I heard me say.
With thine axe thou smeared the slim-tree,
cut and tore the rooted wild-tree;
tending my garden I would be.
Wild weed by the threshold, wild growth by the door.
Lost will I be and far away.
Thy clever axe will strike and tear;
here, come and fell the quick elm-tree!
I'd know thy flesh, and root it up, pull thee onto me.
The flesh-bracelet, pulse-fireband,
flame-vine, snap it from thine arm!
Wild eat, weed-grass, wild growth by the door,
I'll twist thee free, I'll pull thee free.
And lost, my sisters, friends, I be.
Lost will I be and far away.
I'll know thy flesh; thou'lt groan for me.
Gossips and sisters! Oh my friends!
The pulse-bracelet, the wrist-vine,
Bite it and burn with alchemy!
And as the fruit-vine climbs the tree,
I'll clamber, my housey-home, and stay,
long-legs, wild growth, at home in thee.

As the expedition's leader, Wulf Schiefenhövel, and botanist Paul Hiepko interpret the song, Oleto's words draw on the close connection perceived between people and the plant world. Her lover's hair is compared to tree ferns, his strength to branches. As her lover lived in a hostile village in another valley, her elopement means, as she says repeatedly, "lost will I be and far away". The lines "The pulse-bracelet, the wrist-vine,/ Bite it and burn with alchemy!" describe fire-making with a fire-saw, which is a metaphor for lovemaking. These metaphors are her own, shaped into English poetic form by Turner. As the two researchers wrote, "the force and the boldness of its metaphors withstand comparison with our literature".[6]

Coming across this translation and rendering many years after my fleeting visit to Valley X as it was, and Eipomek as it is now, I felt again the privilege of having been so close to a people still living in their timeless, ever-renewed present. They were living survivors of the Papuan ancestry of the Melanesians, their social organisation and practices reflected across the mountains, valleys and islands to the east and fused with the later Austronesian cultures.

In these highland places especially, Papuans had developed an agricultural economy long before those of Mesopotamia or the Indus plain. And in the song of Oleto, they are revealed as men and women, as people, who knew love, and exulted in it.

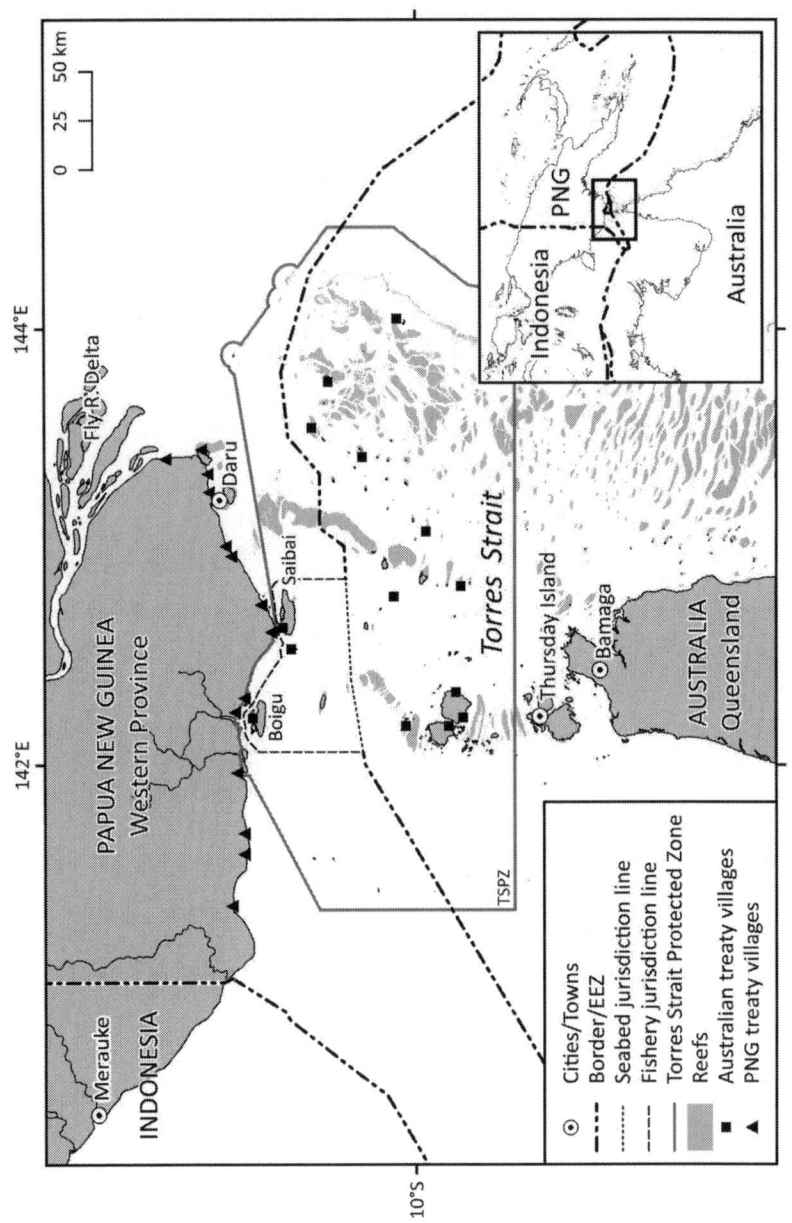

EPILOGUE

Return of the Kanaka

SO, APPROACHING A HALF-CENTURY of independence in most cases, the Melanesians are still discovering themselves and, off and on, each other.

Fijians identify as Melanesian when it suits their diplomatic aims, as more broadly Pacific or Oceanic at other times, and, deep in their hearts, as a unique chosen people. The ni-Vanuatu share a kava culture with Fiji and Tonga and more recently with the Kanaks. The betel-nut habit starts north in the Solomons and extends through Bougainville into Papua New Guinea. Delegates from Vanuatu, the Solomons and the Papua New Guinea can chat in their mutually intelligible versions of Tok Pisin at regional gatherings. Yet, as Ralph Regenvanu told me in Port Vila, Vanuatu's historical and cultural links often seem closer with Tonga.

With hundreds of language groups and many cultural exceptions, generalisations need to be ventured warily. However, attachment to traditional land, a communal language and identity, and memory of ancestors are fundamental to most Melanesian communities. Western-style justice has barely replaced traditional payback and compensation in many places. Politics are clientelist within a Westminster framework and tend to follow the "big man" model, except in the more homogenous Fiji, where stronger parties have formed. Women play a stronger role than outsider stereotypes would have us believe. Some cultures include elaborate male rituals to avoid men becoming captives of female power.[1] More than political systems, the Christian churches provide support for Melanesia's transition to the modern world.

In less than 150 years, since the first imposition of European rule, the Melanesians have adapted to the wider world with remarkable ingenuity. While some early responses took the form of millenarian cargo cults or reversions to *kastom*, there were also initiatives for self-advancement, from the Viti Kabani in Fiji to Maasina Ruru in the Solomons. Such movements were dismissed or suppressed by colonial administrations and churches, who saw their authority threatened or sidestepped.

Populations that seemed threatened with extinction in the 1920s have rebounded. The number of Papua New Guineans was officially estimated at 12.5 million in mid-2024, about four times what it was at independence in 1975 (although the 1975 estimate of about 3 million might well have been an undercount). A census in 2024 got off to a shaky start, and the results were awaited. The growth rate of the population was put at 3.1 per cent a year, which would see the population double in just under twenty-four years. The same goes for the Solomons, with its 720,000 people. Vanuatu, with 335,000 people and an annual growth rate of 2.4 per cent, will have a population of 600,000 by the same year. The stress will be heaviest on cities such as Port Moresby, Lae, Honiara and Port Vila. Fiji's population is hovering at just under 1 million, and Fiji worries about losing its best taxpayers to emigration, but its villagers are shifting into Suva and other towns. The overall picture, however, is that by mid-century, Australia, with an ageing population of perhaps 40 million, could have a near neighbourhood of nearly 30 million younger Melanesians.

At this point in my analysis, it would be typical for an Australian to argue that this population explosion means Canberra must take Melanesia "seriously" and spend more to ensure that the Melanesians are healthy, reasonably prosperous – and content to stay where they are. Otherwise, with the nearest Australian territory – the islands of Boigu and Saibai in the Torres Strait – only 4 kilometres from the Papua New Guinea coast, a Melanesian world of troubles will spill its crime, drug-resistant diseases,

EPILOGUE

job seekers and rebellions into our comfort zone. The proximity of Torres Strait does indeed present these challenges, especially with drug-resistant tuberculosis active in Daru, the centre of the lower Fly region of Papua New Guinea. And the actual territorial border is already quite porous, with local people on both sides allowed rights to cross it and trade in traditional goods and handicrafts.[2]

But Melanesia is already part of the Australian population. People who identified as Torres Strait Islanders in Australia in the 2021 census numbered 39,538, with an additional 42,516 identifying with both Torres Strait Islander and Aboriginal ancestry. Only about 4500 actually live on the islands in the strait, with the rest on the Australian mainland. Their history and culture have similarities with those we have seen elsewhere in Melanesia. Currently undergoing a revival, Torres Strait culture is adapting to a modern context.

In addition, some 7228 Australians say they are descended from the Melanesian cane-field workers who were allowed to stay after the imposition of the White Australia policy. About three-quarters of these Australian South Sea Islanders live in Queensland, close to where their forebears laboured. Like Aboriginal and Torres Strait Islander peoples, they fly their own flag. In Bundaberg, if you stand on an extinct volcano known as the Hummock, the countryside seen stretching towards the coast is a fertile patchwork of green fields of sugar cane, vegetables and freshly tilled red-brown earth waiting to be planted. The fields below were cleared of volcanic rocks by some of the 62,000 Pacific Islanders, mostly from islands in what are now the nations of Vanuatu and Solomon Islands, brought here and to other Queensland and New South Wales sugar towns in the infamous "blackbirding" trade of late colonial days.

Behind the little weatherboard South Sea Islander Church serving Bundaberg's remaining South Sea Islanders is a memorial engraved with hundreds of names, mostly young men from islands such as Tanna and Malaita, who died of overwork and illness on these plantations. The deaths were registered, but the graves were outside the town cemetery and unmarked. The dry-stone walls these "Kanakas" built from the cleared rocks, and probably many graves, are being cleared for more extensive farming.

Australia is now bringing in a new wave of workers to take their place. Jane Smith, granddaughter of a cane-worker kidnapped as a boy from Tanna, provides pro-bono pastoral care and advocacy for the many ni-Vanuatu working the fields around Bundaberg under the seasonal worker scheme, who are worked hard and often struggle to get proper payment and support. "What's the difference between 160 years ago and now?" her husband Geoff, a retired construction union delegate, posed to me on a visit in 2021. "It's the aeroplane, rather than the schooner," he answered himself.

But despite abuses, the scheme has largely been a rewarding experience on both sides. For the thousands of young men and increasingly women coming for six to seven months each year, it infuses savings of several thousand dollars a year into households that are normally close to subsistence, allowing investment in cyclone-proof houses, children's education or small businesses. In many cases, seasonal workers develop strong ties to their host farming families and communities.

As we have seen, there are long queues of applicants registered in Honiara, Port Vila and elsewhere. The addition of a broader category of temporary employment in sectors other than agriculture, such as hospitality and aged care, has drawn more islander men and women. In 2023, Canberra introduced a new "Pacific Engagement Visa", which will admit up to 3000 people each year from the Pacific Islands and Timor-Leste as permanent residents.

So, Australians will increasingly experience more encounters with Melanesians, and find more of them settled nearby, alongside the substantial groups here already from the Polynesian world. It will steadily reverse what the historian Hank Nelson diagnosed in a popular book on Australia's involvement in Papua New Guinea:

> Australians have always been uncertain about that great island to their north. They know it as close but alien; they have ruled half of it, but never possessed it; they are periodically fascinated by it, then they ignore it for years; they put it on their maps of the region but can never

match it in colours with those of their flat, arid, stable homeland; and they see its peoples in fleeting contradictory images as bow and arrow warriors, mission converts, "kanaka" labourers, fuzzy-wuzzy angels and visiting grey-suited politicians ... Australia holds few visible signs of its relationship with Papua New Guinea. Australian genes, language, clothing, food, recreation and gardens show few of the traces that have been part of the back migrations of other colonial powers. Papua New Guinea's influence is strongest in the force that it exerts over thousands of Australian memories.[3]

Along with the Kokoda Trail hike, other longstanding types of contact continue. Churches come together for theological instruction and festivals of prayer and music. Papua New Guineans follow the Australian rugby league competition as fervently as fans in Queensland and New South Wales. An ageing cohort of Australian academic specialists run Pacific research projects. Military veterans and businessmen's clubs help particular schools and local facilities.

But most of the time, Australia pays Melanesia little attention. The region's internal crises come as total shocks: the coups in Fiji, the closure of the copper mine and eruption of civil war in Bougainville, the Kanak uprisings of New Caledonia, the Sandline affair, the near collapse of the Solomon Islands state. Extravagant journalistic races result, as reporters compete to portray the danger and turmoil of Melanesia: news teams arrive in chartered executive jets with portable satellite connections, instead of the rifles and native carriers used by their colonial forebears.

In between such crises, the information vacuum is filled by non-government organisations, which bring delegations of journalists and backbench members of parliament up to see pockets of misery and encourage a flow of donations to help their work with undernourished children, communicable diseases and natural disasters, and to hear about crime and tribal warfare, now carried out with assault rifles rather than bows and arrows. "Africa on our doorstep" was how a federal member of parliament described the region in 2020, after one such sponsored visit.[4]

Periodic wranglings in the region's parliaments – motions of no-confidence, the poaching of rival party members, corruption scandals, court injunctions – result in changes of leadership that are heralded as a break with the past. A clean-up of government is promised. Before long, it becomes clear that most of the old characters and political practices remain.

Another old trope has recently emerged again: the infiltration of a potentially hostile power in the region. Not the French, Germans or Japanese this time, but the Chinese. In common with other parts of the world, a new migration of Chinese fortune-seekers has arrived, mostly from commercially attuned regions of the Chinese coast such as Fujian, where businesspeople are used to pushing official limits at home. They operate stores and fast-food bars across Papua New Guinea and the islands. Resentment is strong among locals, including the older Chinese communities. The visa status of these new arrivals is often murky; they operate on a cash basis; tax officials leave them alone, baffled by language difficulties. This "wild west mercantilism" gets a qualified admiration for its doggedness but is a challenge to sovereignty.

On top of this, Beijing has stepped up its aid, with quick builds of government offices, football stadiums and urban infrastructure by Chinese state-owned corporations and private-sector entrepreneurs. These large projects often get mysteriously rapid clearances and exemptions from employment and labour rules.

In many cases, the main aim of Chinese intervention is simply to secure or reward the diplomatic recognition of the People's Republic of China instead of Taiwan. Expert studies have found that there is no Chinese plan to deliberately snare Pacific governments in a "debt trap", and little risk of such a plan emerging.[5] Overall, Chinese aid is still less than Australian aid, and Australia remains the major aid donor, the main source of budget support and the preferred defence partner for Port Moresby. In terms of soft power, China cannot hope to match Australia in "Jesus, beer, and football", as the Australia Institute's Allan Behm put it to me.

For all the old ties, Australia cops local resentment too: about the onerous conditions for PNG nationals to get visitor visas, about the slowness of inclusion in Australia's seasonal work and other temporary labour intakes, about official advice on travel dangers. The News Corp–owned *Post-Courier* newspaper is a weak monitor of politics, as is its rival, *The National*, owned by Malaysian logging and palm oil firm Rimbunan Hijau. Allan Bird, the East Sepik governor and MP, thinks Canberra should take a "hard stand" on which PNG leaders it embraces. "Draw a line in the sand," he said. "Say this leader is honest and transparent, we'll work with him. Bugger the rest. Because at the end of the day, it's Australian money. They should be targeting, as opposed to just scatter-gunning." Of course, Canberra would argue it has to deal with the leaders that Papua New Guinea elects, not leave the field to malign actors.

The Australian presence on the street in Papua New Guinea is diminishing, with ANZ Bank withdrawing from retail banking there. Westpac planned to follow, but its proposed sale of PNG branches to the locally owned Kina Bank was vetoed by Port Moresby on competition grounds, and then the Albanese government persuaded it to stay.

But the Papua New Guineans do increasingly exert their sovereignty. On becoming prime minister, Marape appointed Sam Koim as chief of the Internal Revenue Commission. He turned his gaze on tax defaulters, including the "wild west" Chinese. As we have seen, some large-scale Chinese investors also had a tougher time under Marape.

Until recently, China largely steered clear of significant military involvement in the region. Countries with armed forces received Chinese uniforms, vehicles and small arms, but not advanced weapons. Some Chinese projects that were given a sinister twist in Canberra's fevered defence circles have turned out to be quite innocuous. A berth for big ships in Vanuatu's northern port of Luganville, for example, was said by some in Canberra to be a future base for China's navy, but was in fact intended for cruise ships filled with tourists.

Yet with Chinese strategic policy growing more assertive since Xi Jinping's ascension in 2012, Australia and its allies have seen a need for counter-displays of power, both hard and soft. Canberra stepped in to displace Chinese firm Huawei from a new high-capacity internet cable to

Papua New Guinea and the Solomons in 2019, at a cost of US$92.5 million. As we have noted, it announced in late 2018 it was joining with Japan, the United States and New Zealand to bring electricity and the internet to 70 per cent of Papua New Guinea's population by 2030.

A multi-billion-dollar fund was allocated to finance these and other infrastructure projects. But US$1.33 billion of it went to financing the acquisition of the Digicel mobile phone network in Papua New Guinea, Vanuatu, Fiji, Samoa, Tonga and Nauru by the Australian carrier Telstra, in order to prevent a Chinese takeover. It is unclear what difference Telstra's ownership of the network is making to the region. After Port Moresby, Lae and other towns were wracked by looting in January 2024, authorities talked of shutting down mobile social media apps blamed for spreading the disorder. Canberra headed off the possibility of Chinese interests gaining control of this powerful mass communication system but seems to have no idea how to use it.

Honiara's diplomatic switch to Beijing and its security agreement with China sent many of Canberra's strategic analysts and journalists into a frenzy of dire forecasts that a military thrust southwards was about to start, requiring a drastic rearmament. The region's leaders are confident that they can work the competition to their advantage, without being captured. "Don't be fearful," PNG prime minister James Marape said to me. "Papua New Guinea will not compromise our democratic values, our Christian values – these are an intrinsic part of us." When I asked if Australia panicked too much about the Chinese influence in his country, he smiled and gave a diplomatic answer: "I won't use the word panic, but there's no cause for concern. I'll maybe qualify that: under my watch, there's no cause for concern. You never know what might happen with others."

In Australia's strategic policy circles, public discussions have rarely addressed an alternative approach to hard military power: a deeper investment in the Melanesian arc, whose people could conceivably outnumber Australians within a few decades, to ensure a belt of resilient, friendly nations.

Only after it was found that the sky had not fallen in, and Chinese missiles were not ranging Australia from Guadalcanal, have more sensible approaches gained favour. We seem to have realised the Chinese cannot be kept out, and the main security threat in Melanesia is internal: human safety. Of course, that too creates the risk of a power like China offering its more authoritarian form of policing. But in December 2023, Anthony Albanese and Marape announced an agreement whereby Canberra would assist Port Moresby to expand its police force to about 10,000 officers, with funding for a new training centre for recruits and specialist investigators. It would not prevent Papua New Guinea from cooperating with other countries on security, but the two governments agreed to coordinate on "the involvement and contribution of third parties". In a ministerial dialogue in June 2024, led on the Australian side by foreign minister Penny Wong, the emphasis was on law and order and human security, with the defence minister, Richard Marles, not present. It marked a distinct shift.

New Zealand meanwhile expanded on the community-policing model it pioneered in Bougainville. The same month as the Australian police initiative was announced, the New Zealand high commissioner in Vanuatu attended the graduation of nineteen new community safety officers at Hog Harbour on Espíritu Santo. Similar teams were operating elsewhere on the islands of Santo, Pentecost, Banks and Torres.[6] This quiet success suggests Australia could learn much from the New Zealand approach. In the islands Australia comes across as too proprietorial, with politicians and journalists constantly referring to the region as "our backyard". Australian conservatives assume that islanders share our historical fear of invasion and would feel reassured by the presence of warships from the same navies that used to bombard their villages. Australian progressives assume that islanders share their liberal views on gender fluidity, same-sex marriage and formal religion.

In a splendid summary of Australian policy, Michael Wesley said that Australia's engagement with the Pacific was a story of "passions outstripping actions, of ambitions outstripping abilities", with "long stretches of lassitude and inattention punctuated by intense periods of concern and engagement". Its tone was "alarmist, quixotic, pugnacious but subsequently deferential, and then ultimately forgetful". It had been niggardly, trying to get Britain to carry out and pay for its strategic bidding and only agreeing to contribute when forced.[7]

The same buck-passing impulse pervades the strategic think-tank analysis coming out of Canberra now: the Chinese challenge requires the Americans, the French, even the British and Germans, long departed from the Pacific, to protect Australia along what that early naval thinker in 1913 called its island "trip-wire".

The Pacific Islanders no doubt wonder whether Australia is really on their side when the chips are down. They want evidence of the Pacific's self-proclaimed *vuvale* (family) member making sacrifices – greater than the more remote and bigger emitters such as China, the United States and India – to combat global warming, which is raising the seas and bringing more frequent and intense cyclones.

For all its talk of putting "first nations" at the heart of its diplomacy, the Albanese government has avoided talk about the Kanak right to self-determination in New Caledonia, seeming to accept the Paris line that no group of French citizens can have more say than the others. It has eagerly swallowed the French assertion that its power can significantly alter the balance against China. The Kanaks are being pushed aside.

On Bougainville, Canberra will soon have to take a position, unless there is an unlikely change of heart by either party to accede to the other's preference, or settle on the kind of compromise being explored by Marape. The can has been kicked down the constitutional road almost as far as possible, almost beyond tolerance for the elected leaders of Bougainville. Weapons are seeping back in, from the PNG mainland and West Papua.[8] A unilateral declaration of independence is quite possible. Leadership from Australia and New Zealand will be highly influential.

It will get harder, not easier, to ignore the mounting unrest against Indonesian rule in Western New Guinea – shown in a better armed guerrilla movement in the highlands, an internet-enabled civil opposition and a sophisticated exile lobby asking the UN to reopen the self-determination question. The conflict could draw in volunteers from Papua New Guinea's restless young highlanders. At the end of Joko Widodo's Indonesian presidency in 2024, the region was in a more intense level of conflict and protest than ever before, and effectively closed to outside observers. His successor,

EPILOGUE

Prabowo Subianto, has a baleful record of military strikes in East Timor and West Papua from his time as an Indonesian special forces officer.

The time may come when more nations join Vanuatu in declaring that the West Papuans deserve more than the cynical realpolitik of 1962–63 that handed them to Jakarta, and that a half-century of Indonesian exploitation and massacres has alienated them. Given the psychological insecurity of Indonesian nationalism, the wealth of Papuan minerals, forests and land, the vested interest of its military in having a domestic combat zone, and Indonesia's revived role as a strategic backstop against a communist power, it is hard to imagine the West Papuans getting much Western support for the independent state they are surely owed by now. But it could be put, initially in second-track diplomacy, that a state of their own within Indonesia, perhaps along the lines of Aceh, which has its own sharia law and police, might be a pathway forwards. Perhaps a more sophisticated Indonesian civil society eventually will accept and appreciate it.

A start to grappling with these fast-emerging new realities could be that Australians put aside their arrogance about their place in the Pacific. For one thing, they could start appreciating that for all their economic poverty, the indigenous peoples of the region have given the world far more original art than they have. Or that the plunder and near-slavery run out of Sydney and Brisbane into the early twentieth century, the suppression of indigenous movements and the ruinous ecological and social side effects of big mines have not left an unalloyed feeling of affinity with Australian among Melanesians.

The more internationally aware islanders were watching the Uluru statement by Aboriginal and Torres Strait leaders. In early 2020 I talked about it with Ralph Regenvanu, who was then the foreign minister of Vanuatu, and I was surprised when he spoke openly and warmly about a domestic Australian subject many foreign leaders would have sidestepped.

Regenvanu said ni-Vanuatu had been heartened by the Uluru Statement from the Heart and its call for an Indigenous voice to be incorporated into the Australian constitution. At the time the idea had been summarily dismissed by the then prime minister, Malcolm Turnbull. "We were hoping that this would be a way forward that everyone could agree on," Regenvanu said. "And we still hope that it can be." He was no doubt disappointed by the negative result when the Albanese government had it put to a referendum in 2023.

But something else he said has resonated in my head ever since. "We very much support the recognition of the Aboriginal people of Australia. We are the original people of the region, they are the original people of the region," Regenvanu said. "This is a black region, it's not a white region." In coming decades, it will become more evidently so.

The population of Melanesia will steadily catch up with that of Australia. The trickle of Melanesians coming into Australia will build into a significant flow back and forth. With wise statesmanship, the region could be embraced as a source of strength and renewal. It could be the way Australia decolonises itself.

ACKNOWLEDGEMENTS

Many helped in this long-brewing project. At the outset: Philip Bowring of the *Far Eastern Economic Review* who sent me on a reporting trip through the Melanesian islands in the 1980s; then two decades later, Alan Oakley of *The Sydney Morning Herald* who let me retrace my tracks.

At various times there were shorter visits and meet-ups, when I learned much from colleagues more deeply versed in the Pacific: Craig Skehan, Sean Dorney, Rowan Callick, Mary-Louise O'Callaghan, Jo Chandler, Lloyd Jones, Steve Marshall, Jon Reid, John Lombard, the late Robert Keith-Reid, Godfrey Scoullar, Campbell Cooney, Johnson Honimae, Nina Ratulele, Makereta Komai, the late Robert Palme.

In Papua New Guinea, I have relied immensely on Stuart Fancy's astute knowledge and generosity over many years. In Rabaul, Susie Alexander and Father Mate Litric helped greatly. In the Highlands, Paias Wingti took me along in 2006 to the peace ceremony recounted here. Over decades, Warren and Joy Dutton at Kiunga have shown me Western Province, and for this book invited me aboard the MV Kuku for the expedition down the Fly River and into Lake Murray, with Captain Stonewig Ame, Redentor Gaggauan and the other crew looking after me. On the way out, Bob Bates of Trans Nuigini Tours hosted me at his Lake Murray resort and flew me out to Mount Hagan. On the election trail in 2022, Malum Nalu and Matrom

ACKNOWLEDGEMENTS

John of the prime minister's staff helped with arrangements and guidance, while Rebecca Kuku of *The National* and Natalie Whiting of the ABC were insightful source. In Port Moresby, Mahalopa Laveil of the University of PNG and Paul Barker of the Institute of National Affairs supplied essential background and commentary. In Bougainville, David and Sophie Kirk hosted me generously in Arawa; Dominic Babatani took me to meet key figures of the 1990s conflict; Joyce Ampa'oi took me up to the ruined Panguna township and told me of her childhood there.

In Fiji, Api, Finau and Kalesi Bavadra hosted me at their home in Viseisei village and showed me around legendary places. At Drauniivi village, Tomasi Naisua taught me its important part in Fiji's colonial-era history, and along with his friend Cau-Cau guided me up and down the sacred mountain, while his cousin Makareta and her family were engaging hosts for my stay. At Vatukacevucevu village, headman Peni Vunica and the village's people saw we were well supplied for the mountain climb and hosted us to kava when we came down. In Suva, Paul Geraghty of the University of the South Pacific was his usual deep and witty source about Fijian culture, and Graham Davis an informed guide to contemporary Fijian affairs.

In Vanuatu, Welly and Monique Warua hosted me at Port Resolution and guided me to the John Frum celebrations. A long time ago, Shaen Egan met me in Luganville and took me to his cattle ranch. More recently from his home in Queensland, he gave me valuable introductions to senior figures in Luganville. These led to an introduction to Peter Terry, who put me aboard his two small ships *Karaa Pha* and *Lara Star* for their trading circuits around the islands of the north; ashore on Malekula, Jack Waiwo, took me across to the remote north-western area. In Port Vila, Ben Bohane and Ginny Stein were ever helpful, and the then-foreign minister, Ralph Regenvanu gave a frank interview greatly informing the themes of this book.

In the Solomon Islands, Ronnie Butala and Silas Malai organised my trip across the island of Malaita and made introductions that made its history come alive. In Honiara, senior journalist Dorothy Wickham gave a sagacious take on contemporary controversies and social issues, as did Fox Qwainas, private secretary to the Archbishop of Melanesia.

ACKNOWLEDGEMENTS

In New Caledonia, my understanding benefitted immensely from Charles Wea, who invited me to spend a day with him at his home village on Ouvéa, scene of the most dreadful incident in the territory's recent history. Mathias Chauchat and Patrice Godin of the University of New Caledonia were invaluable sources about the constitutional, political and social trends and forces. In Australia, fellow *Inside Story* writer Nic Maclellan supplied introductions and his deep knowledge of New Caledonia's politics, while Jean-Francois Vernay has always given me the perspective of a Frenchman who grew up in this outpost in Oceania.

On West Papua, my thanks go to the members of the German Eipo Expedition encountered so long ago, and to Frederick Smith for permission to reproduce his rendition of Oleto's poem. The late Peter King and Jim Elmslie of the University of Sydney's former West Papua Project deepened my understanding, as did meetings with the late Otto Ondowame.

Some years back, Andrew MacIntyre got me embedded for two years in the ANU's Research School of Asia and the Pacific, expanding contact with its amazing range of scholarship. As this book developed, this circle was ever helpful with insights and references, particularly James Batley, Michael Wesley (now at the University of Melbourne), Chris Ballard, Sinclair Dinnen, and Anthony Regan. In Sydney, Kirk Huffman has been a fount of information about the cultures of island Melanesia. Brendan Atkins and Tim Griffiths shared their work on the Frank Hurley-Allan McCulloch expedition into Lake Murray.

This book was commissioned over six years ago, and I thank publisher Chris Feik of Black Inc. for sticking with it years beyond the original delivery deadline. There were always many more places to explore in Melanesia: deeper into the Sepik, the Trobriands, West Papua if permissions were ever forthcoming, the western margins of Melanesia in Maluku and Timor-Leste. But a halt had to be called, and this is the result. Denise O'Dea has been a wise editor in shaping and improving the text, while proofreader Kate Hatch and fact-checker Amelia Willis saved me from numerous errors. Beau Lowenstern came up with the tantalising cover and the interior typesetting.

ACKNOWLEDGEMENTS

The travel involved was lengthy and costly, so I thank the editors who accepted reports along the way that offset some of the expenses: Nick Feik and Michael Williams at *The Monthly*, Erik Jensen at *The Saturday Paper* and Peter Browne at *Inside Story*.

And I thank my wife, Penny, for encouraging me always to pursue a project that at times seemed a Quixotic exercise in delineating a region and its people so often defined by what they weren't.

ENDNOTES

CH. 1 MELANESIA

1   Louis Antoine de Bougainville, *A Voyage Round the World*, translated from the French by John Reinhold Forster, London, 1772, p. 245.
2   J.C. Beaglehole (ed.), *The Endeavour Journal of Joseph Banks, 1768–1771*, State Library of NSW and Angus and Robertson, 1962.
3   Beaglehole, *The Endeavour Journal*, p. 493.
4   Beaglehole, *The Endeavour Journal*, p. 539.
5   Alan Moorehead, *The Fatal Impact*, Hamish Hamilton, 1966, p.43.
6   Bernard Smith, *European Vision and the South Pacific, 1768–1850: A Study in the History of Art and Ideas*, Clarendon Press, 1960, p 90.
7   Moorehead, *The Fatal Impact*, pp. 83–85.
8   John Bach, *The Australian Station: A History of the Royal Navy in the Southwest Pacific, c. 1821–1913*, UNSW Press, 1986, p. 47.
9   Charles A. Valentine, "Social Status, Political Power and Native Responses to European Influence in Oceania", in Thomas G. Harding and Ben J. Wallace (eds), *Cultures of the Pacific*, Free Press and Collier-Macmillan, 1970, p. 384.
10 Alfred Russel Wallace, *The Malay Archipelago: The Land of the Orang-Utan, and the Bird of Paradise. A Narrative of Travel, with Studies of Man and Nature*, Harper, 1869, pp. 584–596.
11 Pamela Swadling, *Plumes from Paradise*, Sydney University Press, 2019.
12 Helen Gardner, "The 'Faculty of Faith': Evangelical Missionaries, Social Anthropologists and the Claim for Human Unity in the Nineteenth Century", and Christine Weir, "'White Man's Burden', 'White Man's Privilege': Christian

ENDNOTES

Humanism and Racial Determinism in Oceania 1890-1930", in Bronwen Douglas and Chris Ballard (eds), *Foreign Bodies, Oceania and the Science of Race 1750–1940*, ANU Press, 2008.

13 Hank Nelson, *Taim Bilong Masta: The Australian Involvement with Papua New Guinea*, Australian Broadcasting Corporation, 1982, p. 121.

14 Gavin Souter, *New Guinea: The Last Unknown*, Angus and Robertson, 1963, pp. 30-43.

15 Joanne Wallis and Michael Wesley, "Unipolar Anxieties: Australia's Melanesia Policy after the Age of Intervention", *Asia and the Pacific Policy Studies*, vol. 3, no. 1, 2015, pp. 26-37.

16 Cyril Pearl, *Morrison of Peking*, Angus and Robertson, 1967, pp. 41-54.

17 Bruce Hunt, *Papua New Guinea and the Defence of Australia Since 1880*, Monash University Press, 2017, p. 9.

18 Michael Waterhouse relates this in his *Not a Poor Man's Field: The New Guinea Goldfield to 1942, an Australian Colonial History*, Halstead, 2010.

19 Bronwen Douglas and Chris Ballard (eds), *Foreign Bodies: Oceania and the Science of Race 1750–1940*, ANU Press, 2008, p. 287.

20 An eminently readable account of this discovery is: Matthew Spriggs and David Reich, "An Ancient DNA Pacific Journey: A Case Study of Collaboration between Archaeologists and Geneticists, *World Archaeology*, vol. 51, no. 4, 2020. See also a fine summary of multidisciplinary work on the Papuan world in Chris Ballard, "Synthetic Histories: Possible Futures for Papuan Pasts", *Anthropology*, vol. 39, no. 4, 2010, pp. 232-257.

21 Tarcisius Kabutaulaka, "Re-Presenting Melanesia: Ignoble Savages and Melanesian Alter-Natives", *The Contemporary Pacific*, vol. 27, no. 1, 2015, pp. 110-146.

CH. 2 FIJI

1 Peter France, *The Charter of the Land: Custom and Colonisation in Fiji*, Oxford University Press, 1966.

2 Aubrey Parke, *Degei's Descendants: Spirits, Place and People in Pre-cession Fiji*, ANU Press, 2014.

3 Robert Nicole, *Disturbing History: Resistance in Early Colonial Fiji,* University of Hawaii Press, 2010.

4 Peter Worsley, *The Trumpet Shall Sound: A Study of "Cargo" Cults in Melanesia*, Schocken, 1968.

5 Martha Kaplan, *Neither Cargo Nor Cult: Ritual Politics and the Colonial Imagination in Fiji*, Duke University Press, 1995.

ENDNOTES

6 Kaplan, *Neither Cargo Nor Cult*, p. 65.
7 Kaplan, *Neither Cargo Nor Cult*, p. 94.
8 Nicole, *Disturbing History*, p. 87.

CH. 3 VANUATU

1 Tom Harrisson, *Savage Civilisation*, Victor Gollancz, 1937, p. 156.
2 Harrisson, *Savage Civilisation*.

CH. 4 ESPIRITU SANTO

1 Richard Shears, *The Coconut War: The Crisis on Espíritu Santo*, Cassell, 1980.
2 Gregoire Nimbtik, "'Worlds in Collision': An Inquiry into the Sources of Corruption within Vanuatu Government and Society", doctoral thesis, RMIT, 2016.
3 Siobhan McDonnell, *My Land, My Life: Dispossession at the Frontier of Desire*, University of Hawaii Press, 2023.
4 Anna Naupa, "Making the Invisible Seen: Putting Women's Rights on Vanuatu's Land Reform Agenda", in Siobhan McDonnell, Matthew Allen and Colin Filer (eds), *Kastom, Property and Ideology*, ANU Press, 2017, p. 308.
5 The latest of these surveys, *Wellbeing in Vanuatu: 2019–2020 NSDP Baseline Survey*, is online at https://vbos.gov.vu/sites/default/files/Wellbeing_report.pdf

CH. 5 NEW CALEDONIA

1 Alan Moorehead, *The Fatal Impact: An Account of the Invasion of the South Pacific 1767–1840*, Penguin, 1967.
2 Christophe Sand, "Archeology of a Piece of Gondwanaland: The Past of New Caledonia", in Ethan E. Cochrane and Terry L. Hunt (eds), *The Oxford Handbook of Prehistoric Oceania*, 2018, pp. 185–205.
3 Stephen Henningham, *France and the South Pacific: A Contemporary History*, Allen and Unwin, 1992.
4 David Chappell, *The Kanak Awakening: The Rise of Nationalism in New Caledonia*, University of Hawaii Press, 2013, p. 55.
5 Nic MacLellan, "Oil and Water", *Inside Story*, 23 July 2024.
6 Denise Fisher, "A Surprising Litmus Test for New Caledonia's Independence Parties", *The Interpreter*, Lowy Institute, 11 July 2024.
7 Nicholas Kurtovich, *Le temps suspendu: Une autre histoire du rêve d'indépendance en Nouvelle-Calédonie*, Luc Deborde, 2021.
8 Chappell, *The Kanak Awakening*, pp. 423–424.

ENDNOTES

CH. 6 SOLOMON ISLANDS

1. Jack London, *The Cruise of the Snark*, Penguin, 2004 (1911), p. 157.
2. Roger M. Keesing and Peter Corris, *Lightning Meets the West Wind: The Malaita Massacre*, Oxford University Press, 1980, p. 30.
3. Caroline Mytinger, *Headhunting in the Solomon Islands*, Macmillan, 1942.
4. Keesing and Corris, *Lightning Meets the West Wind*, pp. 79–80.
5. Mytinger, *Headhunting in the Solomon Islands*, pp 51–52.
6. Keesing and Corris, *Lightning Meets the West Wind*, pp. 162–164.
7. Keesing and Corris, *Lightning Meets the Wind*, p. 195.
8. David W. Akin, *Colonialism, Maasina Rule, and the Origins of Malaitan Kastom*, University of Hawaii Press, 2013, p. 25.]
9. Akin, *Colonialism*, p. 109.
10. Akin, *Colonialism*, p. 332.
11. Michael Wesley, *Helpem Fren: Australia and the Regional Assistance Mission to the Solomon Islands*, Melbourne University Press, 2023, p. 32.
12. Wesley, in *Helpem Fren*, gives the best account of RAMSI.

CH. 7 MALAITA

1. A detailed account of this contest is in Edward Acton Cavanough, *Divided Isles: Solomon Islands and the China Switch*, La Trobe University Press and Black Inc., 2023.

CH. 8 BOUGAINVILLE

1. Bill Brown, "A Kiap's Chronicle", *PNG Attitude*, https://www.pngattitude.com/a-kiaps-chronicle.html
2. Peter Elder, "Between the *Waitman*'s Wars: 1914–42", in Anthony Regan and Helga-Maria Griffin (eds), *Bougainville Before the Conflict*, ANU Press, 2015.
3. Don Vernon, "The Panguna Mine", in Regan and Griffin (eds), *Bougainville Before the Conflict*.
4. National Research Institute of Papua New Guinea, "Financing for Fiscal Autonomy: Fiscal Self-Reliance in Bougainville", available at https://pngnri.org/index.php/hosted-programs-projects/bougainville-referendum-research-project

CH. 9 PAPUA NEW GUINEA

1. The best account of this system is in T. Scarlett Epstein, *Capitalism, Primitive and Modern*, ANU Press, 1968.
2. See S.S. MacKenzie, *The Australians at Rabaul: The Capture and Administration of the German Possessions in the Southern Pacific*, Angus and Robertson, 1938.

ENDNOTES

3   David Marr, "His Master's Voice", *Quarterly Essay* 26, 2007.
4   Errol Flynn, *My Wicked, Wicked Ways*, Aurum Press, 2005.
5   Peter Stone, *Hostage to Freedom: The Fall of Rabaul*, Oceans Enterprises, 1995.
6   Morio Kita, *The House of Nire,* translated by Dennis Keene, Kodansha/Fontana, 1990, p. 587.
7   Shigeru Mizuki, *Soin Gyokusai Seyo*, translated by Jocelyne Allen as *Onward Towards Our Noble Deaths,* Drawn and Quarterly, 2011.
8   Harry West, "Reminiscences of a District Commissioner", PNG Association of Australia, 31 October 2004, https://asopa.typepad.com/asopa_people/files/harry_west.pdf
9   Act Now PNG, "SABL: A Form of Customary Land Theft", https://actnowpng.org/sites/default/files/publications/SABL Factsheet.pdf
10 John C. Cannon, "Forest Loss Increases Violence Against Women", PNG Attitude, 23 May 2020, https://www.pngattitude.com/2020/05/forest-loss-increases-violence-against-women.htm
11 "The True Price of Palm Oil", *Global Witness*, 7 October 2021, https://www.globalwitness.org/en/campaigns/forests/true-price-palm-oil/

CH. 10 PORT MORESBY

1   Peter Phelps, *The Bulldog Track*, Hachette Australia, 2018.
2   Hal B. Levine and Marlene W. Levine, *Urbanization in Papua New Guinea: A Study of Ambivalent Townsmen*, Cambridge University Press, 1979.
3   John Cox, Grant W. Walton, Joshua Goa and Dunstan Lawihin, in Stephen Howes and Lekshmi N. Pillai (eds), *Papua New Guinea: Government, Economy and Society*, ANU Press, 2022.
4   PNGi, "The Midas Touch: How Peter O'Neill and His Associates Have Made a Killing, Part 1", "The Big Skim: Peter O'Neill Inc. Meets Don Sawong and Tos Barnett (The Midas Touch Part 2)", and "Lift Off: Prime Minister, Millionaire (The Midas Touch Part 3)", June and July 2017, https://pngicentral.org/
5   Grant W. Walton and Sinclair Dinnen, "Crime and Corruption", in Howes and Pillai, *Papua New Guinea.*

CH. 11 WESTERN PROVINCE

1   The D'Albertis expeditions form a chapter in Gavin Souter, *New Guinea: The Last Unknown*, Angus and Robertson, 1963.
2   Brendan Atkins, *The Naturalist: The Remarkable Life of Allan Riverstone McCulloch*, NewSouth, 2022, p. 98.

ENDNOTES

CH. 12 THE HIGHLANDS

1. Michael Waterhouse, *Not a Poor Man's Field: The New Guinea Goldfields to 1942 – An Australian Colonial History*, Halstead Press, 2010, p 75.
2. James Griffin, "Michael James (Mick) Leahy", *Australian Dictionary of Biography*, https://adb.anu.edu.au/biography/leahy-michael-james-mick-7134
3. Ian Downs, *The Last Mountain: A Life in Papua New Guinea*, University of Queensland Press, 1986, p. 176.
4. Julius Chan, *Playing the Game*, University of Queensland Press, 2016, p. 121.

CH. 13 THE SEPIK

1. S.S. MacKenzie, *The Australians at Rabaul: The Capture and Administration of the German Possessions in the Southern Pacific*, Angus and Robertson, 1936, p. 10.
2. Duncan Gabi, "The Day the Crocodile God Walked", PNG Attitude, 17 January 2021, https://www.pngattitude.com/2021/01/the-day-the-crocodile-god-walked.html
3. Tim Flannery, *Throwim Way Leg*, Text Publishing, 1998, pp. 186–187.
4. John Paul II, Post-Synodal Apostolic Exhortation, *Ecclesia in Oceania*, 2001, https://www.vatican.va/content/john-paul-ii/en/apost_exhortations/documents/hf_jp-ii_exh_20011122_ecclesia-in-oceania.html
5. G.W. Trompf, *Melanesian Religion*, Cambridge University Press, 1991, p. 146.
6. Trompf, *Melanesian Religion*, pp. 156–159.

CH. 14 WEST PAPUA

1. For a more detailed account, see the chapter "The Eastern Margin" in my book *Demokrasi: Indonesia in the Twenty-First Century*, Black Inc. and Palgrave Macmillan, 2014.
2. Matt Easton, *We Have Tired of Violence*, The New Press, 2022, pp. 255–256.
3. Greg Poulgrain, *JFK vs Allen Dulles: Battleground Indonesia*, Skyhorse, 2020.
4. A credible hypothesis for his murder after he swam ashore from a disabled boat is in Carl Hoffman, *Savage Harvest*, William Morrow, 2014.
5. The best survey in English is Anton Ploeg, "The German Eipo Research Project", *Journal de la Société des Océanistes*, 118, 2004.
6. Ploeg, "The German Eipo Research Project".

EPILOGUE

1. See M.R. Allen, *Male Cults and Secret Initiations in Melanesia*, Melbourne University Press, 1967.

ENDNOTES

2. See Mark Moran and Jodie Curth-Bibb (eds), *Too Close to Ignore: Australia's Borderland with Papua New Guinea and Indonesia*, Melbourne University Press, 2020.
3. Nelson, *Taim Bilong Masta*, p. 11 and p. 219.
4. "Africa on Our Doorstep: The Health Crisis a Short Plane Ride from Australia", *Sydney Morning Herald*, 4 January 2020.
5. "Ocean of Debt? Belt and Road and Debt Diplomacy in the Pacific", Lowy Institute, 2019, https://www.lowyinstitute.org/publications/ocean-debt-belt-road-debt-diplomacy-pacific
6. Radio New Zealand, "Villagers Welcome Community Policing Graduates", 13 December 2023.
7. See the chapter "Lineages" in Wesley, *Helpem Fren*.
8. John Braithwaite, *Peaceful Independence for Bougainville*, ANU Working Paper, September 2024.

INDEX

Aba, Johnny 158
Aboriginal artefacts 239–40
Aboriginal Australians 11, 16, 289, 298
Abwatuntora 61
Aceh 297
Adelaide (ship) 99, 127–8
Adventure (London) 123
Aeneas (ship) 133
Africa 134
The Age 16
Ah Sim's Hotel, Rabaul 184–5
Ahern, Bertie 170
Aiambak 228, 230
Aiyaz Sayed-Khaiyum 37
Aki, George Joshua 251
Akin, David 129, 130, 131, 132, 133
Albanese, Anthony 295, 296, 298
Alebua, Ezekiel 135
Alexander, Susie 178, 195–6
Algeria 100, 105
Algiers 99
Ambae Island 87
Ambrym 52, 78
Ambunti 264–5, 271
Ame, Stonewig 224, 225, 231, 233–4
Amil, Bruce 60
Amil, Sethla 59–60, 89

Ampa'oi, Joyce 158, 167
Ampa'oi, Severinus 159, 160, 167
Anderson, George 14
Aneityum 65, 66
Anglican Board of Missions 235
Anglican Church 121, 132
Angolo, Sima 149
Angoram 246
Anifelo (son of Basiana) 128, 132
Aniwa 64
Anova-Ataba, Apollinaire 101
ANZ Bank 293
Aoba 78
Arawa 154, 155–6, 165, 171
Arfak Mountains 227
The Argus 16
Ark of God (schooner) 124
Armit, William 16
Aropa 154
Asia-Pacific Economic Cooperation
    Summit (2018) 194, 211, 220
Asilaua, Elijah 150
Astrolabe Bay 14
Ataï (chief) 98
Atkins, Brendan 238, 240, 241
Atori 145
Auki (ship) 126–7

INDEX

Auki (town) 133
Australian Army 186–7
Australian Coastwatchers 164, 188
Australian Constitution (1901) 18
Australian Federal Police 207
Australian Museum 144, 234, 235, 238, 239–40
Australian National University 210–11, 259
Australian Station, Royal Navy 17, 18
Austronesians 23–4
Awin people 232

Babala (Bougainville leader) 164
Babatani, Dominic 168
Babate, Kolis 189, 191
Backès, Sonia 113, 118
Baddeley, Walter 131
Bainimarama, Frank 31, 36, 37
Baining people 178
Baker, Thomas 28
Balade 98
Bali 274
Baliem Valley 278, 280
banana boats 153–4
Bancarel, Père 54
Banks, Joseph 6
Barker, Paul 218, 254, 256
Barnes, Charles 160–2
Barnett, Justice T.E. 'Tos' 193, 213
Barnier, Michel 117
Barrick Gold 246
Barton, Edmund 18
Basiana (warrior) 126–7, 128, 145
Bastide, Roger 102
Bates, Bob 230–1, 248
Batley, James 173, 174–5
Bauan language 30
Bavadra, Api 31–2, 35, 38–9
Bavadra, Finau Moce 31–2, 39
Bavadra, Timoci 34, 36, 37
Bayrou, François 118
Beagle (ship) 11
Behm, Allan 292

Bell, George 127
Bell, William 125–7, 143, 145
Belt and Road Initiative 219
Benedict XVI, Pope 265
Benin Bronzes 239
Beqa people 30
betel nuts 196, 197, 198, 199, 211, 287
BHP 228–9
Bhutan 88
Biak 274, 275
Big Nambas 57, 59, 61
Bird, Allan 173, 254, 256, 270, 293
Bird of Paradise Hotel, Goroka 252
Bislama 80, 88
Bismarck Archipelago 22
Bismarck Sea 261
Black, John 246
Black Pride movement 79–80
blackbirding 15–17, 60, 65, 123, 125–6, 163, 289
blackwater fever 9, 124
Bligh, William 9
Boboa Island 241, 243
Bohane, Ben 136
Boigu 288
Bougainville 153–75
  Australia's relationship with 296
  barriers to independence 171–3
  citizens vote for independence 170–1, 191
  civil war 168–9, 173
  colonial days 154–5, 159, 163–4
  independence movement 156
  Japanese invade 130, 164, 171
  map of *152*
  mining in 158–9, 160–2, 166, 171
  PNG soldiers in 167–8, 173
  police in 167, 217, 295
  rebels supplied by banana boats 154
  traditional subsistence farming 163
  under German rule 122, 163
Bougainville Copper Ltd 155, 159, 162, 168, 171, 174, 191, 228, 269

INDEX

Bougainville Ex-Combatants Core Group 170
Bougainville Revolutionary Army 167–9
Bounty mutiny 184
Boyd, Benjamin 65
Brian Bell Group 219
bribery 195
Britain, in the Pacific 5–6, 15, 17, 18, 122, 123
Brosnan, Pierce 156
Brown, Bill 160, 161–2, 166
Brown, George 178
buai 196, 197, 198, 199
Buka Island 122, 163, 164, 169
Buleban, Sophia 62
Bulldog Track 203
Bulolo 202, 243
Buluk (chief) 75, 76
Bundaberg 289–90
Buritori, Constable 232
Burns Philp
    assists in carve-up of German assets 19, 182
    competes with French for business 54
    Cranbrook old boy as manager of 55
    decline of 79
    Mytinger uses steamship of 124
    racist policy of 189
    replaced by Chinese as competitors 90
    runs steamers to Australia and Manila 183
    ship delivers supplies to Bougainville 159
    Stevens captains trading ship for 76
    stores of looted 187
    trader donates slit-drum to museum 240
Burton, John 20
Butala, Ronnie Jethro 141, 148
Butuka Academy, Port Moresby 218
Bwatnapne 61

Caggauan, Redentor 226, 228, 231, 234, 236
Cakobau, Sir George 36
Cakobau, Seru Epenisa 10, 15, 28, 29, 35, 39, 40
Caldoches 102, 119
cannibalism 6, 9, 15, 17, 28, 35, 178, 267
canoes 23–4
Cargo Cult to Christ (McKean) 73
cargo cults 39, 57, 164, 288
Carroll, Lewis 123
Catholic Church
    in Bougainville 164, 165, 169
    Catholic education system 189
    in New Caledonia 97
    in Papua New Guinea 182
    in Sepik River region 264, 265–7
    sympathetic to aims of Maasina Ruru 132
    in Vanuatu 54, 68
    in the Western Province 236
Cau-Cau 46
Champion, Claude 14
Chan, Sir Julius 169, 183, 188, 189, 249–50
Chan, Michael 196
Chand, Satish 171
Chandernagore (ship) 178
Chappell, David 100
Chauchat, Mathias 114, 116
Chaudhry, Mahendra 35, 37
Chebu (ship) 177
chief system 35–6
Chimbu people 245
Chin Pak 183
China
    builds berth in Luganville 293
    builds foreign ministry in Port Vila 90
    builds stadium in Honiaria 146–7
    Chinese settlers in Rabaul 19
    early Chinese traders in Vanuatu 54–5, 79, 90, 146–7
    France as a bulwark against 112
    in Melanesia generally 292
    in Papua New Guinea 183, 188, 217–21, 223, 230, 270–1, 292, 293–5
    recognised by Solomon Islands 139, 146, 148, 219, 294
    recognised by Vanuatu 80

INDEX

China (cont.)
    rolls out red carpet for O'Neill 219
    Sogavare seeks aid from 139
    in the Solomon Islands 146–7, 149–51
    steps up aid to Melanesia 292
    in Vanuatu 60, 90, 293
Chirac, Jacques 105, 106, 107, 108
Choiseul 17, 122, 153
Christianity
    in Bougainville 163–6
    Diderot on hypocrisy of 8
    evangelism in the 19th century 9
    in Fiji 10, 30, 32, 35, 37
    in Malaita 132
    in New Caledonia 101
    role in Melanesia's modernisation 288
    in Sepik River region 264, 265–9
    South Seas Evangelical Church 125
    in Tonga 10
    in Vanuatu 66–8, 69–70, 82
    versus evolutionism 13
    witchcraft practised with 29
    see also Anglican Church; Catholic Church; Methodist Church; missionaries; Presbyterian Church; Seventh Day Adventists
Cilento, Raphael 129
Clapcott, Mr (planter) 56
clientelism 252, 253
Cockade (ship) 133
coffee industry 247–8, 249, 250
Cole, Diana 277
Collins and Leahy 246
colonialism 114, 124, 129
Colyer Watson (company) 189
Commerson, Philibert 6
Commonwealth Bank of Australia 182
Comoro Islands 118
Compagnie Française 53
Connolly, Peter 219
Conrad (driver) 197–9
Conrad, Joseph 261
Contest (ship) 133

Conzinc Riotinto Australia 160
Cook Islands 66, 116
Cook, James 5–8, 12, 52, 64, 97
copper mining 223–4
Corris, Peter 124, 128, 129
corruption
    in New Britain 195
    in Papua New Guinea 207, 213–16, 253, 259
    in Vanuatu 83–5
Corsica 99
cotton industry 65
Coultas, William 130
Covid-19 pandemic 112, 121, 255, 258, 274
Cragnolini, Sir Luciano 217
Cranbrook School 55–6
crocodiles 149–50
Cuba 80
Curacoa (ship) 67, 122
Cyclone Harold 121, 140
Czuba, Fr Jan 256, 265

D'Albertis, Luigi Maria 14, 227
Dampier, William 178
Dani people 278, 280
Daru 289
Darwin, Charles 11, 13
Dauth, John 105
Davies, Roy 132, 133
Davis, Graham 33
de Bougainville, Louis Antoine 5, 6, 8
de Dekker, Paul 119
de Gaulle, Charles 99–100
de Mendaña y Neira, Álvaro 122
de Quirós, Pedro Fernandes 76, 91
de Rays, Marquis (Charles Bonaventure du Breil) 178–9, 182
Declercq, Pierre 103, 108
decolonisation 22, 115, 117–18, 134
Degei 27–8, 34, 38, 40, 41, 44, 48
Deloitte 216
Derby, Lord 15
d'Estaing, Valery Giscard 102

INDEX

Deutsche Neuguinea Kompagnie 16
Dianou, Alphonse 106–8
Diderot, Denis 8
Digicel 294
Dili, Amsida 237
Dillon, Peter 64
Dinh Van Tho 54
Dinnen, Sinclair 208, 209, 216–17
Diro (ship) 213
Diro, Ted 213
disease 66, 98, 124
Disturbing History (Nicole) 40
Divine Word University, Madang 256
Doa, Samson 234, 236
Douglas, Bronwen 98
Downer, Alexander 172
Downs, Ian 245
Dramdram 59
Drauniivi 38–9, 42–5
du Breil, Charles Bonaventure, Marquis de Rays 178–9, 182
Duff (ship) 9
duk-duk (secret societies) 180
Duke of York Islands 178, 179
Dukumoi, Mosese 41–3
Dumont d'Urville, Jules-Sébastien-César 8, 11, 12
Dutch East Indies 6, 15, 21
Dutton, Warren 232, 234
Dwyer, Michael 244

earthquakes 186, 255, 258, 275, 277–9, 282
East Africa 24
East New Britain 188
East New Britain Resources Group 194–5
East Timor 80
Easter Island 24
Eastern Highlands Province 244
Edie Creek goldfield 184, 243
Edmundson, Anna 240, 241
Efate 76, 77, 85, 240
Efogi 202
Egege 233

Eipo people 280, 281–5
Eipomek 285
Ela Beach, Port Moresby 205
Elder, Peter 164
Eluay, Theys 274
Emanuel, Jack 191
Endeavour (ship) 6, 12
Enga highlands 217, 220, 223
Engan people 178
Epstein, Scarlett 185, 188
Erberia (opera) 156
Eretoka Island 85
Erromango 6–7, 64–6
Espíritu Santo 75–93
    chief minister orders blockade of 78
    displacement of bush people 75, 76
    French settlers in 53, 79, 118
    independence movements 75–8
    Luganville 52–3
    safety officers graduate on 295
Etienne (chief) 57
eugenics 20
Eureka (ketch) 235
ExxonMobil 252, 254
Eyerdam, Walter 130

Fa-Malinkele Valley 279
Facebook 259
Fairlady (ship) 149, 153
Fallowes, Richard 130
Falun Gong 147
The Fatal Impact (Morehead) 97
Fatima (mission station) 265
Fayaoue 106–7
Fifi'i, Jonathan 143, 144
Fiji 27–49
    Cakobau as king of 10, 15, 28, 29, 35, 39, 40
    ceded to British crown 10, 15
    Christianity in 10, 30, 32, 35, 37
    coup (2000) 35, 37, 291
    enacts Native Companies Law 44
    ethno-nationalism in 36–7

INDEX

Fiji (*cont.*)
    Fijians as Melanesians 287
    gains independence 22, 77
    Great Council of Chiefs 28, 36, 37, 42
    imports workers from India 27
    invaded by Polynesians 27
    invaded by Tongans 31
    Kaunitoni legend 33
    Labour forms government 35
    language and dialects in 30
    map of 26
    massacre of villagers by troops 40
    measles epidemic 66
    missionaries in 17
    mobile phone network 294
    political divisions 37, 39–40
    population of 288
    racial conflict 44
    religion before Christianity 29–30, 35
    resistance movements 38, 39–40, 41–3
    sugar industry 27
Fiji Museum 28–9
Fiji Water 27, 45
fire walking 30
First World War 18, 19, 181
Firth, Raymond 188
Fisdiepas, Daniel 109
Flannery, Tim 265
FLNKS 103–4, 106–7, 109, 116
Fly River 14, 223–37
Flynn, Errol 20, 183–4
Folau, Israel 48
France
    administration of New Caledonia 98–119
    annexes New Caledonia 17
    Fifth Republic 99
    in Tahiti 5–6
    in Vanuatu 77, 78
Freeport mine 269
Frieda River 269
Friendly Islands (Tonga) 6, 7
Front de Libération Nationale Kanak et Socialiste (FLNKS) 103–4, 106–7, 109, 116
Front Nationale 105
Frum, John 68–72, 77, 130
Furari, Constable 232
Futuna 8, 64
fuzzy-wuzzy angels 21

Gaa, Rocky 145
Gaa, Salathiel Salana 145
Gaa, Samson 145
Gabi, Duncan 262–3, 268, 269, 270
Gaisseau, Pierre-Dominique 278
Gardner, Helen 13
Garnaut, Ross 229
Gazelle Peninsula 178, 180, 188, 245
Geddie, John 66, 67
Génil (ship) 179
Geraghty, Paul 11, 29–31
German East Asiatic Fleet 180, 181
German New Guinea Company 16, 179
Germany
    in Bougainville 163
    divides Solomons with Britain 122
    in the Duke of York Islands 178
    loses territory after First World War 19
    mounts punitive expedition in Mioko 179
    in New Guinea 15, 16–17, 179–81, 261
    in Second World War 99
    swaps Choiseul for Western Samoa 16–17
Gioni, Nick 157, 158
Gizo 153
Gladstone, William 16
global warming 296
Global Witness 194, 195
Goa, Daniel 116
Goa, Patricia 115
Godin, Patrick 115, 116
Goilala people 207
gold mining 220, 246, 255–6

INDEX

gold rushes 15, 20, 183, 243–4, 245
Gomès, Philippe 112
Goroka 247, 251, 252, 258–9
Goroka Valley 244
Gorton, John 190
Gossanah 96, 107, 109, 110
Grand Terre 98, 103, 106, 107, 114
Great Depression 129
Green River 273
Greenpeace 103
Griffin, James 245
Griffiths, Tim 238, 241
Guadalcanal 65, 123, 124, 130, 131, 135, 136
Guale people 135, 136
Guiart, Jean 102
Guinea 99–100
Gulf of Papua 15
Gwee'abe 126, 128, 143
Gygès, Christopher 112

Hagai, Francis 165
Hahalis Welfare Society 165
Hannet, Leo 165
Harris, Geoff 232
Harrison, G.C. 127–8
Harrisson, Tom 54, 65, 66, 67
haus tambaran 262–3, 265, 267, 270
Hawai'i 10, 24, 238–9, 250
Haweis, Thomas 9
Heeschen, Volker 278, 280, 283
Hela 217
Henningham, Stephen 100
Henri Bonneaud (ship) 79
Herbert River 233, 235
Heritage, Geoff 277–8
Hershey Company 195
Hienghène 105, 106, 110
Hiepko, Paul 285
The Highlands, Papua New Guinea 243–59
    author interviews Paias Wingti in 250–1
    ban on entry for Europeans 245–6
    clientelism in 252, 253
    coffee plantations 247–8, 249, 250
    construction of highway into 247–8
    earthquake (2018) 255
    European settlement 247–8
    first white explorers 244–5
    'Middle Kingdom' discovered 245
    missionaries in 269
    natural gas industry 252–3
    postwar labour scheme 247
    in Second World War 245
    violence in election campaigns 252, 259
Hog Harbour 54, 295
Holt, Harold 162
Honiara 122, 139, 146, 288
Hordern family 235
Hospers, John 76
Houenipwela, Rick 137
Howard, John 136, 182
Howard, Stan 182
Huawei 293
Hughes, Billy 238
Hughes, Tony 137
Hughes, William 19
Huli people 252
human sacrifice 9
Hurley, Frank 234–40
Hurley-McCulloch Collection 237–41

Iaken, Josaiah 73
Iloilo, Josefa 34
indentured labour 19
India 134
Indonesia
    'Act of Free Choice' gives Western New Guinea to 275
    applies 'Unitary State' label 274, 275
    New Order regime 276
    promotes nickel industry 114
    strafes and napalms West Papuan villages 280
    in West Papua 274–5, 280, 296–7
    see also West Papua

INDEX

Indonesian Communist Party 276
Industries Federation of New Caledonia 117
infanticide 9
influenza 98
Ingram, Sue 137
Investment Corporation Fund of Papua New Guinea 214
Investment Corporation of Papua New Guinea 214
Ireupuow 64, 69
Irian Jaya 275
Isabel 122, 123, 130, 132
Isamel 78
Islam 13
Italians, in Australia 179
iTaukei people 33, 36-7

Jamai, Gib and Sadawa 233
Jambura, Clarence 234, 236, 241
Japan
    joint electricity project for PNG 294
    in Second World War 21, 130, 164, 171, 178, 186-8, 202-3, 245, 246
Java 274
Jayapura 274, 275
Jiwaka 217
John Paul II, Pope 249, 265-6
Johnson, Irving 69
Jones, Lloyd 157
Jorédie, Léopold 109
Joske, A.B. 41-3
Jospin, Lionel 111
Junkers G31 aircraft 243-4

Kabutaulaka, Tarcisius 25
Kadavu Island 42
Kai Islands 12
Kaimari 238
Kainantu 244, 247
Kaiser-Wilhelmsland 179
Kaku (businessman) 57
Kambong, Manesa 231

Kanakas 18-19, 103, 289
Kanaké, Téâ 103
Kanaks, in New Caledonia 77, 80, 95, 98-118, 291, 296
Kanaky 103
Kapiel 77, 78
Kaplan, Martha 39, 44
Kaputin, John 189, 190, 191
Kar Kar Island 182
Karaa Pha (ship) 58-9, 60-1
Karaperamun 69, 73
kastom
    reversion to 288
    in Sepik River region 268
    in Vanuatu 54, 56, 62, 66, 70, 72, 76, 80, 82-4
Kata, Pastor 32
Kaunitoni legend 33
Kauona, Sam 168, 170, 174
kava 47, 73, 89, 287
Keesing, Roger 124, 128, 129, 144
Keke, Harold 136, 137
Kelua 250-1
Kemakeza, Allan 136
Kempeitai (military police) 188
Kennedy, John F. 275
Kereka 201
Kiap, John 258
kiaps 22, 154-5, 160, 161, 209, 232
Kieta 154, 155, 157, 163
Kimbe 196, 199
Kina Bank 293
The King of Kings (film) 70
Kingitanga movement 10
Kita, Morio 187
Kiunga 223-4, 226
Koim, Sam 214, 221
Kokoda Track 21, 201-2, 204, 291
Kokopo 177, 181, 185
Kolombangara Island 149
Koné 115, 116
Konie, Albert 191, 268, 270
Korogu 262

INDEX

Korokoro, Genevieve 170, 172
Kramer. Bryan 215–16
Kuku, Rebecca 211–12
Kuku (ship) 224–8, 230–4, 236
Kukukuku people 244
Kuni language 236
Kurtovitch, Nicolas 119
Kwaio people 125, 128, 129, 143, 145

labour trade 17, 18, 19, 65, 123, 125–6
   see also blackbirding
Ladoa, Paul 143–5, 146
Lae 185, 203, 245, 248, 288
Lafleur, Jacques 103, 108, 110
Laiagam 248
Lake Murray 230–6, 241
Laloki River 15
Lang, John Dunmore 14–15
Langa Langa Lagoon 123, 140, 150
languages
   in Fiji 30
   language groups in Melanesia 11, 22
   links between Tonga and Vanuatu 8
   spread of Papuan languages 24
   Tryon-Hackman Line 149
   in Vanuatu 80, 88
   see also specific languages, e.g. Tok Pisin
Lani people 278, 280
Lapita pottery 22, 23, 28, 97
Lara Star (ship) 61–3
Lark Force, Australian Army 186–7
Lau, Sandra 218
Laveil, Maholopa 254
Lawes, William 16
Lawson, J.A. 13
Le Pen, Jean-Marie 105, 106, 107
Le Pen, Marine 112, 114, 117
League of Nations 19, 182, 183, 188
Leahy brothers 20, 245, 246, 247
Leahy, Danny 246, 249
Leahy, Jim 246
Leahy, Mick 243, 244–6, 248
Leahy, Paddy 244

Lecornu, Sébastien 112
Leenhardt, Maurice 102
Lenormand, Maurice 99, 100
Leo, Sarah 197, 199
Leong Awa 55–6
Lest We Forget: A Review of 20 Unresolved Issues of National Concern, 2007–2017 214
L'Éveil Océanien 119
Lever Brothers 129
Lew, Anne 90
Libya 80, 103
Lihir Island 224
Lillies, Kenneth 127, 145
Lini, Walter 77, 78, 80, 81, 85
Litric, Fr Mate 196, 267–8, 269
Litzlitz 52, 59, 60
Lo Chan Moon 55
Lo Puchy 54–6, 57, 79
Lo, Richard 55–6, 90
Lo Sin Chao 55
logging industry 192–3
Lolo (passenger) 58
Loltong 61
Lomolomo 34
London, Jack 123–4
London Missionary Society 9, 15, 65, 96
Losinwei 59
Loustau, Henri 99, 100
Loyalty Islands 15, 17, 24, 65, 96, 106, 118, 121
Lu, Ru 'Dora' 217
Luganville 52–4, 63, 68, 75, 77–8, 80, 90, 293

Ma'afu 28, 29, 31
Maasina Ruru 131–3, 134, 143, 145, 288
Macarthur, Douglas 275
MacGregor Collection 239, 240
Machoro, Eloi 105, 108
Mackellar, Cameron 219
Mackenzie, Seaforth 261
Macmillan, Harold 134

319

INDEX

Macron, Emmanuel 111–12, 113, 114, 116, 117
Madagascar 24
Madang 182, 184, 218
Makirato 132
Malai, Silas 141–4
Malaita 139–51
    British avenge murder of Bell 127–8, 143
    British impose tax on locals 125–6
    British set up district office in 125
    communities follow customary life on 144
    Jack London in 123
    Maasina Ruru movement 131–3, 134, 143, 145
    Malaita Council 134, 143, 145, 150
    migration to Honiara 135
    missionaries in 125
    resistance to Europeans 125–9, 130–4
    Sogavare cuts off aid to 147–8
    Taiwanese aid to 146
    US signs up labourers for Guadalcanal 131
Malaita Eagle Force 136
malaria 9, 66, 124
Malaya 134
Malays 12–13
Malaysia 135, 212
Malekula 6, 7, 52, 53, 57, 60, 61, 78
Malekula Native Company 57, 165
Malo, Akana 237
Manamp, Yerima 246
Manele, Jeremiah 150
Manning, David 215
Manokwari 12
Māori 6, 10
Mapou, Louis 95
Mara, Ratu Sir Kamisese 29, 35, 36
Marape, James
    announces plans for third army battalion 217
    appoints Koim as tax chief 293
    background 257
    blamed for payroll glitch 213
    campaigns in federal election 252–3
    clientelism of 253
    compared with O'Neill 256
    early life 251
    increases scrutiny of Chinese businesses 220
    joins Pangu Party 251–2
    launches subdevelopment 212
    moves Kramer into justice department 216
    negotiates agreement over policing 295
    plays down Chinese influence 294
    promises aid to Bougainville 170
    promises to double police force 216
    reluctant to give Bougainville independence 172, 173
    replaces O'Neill as prime minister 170, 215, 255
    responds to 2024 riots 210–11
    wins 2022 election 259
Marape, Rachael 251
Maré 110
Marianas 116
Markham River Valley 247–8
Marles, Richard 295
Marquesa Islands 6, 24
Mata, Roi 85
Mataram (ship) 124, 127
Mataungans 190, 191
Mateparae, Sir Jerry 173
Mathias, Craig 149
Mathias, Elten 61
Matignon Accord 108–9, 110
Matupit 185
Mawe, Natasha 257–8
Mayotte 118
McConville, 'Peanuts' 163
McCulloch, Allan Riverstone 234–41
McGeaver, Patrick 265
McKean, Robert Charles 73

INDEX

measles 98, 124
Megawati Sukarnoputri 274
Mek dialect 278, 280, 281
Melanesia 5–25
   Anglican archdiocese of 121
   Australia's relationship with 290–8
   Chinese in 292
   Dumont d'Urville coins term *Mélanésie* 12
   early European impressions of 6–9, 10–11, 12
   foreign aid to 292
   identifying as Melanesian 25, 287
   linguistic and cultural diversity 287
   map of 4
   origins of Melanesian people 22–4
   political and judicial systems 287
   population of 288, 298
   racial categorisation of 8–9, 11, 20, 24–5
   role of Christianity in 288
   trade in Melanesian labourers 15
   traditional religion and beliefs 265–8
   see also Fiji; New Caledonia; Papua New Guinea; Solomon Islands; Vanuatu; West Papua
Melanesia 2000 (festival) 102
Melanesian Progressive Party 81
Melanesian Spearhead Group 31, 113, 116, 174
Melanesianism 25
Mélenchon, Jean-Luc 117
Melsisi 62
Melville, Herman 9
Mendi 248, 257
Mesiamo (resistance fighter) 164
Messmer, Pierre 100–1
Metallurgical Corporation of China 271
Methodist Church 32, 37, 39, 40, 182
Metzdorf, Nicolas 118
Michel, Thomas 279
Michener, James A. 53
Micronesia 11
Miklouho-Maclay, Nikolai 14

mining
   in Bougainville 158–9, 160–2, 166, 171
   copper mining 223–4
   Freeport mine 269
   nickel mining 100, 110, 114
   Ok Tedi mine 223, 228–9, 257, 269
   Porgera gold mine 220, 246, 255–6
   proposed Frieda River mine 269–70
Minota (ship) 123–4
Mioko 179
missionaries
   diseases brought by 66, 124
   in Fiji 17
   in the Highlands 269
   in Malaita 125
   murder of 40, 65, 69
   in New Caledonia 96–7
   in New Guinea 14–15, 182
   in the Sepik River region 265–9
   in Tahiti 9–10
   in Vanuatu 51–2, 57, 65–7, 69–70
   in West Papua 279–80
   wrangle with evolutionists 13
Missionary Aviation Fellowship 276
Missionary House, Mount Hagen 248
Mister Pip (Jones) 157
Mitterand, François 103, 104, 105, 106, 107, 108
mixed marriages 21, 22
Mizuki, Shigeru 188
Moderates 77, 78
Moluccas 13
Momis, John 165, 169, 189
Momoedonu, Ratu Tevita 34–7, 89
monarchy 10
Monroe Doctrine 174
Montevideo Maru (ship) 187
Morauta, Mekere 229
Morehead, Alan 97
Moresby, John 15
Mormons 70
Moro, Pelise 135
Morrison, George Ernest 16

INDEX

Mount Giluwe 243
Mount Hagen 245, 247–50, 253, 258
Mount Hagen Club 248
Mount Tambora 24
Mount Yasur 63
Mouvement Autonomiste des Nouvelles-Hébrides 77
Muji (warrior) 236–8
Munda 154
Murouroa Atoll 100
Murray, Hubert 17, 19, 205, 237, 239
Murtopo, Ali 276
Musingku, Noah 156
Mytinger, Caroline 124, 126, 127, 155, 184–5

Nagriamel 76–8, 79
Naipao, James 210
Naisseline, Nidoïsh 101
Naisseline, Omayra 118
Naisua, Leone 38
Naisua, Tava 38, 47, 48
Naisua, Tomasi 39, 45
nakamals 70, 86–7
Nakauvadra Range 27–8, 31, 40, 42, 47
Nakoro, Elia 29
Nakorowaiwai 40
Namulo, Temesi 39
Nankervis, Vivian 124
Napoleon III, Emperor 98
Narokobi, Bernard 25
Narua, Werry 63–4, 72
Nasioi people 162–3, 166
The National 194, 211–12, 293
National Geographic 69
National Museum of Australia 239
National Museum of Papua New Guinea 241
National Provident Fund (PNG) 214
natural gas industry 252–3
The Naturalist 238
Nauru 294
Navosavakadua 41–3
navota 92

Nawai, Apolosi 43–4
Nazi Germany 99
Neither Cargo Nor Cult (Kaplan) 39
Nelke, Wolfgang 280
Nelson, Hank 290
Neva (boat) 227
New Britain 23, 178–90, 192, 195, 211
New Caledonia 95–119
　civil war (2024) 116–17
　Cook in 8, 97
　France annexes 17, 98
　French administration of 98–119
　French push Melanesians off best land 98
　history before arrival of Europeans 97–8
　independence movement 22, 79
　Kanaks in 77, 80, 95, 98–118, 291, 296
　map of 94
　Matignon Accord 108–9
　migration from France and Polynesia 100–1
　missionaries in 96–7
　Nouméa Accord 111, 113, 118
　opts to remain part of France 100
　political upheaval in the 1980s 103–9
　Port Breton survivors arrive in 179
　proposal for partition 118
　referendums for independence 111–13, 115
　uprising (1988) 106–9
New Georgia Island 149, 154
New Guinea
　Australia seizes German possessions 261–2
　Australian administration of 182
　during the First World War 182
　early European impressions of 13–15
　economic exploitation of 15, 19–20
　expatriate life 185
　Germans in 15, 16–17, 179–81, 261
　gold discovered in Wau Valley 183
　gold rush 20

INDEX

Japanese in 21, 178, 186–8
languages in 11
Malay forays into 13
migration to 23
missionaries in 14–15, 182
New Guinea and Papua merge 22, 188, 203
Portuguese in 12
Queensland attempts to annex 16
Syme finances expedition to 16
Wallace's impressions of Papuans 12
see also The Highlands; Papua New Guinea; The Sepik; Western Province
New Hebrides see Vanuatu
New Ireland 23, 178, 188
New Popular Front 117
New Zealand 6, 24, 60, 116, 217, 294, 295
Nggela 130, 132
Ngongosila Island 145
Nia Tero 147
nickel industry 100, 110, 114
Nicole, Robert 39–40, 41, 44
Nimbtik, Gregoire 83–4, 85, 86, 134
Niyaura language 262
the 'Noble Savage' 5–6, 8
Noël (chief) 98, 101
Nori (orator) 131–2, 134, 143
Nori, Andrew 136
Norsup 60
North Fly Rubber Limited 224, 232
Noto'l (priest) 130
Nouméa 95, 102, 111, 114, 118, 179
Nouméa Accord 111, 113, 118
nuclear testing 77, 80, 100

Oceanic languages 11
Oil Search 254
Ok dialect 281
Ok Tedi mine 223, 228–9, 257, 269
Ok Tedi River 226
Oleto (Eipo widow) 283–5
Oliver, Michael 76

Olo language 265
Omban 279
Ona, Francis 156, 168, 169
O'Neill, Peter
  compared with Marape 256
  defeats Somare 193, 229
  demands BHP renegotiates divestment of mine 229
  downfall of 254–5
  fiscal record 254
  investigation of deals 213–15, 216
  life before parliament 253
  Marape leaves party of 251
  promises anti-corruption commission 214
  rapport with Chinese businesswomen 217
  reluctant to interfere in agribusiness 194
  replaced by Marape as prime minister 169, 170, 215, 255
  sets up inquiry into logging leases 193
  visits to China 219
  wins seat in parliament 253
O'Neill, Robert 191
Ontong Java 24
Operation Delouse 132–3
Out of Africa movement 22
Ouvéa 96, 106
Owen Stanley Range 201, 202

Pacific Engagement Visa 290
Pacific Games (2011) 111
Pacific Games (2015) 217
Pacific Games (2023) 146, 148
Pacific Islands Forum 113, 147, 173–4
Pacific Islands Regiment 190–1
Pako (cargo cult leader) 164
Pakoro, Adrien Jean-Marie 61–2
palm oil industry 193, 194, 195
PanAust 270
Pandi River 198
Panfilo, Francesco 194

INDEX

Pangu Party 251–2, 255, 259
Panguna 155, 158–9, 167
Papua New Guinea 177–99
    allies offer electrification program to 220
    Australia's relationship with 290–6
    border with Indonesia 273–4
    borrows $1.3 billion 254
    in Bougainville 157, 167–8, 173
    censuses 209, 288
    Chinese in 183, 188, 217–21, 223, 230, 270–1, 292, 293–5
    corruption in election campaigns 253, 259
    delays decision on Bougainville 172–3
    gains independence 22, 166
    geographical separation from Australia 23
    gold rush 20
    government priorities in spending 211
    government scandals 213
    House of Assembly 191
    infrastructure projects 294
    Internal Revenue Commission 221, 293
    Japanese in 202–3, 245, 246
    justice system 208–9, 214–16
    link between diplomatic recognition and aid 219–20
    mobile phone network 294
    national elections (2017) 259
    national elections (2022) 209–10, 259
    nationalises Ok Tedi mine 229
    Papua and New Guinea merge 22, 188, 203
    police in 206–8, 210, 215–17, 295
    political slush funds 83
    population of 288
    Port Moresby becomes new capital of 188
    promises aid to Bougainville 170
    revenue from Bougainville mining 159, 161–2
    sends mercenaries to Bougainville 169
    sends troops to Vanuatu 78
    third army battalion announced 217
    village life versus urban life 210–11
    violence in election campaigns 252, 259
    wealth disparities 211–13
    withdrawal of Australian banks from 293
    see also Bougainville; The Highlands; New Guinea; Port Moresby; Sepik River; Western Province
Papua New Guinea Defence Force 226
Papuan languages 11
Paris Peace Conference (1919) 19
Parke, Aubrey 33–4
Parkes, Sir Henry 179
Parkop, Powes 211, 212–13
Parramatta (ship) 261
Paton, John 66–7
Peace Child (Richardson) 280
Peacock, Eugene 76
Pearls and Savages (film) 235
Pedroza, Eusebio 158
Pence, Mike 220
Pentecost 60, 62
People's National Congress 255
Pétain, Phillipe 99
Phoenix Foundation 76
Piano, Renzo 110
Pidia 157
Pisani, Edgard 104
PNG Sustainable Development Program 229
PNGi Portal 214
Po Ah 55
Poida, Kasiken 72, 73
Police Motu (language) 224
polio 255
Polynesia 8–11, 22, 119, 250
Pomio, New Britain 193–4
Pompidou, Georges 102
Pons, Bernard 105, 107–8

INDEX

Porgera 269
Porgera gold mine 220, 246, 255–6
Porgera River 246
Port Arthur 221
Port Breton 178–9
Port Moresby 201–21
   ambivalence towards urbanisation 210–11
   Australian governor resides in 22
   becomes capital of Papua New Guinea 188
   Chinese-built Noble Centre denied permit 221–2
   Chinese in 217–21
   crime in 204–9, 211
   first European settlement of 15
   hosts Pacific Games 217
   inaccessibility by road 201, 202–3
   lack of infrastructure 210
   overview of 203–5
   population of 210, 288
   riots over payroll glitch 208, 213
   in Second World War 202–3
Port Resolution 7, 69, 122
Port Resolution Yacht Club 64
Port Sandwich 6, 53, 54
Port Vila 68, 78, 80, 86, 89, 288
Portuguese, in Papua 12
Post-Courier 155, 255, 293
Prabowo, Subianto 297
Prasad, Hoolikantimath 51
Presbyterian Church 66–7, 69–70, 73
President Coolidge (ship) 53
prisoners of war 187
P.T. Barnum's circus 28

Queensland 15, 16
Queensland Kanaka Mission 125
Queensland Museum 239, 240
Quinto, Ruth 90
Quinto, Steve 90

Ra region, Fiji 29, 34, 37, 40–1

Rabaul 19, 21, 130, 177, 181–9, 190, 269
Rabaul Hotel 177–8, 184, 195
Rabaul Yacht Club 196
Rabuka, Sitiveni 34, 36, 37
racial categorisation 8–9, 11, 20
racism 11, 20–1, 25, 129, 189
Ragh, Ragh 'Charley' 57
Rairi, Sainivati 48
RAMSI 136–7, 175
Ramu Nickel 220, 270–1
Ranmawat 62
Rapanui 24
raskol gangs 204, 215, 218, 258
Ratzinger, Cardinal Joseph 265
Ravulo, Kalaveti 47, 48
Regenvanu, Ralph 81, 83–7, 287, 297–8
Regenvanu, Sethy 80–1
Regional Assistance Mission to the Solomon Islands (RAMSI) 136–7, 175
Rennell-Bellona group 24
The Resistance (Bougainville) 168
Resolution (ship) 6–7, 52, 64
Réveille Canaque 101
Richardson, Don 280
Rimbunan Hijau group 193–4, 195, 293
Rio Tinto 155, 171
Riverina district, New South Wales 65
Robert, Jean-Jacques 77
Robinson Crusoe (film) 156
Rocard, Michel 108, 109
Rockefeller Foundation 129
Rockefeller, Michael 275
Roosevelt, Frankllin D. 68
Rotuma 11–12, 41, 42, 44
Roughan, John 137
Rousseau, Jean-Jacques 5
Royal Australian Air Force 78
Royal Australian Navy 10–11, 18, 127, 133, 181
Royal Navy 10, 15, 17, 18
Royal Papua New Guinea Constabulary 208, 216
Royal Solomon Islands Police 136

INDEX

Ruavatu 124
rubber industry 232
Ruben, Api 58–9
Runovoro (prophet) 56
Ryan, Peter 203

Sacred Heart Society 182
Sahul shelf 23
Saibai 288
Sain, Ken 205–6, 215
Salan, Raoul 99
Sammy (kiap) 155
Samoa 10, 15, 22, 24, 66, 294
Samson (lay pastor) 69–70
Sand, Christophe 98
sandalwood trade 64–5
Sandars, Eustace 132
Sandline International 169, 291
Sanduan Province 273
Santa Ana Island 150
Santa Cruz group 23
Sarawak 193
Save the Sepik group 270
Savo 130
Sawong, Don 213–14
Schiefenhövel, Wulf 285
Sean (businessman) 196–7
Second World War
    Australia's Lark Force 186
    effect on people in Espirito Santo 56
    Germany in 99
    Japan in 21, 130, 164, 171, 178, 186–8, 202–3, 245, 246
    United States in 21, 52–3, 130–1
Segond Canal 52–3
Semoso, Francesca 173
Sepik River 261–71
    declared a restricted area 262
    German settlements along 261
    haus tambaran in 262–3, 265, 267, 270
    Jim Taylor's expedition through 246
    missionaries in region of 265–9
    proposed Frieda River mine 269–70

Seventh Day Adventists 57, 61, 68, 126–7, 182, 236
Shackleton, Ernest 234
sharks 150
shells, as currency 180
Shoalhaven (ship) 133
Shortland Islands 122
Sia, Francis 141
Sibu, Malaysia 193
Sinalagu 127, 142, 143
Singapore 221
Siwai people 156
Skehan, Craig 136
The Sky Above, the Mud Below (film) 278
smallpox 98
Smith, Graeme 219–20
Smith, Jane 290
Smol Nambas 57, 59
Snark (ketch) 123, 124
social media 89
Société Le Nickel 98
Société Minière du Sud Pacifique 110
Sogavare, Manasseh 137, 139, 146–8, 150
Sogete/Mukus Integrated Rural Decelopment Project 194
Sohano 165
Solomon Islands 121–37
    Boyd killed in 65
    British neglect in the 1930s 129
    Chinese in 146–7
    declared a protectorate by Britain 17, 122
    development politics 135
    disconnect between village and nation-state 137
    divided between Germany and Britain 122
    fear of Bougainville's independence in 174
    gains independence 22, 77, 134
    Guale uprising 135–6
    influx of cash from seasonal work 146
    interventions to restore peace 136–7, 139, 147, 291

INDEX

Japanese in 21, 130, 187
languages in 11, 24
Malaitans in Honiara 135, 139
map of *120*
police in 136
political chaos 136, 137, 139
political slush funds 83
population of 288
recognises Beijing 139, 146, 148, 219, 294
removes restrictions on logging 135, 137, 139
resistance to Europeans 125–9, 130–4
Royal Navy attempts to protect 17
signs security agreement with China 147
see also Malaita
Solomon Islands Labour Corps 131
Somare, Michael
   defeated by O'Neill (2011) 193, 214, 229, 253
   founds Pangu Party 251
   hallmarks of second term of 253–4
   interviewed by author 249
   Mataungans join new government of 191
   negotiates return of artefacts 240
   opposes urbanisation 210
   as PNG's first prime minister 191, 210
   steps up issuing of logging leases 193, 194
Sopé, Barak 81
sorcery 241, 267–8
Souter, Gavin 14
South Sea Islander Church, Bundaberg 289
South Sea Islanders, in Australia 289–90
South Seas Evangelical Church 125, 132
Southern Cross (ship) 121
Southern Moana (ship) 51
Spanish influenza 66
Speight, George 35, 37
Spencer, Stella 44
Stephens, Thomas Carfield 75

Stevens, Fabiano 92–3
Stevens, Jimmy 75–8, 79, 92
Stevens, Lotty 92
Stevenson, Robert Louis 67
Strickland River 231, 232–3, 235
Suharto, President 274, 276
Suidani, Daniel 146, 147, 148, 150
Sukarno, President 274, 276
Sukuna, Ratu Sir Lalu 28–9, 44
Sulawesi 274
Sulphur Bay 70, 72, 73, 78
Suma, Ated 62
Sumatra 13
Sumbawa 24
The Sun 235, 238
Sunda shelf 23
The Sydney Morning Herald 73
Syme, David 16
syphilis 98
Szarka, Gerald 232

Tabubil 228
Tabwémasana 77
Tahi, Merilyn 87
Tahiti 5–6, 8, 9, 100
Taimareho I (ship) 140
Taiwan 139, 146, 219, 292
Takaku, William 156–8
Taki, Allan 145–6
Tales of the South Pacific (Michener) 53
Talifilu, Celsus 147
Tama, James 121
Tamlumlum, Paul 57
Tammur, Oscar 190
Tan Eng Kwee 194
Tanganyika 33
Tanguay, Jamie 88
Tanna 7–8, 63–73, 77, 118, 122, 130
Taro 153
Tarowai, Maliwan 73
Tavore, Alphons 168
Tavurvur (volcano) 195–6
Taylor, Jim 243, 245–6, 247, 248

INDEX

Telefomin 232
Telstra 294
Tenmaru 61
Tennant, Doug 194–5
Teosin, John 165
Terry, Peter 57–8, 61
Tevanu Star (ship) 61–2
Teven, Johannes 271, 273
Theseus (ship) 133
Thomson (driver) 141–2, 145
Thursday Island 16
Tiendanite 101, 104
Timor-Leste 24, 250, 290
Tingal-Lémé, Magalie 116
Tinkoria, Miriam 183
Tiong Hiew King 193
Tjibaou, Emmanuel 118
Tjibaou, Jean-Marie 101–6, 108–10, 118
Tok Pisin language 236, 287
Tolai people 178–82, 185, 187–91, 245, 268
Tonga 6–8, 10, 22, 24, 250, 287, 294
Tonkinese, in Vanuatu 53, 54, 55, 79, 90
Torres Strait 12, 16, 288–9
Torres Strait Islanders 289
Torricelli Mountains 265
Towns, Robert 65
Townsville 65
trade 13, 17
Transparency International 214
Trompf, Garry 267, 269
Trump, Donald 220
The Trumpet Shall Sound (Worsley) 39
Tryon-Hackman Line 149
Tsek (cult leader) 56–7
Tsiamalili, Peter 173
tuberculosis 98, 255, 289
Tuka movement 38, 39, 41–2
Tulagi (ship) 159
Tulagi (town) 122, 128, 130
Tupou, Sela 75
Turnbull, Malcolm 297
Turner, Frederick 283, 285

Tzen Niugini 195

U-Vistract 156
Ukraine war 255
Uluru Statement from the Heart 297–8
Umaka, Adrian 237, 241, 268
Unevangelized Fields Mission 277
Union Bank of Switzerland 254
Union Calédonienne 99–100, 101, 116
United Nations 114, 116, 188
United States
   aid to Malaita 147–8
   annexes Hawai'i 10
   joint electricity project for PNG 294
   relationship with the Marianas 116
   in the Second World War 21, 52–3, 130–1
   in Vanuatu 68
Uriba, Jerry and Koleni 233
Usakof 234, 236–7, 239

vaccinations 255, 258
Vaileka 45
Vale Lebo 41
Valentine, Charles A. 11
Valley X 278, 279, 285
Vanafo 76, 79, 91–2
Vanimo 273
Vanua'aku Pati 77–9, 81
Vanuatu (formerly New Hebrides) 51–73
   Australian Museum donates slit drum to 240
   Boyd kidnaps islanders from 65
   chiefs as political mediators 86
   Chinese in 54–5, 79, 90, 146–7, 293
   Christianity in 66–8, 69–70, 82
   constitutional issues 82, 86
   Cook visits 6, 52
   corruption and nepotism in 83–5
   duality of state and *kastom* 82–8
   foreign policy 81–2
   France uses labour from 17
   French settlers in 53–4, 77, 118

INDEX

gains independence 22, 79–80
independence movements 75–8
John Frum movement 68–70
kastom 54, 56, 62, 66, 70, 72, 76, 80, 82–4
labourers kidnapped to work in Queensland 289
land reform 85–6
languages in 80, 88
map of 50
measles epidemic 66
measures of happiness in 88–9
missionaries in 51–2, 57, 65–7, 69–70
mobile phone network 294
National Council of Chiefs 82, 85
Ni-Vanuatu as Melanesians 287
original inhabitants 24
Papuan ancestry of 22, 24
as part of the Anglican archdiocese 121
PNG troops in 78–9
police in 295
political system before Europeans 85
population of 288
president kidnapped in pay dispute 86
real estate development 76
recognises Beijing 80
replacement of traditional wealth with money 89
resistance movements 56–7
Royal Navy attempts to protect 17
seasonal work scheme in Bundaberg 290
in the Second World War 21
social values 89
subordinate position of women in 86–7
traditional communities in 85–6, 87–8
visited by Tongan canoes 8
see also Espiritu Santo
Vatukacevaceva 46, 47
Vemerana Federation 78, 92
venereal disease 9
Vernon, Don 166

Versailles Treaty (1919) 182
Victor Emanuel Range 261
Victoria, Queen 40
Vietnam 13, 53, 100
Viseisei 31–2, 33, 38
Viti Kabani 38, 43–4, 288
Vogelkop 15
The Voice referendum (2023) 297–8
volcanoes 185, 195–6
von Bellingshausen, Thaddeus 9
Votai, Seremaia 46, 48
Vuda 33
Vulcan 185
Vunapalading 197, 199
Vunica, Peni 46, 47

Wabadala, Max 224
Wabag 248
Wahgi River 244
Wahgi Valley 245
Wahid, Abdurrahman 274
Waiwo, Jack 59
Walker, Barry 155
Wallace, Alfred Russel 12, 24, 61
Wallacea 23
Walton, Grant 216
Wan, Isaac 71
Wanandi, Jusuf 276
Wanderings in the Interior of New Guinea (Lawson) 13
Wang Yi 147
Wantepe, Nathan 251
war veterans land scandal 182
Warner, Margaret 124, 184
Warramunga (ship) 133
Warrego (ship) 261
Wartuam, Ruth 198
The Washington Post 280
Waterhouse, Michael 244
Watt, Agnes 67
Watut River 244
Wau 20, 202, 243
Wau Valley 183

INDEX

Wea, Charles 95–7, 110, 115
Wea, Djubelly 107, 108, 109, 110
Wea, Maki 107
Weather Coast, Guadalcanal 135
Weir, Christine 13
Wenda, Benny 81
Wesley, Michael 134, 295
West, Harry 189, 190
West Papua 273–85
  becomes part of Indonesia 275
  border with PNG 273–4
  carved up into provinces 275
  early contact with Europeans 278
  Eipo people 280, 281–5
West Papua (cont.)
  ethnic Papuans in 274
  German researchers in Baliem Valley 279–80
  immigration from Java and Bali 274
  independence movement 79, 80, 81, 274, 276, 296–7
  Indonesia destroys bases of Free Papua Movement 276
  Indonesia strafes villages 280
  map of 272
  missionaries in 279–80
  Morning Star flag banned in 274
  rendering of Eipo song into poetry 283–5
  restricted entry into 275
  troops massacre protesters 274
  unrest against Indonesian rule 296–7
  visit by author in 2013 274
Western Province, Papua New Guinea 223–41
  journey up Fly River by author 224–34, 236
  map of 222
  travel in 223

Western Samoa 17, 122
Westpac 293
Wewak 264
whaling ships 9
Wheatsheaf (ship) 126, 127
White Australia Policy 18, 19, 125, 218, 289
Whiting, Natalie 252
Whitlam, Gough 190
whooping cough 66
Wickham, Dorothy 148, 150–1
Widodo, Joko 275, 296
Wiles, Alma 61
Wiles, Norman 61
Wilkes, W. 67
Williams, John 65, 69
Wilson, Woodrow 19
Wimb, Wingti 249
Wingti, Paias 213, 249–51
Winrock 148
witchcraft 29–30, 59–60, 82, 267–8
women
  in Melanesia generally 287–8
  in Vanuatu 86–7
  in West Papua 283
Wong, Penny 295
World Bank 192, 203
W.R. Carpenter (company) 19, 54, 124, 182

Xi Jinping 219, 220, 293
Xstrata 110
Xueqiang, Liu 51

Yamuga people 251
Yankee (yacht) 69
Yeiwéne, Yeiwéne 109, 110
Yonggom people 228, 232
Young, Florence 125, 145
Yule Island 227
Yumei, Ni 217–18